W9-CKK-049

For Jane Ross —

With deep appreciation for
all your help and
thoughtfulness —

Sandy

Going Nuclear

Going Nuclear

Leonard S. Spector

A Carnegie Endowment Book

BALLINGER PUBLISHING COMPANY
Cambridge, Massachusetts
A Subsidiary of Harper & Row, Publishers, Inc.

Copyright © 1987 by Carnegie Endowment for International Peace.
All rights reserved. No part of this publication may be reproduced, stored
in a retrieval system, or transmitted in any form or by any means, electronic,
mechanical, photocopy, recording or otherwise, without the prior written
consent of the publisher.

International Standard Book Number:0-88730-144-4 (CL)
0-88730-145-2 (PB)

Library of Congress Catalog Card Number: 86-32115

Printed in the United States of America

Library of Congress Cataloging-in-Publication Data

Spector, Leonard S.
  Going nuclear.

  Bibliography: p.
  Includes index.
  1. Nuclear weapons. 2. Nuclear nonproliferation. I. Title.
U264.S626   1987   355.8'25119   86-32115
ISBN 0-88730-144-4
ISBN 0-88730-145-2 (pbk.)

To my mother and the memory of my father

Contents

Foreword

This is the third annual report in the Carnegie Endowment's series on the spread of nuclear weapons. Initiated in 1984 with the publication of *Nuclear Proliferation Today* and continued in 1985 with the release of *The New Nuclear Nations,* the series is intended to increase public awareness of the danger of nuclear proliferation and to stimulate greater attention to this important issue by policymakers, the media, and the scholarly community.

The recent developments reviewed in this volume signal that nuclear proliferation may be entering a new and increasingly dangerous phase. First, an additional nuclear-threshold state—Pakistan—has reportedly acquired the capability to manufacture nuclear arms, joining the ranks of Israel, India, and South Africa. Not only would Pakistan's ascendency represent the first new addition to this group for the better part of a decade, but it would mean that nuclear weapons may now be available to two neighboring states that have fought major wars and between which tensions continue to run high—a situation that holds unprecedented risks of nuclear confrontation.

Second, new disclosures suggest that Israel's nuclear arsenal may number a hundred or more weapons and may include thermonuclear devices and nuclear-tipped short-range missiles. If true, this would mean that the international community is now confronting the first case of so-called advanced proliferation outside the major powers. Like the reports that Pakistan has now crossed the nuclear-weapons threshold, the new disclosures concerning Israel's nuclear activities reveal the shortcomings of international efforts to restrain the spread of these dangerous armaments in recent years.

Finally, as domestic unrest grows in a number of nuclear-threshold countries, dramatically including South Africa and Pakistan, the risk that nuclear weapons or the ability to manufacture them might end up in the hands of opponents or successors of one of these regimes is growing markedly. With some factions in these struggles for power espousing radical ideologies of either right or left, the potential consequences for international security could be grave indeed. This added dimension to the dangers of proliferation is explored in depth in Chapter II of *Going Nuclear,* which draws on historical cases enriched by newly obtained documentation to highlight the unpredictable dangers posed by the process of nuclear inheritance.

Going Nuclear has been prepared by Leonard S. Spector, who also authored *The New Nuclear Nations* and *Nuclear Proliferation Today.* A Senior Associate at the Endowment, he has worked in the field of nuclear non-proliferation for over ten years, first at the Nuclear Regulatory Commission, and then on the staff of the Senate Energy and Nuclear Proliferation Subcommittee, where he served as chief counsel from 1978 to 1980. While with the Subcommittee, Mr. Spector assisted in drafting the 1978 Nuclear Non-Proliferation Act, the basic law governing U.S. policy today. His writings on non-proliferation and related nuclear energy issues have appeared widely.

As always, Endowment sponsorship of this report implies a belief only in the importance of the subject and the credentials of the author. The views expressed are his. Comments or inquiries are welcome and may be addressed to the Carnegie Endowment for International Peace, 11 Dupont Circle, N.W., Washington, D.C. 20036.

Thomas L. Hughes
President
Carnegie Endowment
for International Peace

Acknowledgments

This project reflects the contributions of many individuals and institutions to whom I wish to express my thanks.

Going Nuclear has been prepared under the auspices of the Carnegie Endowment for International Peace and is sustained by grants from the Carnegie Corporation of New York and the Rockefeller Brothers Fund. I greatly appreciate their support. I also wish to thank the Endowment's president, Thomas L. Hughes, for his continuing commitment to this project.

I am particularly indebted to Larry L. Fabian, the secretary of the Endowment, whose advice has been instrumental to the success of the Endowment's first two annuals on the spread of nuclear weapons, *Nuclear Proliferation Today* and *The New Nuclear Nations,* and to the preparation and dissemination of this report.

I am also especially grateful to Dr. Barry M. Blechman, who initially proposed the publication of an annual review of nuclear proliferation. Dr. Blechman has served as senior editorial advisor to the project, which has been considerably assisted by his thoughtful recommendations.

In addition, I wish to thank Carnegie Endowment interns Kavita Ramdas, Carol Kuntz, and Theodore Hirsch, whose careful sifting and organization of source materials provided the essential data for this book. Ms. Kuntz's and Mr. Hirsch's historical research on past instances of contested successions to nuclear assets were also invaluable contributions. I also want to thank Jane Ross for her unstinting assistance in preparing the numerous revisions of the manuscript and for her help in managing the project as it passed through its various phases.

Going Nuclear has been greatly aided by an informal group of advisors that assisted in reviewing the manuscript for accuracy and completeness. In addition to Dr. Blechman, the group included Dr. Joseph Nye, a principal architect of U.S. non-proliferation policy during the Carter administration as deputy to the under secretary of state for security assistance; Dr. Albert Carnesale, academic dean, John F. Kennedy School of Government; Mr. Charles Van Doren, former assistant director of the Arms Control and Disarmament Agency; and Mr. Myron Kratzer, former assistant secretary of state for oceans and international environmental and scientific affairs. I greatly appreciate their contributions in enhancing the text's balance and comprehensiveness. The views contained in this report, however, are my own, and the participation of these individuals does not necessarily constitute an endorsement on their part of specific statements or conclusions.

In addition, a number of other experts and investigators provided important assistance that I would like to acknowledge. Warren H. Donnelly of the Congressional Research Service was most helpful in making various research materials available, and Paul Leventhal of the Nuclear Control Institute also provided valuable assistance in this regard. I also wish to thank David Albright, Pauline Baker, Lawrence Barcella, Stephen Cohen, Georges Fischer, Bertrand Goldschmidt, Thomas W. Graham, Rodney Jones, Selig Harrison, Geoffrey Kemp, Richard Lansdale, Gary Milhollin, Neil Moore, Harald Muller, Barry Renfrew,

Ze'ev Schiff, Leonard Weiss, and Peter Zimmerman for their comments and insights.

My thanks also to John Fialka, Simon Henderson, Peter Hounam, Egmont Koch, Christer Larsson, Pearl Marshall, and Vyvyan Tenorio. Without the investigative work of all of these journalists—and that of the numerous others whose names appear in the notes to this volume—this book could not have been written.

I also want to express my appreciation to Mike O'Hare for his encouragement; to Endowment librarian Jane Lowenthal and to Monica Yin and Jenny Grimsley for their superlative work in obtaining research materials; to Rosemary Gwynn for her unfailing aid in seeing to the project's staffing needs; and to Yi-Li Wu and Shelley Stahl for their eagle-eyed proof-reading.

Thanks also to Heidi Shinn for her fine job copy-editing the text; to Steve Smith for his care in setting it into type; to Diana Regenthal for her work in indexing this and previous volumes; and to Brad Wye, who prepared the maps used in the text.

Leonard S. Spector
Senior Associate
Carnegie Endowment
for International Peace

Chapter I:
Overview

Like the buildup of the superpowers' nuclear arsenals, the continuing spread of nuclear weapons to additional nations poses incalculable risks to the world community. Many believe that a nuclear confrontation involving one of the emerging nuclear nations is the most likely catalyst of a future nuclear holocaust. Indeed, few would predict the outcome of a nuclear crisis initiated by a regional power in the Middle East or South Asia, where the United States and the Soviet Union are now so vitally engaged.

Even a nuclear war that remained confined to a particular region could cause extraordinary devastation. If new estimates of Israel's nuclear might are accurate, it now has the weaponry to level every urban center in the Middle East with a population of over 100,000. South Africa could theoretically do the same in Southern Africa. India will shortly have enough nuclear-weapons material unrestricted by external non-proliferation controls to cause untold destruction in all of Pakistan's principal cities, and it appears that it will not be long before Pakistan will be able to wreak comparable havoc throughout northwestern India.

Since the People's Republic of China conducted its first

nuclear test over two decades ago in 1964, no country has officially joined the nuclear-weapons club, whose other declared members today are the United States, the Soviet Union, Great Britain, and France. Nevertheless, the number of countries able to manufacture nuclear weapons and apparently ready to do so in response to regional pressures has mounted steadily.

Israel apparently achieved this status in the late 1960s. India did so by 1974 when it conducted its first and only nuclear test—something no other nation beyond the five declared nuclear powers has done—which it termed a "peaceful nuclear explosion." South Africa became a de facto nuclear state in 1980 or 1981, as it gained the capability to produce nuclear-weapons material. Pakistan stands at this threshold today. Argentina, Brazil, Iran, Iraq, and Libya, although they lack the ability to manufacture nuclear explosives, have all taken steps in this direction in the past decade.

While relatively stable nuclear relationships have emerged among the five declared nuclear powers, the spread of nuclear arms to the new nuclear nations presents a host of unpredictable dangers. Many of these states are located in highly volatile regions and a significant number have engaged in armed conflicts in recent years. The Iran-Iraq war, Israel's invasion of Lebanon, Argentina's occupation of the Falklands, and South Africa's incursions into Angola and other nearby countries are but some examples of the uncertainties of military decision making in the emerging nuclear states that may some day lead to nuclear confrontation.

The spread of nuclear weapons also increases the danger that nuclear arms may fall into the hands of radical, anti-status quo forces as the result of war, revolution or coup d'état. This danger afflicted two of the declared nuclear powers during the early stages of their nuclear-weapons programs, France and China. It is a particular concern in countries experiencing internal instability today, such as South Africa and, to a lesser extent, Pakistan, a subject examined in depth in Chapter II.

With the proliferation of nuclear capabilities, the threat of nuclear terrorism also grows. Indeed, according to a major international study released in 1986, the probability of nuclear terrorism, though low, is increasing today because of a confluence of factors, including "the growing incidence, sophistication, and lethality of conventional terrorism," the "apparent evidence of state support, even sponsorship, of terrorist groups," and growing world-wide stocks of nuclear-weapons material.*

The spread of nuclear weapons is also increasing the likelihood of conventional war, as governments have been tempted to strike preemptively against the nuclear installations of potential adversaries. Israel, Iraq, and Iran have already carried out raids against foreign nuclear plants, and there is evidence that Libya and India have contemplated similar action.

For these reasons the international community has struggled to contain the spread of nuclear arms. This book describes the progress and the setbacks of the past year.

Slowing the Spread

Acquiring the capability to produce nuclear arms often takes decades, starting with training programs and the establishment of nuclear research centers. The most difficult obstacle is obtaining nuclear explosive material, either highly enriched uranium or plutonium. To obtain the former material, natural uranium must be improved to weapons grade in a highly complex enrichment plant. Plutonium is produced in uranium fuel when this is used in a nuclear reactor. The used fuel must then be transferred to a reprocessing plant where plutonium is extracted from other fuel constituents. For nuclear threshold countries, building the facilities for either process has proved a considerable technological

---

*"Report of the International Task Force on Prevention of Nuclear Terrorism" (Washington, D.C.: Nuclear Control Institute, June 25, 1986), p.1.

challenge, requiring many years' effort even with active foreign assistance.

With the exception of India's 1974 detonation, none of the emerging nuclear countries is known to have conducted a nuclear test and most, if not all, appear unlikely to do so for the foreseeable future. This has served as a valuable constraint on proliferation by reducing the risk of wide-open escalation of nuclear weaponry akin to that of the nuclear-weapon states. The absence of testing has also dampened pressures on neighboring states to develop their own nuclear capabilities.

Reliable early generation atomic weapons, however, can be developed without testing; indeed, the type of bomb dropped on Hiroshima had never been tested. Moreover, as discussed later in this book in greater detail, new evidence concerning the Israeli nuclear program suggests that advanced atomic weapons, employing some concepts of the hydrogen bomb, and nuclear weapons small enough to serve as ballistic missile warheads can be developed without testing, at least by scientifically advanced nations. Developing true hydrogen bombs, weapons hundreds of times as powerful as the atom bombs used in World War II, still apparently remains out of reach without nuclear-weapons testing, however.

The international non-proliferation regime places additional constraints on the manufacture of nuclear arms. Its linchpin is the safeguards system of the International Atomic Energy Agency (IAEA), a Vienna-based international organization founded in 1957 and comprising more than 100 member states. The Agency's safeguards consist of reporting requirements, audits, and on-site inspections, which it applies to the vast majority of nuclear installations in non-nuclear-weapon countries to verify that these facilities are not used to support nuclear-weapons programs. Despite certain shortcomings, these safeguards can probably detect most illegal uses of these plants and therefore pose a significant deterrent to proliferation. But safeguards are less effective against the misuse of highly enriched uranium or plutonium, both directly usable for nuclear weapons. If it had made the necessary preparations, a country possessing either substance could abrogate safeguards and build weapons before the international community could intervene.

The 1968 Treaty on the Non-Proliferation of Nuclear Weapons (NPT), now ratified by over 130 non-nuclear-weapon states, is a second key element of the regime. Non-weapon-state NPT signatories pledge not to manufacture nuclear arms and agree to accept IAEA safeguards on all of their nuclear installations, while all parties agree to require safeguards on all of their nuclear exports. Argentina, Brazil, India, Israel, Pakistan, and South Africa have not ratified the treaty, however, and each possesses unsafeguarded nuclear facilities. Moreover, although Iran, Iraq, and Libya are parties to the pact, their lack of respect for other norms of international behavior has called into question their commitment to the accord.

The Nuclear Suppliers Group, formed in 1974, at a time when several exporting states had not ratified the NPT, has also required IAEA safeguards on all of its participants' nuclear exports. Its most prominent members are Belgium, Canada, France (the only non-NPT participant today), Great Britain, Italy, Japan, the Netherlands, the Soviet Union, Sweden, Switzerland, the United States, and West Germany. The People's Republic of China is not a member, but it has pledged that it will require safeguards on its future exports. Since the mid-1970s the nuclear suppliers, largely at U.S. urging, have also greatly restricted exports of enrichment and reprocessing technology. (Before it unilaterally adopted more restrictive policies on nuclear transfers in 1984 and 1985, China, which is not a party to these understandings, is believed to have helped Pakistan to develop its uranium enrichment capability—and to design nuclear arms themselves.)

Several individual supplier nations have adopted export policies that go beyond those adopted by the suppliers as a group. The 1978 U.S. Nuclear Non-Proliferation Act, for example, prohibits the sale of nuclear reactors and fuel to nations that have not placed *all* of their nuclear installations under IAEA safeguards. (More details on the technological requirements for nuclear weapons and related international institutions and treaties may be found in the appendices.)

Despite the intensity of their own nuclear rivalry, the United States and the Soviet Union have cooperated actively to strengthen the non-proliferation regime. U.S.-Soviet tensions in the Middle East and other troubled areas, however, have often impeded their respective efforts to arrest proliferation by their regional allies. Moreover, many fear that it will only be a matter of time until the unwillingness of the superpowers to restrain their own nuclear arsenals begins to undermine the non-proliferation system.

In some respects, international efforts to curb proliferation are gaining strength. The renunciation of nuclear weapons is slowly becoming a norm of international conduct, as demonstrated by the increasing number of parties to the Non-Proliferation Treaty and the slow rate at which new nations are crossing the nuclear-weapons threshold. The recent decisions of China, Argentina, South Africa and, apparently, Brazil to require IAEA safeguards on their exports also indicate the vitality of this control. Moreover, the nuclear-supplier nations appear to be exercising greater care than ever before in restricting exports that could aid additional nations to develop nuclear capabilities, although their controls remain imperfect.

International pressure aside, self-interest has also played a significant role in retarding proliferation. The nuclear threshold nations have avoided overt nuclear arming, for example, partly for fear that this might stimulate rival powers to do the same or to enlarge pre-existing nuclear capabilities; concerns over possible preemptive action, noted above, have also been a restraining influence. In addition, military considerations dictate that along with nuclear weapons themselves, costly delivery systems must be acquired, customized, and maintained, all of which can impose a heavy burden on a developing economy. National leaders in states with deep ethnic or regional divisions must also consider domestic security, including whether the development of specialized nuclear forces will allow one or another group to gain unacceptable political leverage as the appointed guardian of the nation's nuclear arms and whether such arms might fall into the hands of the regime's domestic adversaries.

These various factors have not yet arrested the trend toward further proliferation, but they appear to have reduced the attractiveness to emerging nuclear powers of outright development of nuclear weapons—the model followed by the five declared nuclear-weapon states. Instead, Pakistan seems likely to continue following the more ambiguous approach of Israel, South Africa, and (since 1974) India of acquiring a nuclear capability without overtly manufacturing weapons or conducting nuclear tests. Argentina, Brazil, Iran, and Iraq also appear to have followed this model.

While such indeterminate nuclear-weapons capabilities may well present fewer overall risks than full-fledged programs under which nuclear arms are integrated into national military forces and can be used almost instantaneously, a world with six, or possibly more, de facto nuclear-weapon states, which could count on having such arms in any protracted conflict, still poses serious dangers. Nor is there any guarantee that as more nations reach this level of nuclearization, they will remain at this plateau or that still others will not be encouraged to follow their example. For these reasons, international efforts to curb the spread of nuclear weapons continue to aim at preventing nations from reaching even this ambiguous stage of nuclear arming. As the events of the past year indicate, these efforts have met with only limited success.

Nuclear Proliferation Today

The developments from mid-1985 to the fall of 1986 chronicled in this book are profoundly troubling. New information on the Israeli nuclear program reveals that the scale of proliferation in that country has been far greater than previously recognized. Details, published here for the first time, concerning Libya's attempt to purchase nuclear weapons in 1981 and newly unearthed evidence that the Shah of Iran had launched a nuclear-weapons research program—which presumably has been inherited by the Khomeini government—underscore the risk of proliferation by these nations. The threat of a nuclear arms race between India and Pakistan has also intensified, amidst increasing evidence that Pakistan has manufactured all of the components necessary to produce nuclear weapons for the first time. Worsening racial strife in South Africa, meanwhile, may lead Pretoria to reconsider its policy against nuclear testing and raises the fearful possibility that its nuclear-weapons capability might fall into the hands of extremists—of the right or the left. Only in Latin America are trends more favorable, as Argentina and Brazil took steps to dampen their long-standing nuclear rivalry.**

The Nuclear Inheritors. With two nuclear-threshold nations, South Africa and Pakistan, now experiencing serious domestic unrest that could lead to the collapse of internal order or to the advent of anti-status quo governments, there is a growing risk that radical forces may gain control of nuclear weapons or the ability to manufacture them—a possibility that may pose one of the gravest dangers of the next decade. Although radicals have never acquired lasting control over such nuclear assets as the result of war, revolution, or coup d'état, there is historical precedent for the key elements of this scenario. In 1961, a group of right-wing French generals based in Algeria appears to have briefly taken control of a nuclear device at France's Sahara nuclear test site during an unsuccessful coup attempt, and an insubordinate province chief in the People's Republic of China, until he was ousted in 1968, similarly threatened to take over China's

---

**The developments summarized here are discussed in detail in the respective sections dealing with particular countries, along with detailed citations that will not be repeated.

Lop Nor nuclear-weapons assembly and testing site during China's Cultural Revolution. In Iran in 1979, on the other hand, a radical, anti-status quo government took power and gained permanent control over an extensive nuclear infrastructure, although this did not include nuclear arms or the ability to produce them. Finally, the United States was able to prevent, by means of a last-minute rescue mission, a modest quantity of non-weapons-usable reactor fuel from falling into the hands of North Vietnamese forces when they overran South Vietnam in 1975; preventing radicals from inheriting far more sensitive nuclear assets in South Africa or Pakistan, however, would pose a daunting, and possibly insurmountable, challenge.

Asia. Despite an auspicious December 1985 agreement between India and Pakistan not to attack each other's nuclear installations, a subsequent chilling of Indo-Pakistani relations and unsettling domestic political developments in each nation dimmed prospects for a further easing of regional nuclear tensions. Meanwhile, both nations continued to advance their nuclear-weapons capabilities. India obtained for the first time weapons-usable plutonium unencumbered by any non-proliferation controls, while Pakistan, where senior political figures have now begun openly advocating the development of a nuclear deterrent, may have acquired its first stocks of highly enriched uranium (the alternative nuclear-weapons material), which it would be similarly free to use for nuclear arms. If Pakistan has in fact crossed this threshold and if both nations have taken steps to prepare other needed components, as some reports suggest, it is possible that they could assemble a number of aircraft-deliverable atomic bombs within a matter of months. For the time being, however, it appears that neither is likely to conduct a nuclear test or openly declare its possession of nuclear arms.

An important positive development in Asia was North Korea's adherence to the Non-Proliferation Treaty, which will go far toward alleviating concerns that a large, indigenous nuclear-research reactor, now under construction there, might be used for the development of a nuclear-weapons capability.

The Middle East. A detailed exposé of Israel's nuclear program published in October 1986 indicates that it is far more advanced than previously recognized and, accordingly, that the pace of proliferation in the region has been more rapid in recent years than generally acknowledged. The exposé, based on information and photos supplied by a technician formerly employed at Israel's classified Dimona nuclear complex, indicates that Israel may now possess between 100 and 200 nuclear weapons—not the 20 to 25 previously estimated—and that some of them may employ nuclear fusion, the principle of the H-bomb, which would make them tens of times more powerful than the atom bombs used in World War II. New evidence also appears to confirm that Israel deployed the short-range (400-mile) Jericho II missile, capable of carrying a nuclear warhead, in the early 1980s. If these various reports are accurate, Israel has vastly increased its nuclear might since 1980.

Libya, Iraq, and Iran are not known to have taken specific steps towards nuclear arming during the period covered by this volume. There has been evidence in past years of Libyan and Iraqi interest in acquiring such arms, however, and Iranian nuclear activities (included in this survey for the first time) also merit attention, given that nation's radical foreign policy and its inherited nuclear infrastructure. Iraq's continued violation of international arms control norms by repeatedly using chemical weapons against Iran and Syria's possession of advanced Soviet surface-to-surface missiles, reported development of an indigenous chemical-weapons capability, and possible Soviet nuclear guarantees are additional factors that could increase the risk of escalation to the nuclear level in any future Middle East conflict.

Latin America. The advent of civilian governments in Argentina and Brazil in late 1983 and early 1985, respectively, along with a series of subsequent bilateral initiatives aimed at easing the countries' long-simmering nuclear rivalry, promise to reduce substantially the threat that either will build nuclear weapons. Elements in both nations supportive of more open-ended nuclear development continue to wield significant power, however, and have retarded the adoption of more far-reaching non-proliferation restraints, while obtaining continued support for previously initiated projects that may ultimately permit the production of unrestricted nuclear-weapons material.

The revelation in August 1986 that the Brazilian military may have taken steps to build a nuclear test site at a remote army reservation raised additional questions about the direction of the Brazilian program. Argentina, however, accepted the assurances of Brazil's civilian leaders that the site was not intended for this purpose, and bilateral non-proliferation discussions do not appear to have been affected. (Brazil is not expected to possess unrestricted nuclear-weapons material for a number of years, so the development of a test site would have been quite premature, in any event.)

South Africa. South Africa has had the capability to produce nuclear weapons since 1980 or 1981. Given its past activities indicating an intent to develop such arms, there is reason for concern that since 1985 it has slowly added to its stocks of nuclear-weapons material or, if it has indeed decided to build nuclear arms, added several weapons to an undeclared nuclear arsenal of perhaps a dozen atomic bombs.

It has been widely assumed that South Africa will not conduct a nuclear test for fear of complicating relations with the West. With these ties already under increasing stress during 1986 because of Pretoria's racial policies, however, the added diplomatic costs of a test—which would give a major boost to white morale—may not loom as large in Pretoria's calculations as they once did. Another danger inherent in South Africa's nuclear capability is the risk, noted earlier, that a radical faction within the country may gain control over nuclear weapons or nuclear-weapons material and blackmail other elements in the nation or outside states to advance its political goals.

Controls and Safeguards. The International Atomic Energy Agency demonstrated its vitality by serving as the forum for the drafting of two major international conventions on nuclear accidents in the aftermath of the April 1986 disaster at the Soviet Chernobyl reactor. Similarly, at the IAEA General Conference in late September, a bid by several Arab states to impose sanctions against Israel was withdrawn for lack of support, seeming to end years of turmoil in the Agency that had led to repeated threats by the United States to withdraw from the organization. The matter was laid to rest only days before the revelations about Israel's nuclear program were published, however, raising the possibility that the sanctions issue will lead to renewed controversy at the 1987 General Conference.

With respect to controls over nuclear transfers, finally, a number of episodes of clandestine trade in nuclear-related equipment and materials were reported. These include Pakistan's acquisition of specially hardened steel from West Germany; Pakistani and Indian efforts to obtain Swedish flash X-ray machines, used for testing nuclear-weapons components; and India's unannounced importation of heavy water (used in its nuclear reactors).

* * *

The events of 1985-86 are analyzed in detail in the chapters that follow, beginning with an in-depth look at the dangers of nuclear inheritance. Subsequent chapters examine developments in each of today's emerging nuclear-weapon states—India, Pakistan, Israel, Libya, Iraq, Iran, Argentina, Brazil and South Africa—with introductory sections that briefly highlight related regional developments. Events relating to international non-proliferation controls and safeguards are discussed in the final chapter.

Chapter II:
The Nuclear
Inheritors

"At one of their research centers we were concerned that paper studies and computer analyses
of nuclear weapons were under way . . . that
they had gotten a charter from the Shah."

> *Former Carter administration official de-
> scribing Iran's nuclear-weapons research
> under the Shah—now presumably in the
> possession of the Khomeini regime.*

From the beginning of the nuclear age, the possibility that
war, revolution, or coup d'état might lead to abrupt changes
of control over nuclear weapons or other nuclear assets has
greatly magnified the dangers posed by the spread of nuclear
arms. With two nations at the nuclear-weapons threshold
now confronting serious domestic instability that could lead
to the collapse of internal order or to the advent of anti-
status-quo governments, the risks of nuclear inheritance
may pose one of the gravest dangers of the next decade.

Changes in the control of nuclear assets are relatively
commonplace: such a shift occurs, for example, every time
there is a change of leadership in Washington, Moscow,
Beijing, or New Delhi. When a contested transfer of power
abruptly shifts nuclear assets to individuals or political movements whose alignment is fundamentally different from
those previously in control, however, the process can have
serious and unpredictable impact on the risk of nuclear war
and international stability. Nuclear materials, installations,
technology, scientific talent, and, it appears, even nuclear
weapons themselves, already have been the subject of such
contested inheritances. In the past, struggles for the control
of nuclear assets have been incidental to larger struggles for
power. Still, contested nuclear successions in World War II
helped change the course of history, and their potential to
do so again is increasing.

So far, each of the six most advanced emerging nuclear

powers—Argentina, Brazil, India, Israel, Pakistan, and South Africa—has restrained its nuclear aspirations to a degree, in large part because of international pressure led by the major powers. Even as they have advanced toward, and in some cases crossed, the nuclear-weapons threshold, none of these emerging nations has declared itself to be a nuclear-weapon state or announced the intention to become one. More important, none of these nations has brandished its nuclear capability in order to threaten its neighbors or to establish itself as an independent, revolutionary force in world affairs. At the same time, governmental transitions in these nations, if sometimes outside constitutional processes, have been generally peaceful so far, and successor governments have been cautious in altering the strategic outlook and overall foreign policies of their predecessors.

The future may be very different. Many fear that South Africa's next government—whether white or black—will come to power by the violent displacement of the current regime, and the same might happen in Pakistan. Today, relative moderates lead the opposition in both countries, but radical factions are also part of the power struggle — neo-Nazi white extremists and militant pro-communist blacks in South Africa, Muslim fundamentalists and anti-Western populists in Pakistan; few observers would venture a prediction of the ultimate winner in either case. Although far less likely, both Argentina and Brazil have had experience with extremist political movements and coups d'état, and have the potential for populist uprisings, if economic conditions become severe enough. Only in India—which is also experiencing serious domestic unrest—and in Israel are there well-established traditions of constitutional succession.

A prolonged and tumultuous internal struggle in any of these nations would contain enormous dangers. Violent factions seeking to destabilize existing regimes could attack nuclear facilities or even seek to gain control of nuclear weapons (if the nation possessed them) in order to discredit governmental authorities and demonstrate their own potency. In truly chaotic internal situations, nuclear facilities, materials, or weapons could fall into the hands of mobs or organized criminal elements.

If radical new leaders come to power in any of the near-nuclear states through the violent displacement of the old order, possibly following years of bitter struggle, these individuals could seize upon their inherited nuclear capabilities as powerful political instruments. If the nuclear-weapons threshold had been crossed by the old regime, as it has been in South Africa and, it seems, in Pakistan, the succession to a de facto nuclear arsenal could immediately make the new leadership a force to be reckoned with in international affairs. In an effort to establish its legitimacy, the new leadership could be tempted to trumpet its inherited nuclear status with a test or a declaration that it possessed nuclear arms in order to demonstrate its permanence and its control over the affairs of the nation.

Moreover, for any radical regime committed to an ideological, political, or even religious vision of the "proper" world order, an inherited nuclear-weapons capability would offer unparalleled opportunities to support other nations or movements with similar revolutionary ideals. Indeed, the new revolutionary government could find itself virtually propelled to the vanguard of a bloc of states and subnational organizations dedicated to changing the international status quo.

At the same time, one of the most important restraints on possible nuclear adventurism by the nation's former leaders, namely the desire to maintain close relations with the major powers, particularly the United States, could be swept away. In the wake of such a violent transfer of power, ties to those perceived to be allies of the former regime are likely to be severely strained, if not ruptured altogether. Revanchist sentiments, moreover, would provide added incentive for adopting external policies antagonistic to those former allies who, given today's alignments, tend to be nations seeking to stabilize the international order.

In sum, in the volatile aftermath of a tumultuous assumption of power, the new radical leadership of a country that had crossed the nuclear-weapon threshold could perceive reasons to proclaim the nation to be a nuclear-weapon state and to utilize its nuclear assets for a variety of dangerous purposes. With external constraints crumbling, it could launch a campaign of nuclear confrontation and blackmail vastly overshadowing the mayhem caused by today's radical but non-nuclear regimes in Iran and Libya. Virtually overnight, the world community might confront a hostile, unpredictable, and highly dangerous new member of the nuclear club.

It is a time-honored truth that the spread of nuclear weapons to additional nations ultimately depends upon the capabilities and the intentions of potential nuclear states. Fortunately, the development of the necessary nuclear infrastructure requires a number of years, probably a decade or more for newly industrializing nations. Similarly, the historical record suggests that a government's decision to develop nuclear arms is likely to become known by other concerned states, or at least strongly suspected, many years before such arms can be obtained. As a result of this critically important lag, rivals of the proliferating state and the international community have had sufficient time to develop strategies, both diplomatic and military, for trying to forestall new entrants to the nuclear club, or at least to contain the impact of their arrival.

Israel's destruction of Iraq's large research reactor outside Baghdad in 1981 is the most dramatic recent example of the former, preemptive approach. After evaluating Iraq's actual and planned expansion of its nuclear infrastructure and observing signs that Baghdad intended to develop nuclear arms, Israel took action, first through diplomatic initiative and then through military force. Whether the raid was justified remains a matter of debate. It is now widely accepted, however, that Israel acted years before Iraq could possibly have acquired nuclear arms, taking advantage of the interval, described above, between Iraq's charting of its nuclear objective and the attainment of its goal.

Similarly, in the mid-1970s, the United States discerned that both Taiwan and South Korea were taking steps toward developing nuclear arms. Well before either nation could have achieved this status, Washington was able to use its long-standing ties to Taipei and Seoul to persuade both to abandon their weapons programs. In the case of Libya, a growing international embargo on nuclear sales to Tripoli has arrested its nuclear development many years before it could possibly develop an indigenous nuclear-weapons capability.

Finally, U.S. and international efforts to discourage the development of nuclear weapons by Israel, India, South Africa, and Pakistan began well before any of them had gained nuclear capabilities. Though in some cases muted by other considerations and only partially successful, these external pressures, brought to bear over the years on a series of similarly oriented governments in each country, have gradually led these emerging nuclear states to exercise at least a measure of caution in their nuclear affairs.

What makes the danger of radical governments gaining control of existing nuclear capabilities so grave is the abruptness of the political change in the emerging nuclear nation and the simultaneous tearing asunder of that nation's preexisting external relations. In such circumstances, the time between the new leadership's decision to acquire and brandish nuclear weapons and the achievement of these objectives would be drastically foreshortened, making it difficult for outside forces to reestablish the nuclear restraints that had enmeshed the former regime or to construct new kinds of dampers. Indeed, the basic diplomatic relations essential for the most minimal initiatives on this front may have been completely severed.

How likely is it that radicals will seize power and inherit the bomb in an emerging nuclear state? Obviously this will depend in each potential case on the relative strength of such factions and on the political dynamics of the particular country involved. But contested nuclear inheritances are not as uncommon as one might believe; since 1960 they have taken place or have been threatened in France, China, Vietnam, and Iran. Fortunately, none resulted in a lasting shift of control over nuclear arms or over the ability to manufacture them.

These episodes, discussed in detail in the following sections of this chapter, are sobering, although none directly parallels the scenario of radicals successfully seizing power in an undeclared nuclear-weapon state. The French and Chinese cases involved the actual or threatened succession to nuclear weapons by right-wing and conservative factions, respectively, but neither ultimately displaced the national government. Nonetheless, the cases illustrate the essential element of contested nuclear inheritances: the acquisition of nuclear assets as new forces take control over the territory where such assets are located.

The Vietnam case holds a very different lesson. Here the nuclear asset at issue was an incidental amount of non-weapons-grade uranium fuel, but the United States was determined to prevent its falling into North Vietnamese hands. This required heroic efforts, a measure of the difficulty that may be encountered in future cases where more significant nuclear legacies are at stake.

Iran may be the most troubling case. There, radicals ultimately took power, but did not inherit nuclear weapons or the ability to make them. Nonetheless, significant nuclear assets were taken over by the revolutionary government without external complaint, largely because of the complex political situation at the time. Had a nuclear-weapons capability been part of this legacy, some in the new regime, judging by their statements in 1979, might have eagerly exploited this capability to advance the nation's Muslim revolution beyond its borders.

Background: World War II

Although the four episodes mentioned above are the most relevant for understanding the danger of nuclear inheritance today, it is illuminating to recall that the threat posed by nuclear succession has been apparent since the mid-1930s, when Hitler and Mussolini came to power in two nations where some of the most advanced scientific research into atomic fission was being conducted—research that shortly formed the foundation for the development of atomic weapons.

A number of eminent nuclear physicists from these nations soon emigrated to the United States, but Werner Heisenberg, among Germany's top nuclear investigators, continued his work in Berlin and Leipzig and played a leading role in the Nazi government's ultimately unsuccessful atomic-weapon-development program.[1] Germany's access to scientific talent of this caliber greatly contributed to U.S. concerns that Hitler might succeed in building atomic weapons, concerns that, in turn, were the principal spur to President Roosevelt's decision to initiate the U.S. nuclear-weapons program in 1941.[2]

Hitler also advanced his nuclear-weapons program by conquest, as Germany succeeded to necessary subsidiary capabilities previously developed by other European nations. Hitler's invasion of Czechoslovakia in 1939, for example, gave Germany access to the Joachimsthal uranium mines, thereby securing a supply of this then rare element. Similarly, the German occupation of Norway in 1940 placed the Norwegian Hydro-Electric Company's Vemork plant, the world's only commercial producer of heavy-water needed to operate certain types of nuclear reactors, under German control. Allied concerns over the latter inheritance were so grave that they arranged for the Vemork heavy-water stocks to be evacuated to France before the plant fell to the Germans.[3] Furthermore, in November 1942 and January 1943, Britain mounted commando raids to sabotage the facility. The second attack successfully destroyed the plant's high-concentration room and set back the German atomic-weapons program by many months. A November 1943 Allied bombing raid and another sabotage operation in February 1944, which sank a ferry transporting hundreds of liters of heavy-water, ensured that heavy-water supply would remain a bottleneck in the German atomic-bomb program throughout the war.[4]

As Soviet forces swept across Eastern Europe in 1944, Moscow, in turn, took control of the Joachimsthal uranium mines.[5] This strategically important inheritance undermined a U.S. effort, begun in 1942, to obtain a "preclusive monopoly" over the world's known uranium deposits in an attempt to forestall the possibility of eventual Soviet nuclear arming.[6]

After the fall of Germany, American and Soviet teams also vied to gain access to the Germans' scientific talent and to the fruits of German wartime research and development in the nuclear field. The U.S. effort was spearheaded by the "Alsos" mission, a top-secret group of soldiers and scientists charged with acquiring information, personnel, and hardware relating to the German atomic-bomb program made available by Allied advances.

According to a detailed history of the Nazi atomic program, the capture of Strasbourg in November 1944 revealed to the Alsos team for the first time the precise locations of German nuclear research activity and spurred the Americans to race to facilities that would be beyond the U.S. occupation zone after the war.[7] The Nazis, it was discovered, were building reactors at two sites, one in Hechingen, under the direction of Professor Heisenberg, and one in Stadtilm, under Dr. Kurt Diebner; Hechingen was situated in what was to be the French occupation zone and, Stadtilm, in the Russian. Both locations were overrun by U.S. troops in April 1945, and the American forces captured an impressive array of nuclear facilities. A number of atomic scientists like Heisenberg, Diebner, Walther Gerlach, and the discoverer of atomic fission, Otto Hahn, were also taken into custody by the Alsos team.

Although this inheritance did not confirm the wartime fears of a nearly completed German bomb, these and other German facilities were deemed sensitive enough by the Alsos team to warrant measures to prevent their falling into the hands of the Soviets—or into those of other American allies. Acting on information obtained in Strasbourg indicating that a metal refining plant at Oranienburg was crucial to the German bomb program, American planes bombed the installation to preclude its acquisition by the advancing Russian troops. Similarly, the cave housing Heisenberg's uranium reactor near Hechingen was blown up by the Americans as the French began to occupy the region, an act prompted by American fears of a nuclear-capable left-leaning French government after the war.[8]

Although the United States obtained the lion's share of the German nuclear spoils, conquest also provided the Soviet Union an inheritance of considerable value. In addition to the Joachimsthal uranium mine in Czechoslovakia, the Russians appropriated uranium stockpiles at Rheinsberg and a uranium-smelting plant that had been evacuated to Stadtilm. By far the greatest boost to the Russian nuclear-weapons program, however, came from their roundup of German atomic scientists. Included in this sweep were Professor R. Dopel, Professor Gustav Hertz, and the uranium processing specialist Dr. Nikolaus Riehl, who played an integral role in the next decade of Soviet nuclear-weapons development.

These events, of course, involved the major powers and considerably predated even the earliest elements of the non-proliferation regime as it now exists. Though of less immediate relevance to proliferation today than the events in France, China, Vietnam, and Iran examined below, the nuclear successions of World War II and its immediate aftermath stand as powerful reminders of the importance of inheritance as a mechanism for advancing the nuclear-weapons aspirations of anti-status-quo—as well as more conservative—powers.

France, 1961

For two days during an attempted coup d'état in late April 1961, insurgent French military forces in Algeria may have gained control over a nuclear weapon being readied for testing at France's Reganne test site in the Sahara.[9] The coup attempt, led by four retired French generals, was triggered by bitter right-wing opposition to French President Charles de Gaulle's Algerian policy. In September 1959, after years of bloody guerrilla warfare between French and Muslim nationalist forces, de Gaulle had offered independence to the long-time French territory.[10]

The attempted coup, later known as the "Revolt of the Generals," began in the pre-dawn hours of Saturday, April 22, when rebel units, principally from the Foreign Legion, paratroops, and other special forces, seized key points in Algiers and arrested a number of top regular army officers and civilian administrators there. No resistance was offered, and by morning the rebels effectively controlled the city.

Several hours later, the leader of the rebellion, General Maurice Challe, a former commander-in-chief in Algeria, read a communiqué on Radio Algiers seeking to rally other French forces in Algeria to his cause:

I am in Algiers with Generals Zeller [former air force chief-of-staff] and Jouhaud [former army chief-of-staff] and in contact with General Salan [like Challe, a former commander-in-chief in Algeria] in order to keep our oath: to retain Algeria. An irresponsible government is getting ready to deliver Algeria to the Muslim nationalist rebellion. Do you want Mers-el-Kebir and Algiers to become Soviet bases overnight? . . . The new command reserves the right to extend its action to metropolitan France and to rebuild a republican constitutional system that has been gravely compromised by a government whose unlawfulness is staring the nation in the face.[11]

Though Challe's threat to bring his rebellion to mainland France sounds extraordinary today, it came only three years after his co-conspirator, General Raoul Salan, had attempted a coup during which Algerian-based troops had in fact prepared for an invasion of metropolitan France—and during which they had successfully taken over the island of Corsica and established, as they had in Algeria, a Committee of Public Safety, which displaced the legitimate civilian authorities.[12]

The 1958 crisis had triggered the fall of the Fourth French Republic and led to de Gaulle's return to power. To ensure stability, de Gaulle had not prosecuted the central figures in the 1958 coup attempt but had quietly retired them or shifted them to honorary posts. Following de Gaulle's decision in September 1959 to grant self-determination to Algeria, however, right-wing plotting began anew.

In January 1960, de Gaulle removed the chief of French forces in Algeria for publicly declaring that the French army would never leave the region. The action led extremist anti-independence European settlers, known as "pieds noirs," to take over the central portion of Algiers and hold it for a week in protest. This time, the armed forces remained loyal to Paris throughout the disturbance, called the "Revolt of the Barricades," but discontent among right-wing military figures continued. By late 1960, planning for the Generals' Revolt was under way and, despite a January 1961 referendum that showed three-to-one support for de Gaulle's Algeria policy, in early April, Salan, now retired, formed the clandestine Secret Army Organization (OAS), dedicated to maintaining French control over Algeria.

During the remainder of the first day of the 1961 coup attempt, April 22, Challe and his co-conspirators pressed senior officers of the army, navy, and air force in Algeria to join them, with mixed success. Additional Foreign Legion and other special units rallied to their side, as did the chief of the air force in Algeria, but most air force units, a small naval force at Mers-el-Kebir, and the commanders of Algeria's two other major cities, Oran and Constantine, among others, held back.

As these events unfolded, French technicians were readying the nation's fourth nuclear test at the Reganne test site in Algeria, some seven hundred miles south of Algiers. Activities at the site were jointly controlled by the French Atomic Energy Commission (CEA) and the French Army. Judging from France's three previous tests, the device being prepared probably was designed to have a yield at least comparable to that of the Hiroshima bomb, although details remain classified.[13]

Subsequent revelations have made clear that the insurgent generals in Algiers were aware of the existence of the device and attempted to exercise control over it at least to the extent of keeping it intact by delaying the planned test.[14] During the first day of the coup — April 22 — General Gustave Mentre, joint services commander of the Sahara region, which included the Reganne test site, joined the rebellion. At his headquarters, located in Algiers, he signed an order referring to General Challe as having "taken in hand the destiny of Algeria" and declaring that the forces in the Sahara must "obey his [Challe's] orders."[15] Subsequently, a specific order to halt the test was issued by the insurgent military leaders in Algiers.[16]

On Sunday, April 23, the revolt gained momentum, as Oran and Constantine came under the control of the insurgents and General Salan arrived in Algiers from Spain, where he had been living, after eluding Spanish authorities. Still at issue, however, was whether the rebels could gain substantial military and political backing in France; without it, the Algerian forces, which depended on the mainland for regular supplies of food, munitions, and medical provisions, had little chance of realizing their objectives.[17]

In Paris, virtually all political parties rallied to the central government.[18] De Gaulle, in an impassioned radio and television address Sunday evening, announced that he was assuming special emergency powers to crush the rebellion and called on the population for support. At the same time, he forbade French troops from carrying out the insurgents' orders.[19]

At 11:30 P.M. that night, French Premier Michel Debré appeared on television to warn that an invasion of mainland France by insurgent paratroops was imminent, probably near Paris. Paris area airports were closed; obstructions were placed on their runways; and police, troops, and tanks were placed on guard at strategic points near the capital.[20] In a statement broadcast every quarter hour throughout the night, Debré declared that any attempted landing would be met with force and told the populace: "Flights and landings are forbidden at all aerodromes of the Paris region, beginning at midnight. When the sirens sound, go there—on foot or in cars—to convince these misled soldiers of their grave errors."[21] The government's efforts apparently succeeded. Although rebel paratroopers were said to have gathered at an airfield in Algiers and had been prepared to board planes for France, the invasion failed to materialize.[22]

Monday, the 24th, de Gaulle responded to the invasion threat by blockading Algeria, in the hopes of slowly wearing down the rebels' efforts to sustain themselves.[23] New reports indicated that key elements of the air force and navy in Algeria were standing by the central government. Throughout France, ten million workers held a one-hour strike to protest "fascism." Although Debré reinstituted his alert against an invasion for a second night, the preparations again proved unnecessary.[24]

In Algeria, the revolt entered a period of uncertainty. The headquarters staff of the Foreign Legion based at Sidi-bel-Abbes shifted its allegiance to the rebels. But at Constantine, the commander who only the day before had thrown in his lot with the insurgents, returned his allegiance to Paris.[25] It is also now clear that sometime on Monday preparations were being pursued at Reganne to detonate the nuclear device despite the order from Algiers against taking this step.

On Tuesday, April 25, the rebels suffered two more setbacks. An attempt by insurgent paratroops to wrest control of the Mers-el-Kebir naval base from loyalist troops was repulsed, and at 6 A.M. France's fourth nuclear test was conducted at Reganne.[26] With support ebbing in Algeria and the prospects increasingly bleak for rallying aid in France, the revolt collapsed. General Challe, after agreeing to surrender to Paris, fled with his three principal co-conspirators, but was soon arrested.[27]

The April 25 atomic explosion was announced by French authorities in Paris as being of "weak power" and was widely thought by outside experts to have been an unsuccessful "fizzle."[28] The more prevalent view today is that the test was mounted in haste at the instructions of the Paris authorities to ensure that the device was destroyed and did not become a bargaining chip in the hands of the insurgent generals.[29] In this sense, the test would have been a precautionary action, not unlike the alerts in Paris, aimed at denying any possible advantage to the rebels.

How the chain of command operated at the Reganne site is uncertain. The base itself was under the immediate command of a General Thiry, whose allegiance during the coup attempt is not clear.[30] Apparently he reported to General Mentre, who had sided with the rebels on April 22. At his subsequent trial, however, Mentre claimed that by April 25 he had switched his allegiance back to Paris and had, in fact, been instrumental in ensuring that its instructions to detonate the device were carried out.[31]

While the matter remains murky, there is a reasonable basis for believing that the test site and the test device were under rebel control from the start of the coup on April 22 until sometime on April 24, when the insurrection began to disintegrate and a number of vacillating participants, including Mentre, sought to reaffirm their loyalty to Paris. It is also possible, however, that throughout this period the Reganne test site, like the Mers-el-Kebir naval base, was firmly under the control of troops and technicians loyal to the national government—despite Algiers' attempts to direct events at the Sahara nuclear base.

How the rebel generals might have used the Reganne device is unclear. Their overall strategy seemed to be one of using military force to establish control over a growing list of geographic and military assets, first in Algeria and then in metropolitan France, so as to catalyze still further military and political opposition to de Gaulle's Algeria policy until his government fell. In this context, control—or even apparent control—over the Reganne nuclear device would have been one of many symbols of the insurgents' growing strength through April 24, a symbol roughly analogous to the winning of Oran or Constantine. Although press accounts do not reveal whether Challe and his cohorts used their apparent control over the nuclear device in this way, it may well have been one of the factors they cited in trying to persuade others to join their cause. In the face of the overwhelming support for de Gaulle that the French polity displayed, however, it seems unlikely that even open invocation of the possession of the Reganne device would have rallied enough political support to the rebels' cause to win the day.

In addition to this symbolic role, the Reganne device was not without military significance. Early in the revolt, Paris must have taken stock of the military strength potentially available to both sides if a showdown became inevitable. Of France's 1.1 million men under arms, 500,000, including the bulk of the country's seasoned combat troops, were in Algeria, while a large proportion of those in France were recruits undergoing training.[32] Similarly the availability of aircraft and warships was a critical factor in weighing the potential for an invasion of metropolitan France. Although it is hard to imagine that nuclear arms would ever have been used in the struggle, it is equally hard to imagine that Paris, as it calculated the military balance, would have failed to appreciate the blackmail potential of the Reganne device in the insurgents' hands. Quite possibly it was this potential military threat, rather than the weapon's value as a political symbol, which led government officials to press for the prompt detonation of the device.

Since the Revolt of the Generals ultimately failed, the episode obviously does not illustrate the danger to international order that might result if radical forces inherited nuclear arms upon taking over a national government. Nonetheless, the episode provides an historical precedent for a crucial element of this scenario, since it involved a contested inheritance of a nuclear device—or at the least, a very close call. Thus the case shows that the ultimate nuclear succession can indeed occur.

It also reveals, of course, the attempt to use control over

nuclear weapons in order to gain national power in the first place. In effect, the fact that a nuclear weapon was vulnerable to seizure created a potential new basis for leverage in the struggle for national ascendency. While the extent to which the generals in Algiers attempted to use this leverage remains one of the many unanswered questions about this episode, the case stands as a warning that the presence of nuclear weapons is likely to add a dangerous new dimension to future civil conflicts in emerging nuclear-weapon states, a dimension that radical anti-government groups, among others, might seek to exploit.

The People's Republic of China, 1967-1968

For six months and possibly longer during China's tumultuous Cultural Revolution, the party boss of Xinjiang (Sinkiang) Province, Wang Enmao, is believed to have threatened to take over China's Lop Nor nuclear-weapon assembly and testing site located there, as part of an effort to maintain his authority in the face of a bid by Beijing to unseat him. Though Wang's threat was never carried out—and thus no actual succession to a nuclear capability took place—the episode reveals once again how nuclear weapons can abruptly change hands through the ebb and flow of political tides in the territory where they are situated.

Wang Enmao had governed Xinjiang since the mid-1950s as the commander of the Xinjiang Military Region and its top political commissar.[33] The area was one of high strategic importance, quite apart from the Lop Nor nuclear site, because of its significant agricultural output and its mineral resources, which included major oil fields and most of China's uranium reserves. Xinjiang, which borders the Soviet Union, had also been the target of Soviet subversive activities for many years, including Soviet-inspired movements to establish independent "East Turkestan," "Uighur," and "Ili Kazak" republics in the region between 1954 and 1958. In 1962, two years after the serious rift in Sino-Soviet relations, Beijing had had to use force to suppress a resurgence of the movement for an East Turkestan republic, and some 100,000 refugees had fled to the Soviet Union. For years afterward, the Xinjiang border was the site of repeated clashes between Chinese and Soviet troops.[34]

On August 8, 1966, the Chinese Communist Party's Central Committee formally launched the Great Proletarian Cultural Revolution, a radical campaign led by Chairman Mao Zedong and Defense Minister Lin Biao to purge the party of conservative elements—principally those who over the years had attained privilege and rank contrary to the leveling ideology of Chinese communism. Ideology aside, the effect of the Cultural Revolution was to create a virtual civil war between old-guard and radical forces within Chinese society, which was to last for a decade. In Xinjiang, it led to an extended, violent confrontation between the powerful, long-entrenched Wang and the newly radicalized central government in Beijing.

Within months after the Cultural Revolution was declared, hundreds of pro-Mao/Lin Biao revolutionaries, known as Red Guards, came to Xinjiang from Beijing and, with local sympathizers, pressed for the ouster of the regional party's leadership through a series of demonstrations, poster campaigns, and hunger strikes. Initially, regular army units (i.e., units of the People's Liberation Army) in the region sided with local authorities and assisted in maintaining order and in providing security to ensure uninterrupted agricultural production. By late December 1966, however, clashes between anti-Wang Red Guards and local party veterans intensified, and some army units were reported to be supporting the anti-Wang forces. At this point, Beijing was urging the Red Guards around the country to destroy the existing party machinery and to replace it through the "revolutionary seizure of power from below."[35]

In December 1966, Wang travelled to Beijing, apparently seeking to negotiate an understanding with Mao and Lin. During or shortly after these negotiations, Wang is believed to have made an indirect threat to seize the Lop Nor site, declaring that the facilities there "belonged to the people and [that] he would see to it that they will not become a tool in the hands of any faction in the bitter internal fight."[36] Inasmuch as China had used Lop Nor to conduct its fourth nuclear test on October 27 and its fifth on December 28, the site appears to have been under firm central government control at least through the end of 1966.

Wang's December mission to Beijing was apparently fruitless, and January saw a dramatic heightening of armed conflict in Xinjiang, with different elements of the People's Liberation Army supporting opposing sides in the struggle. Reported sabotage at the strategic Karamei oil fields and attacks by pro-Wang forces against pro-Beijing People's Liberation Army troops guarding the Sino-Soviet border contributed to the turmoil.[37]

At the end of January, Wang appears to have again threatened to take over the Lop Nor site if the central authorities did not control the radicals challenging him.[38] Apparently acknowledging Wang's strength and the importance of maintaining order in the sensitive border province, in mid-February Beijing agreed to place implementation of the Cultural Revolution under Wang's control, and later in the month Premier Zhou Enlai announced that revolutionary activities would be suspended.[39] Whether Wang's nuclear threat influenced this decision is not known.

Nonetheless, violence between pro-Wang and pro-Beijing forces in the province continued. During the spring and early summer of 1967, according to a leading Western historian of the period,

The anarchist trends among the Red Guard factions in Sinkiang [sic] prompted renewed speculation in Hong Kong that Wang had threatened to seize the Lop Nor nuclear facilities and had ordered military units under his command to take over the Gaimusi Arsenal. One source even claimed that Wang and Mao had arrived at an "unofficial truce," whereby Wang would agree to keep off the Chinese nuclear facilities in exchange for Mao's continued public backing. Whether or not such an understanding was actually reached, China detonated her first hydrogen device at the Lop

Nor site [on June 17, 1967] thus indicating that the facility was operational and probably had not been taken over by Wang.[40]

Although this source does not go so far, it seems reasonable to assume that continued test activity at Lop Nor was a strong indication of central government control.[41]

At a rally in mid-March, Wang was hailed as a faithful follower of Mao, suggesting that he had reached a *modus vivendi* with Beijing, but violence in the Xinjiang region continued for the remainder of 1967, one estimate reporting that there were more than 600 armed clashes before year end.[42]

In late 1967, Wang, still apparently a power to be reckoned with, again visited Beijing for talks. The trip coincided with China's next nuclear test, its seventh, conducted at Lop Nor on December 24. This test appears to have been a fizzle. Based on samplings of airborne radioactive debris, the U.S. Atomic Energy Commission concluded that the blast was an attempted H-bomb test, but had a yield of only twenty kilotons, (equivalent to 20,000 tons of TNT)—the yield of a relatively small atomic weapon—rather than a yield comparable to the three-megaton yield of China's first hydrogen device (equivalent to 3 million tons of TNT), tested the previous spring.[43]

Although the unexpectedly low yield parallels France's April 1961 fizzle at Reganne, published sources do not give any direct evidence that the Lop Nor misfire was the result of a deliberate effort by Beijing to destroy the device in order to prevent it from falling into the hands of pro-Wang forces. Beijing, however, made no public mention of the detonation, breaking tradition with the announcements and celebrations that followed all previous tests.[44] Furthermore, prior to most previous detonations, the Atomic Energy Commission, using reconnaissance satellite data, had been able to detect Chinese test preparations in time to alert the Congressional Joint Atomic Energy Committee; this time no such warning had been given.[45] These factors would be consistent with a test conducted in haste because of a threat to the Lop Nor site by pro-Wang forces. Other explanations, including an unplanned or premature detonation, are also plausible, however.

During 1968, Beijing slowly consolidated its hold over Xinjiang amid continuing violence. In May, Wang again traveled to the capital, where he remained through July; during this time, additional troops loyal to Mao and Lin were sent into Xinjiang. In August, Wang was ousted as regional military commander, and in September, the Xinjiang Revolutionary Committee was formed, chaired by a long-time colleague of Lin, a step that effectively displaced Wang's regular Chinese Communist Party apparatus.[46]

Although there appear to be no further published reports of Wang's threatening Lop Nor, China did not conduct another nuclear test until December 27, 1968—a full year after its previous, apparently failed, nuclear detonation. The delay has been attributed to ideological conflicts within China's nuclear establishment.[47]

Wang's power continued to decline during 1969. When he appeared at the April 1969 Party Central Committee meeting in Beijing, he had been demoted from representative to alternate and within another month he dropped from view altogether.[48]

Wang never sought to displace the authorities in Beijing and was more a conservative than a radical force. Thus as in the case of the French generals' revolt, the episode is not an example of radicals' simultaneously taking control of a national government and inheriting nuclear arms. Nevertheless, a central component of that scenario—the succession to nuclear weapons as the result of the assertion of political control over the territory where they are located—was repeatedly threatened. Though in the end such a transfer never actually came to pass, the episode provides further evidence that the inheritance of nuclear weapons by leaders profoundly antagonistic to those previously controlling them must not be dismissed as an improbable contingency; it is an inevitable risk in any nuclear-capable state confronting pressures—internal or external—for fundamental political change.

The episode also highlights the difficult choices policy-makers may face in order to prevent nuclear successions. Judging from Beijing's silence, the December 24, 1967, fizzle was a significant setback for its nuclear-weapons program. If the Lop Nor site was, in fact, being threatened at the time by pro-Wang forces, decision makers at the site and in Beijing must have agonized over whether to accept such a setback by prematurely detonating one of China's few, very costly, hydrogen bombs or run the risk that it might fall into Wang's hands. The choices confronting officials hoping to prevent future nuclear inheritances are likely to be no less difficult.

Finally, although the focus here has been on the risk that new national leaders will misuse inherited nuclear weapons once they have attained power, Wang's nuclear threats, like the French coup attempt, also demonstrate the possible role of inherited nuclear weapons as levers for attaining domestic political power in the first instance. The risk of nuclear succession as insurgents assert control over portions of national territory could greatly magnify the dangers of civil strife in the undeclared nuclear-weapon countries. Indeed, in turmoil like that of the Cultural Revolution, the possible seizure of nuclear weapons by armed gangs of peasants or radical students (who might coerce technicians at a given nuclear site into providing assistance) cannot be ruled out.

South Vietnam, 1975

In April 1975, as it completed its conquest of South Vietnam, North Vietnam took over a small nuclear-research reactor located at Da Lat, 170 miles northeast of Saigon, which the United States had transferred to the Saigon government in 1963.[49] Through a last-minute recovery mission, however, U.S. nuclear specialists were able to remove the reactor's fuel only a week before Da Lat was abandoned to Communist forces, thereby rendering the unit temporarily unusable. Hanoi, with Soviet assistance, reopened the facility in 1984.[50]

Neither South nor North Vietnam had the capability to build nuclear weapons, nor does the Democratic Republic of Vietnam have this capability today. Moreover, the extremely small size of the Da Lat reactor and the relatively low enrichment of its fuel meant that neither could have contributed significantly to the manufacture of nuclear weapons, except over the course of many years. Nonetheless, the 1975 episode is important because it is one of the few actual cases of post-World War II nuclear inheritance and because it graphically demonstrates the difficulties outside powers may encounter in preventing even a modest nuclear succession from taking place.

The Da Lat reactor project was launched in 1959, when the United States awarded the Saigon government a $350,000 grant under the U.S. Atoms for Peace program. The 250-kilowatt reactor, a TRIGA Mark II model, was similar to a number of research reactors located at U.S. universities and abroad. It was fueled with approximately twelve kilograms (26 pounds) of twenty-percent-enriched uranium.[51] By way of comparison, fifteen to twenty-five kilograms (33 to 55 pounds) of uranium enriched to ninety percent or more are needed to build an unsophisticated atomic weapon. Under the terms of a 1959 agreement for nuclear cooperation with the United States covering the transfer of the installation, the facility was owned by the Saigon government, but its fuel was leased from the United States. The agreement also contained a number of nonproliferation restrictions on the use of the plant, including a guarantee that it would not be used for the development of nuclear arms and that the United States would have the right to inspect the plant to verify Saigon's adherence to this pledge.[52] Under a 1965 trilateral agreement with the International Atomic Energy Agency (IAEA), the United States agreed to suspend its verification or "safeguards" rights as long as the IAEA applied its safeguards to the installation.[53] (This suspension of U.S. safeguards rights in favor of the IAEA is the standard approach in all U.S. nuclear accords with non-nuclear-weapon states.)

In 1971, South Vietnam ratified the Non-Proliferation Treaty. This pact also placed South Vietnam under the obligation to apply IAEA safeguards to the Da Lat reactor, since the treaty requires all of a party's nuclear activities to be placed under IAEA oversight. North Vietnam was not a party to the pact in 1975, and, shortly after its victory that year, Hanoi notified the United States, Great Britain, and the Soviet Union (the depository countries for the treaty) that it did not consider itself bound by the pact. It did not adhere to the treaty until 1982.

By January 1975, North Vietnam had begun its conquest of the South, taking Phuoc Long Province, north of Saigon on January 6.[54] On March 15, South Vietnamese President Nguyen Van Thieu ordered that the northern provinces of Vietnam be abandoned. The northern capital of Hué fell five days later. The last evacuation of Americans from Saigon would take place in little more than a month, on April 29, and Saigon would fall on April 30.[55]

During mid-March, staff members of the U.S. Energy Research and Development Administration (ERDA) brought the question of the impending loss of the Da Lat reactor to the attention of top agency officials, seeking authorization to arrange for the removal of the Da Lat fuel.[56] The reactor had once before been the subject of concern, during the January 1968 Tet offensive, when Defense Department aides had feared that it might come under enemy fire during the assault on Da Lat and when one of the top specialists at the Da Lat Institute of Nuclear Research (which housed the reactor) was among those rounded up by the insurgents and executed.[57] A contingency plan for dismantling the reactor was prepared in 1969, but the unit then received scant attention until the March 1975 crisis.

On March 24, after meetings with the State and Defense Departments, ERDA launched a mission to recover the fuel. By this point, Tuyenduc Province, which contains Da Lat, was already under North Vietnamese attack.

Concern that the reactor might provide North Vietnam a ready nuclear-weapons capability obviously was not a factor. However, the loss of strictly regulated, U.S.-owned nuclear material to conquering enemy forces, who had no legal obligation to keep the material under IAEA or U.S. safeguards, would have dealt a serious blow to the regime of orderly non-proliferation controls the United States had been trying to build for decades. It would also have caused further injury to U.S. prestige, already seriously battered by South Vietnam's collapse. As noted below, the State Department would stress the potential interruption of safeguards as the principal reason for the mission, but according to one of the officials who ordered the effort, its real purpose was to protect the Ford Administration and, it appears, the U.S. nuclear export program from embarrassment. Indeed, in a March 27 cable tasking various units to assist the effort, the Joint Chiefs of Staff acknowledged this explicitly, declaring that the State Department and ERDA had determined that the fuel "must be removed and transported out of country due to the political repercussions that could arise should the fuel fall into North Vietnam hands."[58]

Removal of the Da Lat fuel posed a number of difficult problems. The first was that the permission of the South Vietnamese government would be needed to recover the material. A U.S. request to take this step, however, could give the appearance that Washington had given up all hope of Saigon's holding back the North Vietnamese. Seeking to gloss over this awkwardness, on March 25, Washington cabled the U.S. Embassy in Saigon to stress that South Vietnam's failure to make payments on its lease for the fuel meant that the U.S. legally had the right to reclaim the material:

Embassy Saigon is requested to seek GVN [Government of Vietnam] agreement to the removal and safeguarding of the nuclear fuel at the Da Lat reactor soonest. Under the terms of the lease agreement signed by the United States and the GVN, GVN is required to return the nuclear fuel to USG [U.S. Government] if it cannot make appropriate payments. The lease expired on 12/31/74 after the GVN notified US that it was unable to make the payments. Although the provisions of the lease agreement provide the basis for repossession by the United States, the real purpose in removing the fuel is to insure that adequate safeguards continue to be applied and prevent misuse of the fuel should the reactor fall into the hands of the North Vietnamese. Inasmuch as the reactor has not been in operation for some time, removal of the fuel would not interfere with any ongoing research at Da Lat. Furthermore, the USG is prepared to arrange for new fuel for the reactor, when appropriate, should the GVN wish to resume reactor operation. Prompt GVN approval and Embassy reply required to permit [removal] mission to proceed.[59]

Saigon's approval was apparently obtained with little difficulty.

Dealing with the IAEA presented a second set of problems for the U.S. specialists planning the mission. Normally, the IAEA would be informed before the removal of safeguarded enriched-uranium fuel from a nuclear installation for transfer to another nation. To have alerted the IAEA to U.S. plans formally, however, would also have alerted North Vietnam's ally, the Soviet Union—whose nationals held important posts in the IAEA bureaucracy—about the impending removal mission. If Hanoi learned Washington's intentions, it could have attempted to foil the U.S. plan by accelerating the capture of Da Lat.

To avert this possibility, while still adhering to the principle of continuous IAEA coverage, on March 25 the State Department sent the following instructions to the U.S. Mission to the IAEA in Vienna:

Request you advise Director General IAEA confidentially of actions being taken and basis for doing so, pointing out that USG recognizes that fuel is under IAEA safeguards and that necessary transfer forms will be executed in due time. . . . [60]

Ironically, as Washington was readying this behind-the-scenes initiative with top IAEA officials, the IAEA staff was becoming concerned over the status of the Da Lat unit.

Cabling back that he had made arrangements to meet with IAEA Director General Sigvard Eklund and IAEA safeguards chief Rudolf Rometsch that afternoon, U.S. Ambassador to the IAEA Gerald Tape went on to note:

IAEA safeguards staff member independently called Misoff [Mission officer] today to inquire as to whether we had any info re status of research reactor at Da Lat, noting concern over press reports of deteriorating situation in Vietnam, and fact that they had not rpt [repeat] not received any materials reports from GVN for some time, which are required pursuant to Vietnam/IAEA NPT [Non-Proliferation Treaty] safeguards agreement. Misoff mentioned that we had seen one recent report that research reactor at Da Lat was in no immediate danger, but that situation was being kept under review. (We did not mention contents reftel [i.e. contents of the cable received earlier in the day from Washington about the planned recovery mission]). In any event, Agency is sending cable today to GVN reminding appropriate authorities of reporting requirements and urgently requesting current report on status of reactor and fuel.[61]

Ironically, Saigon appears to have undercut Washington's attempt at secrecy by responding to the IAEA's inquiry by a cable dated March 27, informing the agency that the Da Lat fuel was to be "provisionally" removed to the United States on March 31.[62] Whether North Vietnam received any advance warning of the U.S. recovery mission is not known, but there appears to have been no attempt to interfere with the U.S. effort.

Washington's diplomatic headaches, however, paled in comparison to the logistical difficulties of removing radioactive fuel from a war zone. Although the fuel itself weighed only twelve kilograms, it had to be shielded during transport for safety reasons in specially configured, concrete-filled, 55-gallon drums weighing a ton each. Thirteen of the drums were required for the fuel, which was in the form of sixty-seven used elements and two fresh ones. Skilled specialists to remove the fuel from the reactor and oversee its safe shipment had to be identified and brought to the site, and arrangements for storing the potentially dangerous material after its recovery had to be worked out.

Astonishingly, by April 1 all of these details had been dealt with—and the fuel had been successfully removed from Vietnam. On March 27, two ERDA experts, John Horan and Waldemar "Wally" Hendrickson, from ERDA's Idaho Falls Operations Office, arrived in Da Lat; both were familiar with the fueling and unloading of TRIGA reactors. R. Neil Moore, the ERDA official in charge of the operation's logistics in Washington, D.C., obtained the needed thirteen fuel transport casks from the Armed Forces Radiobiology Research Institute in Bethesda, Maryland, which housed a TRIGA reactor similar to that in Da Lat. On March 27-28, the casks were airlifted by specially arranged U.S. Air Force transport to Da Lat via Clark Air Force Base in the Philippines and Tan Son Nhut Air Base in Saigon, along with a one-ton forklift, personal radiation meters, special underwater lamps, grappling devices, and a set of hand tools that Moore purchased from a Sears store while enroute to Washington's Andrews Air Force Base, where the various items were being assembled.[63]

On March 30, Horan and Hendrickson extracted the fuel from the reactor. Even this was no easy task, because one of the American technicians first had to hook the fuel, which was immersed in several feet of water, with a grappling tool attached to the end of a flexible cable as he lay prone over the reactor pool—a "fishing" effort that took hours. On April 1, the fuel arrived at Johnston Atoll, where it was temporarily placed under the jurisdiction of the Army's Defense Nuclear Agency.[64] The material was later shipped to ERDA's Richland, Washington reservation. Contrary to some press reports at the time, the Da Lat reactor itself was not destroyed, although Horan and Hendrickson had instructions to fill the unit with concrete if removing its fuel proved impossible.[65]

On April 1, the IAEA was officially notified that the fuel had been removed to U.S. territory.[66] In a poignant afternote to the operation, Le Van Thoi, Director General of the Saigon Atomic Energy Office, wrote Horan and Hendrickson on April 19 to thank them for their efforts. The note concluded, "Like you, we all look forward to a day in the near future when we can cooperate in many other projects, one of which should be the reactivation of our Da Lat reactor."[67] Saigon fell barely two weeks later.

Ironically, it was after the fuel was safely in U.S. hands that IAEA oversight missed a beat. Owing to the exigencies of the moment, the Agency had not validated the quantity of fuel shipped out of Vietnam. In principle, it could have inspected the fuel after its arrival at Johnston Atoll. American diplomats were not enthusiastic about this possibility, however. On April 2, Washington cabled the U.S. mission to the IAEA:

We recognize Agency concern with respect to its safeguards responsibilities, in light of circumstances which made verification of quantities and composition of material before removal from Vietnam impossible. If Agency requests opportunity to verify quantities and composition, every effort will be made to accomodate. However, making arrangements for inspection visit while material is on Johnston Atoll might be difficult, since it is in U.S. military area. In any case, there is no facility on Johnston suitable for safe opening of casks. Recommend, therefore, that any requested verification be postponed until material is in U.S. Agency would then have had adequate time to plan inspection procedure and prepare instrumentation necessary to permit meaningful verification.[68]

In the end, it appears that the United States filed a standard technical report describing the material it had removed from Da Lat, and the IAEA accepted this as sufficient compliance with its safeguards standards.[69]

Although the Democratic Republic of Vietnam inherited the Da Lat reactor itself, Washington was ultimately successful in ensuring the orderly disposition of the reactor's fuel and the formal adherence to IAEA safeguards requirements. To restart the reactor, Vietnam had to rely on Soviet assistance, which apparently was conditioned on Hanoi's adhering to the Non-Proliferation Treaty.

Yet recovery of the U.S. fuel had required an extraordinary effort, even though only twenty-six pounds of low-enriched uranium was involved. Moreover, a critically important *political* factor had been essential in galvanizing Washington to action, although this factor was never explicitly recognized; this was the certainty that the fuel was going to be lost to a hostile government. As described in the next section dealing with Iran, where the political situation is more ambiguous and where those hoping to forestall a contested nuclear inheritance also have an interest in establishing good relations with the factions seizing power, efforts to block nuclear succession can be paralyzed.[70]

Iran, 1979

When the Shah of Iran, Mohammed Riza Pahlavi, was deposed by a popular revolution in January 1979, Iran possessed a substantial nuclear infrastructure, although one that did not permit the manufacture of nuclear weapons. In November 1979, after months of turmoil within Iran, the radical Muslim fundamentalist government of Ayatollah Ruhollah Khomeini came to power and took control of the Shah's nuclear legacy.

Although the evidence remains incomplete, it now appears that, in parallel with his highly publicized nuclear-power program, the Shah had initiated an undeclared nuclear-weapons research project. It is reasonable to assume that this, too, was part of the Khomeini government's nuclear inheritance, although the flight of trained nuclear personnel after the 1979 revolution may have reduced the strategic potential of this legacy. There is also evidence indicating that some elements that gained power in the chaotic aftermath of the Shah's downfall made specific inquiries to determine the level of the country's attainments in the field of nuclear-weapons development and expressed interest in building an "Islamic" bomb.

Until its abrupt truncation in 1979, Iran's nuclear program was by far the most ambitious in the Middle East. Drawing

on a scientific and technical base that had been slowly growing since the 1950s, in 1974 the Shah established the Atomic
Energy Organization of Iran (AEOI) to implement a grandiose nuclear energy plan that called for the construction of
twenty-three large nuclear-power plants within two decades.[71] Though Iran's nuclear infrastructure at the time consisted of a single U.S.-supplied research reactor at Tehran
Nuclear Research Center, within months of its creation the
AEOI, backed by Iran's enormous oil wealth, was negotiating with the United States, France, and West Germany for
the purchase of over a dozen large nuclear-power plants. By
the time of the Shah's fall in January 1979, two West German units were more than half completed at Bushehr, site
preparation work had begun for two additional French-
supplied power reactors near Darkhouin, and thousands of
Iranian nuclear specialists were being trained in these countries, and in the United States, Great Britain, and India.[72]

In addition, the AEOI had negotiated an elaborate set of
arrangements to ensure adequate long-term supplies of low-
enriched uranium fuel for the nuclear power plants it was
building. The arrangements included extendable ten-year
fuel contracts with the United States, Germany, and France,
concluded in 1974, 1976, and 1977, respectively, and the
purchase in 1975 of a ten-percent share in a major enrichment plant being built in France by the EURODIF consortium, which included France, Belgium, Spain, and Italy. Negotiations were also under way for Iran to buy a portion of a
second enrichment plant planned by another French-led
consortium, COREDIF.[73]

In parallel to these open, commercial activities, however,
it appears that the Shah may have initiated a three-pronged
undeclared nuclear-weapons research program, which included work on two technologies for producing weapons-
grade nuclear material—enrichment and reprocessing—and
on designing nuclear weapons themselves.[74] The enrichment
effort was apparently initiated in 1976, when negotiations
are believed to have begun between the Tehran Nuclear Research Center and Dr. Jeffrey Eerkens, an American scien-

tist, to underwrite Eerkens' development of specialized lasers he had designed for the enrichment of uranium.[75] Eerkens had previously worked on classified U.S. uranium-enrichment projects for the AiResearch Corporation, one of the major government contractors in the field. Eerkens' negotiations with Iran eventually led to the export to Tehran in 1978 of four experimental lasers that Eerkens claimed at the time could together produce a kilogram (2.2 pounds) of five-percent enriched uranium per day—a capability that would also theoretically permit the production of 15 kilograms (33 pounds) of highly enriched uranium in ninety days, potentially enough for a nuclear weapon.

According to a 1980 investigation of Eerkens' activities by the General Accounting Office, in 1976, while he was still employed by AiResearch, the scientist requested the approval of the Energy Research and Development Administration to discuss his laser enrichment process with the Iranians. ERDA had previously turned down an AiResearch proposal seeking support for the Eerkens' enrichment laser, since ERDA considered other laser enrichment methods more promising. Nonetheless, ERDA's division of classification believed Eerkens work had sufficient potential to be a proliferation risk, and it objected to his discussions with Iran.[76]

This decision notwithstanding, Eerkens appears to have traveled to Tehran in 1976 to discuss Iranian funding for his work.[77] In October of that year, he founded the small Los Angeles-based company, Lischem, to manufacture the specialized lasers. Four months later, in a February 23, 1977, letter to Eerkens, Dr. Ehsanollah Ziai of the Tehran Nuclear Research Center tentatively agreed to buy six lasers (later reduced to four) able to generate light at what was believed to be the optimum wave length for enriching uranium on a large scale—16-micron infrared light.[78] Eerkens left AiResearch two months later. On two occasions in the spring and summer of 1977, the head of the Tehran Nuclear Research Center, Dr. Mojtaba Taherzadeh, met with Eerkens in Los Angeles and, according to the minutes of the second meeting obtained by the *Los Angeles Times,* Taherzadeh agreed to help finance Lischem. In December, working through an Iranian businessman in Los Angeles, possibly for the purpose of disguising the source of Eerken's funds, Taherzadeh's research center provided a letter of credit for $600,000 to underwrite the project.[79]

In 1978, Eerkens sought an export license for the lasers from the Department of Energy (the agency that had absorbed ERDA's functions in a 1977 reorganization). On the application, however, he stated only that the lasers were for laboratory plasma research, and he apparently modified the lasers by filling them with carbon-dioxide so that they would produce 5-micron, rather than 16-micron, light. Eerkens told the *Los Angeles Times* that by refilling the lasers with another gas, chlorine mono-fluoride, they would produce the 16-micron light stipulated in the Iranians' contract—a strong indication that, however described in the export license application, the lasers were intended for uranium enrichment.[80]

The Energy Department recognized that Iran might try to use the devices for enrichment, but the particular experts that the Department consulted in ruling on the export license were skeptical that the process would work, and the Department granted the license on June 20, 1978.[81] A number of other well respected experts interviewed during subsequent investigations by the *Los Angeles Times* in 1978 and by the General Accounting Office in 1979-80, however, believed the Eerkens process had considerable potential and implicitly criticized the Energy Department's decision.

The lasers, weighing some three tons, were shipped to Tehran in October 1978, three months before the Shah's downfall. At that point Eerkens was attempting to obtain U.S. permission to go to Iran to help set them up, but he abandoned this effort shortly after the Shah's ouster.

Eerkens claimed that Iran was interested only in producing low-enriched uranium for nuclear-power-reactor fuel. There is reason to suspect, however, that the Eerkens lasers were part of a quiet Iranian effort, operating outside its nuclear-power program, to obtain the technology needed to build nuclear arms.

First, there was no need in Iran's nuclear power program, despite its ambitiousness, for a domestic enrichment capability. As noted above, by 1977 Iran had already contracted to purchase ample quantities of power-reactor fuel; it was also a part owner of the EURODIF enrichment plant; and it was negotiating to obtain a share of a second multinational enrichment facility. Although the insecurity of external fuel supply is often cited as a justification for developing a domestic enrichment capability, this redundancy in Iran's external fuel supply arrangements, the nation's status as an NPT signatory, and the global drop in demand for uranium ensured that the Shah would have no difficulty fueling a peaceful nuclear-power program. By 1978, moreover, Iran was taking a second look at that program, and there was good reason to believe that it was about to be significantly scaled back, reducing the demand for low-enriched uranium fuel.[82]

Secondly, gaining access to one of the most sensitive areas of nuclear research by quietly financing the start-up of an American R & D firm was hardly consistent with the open commercial arrangements Iran was making to meet its power-reactor-fuel requirements. Eerkens' 1976 visit to Iran, despite ERDA's objections and his less-than-candid export license application for the lasers, also suggest that more was involved than a straightforward arrangement to ensure the future production of electricity.

Evidence has now come to light suggesting that in addition to these enrichment activities, the Tehran Nuclear Research Center was also quietly working on a second sensitive nuclear technology, reprocessing, the technique for obtaining plutonium, the alternative nuclear-weapon material to highly enriched uranium. According to the former head of the AEOI, which controlled the Tehran center:

While there were no plans in Iran, before the revolution, to engage in reprocessing . . . the leadership of the AEOI had adopted a policy of giving the scientists and research teams a lot of leeway regarding the experiments they wanted to conduct. Consequently, on a laboratory scale a great number of experiments were being performed of which some may have involved lines of technology which, in the appropriate configuration, could have been used later on in the process of reprocessing spent fuel. It was a long way to go from here to a pilot reprocessing facility even on a lab scale.[83]

Although plutonium can be used in a mixture with natural uranium to fuel reactors instead of low-enriched uranium, Iran had little need to adopt this alternative—just as it had little need to develop its own enrichment program—because it had arranged for generous supplies of low-enriched fuel from abroad. In addition, these reprocessing activities were apparently conducted in secret. Both factors suggest that any experiments in this field may have been aimed at the long-term development of a nuclear-weapons capability.[84]

More troubling still, however, is separate intelligence data obtained by the United States in the late 1970s indicating that the Shah had set up a secret research group to work on nuclear weapons themselves. According to one knowledgeable specialist, the unit was a "nuclear-weapons design team" whose existence so troubled U.S. non-proliferation aides that a then pending agreement for cooperation with Iran in the areas of nuclear research and power was put on hold. Another official recalled that "at one of their research centers we were concerned that paper studies and computer analyses of nuclear weapons were under way"; it appeared, he continued, that "they had gotten a charter from the Shah." A third U.S. insider described the unit as a group doing "advanced research that didn't look too good," but he did not recall clear evidence of work being performed on nuclear arms.[85] It is not clear when these research activities were initiated or how closely they were associated with the Eerkens laser project or the reprocessing research noted above.

One factor that may have contributed substantially to the Shah's seeming interest in nuclear arms was that by the late 1970s, Iraq, Iran's long-time rival, was in the process of acquiring nuclear installations that could have provided it with a rudimentary nuclear-weapons capability within a decade.[86] Indeed, despite Iran's status as a Non-Proliferation Treaty party, in 1975, a year after India's nuclear test, the Shah declared that, "If ever a country in this region comes out and wants to acquire atomic weapons, Iran must also possess atomic bombs."[87] Israel's concerns over Iraq's nascent capability, it should be recalled, led Israel to destroy Iraq's principal nuclear plant, the Osiraq reactor, in 1981. During the mid- to late 1970s, there was also increasing evidence that Pakistan was moving to acquire nuclear arms. Though Pakistan was not a potential military adversary, the Shah may well have feared that a Pakistani nuclear weapon would undermine Iran's claim to be the region's most technically advanced power.

Whatever the hopes for the Eerkens lasers, Iran's progress on reprocessing, or the accomplishments of the Shah's nuclear-weapons research group, there is wide agreement that any Iranian nuclear-weapons program was still in its infancy in 1979. Still, when Iran's revolutionaries took power, they inherited more than a blank slate in these sensitive areas.

In conjunction with its open peaceful nuclear research activities, the AEOI had signed a contract in 1976 with the General Atomic Corporation, the American manufacturer of the Tehran research reactor, to purchase over twenty kilograms (44 pounds) of highly enriched uranium fuel for the facility. Iran hoped that by increasing the amount of fuel in the core from five to twenty kilograms, it could significantly improve the reactor's efficiency and double its power to ten megawatts.[88] The U.S. embassy in Tehran supported the transfer, apparently hoping that by maintaining good relations on this front, Iran would be encouraged to turn to the United States, rather than France and West Germany, for its planned multi-billion dollar purchases of nuclear-power plants. In an apparent effort to persuade Washington to amend the U.S.-Iran agreement on nuclear research to permit the sale, in May 1977 the embassy cabled:

While we appreciate that request for 20.2 kilograms of highly enriched uranium for Tehran research reactor far exceeds fuel ceiling
provided for in existing bilateral research agreement, we are concerned that refusal will feed GOI's [Government of Iran's] worst
fears concerning reliability of US as future supplier of nuclear materials. Against background of May 4 Presidential announcement
of approval of significant quantities of HEU [highly enriched ura-
nium] to 8 projects in Canada, the Netherlands, Japan, Belgium,
and FRG, suspicions will also be fed that US has and will continue
to differentiate between various customers in favor of the industrial West. Juxtaposition of this development with Secretary's [of
State Cyrus Vance's] imminent arrival and expected discussion of
future US/GOI cooperation in nuclear energy field seems
unfortunate.

Would appreciate urgently therefore . . . indication of whether
it likely amendment to existing bilateral research agreement can
be reached quickly to accomodate export request. . . . [89]

Washington, however, firmly opposed the sale:

The President's concern about inventories of HEU abroad is the
reason behind these guidelines [announced in April 1977 limiting
exports of the material]. Growing volume of HEU in international
commerce poses a special risk as it is readily usable in nuclear
weapons. Such an approach is not meant to impugn the nonproliferation intentions or question the motives of countries like Iran.
We are confident the GOI recognizes the serious problems associated with the widespread use of HEU particularly the possibility of
terrorist seizure. . . .

In the meantime . . . application will be kept in suspense.
Should the GOI raise questions about delay in approval of the
HEU export license, you may point out problem of ceiling in
present agreement and our expectation that the issue will be addressed in negotiations for new bilateral [covering nuclear research
and nuclear power]. You may also provide background contained
[above] . . . on our nonproliferation concerns associated with
HEU. [90]

When the Shah fell, the export license, which had been

amended on August 8, 1978 to request 26.2 kilograms (57.6 pounds) of highly-enriched uranium, was still pending. Had the application been approved, or had a renewed request for the material made in the spring of 1979 by Iran's Provisional Revolutionary Government been granted, Iran would now have the essential ingredient necessary to manufacture a nuclear explosive.

Instead, by mid-1979, as Khomeini pursued his anti-modernization, Muslim fundamentalist revolution, the nuclear-power reactor contracts with Germany and France had been canceled, and work ceased on the Bushehr and Darkhouin projects. Iran's fuel-supply contracts and participation in EURODIF have been in limbo ever since.[91] Although in 1984, West German experts visited the partially completed Bushehr reactors to assess what would be needed to complete them, it appears that no German assistance will be provided as long as the Iran-Iraq war continues.[92] (It should be noted that had these reactors been operating at the time of the Shah's overthrow, their spent fuel would have contained enough weapons-usable plutonium for dozens of nuclear weapons, although the material would have been subject to IAEA safeguards and there is no evidence that the Shah possessed a reprocessing capability to extract the plutonium from the spent fuel. Over several years, however, the Khomeini government might have been able to develop one, possibly building on its inherited reprocessing research.)

The status of the Shah's undeclared nuclear-weapons research program remains unknown. Many nuclear experts associated with the Iranian nuclear-power program fled Iran during the anti-modernization campaign that led to the cancellation of the French and German reactor deals. According to the former head of the AEOI, however, many specialists working at the Tehran Nuclear Research Center remained.[93] It is possible these included the experts engaged in weapons-related work, although it appears that the laser enrichment team was disbanded. Indeed, as of late 1983, the Eerkens lasers had not even been uncrated.[94]

The Khomeini government, it may be noted, has maintained and expanded its nuclear research program, opening a second research center at Isfahan in late 1984, for example. The work under the Shah on reprocessing and nuclear-weapons design would provide a valuable foundation for further efforts in the field by the Khomeini government and could possibly reduce the time needed to develop nuclear arms by a number of years.

The five-megawatt, U.S.-supplied research reactor at the Tehran Nuclear Research Center presents separate issues. In contrast to its actions in the case of the Da Lat reactor in Vietnam, the United States did not attempt to remove the fuel from the Tehran installation prior to the fall of the Shah's government, and five kilograms (11 pounds) of highly enriched (93 percent) uranium fuel, still in use at the reactor, fell into the hands of the Shah's radical successors. The amount involved is too small to permit the manufacture of a nuclear weapon, however, and the material remains under IAEA safeguards pursuant to Iran's Non-Proliferation Treaty obligations.[95]

Nonetheless, the very outcome the United States struggled to avoid in Vietnam—having U.S. nuclear material fall into the hands of a hostile government—transpired. And, given Iran's far larger nuclear infrastructure, it is entirely possible that the Tehran reactor may eventually be used to perform studies or provide training to support the development of nuclear arms.

A further setback for Washington was that the bilateral U.S.-Iran nuclear cooperation agreement covering the fuel expired in April 1979, shortly after the Shah was forced from power. Although the United States claims that all the non-proliferation controls in the accord remain in effect despite its expiration, it is not clear that Iran has agreed to this interpretation. Among other restrictions, the agreement gives the United States the right to approve any disposition of the fuel once it is removed from the reactor and the right to inspect the fuel if IAEA safeguards ever cease to apply—for example, if Iran withdraws from the Non-Proliferation

Treaty, as that pact allows, on ninety days' notice.[96]

Though the loss of the fuel and these rights poses only modest proliferation risks, it highlights one of the most important lessons of the Iranian nuclear inheritance, namely the difficulties outside powers may encounter in trying to influence the disposition of a nation's nuclear assets during a period of internal upheaval. During the period of the Shah's decline and during the tenure of the interim Bakhtiar and Bazargan governments which preceded Khomeini, the United States attempted to keep relations with its erstwhile regional ally on as even a keel as possible. This effectively constrained it from taking steps to prevent the transfer of the fuel—or of other, more sensitive nuclear assets such as nuclear-weapons research—to Iran's new leaders.

To have sought the removal of the reactor fuel before the Shah's overthrow would have given the appearance that Washington expected his ouster at the very time that Washington was trying to bolster his authority. To have sought to remove the fuel in the months following his departure would have given the impression that the United States considered the revolutionary government unreliable, a step that would have undercut Washington's effort to maintain businesslike relations with Iran's new leadership and forestall possible Soviet adventurism. In the end, the United States temporized, refusing to renew and amend the U.S.-Iran nuclear pact to permit new exports of highly-enriched-uranium fuel, but tolerating the loss of control over that already in Iran.

Until November 1979, of course, the United States did not fully appreciate the power of Muslim fundamentalism in Iran and thus was unable to predict that a radical anti-Western government would soon take power there. Had the advent of a hostile government been more certain—as it was in Vietnam in 1975—it is possible the United States would have acted more aggressively to block the turnover of the Shah's nuclear assets. As it turned out, Washington's predisposition through late 1979 to avoid stresses with the government in power and American underappreciation of the dangers that loomed ahead led to inaction—with the result that

Khomeini inherited nuclear assets that never would have been transferred to him directly or, one assumes, willingly abandoned to him.[97]

Given the Khomeini government's outspoken calls for the overthrow of the current superpower-dominated world order and Iran's open desire to spread its revolutionary fundamentalism throughout the Muslim world, there is good reason for concern that the Shah's successors would have attempted to exploit their nuclear legacy to develop nuclear weapons had this been feasible. New evidence provided by a former Iranian government energy specialist lends support to this conclusion, at least for the period from 1979 to 1981.

During the first half of 1979, numerous elements within and outside the Bakhtiar and Bazargan governments contended for power, some backed by private armies. During this period, one such strongman, who was an official of the Bazargan government and had close ties to the Khomeini camp, approached this energy aide and made detailed inquiries as to the steps that would be necessary for Iran to develop nuclear weapons, given the country's then existing nuclear infrastructure. Though this did not reflect a coherent government policy on nuclear arming—indeed at this juncture work at the Tehran Research Center was temporarily at a standstill—according to the source, the query went beyond idle curiosity. At the time, according to the former government energy specialist, a number of Muslim religious leaders were actively calling for Iran to build an "Islamic" bomb, apparently in the hopes that this would enhance Iran's prestige among Islamic states and lend status to Muslim fundamentalism as an alternative to secular, Western-oriented modernization and Soviet Marxism.

In 1981, after Khomeini's authority was well established, some Iranian officials continued to express interest in acquiring nuclear arms, although it is not known whether specific actions were taken to pursue this objective.[98] Although the lack of interest in the Eerkens lasers through late 1983 suggests that few such steps were taken during this period, it is possible that Iranian investigators simply considered this technology too esoteric to be of value, particularly without Eerkens' assistance, and decided to pursue other avenues of weapons-oriented research.

The Iranian nuclear inheritance most closely parallels the scenario, described in the opening section of this chapter, of a radical government inheriting nuclear arms from a predecessor regime through a contested seizure of power. Although neither nuclear arms nor the capacity to build them were transferred in this instance, a significant nuclear infrastructure, including some weapons-relevant technology and equipment, was transferred by contested political succession to a militant anti-status-quo government. Moreover, enough highly enriched uranium for a weapon would have been inherited had the AEOI request for U.S. research-reactor fuel been granted, as encouraged by U.S. officials in Iran. In addition, some factions within the ruling revolutionary elite favored the development of nuclear arms to advance Iranian interests beyond its borders.

At the same time, the confused political picture after the Shah's departure and competing policy objectives disarmed the United States and kept it from taking possible steps to forestall Khomeini's succession to the Shah's nuclear assets. Once the hostage crisis began in November 1979, Washington lost the ability to act on the nuclear front, as Khomeini tightened his grip on the country.[99] Indeed, the disposition of the Shah's undeclared nuclear assets may not be known.

The story of the Iranian nuclear legacy is not yet over. The Muslim fundamentalist government, now firmly in control, is reactivating the nation's nuclear program. There is reason for concern that Iran, which has been locked in a bitter six-year war with Iraq and which has shown intense hostility toward both of the superpowers, remains interested in acquiring nuclear arms. In the years ahead it may yet exploit the full military potential of its inheritance.

The Future

Reduced to their basics, the four cases discussed above

teach several elementary lessons. First, nuclear weapons, like other tangible assets, can indeed change hands as political control abruptly shifts over the territory where they are located. This appears to have happened once, in France, and was threatened in China. It can be added that even if the Algerian generals in the French case never did, in fact, exercise control over the Reganne test site, Paris was sufficiently concerned over this possibility to destroy the nuclear device there; Beijing may have taken similar action in December 1967 because of the threat to Lop Nor from pro-Wang forces. Simply put, the succession to nuclear weapons by elements hostile to those controlling them is not implausible; it is a danger that has already presented itself on at least two occasions.

Secondly, it is also not implausible that a radical, anti-status-quo government can sweep into power and inherit significant nuclear assets; nor is it implausible that militants within such a government would desire nuclear arms to advance the country's interests abroad. This is precisely what occurred in Iran in 1979, and there were similar episodes during World War II.

Third, preventing the inheritance of nuclear assets is likely to be costly and complicated, and in some instances it may not be possible at all. The Vietnam case, with its clear-cut political situation and limited quantity of research-reactor fuel, is unlikely to be duplicated. Iran in 1979 is a far more probable model, with national authority in flux and nuclear assets diverse and partly hidden from view.

In sum, though a radical government has never inherited nuclear arms, there is historical precedent for the key elements of this scenario. With radical factions now active in South Africa and, to a lesser extent, in Pakistan and the danger present in both countries that the national government may be displaced, it is a scenario that must be given serious attention.

Although few would venture to predict specific political developments in these two nuclear-weapon threshold states, it is prudent to speculate about the possibilities for nuclear inheritance in each. If the South African government were on the verge of collapse, a range of black-majority forces, some moderate, some extremist, would probably be jockeying to position themselves to take power or to wrest it away from a competing faction in the period of turmoil that could well follow the fall of white minority rule. Simultaneously, white extremists could well be plotting a preemptive coup. Whoever prevailed could inherit extensive and highly dangerous nuclear assets not currently subject to any external non-proliferation controls: a facility capable of producing weapons-grade uranium (the Valindaba uranium enrichment plant); a stockpile of the material; and, possibly, ten or twenty nuclear weapons themselves. If such weapons have been produced, facilities for their manufacture, specialized scientific manpower, and data on nuclear-weapons design and fabrication would also be part of the white government's nuclear legacy—but all of these elements, and the whereabouts of the nuclear weapons would be secret, unknown to outsiders. Plutonium-bearing spent fuel from the Koeberg nuclear-power plants, and the plants themselves, would also be part of the South African nuclear legacy. This material is subject to IAEA safeguards, however, and South Africa has also pledged to France, the supplier of the Koeberg plants, that none of the fuel will be reprocessed domestically to extract its plutonium; nor does South Africa possess the necessary reprocessing facilities.[100]

Extraordinary measures would be required to prevent the inheritance of these nuclear-weapons-relevant assets. Nuclear weapons and stocks of nuclear-weapons material would have to be destroyed, rendered unusable (for example, through the dilution of highly enriched uranium) or removed from the country; industrial-scale facilities would have to be rendered inoperable; and steps would have to be taken to disperse key personnel and destroy technical data. Removal of the highly radioactive, and less militarily sensitive, Koeberg spent fuel might also be considered. The logistical complexity of the Vietnam fuel evacuation would be multiplied many times in the South African case.

Would the current South African government take these steps on its own, eliminating its ultimate weapon in its hour of crisis and destroying a show-piece facility worth tens of millions of dollars? Would it recognize its impending displacement by revolution or coup in time to take such steps if it wanted to? Would outside governments, such as the United States, try to intervene out of fear of a radical takeover or would they hesitate, as the United States hesitated in Iran, hoping to shore up the existing government until the last moment and then to build bridges to its successor? Even if outsiders decided to step in, how would they do so—by bombing Valindaba or mounting a commando raid to seize South Africa's nuclear weapons, assuming they could be located?

A crisis in Pakistan would present comparable dangers. Nuclear assets that might be inherited would again include a uranium enrichment plant probably capable of producing weapons-grade material; stocks of this material, if it had been produced; and, potentially, nuclear weapons themselves (an increasing possibility as time passes)—none subject to external non-proliferation controls. Fabrication facilities, weapon designs, trained manpower, and the Kanupp nuclear power plant in Karachi with its spent fuel—which, like the Koeberg plants is under IAEA safeguards—would also be part of the Pakistani nuclear legacy.

Preventing such a legacy would pose the same problems of locating the assets and choosing a suitable course of action as in the case of South Africa, and the same reluctance to act on the part of the Pakistani government and on the part of the interested outsiders, such as the United States, could be anticipated. The possibility of preemptive military action by India or by Afghanistan (with Soviet backing) during a period of internal Pakistani turmoil would complicate the picture, however, and even this might prove unsuccessful in destroying all of Pakistan's military nuclear assets, given the secrecy that surrounds the program.

Possibly the end of minority rule in South Africa will come about peacefully, as the result of negotiation rather than civil strife, and the forces of moderation will prevail. In

Pakistan, a nascent parliamentary democracy may take root, and that country's future leaders may be selected by ballot rather than by exercising power in the streets. In the end, the current dangers from proliferation in both countries, as serious as they are, might not be further exacerbated by nuclear successions. But such an outcome cannot be guaranteed, and the risk that extremists will ultimately emerge victorious must be recognized.

Strategies can be devised for mitigating the dangers of nuclear inheritance. Ideally, steps should be taken now to envelop militarily significant nuclear assets in these countries in a network of tough non-proliferation controls, particularly IAEA safeguards. While a radical new government could always throw over these restraints, it would suffer serious political costs that would cause it to hesitate before taking such a step—just as even the most radical new governments have hesitated to repudiate their nation's pre-existing international debt. Indeed, even the Khomeini regime has adhered to its IAEA commitments covering the Tehran research reactor and fuel, although, admittedly, this facility does not present the same temptations as a nuclear-weapons capability.

Persuading South Africa and Pakistan to accept IAEA safeguards over their entire nuclear programs has been a longstanding non-proliferation objective, and early achievement is not likely, particularly in Pakistan, where concerns over India's partially unsafeguarded nuclear program are, understandably, a major concern. Nonetheless, the dangers of future nuclear successions mean that increased priority must be given to achieving this goal.

A parallel strategy would be to develop mechanisms to permit the rapid extension of IAEA safeguards to key nuclear assets—nuclear-weapons material and the facilities for producing them—on the request of a government during periods of internal crisis or war. Currently, negotiations on the technical aspects of applying safeguards take months and sometime years. The availability of "emergency safeguards" could be a valuable option for reducing the dangers of undesired successions; moreover, their very existence would tend to reduce the singularity of a special request to the Agency for safeguarding, lessening the loss of face that might be involved for the requesting government. Whether a government that had long resisted safeguards would accept them in extremis is problematic, but the availability of this option would at least be a step toward encouraging this outcome.

U.S. contingency planning for the receipt or rapid removal of nuclear-weapons material on request could also be invaluable. In the Vietnam case, the United States quickly found a suitable temporary repository for the Da Lat fuel at Johnston Atoll, but finding a comparable site for sequestering larger, more hazardous, and more politically sensitive nuclear assets could prove far more difficult. Early attention to the problem could also permit Washington to encourage precautionary steps by the government of the particular emerging nuclear-weapon state under challenge.

Finally, to reduce the threat of unpredictable nuclear inheritances in the future, the United States and other nuclear suppliers could give more explicit consideration to the question of internal and regional stability when deciding on nuclear transfers to particular nations. There appears to have been some reluctance to consider such factors in the past.

In July 1945, a member of the Hungarian Royal Crown Guard gave the U.S. Seventh Army Hungary's greatest national treasure, the crown of St. Stephen, to prevent its falling into the hands of advancing Soviet troops. The crown, a symbol of Hungarian nationhood since it was given to the Hungarian king in the year 1000 by Pope Sylvester II, had been used in the coronation of every subsequent Hungarian king, and no ruler was considered legitimate unless crowned with it. The United States placed the crown in Fort Knox for safekeeping. It was returned to Hungary in January 1978.[101]

Today, nuclear weapons, weapons material, and related items may be the greatest national treasures of the nuclear-threshold states. They, too, are at risk in time of war or upheaval. Unfortunately, finding mechanisms for the safe disposition of these strategically important assets poses a far more difficult challenge. If the most serious dangers of nuclear inheritance are to be avoided, greater attention will have to be given to this complex problem in the years ahead.

Chapter III:
Asia

"If India openly starts a weapons programme, the deep-rooted Pakistani fears of India . . . would put tremendous pressure on Pakistan to take appropriate measures to avoid a nuclear Munich at India's hands in the event of an actual conflict, which many Pakistanis think very real."

Senior Pakistani nuclear scientist, Abdul Qadir Khan, Fall 1985

"If Pakistan gets a nuclear weapon, India will have to think very seriously about its own option. . . . We have every indication and information that leads us to believe that Pakistan has not given up its nuclear weapons program and is bent on having it."

Indian Prime Minister Rajiv Gandhi, April 1986

The danger of proliferation in Asia intensified between mid-1985 and late 1986. Despite an auspicious December 1985 Indo-Pakistani agreement against attacking each other's nuclear installations, a subsequent chilling of relations between the two countries and unsettling domestic political developments in each soon dimmed prospects for a further easing of nuclear tensions.

Both nations, meanwhile, continued to advance their nuclear-weapons capabilities, further reducing the chances of averting a regional nuclear arms race. India, which conducted a single nuclear test in 1974, for the first time obtained weapons-usable plutonium unencumbered by any non-proliferation controls, while Pakistan appears to have acquired its first stocks of highly enriched uranium (the alternative nuclear-weapons material), which it would be similarly free to use for nuclear arms. If Pakistan has in fact reached this threshold and if both nations have taken steps to prepare other needed components, as some reports suggest, it is possible that they could assemble a number of aircraft-deliverable atomic bombs within a matter of months.

The Indian leader, Rajiv Gandhi, appears unlikely to take such a step, unless Pakistan conducts a nuclear test. Pakistan's General Zia ul-Haq, in turn, will probably refrain from such a provocation, which could jeopardize critically needed U.S. assistance and could intensify Soviet pressure from neighboring Afghanistan. In sum, South Asia now has, or may very shortly have, two nuclear-weapons-capable states, hovering uneasily at the nuclear threshold.

Another important and very positive development in Asia during the 1985-86 period: North Korea ratified the Non-Proliferation Treaty in December 1985. Pyongyang's decision is believed to be the result of Soviet pressure initiated at U.S. urging.[1] Apparently in late 1984, Washington became concerned that a large unsafeguarded research reactor that North Korea was building at Yong Byon might be the first stage of a nuclear-weapons development program. The reactor was unusually large, given the early stage of North Korea's nuclear energy and research program, possibly in the twenty to thirty megawatt range, and was a natural-uranium/graphite unit, an out-of-date design, but one well-suited to a clandestine nuclear-weapons development effort.[2] In early 1985, U.S. non-proliferation aides quietly raised the matter with their Soviet counterparts, but received no response until the announcement of North Korea's ratification of the pact. The step means that Pyongyang has formally renounced nuclear arms and, more important, has agreed to place all of its nuclear installations under International Atomic Energy Agency safeguards. Apparently to encourage North Korea's decision, the Soviet Union agreed to expand nuclear trade by supplying it with a commercial nuclear power reactor.

South Korea ratified the treaty in 1976 after abandoning a nuclear-weapons program begun early in that decade.[3]

Largely because of its unwillingness to jeopardize U.S. security guarantees, South Korea is not believed to be reconsidering this stance. Although tensions with the North continue, the fact that the latter has now joined the Non-Proliferation Treaty should avoid the emergence of a situation in which South Korea felt compelled to renew its nuclear-weapons program because of suspicions that the North is developing such capabilities.[4]

In Taiwan, confidence in U.S. security ties may not be as strong as it is in South Korea, but there is no evidence of a reawakening of the Taiwanese nuclear-weapons program of the early 1970s.[5] While the United States has continued to supply Taipei with defensive arms, it has sharply limited the types of weapons provided and their sophistication, and the People's Republic of China continues to apply pressure to restrict such sales. President Reagan's trip to China in April 1984, when he invoked Beijing as a strategic counter to Moscow, demonstrated the growing importance to Washington of Sino-U.S. relations. In 1986, the United States agreed to provide China with advanced technology for the first time to assist it in modernizing its defense forces, a further indication of growing Sino-U.S. ties.[6]

To counter diminishing U.S. military support, Taiwanese leaders have made the most of U.S. aid while developing Taiwan's conventional arms industry, with particular emphasis on air-defense capabilities.[7] The United States has agreed to transfer increasingly sophisticated technology to Taiwan to assist in this effort. This buildup has not extended to nuclear capabilities, however. Taiwanese President Chiang Ching-kuo told the German weekly *Der Spiegel* in May 1983 that his nation would not build atomic weapons, although it had the scientific and technological capability to do so.[8] Similarly, in November 1983, the Taiwanese press reported that Taiwan's cabinet, in a formal response to a question from a legislator, stated that the "government of the Republic of China under its established policy would never develop nuclear weapons. . . . There is no reason to develop nuclear weapons to 'kill our own people.' However,

. . . the government has spared no effort to develop high technology defense industries in this country."[9] No evidence has emerged since to contradict these declarations.

While Japan unquestionably has the capacity to produce nuclear weapons and is developing sizable reprocessing and enrichment capabilities, the strong domestic opposition to nuclear weapons resulting from its history as the first victim of nuclear attack exclude it as a proliferation threat at least for the present. It is conceivable, however, that were North or South Korea or Taiwan to acquire such weapons, Japanese attitudes might change rapidly.

The activities of the People's Republic of China are also critically important to the risk of further proliferation in Asia. China has been a nuclear-weapon state since 1964, when it tested its first nuclear device. Through the 1970s, its policy was not to oppose the spread of such weapons to additional countries, which it saw as a means of diminishing the power of the United States and the Soviet Union. Indeed, during the early 1980s, there were repeated reports that China had made sales of nuclear materials to such countries as South Africa, India, and Argentina, without requiring them to place the imports under IAEA inspection.[10] From 1982 to 1984, several press accounts, usually quoting anonymous U.S. government sources, reported that China was aiding Pakistan's efforts to acquire nuclear arms by providing it with nuclear-weapons design information, weapons-grade uranium, and technical assistance in completing an unsafeguarded uranium-enrichment plant, potentially capable of producing weapons-grade material.[11] Against this background, the Reagan administration suspended the talks it had initiated with Beijing in mid-1981 on an agreement for cooperation in the field of nuclear energy.

In mid-1983, China began a dramatic shift in its posture, and the U.S.-PRC talks were renewed. In January 1984, China joined the IAEA and subsequently advised the United States that in the future it would require IAEA safeguards on its nuclear exports. In a series of statements beginning that month, top Chinese leaders declared China's firm commitment to non-proliferation. Premier Zhao Ziyang stated in an address to the Sixth National People's Congress in May 1984, for example, that China does "not engage in nuclear proliferation by helping other countries to develop nuclear weapons."[12] Based on these developments, a nuclear trade agreement was initialed in Beijing during President Reagan's April 1984 visit.

The administration did not submit the accord for the required review by Congress until July 1985, over a year later, reportedly because of concerns that Chinese nuclear aid to Pakistan was continuing.[13] After further talks, however, China agreed to implement its non-proliferation policy, according to U.S. officials, "in a manner consistent with basic non-proliferation practices common to the United States and other suppliers," an official U.S. circumlocution apparently intended to signify that any Chinese assistance to Pakistan had been halted.[14] China has repeatedly denied that anything beyond normal scientific exchanges ever took place.[15] In the fall of 1985, China also announced it would voluntarily place some of its civilian nuclear installations under IAEA safeguards, matching a step previously taken by all other nuclear-weapon states.

The U.S.-China agreement, the first U.S. nuclear accord with a nuclear-weapon state that is not an ally, went into effect in December 1985 after a lengthy congressional review.[16] Through a joint resolution, Congress required that before a license could be issued for any nuclear exports to China under the agreement, the president—after further negotiations with Beijing—would have to certify that the provisions of the accord would be "effective" in ensuring that U.S. nuclear exports were used exclusively for peaceful purposes.[17]

The pact itself provided only for "visits" and "exchanges of information" with respect to U.S. nuclear exports, but not for the full range of accounting and surveillance procedures akin to those used by the IAEA. The Reagan administration made clear that it considered the agreement sufficient and would not demand such iron-clad procedures from

Beijing in any further negotiations. Nonetheless, Congress, fearing that China would back away from the accord, rejected a provision that would have made U.S. exports conditional on China's accepting verification procedures equivalent to those of the IAEA.[18]

In April 1986, China announced a drastic cutback in its nuclear power program, apparently because of a shortage of foreign exchange.[19] This will effectively preclude any major U.S. nuclear sales to China for the time being, mooting the verification question, at least temporarily. In the meantime, under its offer to accept safeguards voluntarily on some of its civilian nuclear plants, China has announced that its largest nuclear power project, at Daya Bay near Hong Kong, will be placed under the IAEA system.

In mid-September, China signed a nuclear cooperation accord with Pakistan. The agreement provides that all equipment and materials supplied by China will be covered by IAEA safeguards, but the accord does not require as a condition of supply that Pakistan place all of its nuclear installations under the IAEA system. The United States and, at least for the moment, all other Western nuclear supplier countries have made such comprehensive coverage a condition for nuclear trade with Pakistan. It remains possible that China will use the accord as a cover so that it can offer technical assistance—for which safeguards are not apparently required—for more sensitive aspects of Pakistan's nuclear program.[20]

India

A tentative warming of relations in late 1985 led India and Pakistan to a December commitment not to attack each other's nuclear installations. The accord raised hopes that the two countries had taken a cautious first step down a path that might yet avert a nuclear arms race in South Asia. By late-1986, however, much of the momentum toward Indo-Pakistani detente had dissipated. India had quietly continued to advance its nuclear-weapons capability, acquiring for the first time weapons-usable plutonium that is totally free from any non-proliferation controls. India may already have fabricated other components for nuclear arms and is believed to have a team of specialists working on improved nuclear-weapon designs. If it chose to, India could probably deploy a small number of aircraft-deliverable atomic bombs in a matter of months.

Still, it appears that the government of Prime Minister Rajiv Gandhi is maintaining its policy against actually building or testing nuclear weapons. How long this policy may be continued is unclear. New reports that Pakistan has made major advances in its nuclear-weapons program may trigger domestic pressures in India that will push Gandhi to adopt a more assertive nuclear stance, such as the quiet readying of a number of nuclear weapons or, possibly, further nuclear testing and overt deployment of such arms.

Background. The dynamics of the incipient Indo-Pakistani nuclear-arms race are complex. As in the case of U.S.-Soviet nuclear relations, Indian and Pakistani decision-making on this issue takes place against a backdrop of intense mutual suspicion and domestic political considerations, as well as in relation to specific developments in the nuclear programs of the two countries. Centuries old Hindu-Muslim antagonisms, for example, remain a factor in this ultra-modern realm, even among the governing elites in both countries, and the three wars fought between the two states since independence from the British in 1947 have left a legacy of deep distrust.[1]

Pakistan's dismemberment in the 1971 Indo-Pakistani War, in which the independent country of Bangladesh was created out of territory that had formerly been East Pakistan, left India by far the dominant power in the region. India's modernization and expansion of its conventional forces in the past 15 years have heightened its military supremacy—it is generally thought to have a several fold advantage in military equipment and man-power over Pakistan—while its size and its economic development during this period have led inevitably to its political dominance in regional affairs.

Post-1971 Pakistani foreign policy, including new links with other Islamic countries (especially the oil rich members of OPEC) and growing ties to the United States in the aftermath of the 1979 Soviet invasion of Afghanistan, have sought to counterbalance India's regional hegemony. But initiatives seen by Pakistan as essential to avoid becoming a mere satellite of its eastern neighbor have been perceived in New Delhi as unfriendly challenges to India's natural leadership role in the subcontinent. Even domestic political unrest in both nations is seen partly through the prism of these mutual antagonisms, as each accuses the other of being the unseen hand behind anti-government agitation.

While some policymakers in both countries, seemingly including Pakistani President Zia ul-Haq and Indian Prime Minister Gandhi, favor improved relations, other factions remain intensely nationalistic and hostile to rapprochement. This lack of consensus has restricted the maneuvering room of both leaders, leading them to be cautious in their efforts to improve bilateral ties and making accommodation in the nuclear sphere particularly difficult.

The histories of both nations' nuclear programs also critically affect the current state of their nuclear relations. In retrospect, it appears that the groundwork for an Indian nuclear-weapons program was laid in the 1950s.[2] Nonetheless, until the mid-1960s, India's public nuclear stance was one of unequivocally rejecting the development of nuclear arms. In late 1964, however, shortly after China's first nuclear test and at a time when India's defeat in its 1962 border war with China was still vivid, Prime Minister Lal Bahadur Shastri indicated that India might develop nuclear explosives—ostensibly for peaceful purposes, such as civil excavation. Despite further advances in the Chinese nuclear-weapons program, Indira Gandhi, who took over as Prime Minister in 1966, downplayed the nuclear-weapons issue until late 1969, when the development of "peaceful nuclear explosives" was again openly declared to be an objective of India's nuclear program. (In 1968, India declined to sign the Nuclear Non-Proliferation Treaty, which would have required it to renounce nuclear explosives and to place all of its nuclear installations under international inspection. The decision allowed India to retain the option of developing nuclear arms.)

In May 1974, while Mrs. Gandhi was still prime minister, India conducted its first—and only—nuclear test, which it referred to as a peaceful nuclear explosion. The failure of India to respond directly to the Chinese nuclear-weapons program for a decade and the fact that after the 1974 test Mrs. Gandhi did not proceed to build a nuclear arsenal suggest that the test was intended as a political gesture, aimed at enhancing India's international stature, rather than as a military response to a perceived nuclear threat from China. Only since the late 1970s, when confronted with Pakistan's growing nuclear-weapons program, have Indian leaders openly considered exercising the nation's nuclear-weapons option.[3]

In 1972, following Pakistan's defeat in the 1971 Indo-Pakistani War, Prime Minister Zulfikar Ali Bhutto is believed to have launched Pakistan on the path to nuclear arms.[4] At this point, two years prior to India's test (though after India had reiterated its interest in peaceful nuclear explosives), Pakistan may have been seeking to offset its conventional military inferiority, as well as to counter India's emerging nuclear-weapons potential.

Pakistan has consistently denied that it is building nuclear weapons and has repeatedly asserted that its nuclear program is entirely peaceful. The program, parts of which have been shrouded in secrecy, has relied heavily on technology, equipment, and materials imported from the West, often illegally.[5] The cornerstone of the program is a uranium enrichment plant (a facility theoretically capable of upgrading natural uranium to weapons-grade) located at Kahuta. The plant was discovered by the United States in the late 1970s, when the facility was still under construction, and was subsequently acknowledged by the Pakistani government.[6] Pakistan claimed that it was building the costly facility to supply low-enriched uranium fuel for future nuclear-power stations. But construction of the enrichment plant was so premature by normal civilian nuclear energy standards that the facility is presumed by India, the United States, and other observers to be intended for the development of nuclear arms.[7] Since disclosure of the plant, Indian concerns over Pakistani nuclear activities have been exacerbated by repeated revelations of Pakistani nuclear smuggling operations, reports of Pakistani efforts to design nuclear arms and test their components, and the early 1984 announcement that the Kahuta plant had begun producing enriched uranium—though not weapons-grade material.[8]

Indira Gandhi, who after being ousted as prime minister

in India's 1977 general elections, returned to power in 1980, tended to minimize the Pakistani nuclear threat in her public utterances. In early 1980, however, she declared that she would "not hesitate from carrying out nuclear explosions . . . or whatever is necessary in the national interest," and in 1981 and again in 1983 it was reported that India was maintaining a nuclear test site in a state of readiness.[9] In addition, several reports suggested that Mrs. Gandhi had authorized work on improved nuclear-weapon designs and, possibly, the fabrication of nuclear-weapon components.[10]

Moreover, until her assassination in October 1984, Mrs. Gandhi quietly enlarged India's actual capability to produce nuclear arms and, despite strong pressure from the United States, refused to place the key installations involved under IAEA safeguards—in effect, keeping them free of legal constraints that might limit their use for nuclear weapons. The facilities, some of which were completed after Rajiv Gandhi became prime minister following his mother's death, now form the backbone of India's nuclear-weapons potential and remain outside the IAEA system. They include two nuclear power reactors (Madras I and II, commissioned in 1983 and 1985, respectively), the Dhruva research reactor (commissioned in 1985), the refurbished Trombay reprocessing plant (reopened in late 1983 or early 1984) and the Tarapur reprocessing plant (which began operating at full capacity in 1982).[11] Together, these facilities provide India with the theoretical capability to manufacture nearly thirty nuclear weapons annually, a vast increase over the country's 1974 nuclear capability of one bomb per year.[12]

In the months preceding Mrs. Gandhi's death, nuclear tensions with Pakistan increased, spurred by new revelations of Pakistani nuclear smuggling and of reports that China had given it nuclear-weapon-design information.[13] These anxieties were heightened by press accounts stating that Mrs. Gandhi was being urged to launch a preemptive attack against Pakistan's Kahuta enrichment plant.[14] Overall Indo-Pakistani relations also deteriorated seriously, as India accused Pakistan of fomenting unrest by Sikh nationalist

groups in the Punjab region and of making incursions into
Kashmir which led to a series of border clashes. Against this
background, in mid-October 1984, Mrs. Gandhi departed
from her earlier muted statements, and in an address to a
group of army commanders, declared that the Pakistani nuclear program was "a qualitatively new phenomenon in our
security environment," which must add a "new dimension"
to India's defense planning.[15]

On October 31, Indira Gandhi was assassinated by Sikh
members of her bodyguard, and Rajiv Gandhi was appointed prime minister. He was confirmed in the post after a landslide victory in the December 28, 1984, general election. By
April 1985, he had taken his mother's expressions of concern
about the Pakistani nuclear program a step further. In a series of interviews and statements that continued for the next
eight months, he openly accused Pakistan of seeking to build
nuclear weapons and declared that this development was
causing India to reconsider its position against nuclear arming.[16] Indeed, in a June 5 interview in Paris, he hinted that
India had already made the components for nuclear arms
and, if it chose to, could assemble such weapons rapidly:

In principle we are opposed to the idea of becoming a nuclear
power. We could have done so for the past 10 or 11 years, but we
have not. *If we decided to become a nuclear power, it would take a
few weeks or a few months.*

Q. Are you contemplating this?
A. Not yet . . .
Q. . . . Will you or will you not take the decision to produce nu-
clear weapons?
A. We have not yet reached a decision, but we have already
worked on it.[17]

India's verbal attacks against the Pakistani nuclear program took a more ominous turn in early August 1985, following the report on American television that Pakistan had
recently detonated the non-nuclear portion of a nuclear device, a significant milestone toward nuclear arming.[18] On

August 8, following a series of parliamentary calls for action, Indian Atomic Energy Commission Chairman Raja Ramanna announced the start-up of the Dhruva research reactor. Rather than merely extolling India's achievement in commissioning one of the world's largest civilian non-power reactors, the announcement carefully underscored the fact that the plant would give India the ability to produce plutonium from domestic technology and fuel—a none-too-subtle declaration that India had a new source of nuclear-weapons material free from all non-proliferation controls.[19] The announcement, which was widely publicized in Pakistan, appeared to be a clear warning that India's considerable nuclear capabilities would guarantee it superiority in any regional nuclear arms race.[20] (As described below, the plant has been plagued with technical problems and was not operating as of the fall of 1986.)

Political Developments. The drumbeat of official anti-Pakistan nuclear rhetoric continued in subsequent months, with Gandhi seeming to suggest that Pakistan was getting increasingly close to its goal of producing nuclear arms.[21] In September, a high-level U.S. delegation, led by Under Secretary of State for Political Affairs Michael H. Armacost and senior National Security Council staff member Donald R. Fortier, tried to break the cycle of nuclear discord by urging the two nations to undertake a "regional initiative" to avert further nuclear competition.[22] Having previously rejected a series of Pakistani regional arms control proposals, New Delhi gave the American suggestion a chilly reception, claiming that Washington was attempting to avoid its responsibilities for halting the Pakistani nuclear program.[23]

Gandhi's declarations, and those of other Indian officials, on Pakistan's nuclear ambitions appear to have been addressed to several audiences. First, the pronouncements appeared to be a clear warning to Pakistan that if it pursued the course of nuclear competition, it would gain little, since India would quickly out-distance it in any nuclear arms race. Secondly, Gandhi appeared to be attempting to address mounting pro-weapons sentiment at home: by mid-summer

1985, members of Gandhi's Congress(I) Party, as well as the right-wing opposition, were openly calling for India to build nuclear arms in response to Pakistan.[24] Finally, as he made explicit at the time of his June 1985 visit to Washington, Gandhi was attempting to prod the United States to be more forceful in arresting Pakistan's nuclear ambitions. U.S.-Pakistani ties had grown considerably since the late-1979 Soviet invasion of Afghanistan, and although U.S. law provided that the $3.2 billion in U.S. aid to Pakistan would be terminated if Islamabad tested a nuclear device, Gandhi complained that Washington was tolerating Pakistan's continuing progress toward this threshold.

Despite this seeming deadlock, a slow thawing of overall Indo-Pakistani relations became apparent in October as the two countries stepped up bilateral talks on a variety of divisive issues. When Zia and Gandhi met at the United Nations in New York on October 22, an easing of nuclear tensions appeared nearly within grasp. Pakistani Secretary of Foreign Affairs Niaz Naik announced that the two leaders had agreed on the desirability of opening "a process of technical discussions between the two countries on nuclear non-proliferation issues."[25] In a contemporaneous interview, however, Gandhi threw cold water on the report, stating that no agreement had been reached on starting such discussions and reiterating his view that Pakistan was bent on obtaining nuclear arms, despite President Zia's denials.[26] Nonetheless both sides agreed to further high-level talks on two other important issues, increasing trade and improving security along their mutual border (an apparent euphemism for India's desire to stanch the flow of arms from Pakistan to militants in the Punjab.)

Overall relations continued to improve in subsequent weeks. At the end of November, Gandhi invited Zia to attend the mid-December inauguration of India's most advanced research reactor, the Fast Breeder Test Reactor at Kalpakkam. Although Pakistan Atomic Energy Commission Chairman Munir Khan, rather than President Zia, attended the event, India's invitation for high-level Pakistani participation contrasted sharply with the overt anti-Pakistani rhetoric that had accompanied the commissioning of the Dhruva reactor only four months earlier.[27]

President Zia's visit to New Delhi on December 17—his sixth meeting with Prime Minister Gandhi since the latter took office—offered still brighter hopes for alleviating nuclear frictions. The high point of the visit was his joint announcement with Prime Minister Gandhi that they had reached an agreement not to attack each other's nuclear installations.[28] In late September rumors had surfaced in Pakistan that India was about to attack the Kahuta enrichment plant, a plan supposedly conceived by Indira Gandhi but postponed after her death.[29] Although India immediately denied the accusations, Gandhi apparently initiated the no-attack proposal in an effort to lay the issue to rest. The accord, which was to be reduced to writing and formally signed at a later date, did not restrict Pakistani or Indian nuclear activities, as such. Nonetheless, it appeared to be a cautious first step in this direction, raising hopes that more comprehensive measures might follow.

The two leaders also agreed at the December meeting to a step-by-step process for normalizing relations, including the resumption of talks on draft peace treaties, new discussions to end border clashes over a disputed glacier in Kashmir, and the expansion of trade links. An understanding was also reached that these initiatives would culminate in a visit by Rajiv Gandhi to Islamabad during the first half of 1986, the first state visit by an Indian prime minister since 1964.[30]

The next several months were notable for the virtual absence of Indian verbal attacks against the Pakistani nuclear program. The anticipated process of overall normalization, however, soon bogged down, largely, it seems, because of domestic political difficulties on both sides. Pakistani business interests, fearful that cheaper Indian goods would flood their markets, were able to block Pakistan's implementation of the newly negotiated trade understandings with India, thereby undoing one of the few concrete accomplishments of the two countries' new-found spirit of cooperation. In

India, a resurgence of unrest in the Punjab was a still more serious blow.

The Punjab, a strategic northern state in India, has experienced nearly five years of escalating violence and conflict over the demands of Sikh extremists for the establishment of an independent Sikh-led nation.[31] In July 1985, Gandhi reached a compromise settlement with the leaders of the Akali Dal, a moderate party representing the majority of Sikhs in the Punjab state, granting partial autonomy to the region and adjusting the state's borders to increase the Sikhs' political power. Despite opposition to the agreement by separatist Sikh militants, manifested in the August assassination of the president of the Akali Dal, Gandhi's July peacemaking initiative was resoundingly affirmed when the Akali Dal won a landslide victory in the September statewide elections.

The apparent success of Gandhi's Punjabi gambit significantly enhanced his political stature and, along with several other domestic successes, had given him the leeway to proceed with his potentially unpopular opening to Pakistan. Moreover, with India having long accused adjacent Pakistan of arming and harboring Punjabi militants, the restoration of order there permitted these recriminations to subside, paving the way for improved ties. The subsequent upsurge of violence in the region, however, had just the opposite effect, eroding Gandhi's popularity at home and once again casting Pakistan in the role of antagonist.[32]

As a result of these and a series of similar domestic and bilateral setbacks, by early February it was rumored that Gandhi's trip to Islamabad was being indefinitely postponed, a decision that was announced officially in mid-March.[33] With the movement toward rapprochement steadily losing momentum, further negotiations on expanded nuclear restraints became impossible. Indeed, even the formalization of the December agreement against attacks on nuclear installations was placed in abeyance, although both sides are said to consider the understanding to be binding by virtue of their leaders' oral pledges.[34]

In March 1986, India renewed its protests against the Pakistani nuclear program. Possibly New Delhi hoped to chill its neighbor's then ongoing negotiations with the United States on economic and military assistance by publicizing what it knew to be a divisive issue between them.[35] In somewhat milder terms than the pronouncements of the previous fall, the well-publicized annual report of the Indian Defense Ministry, referring to "Pakistan's determined quest for nuclear status," declared:

Whether it would explode a nuclear device after manufacturing it, or retain an untested device, so that further American support may not be prejudiced is a matter of conjecture. For our part, we must be cognizant of the fact that Pakistan has moved closer to acquiring a capability to make nuclear weapons, which has an obvious bearing on our security.[36]

Prime Minister Gandhi was more forceful the following month in telling the lower house of the Indian parliament:

. . . If Pakistan gets a nuclear weapon, India will have to think very seriously about its own option. . . . We have every indication and information that leads us to believe that Pakistan has not given up its nuclear weapons program and is bent upon having it.[37]

Nonetheless, by this point, it appeared that Indian interest in nuclear politics was waning, as more immediate crises in the Punjab, Kashmir, and in neighboring Sri Lanka became the focus of domestic political concern.[38] By the summer of 1986, with accusations flying that Pakistan was contributing to unrest in all of these areas, the spirit of Indo-Pakistani cooperation seen the previous December was largely a memory.

Technical Developments. However cautious Gandhi's statements of India's nuclear intentions may have been throughout the year, from a technical standpoint, India took a major, and potentially provocative, step toward developing a ready nuclear-weapons option. For the first time India obtained nuclear-weapons material—separated plutonium—that was indisputably free from non-proliferation controls and thus available for use in nuclear arms.[39] Ironically, although Indian nuclear aides had boasted the previous summer that the Dhruva research reactor would provide a source of such unrestricted plutonium, technical problems have prevented the reactor from operating since its commissioning.[40] Instead, India's new unrestricted plutonium came from spent fuel produced in the Madras I nuclear power reactor, which was inaugurated in July 1983.[41]

Since India is not a signatory of the Non-Proliferation Treaty, it has no legal obligation to refrain from manufacturing nuclear weapons, nor is it bound to place all of its nuclear plants under the audits and inspections ("safeguards") of the International Atomic Energy Agency (IAEA), as the treaty requires. These safeguards are intended to verify that nuclear materials are not being used for nuclear weapons. Some of India's nuclear installations that were imported from abroad are under IAEA oversight because the supplying country imposed this requirement. India built the Madras I reactor on its own, however, so that this supplier-country rule does not apply to the plant. Although India could have put the facility under IAEA safeguards voluntarily as a means of reassuring Pakistan and others that it would not use plutonium produced in the plant's spent fuel for military purposes, India has declined to take this step.

Until India extracted the plutonium from the Madras I spent fuel, all of its separated plutonium had come from two sources: the twin, safeguarded Rajasthan nuclear-power plants and the Canadian-supplied Cirus research reactor, which, though not safeguarded, is subject to limited non-proliferation controls. The plutonium that has been separated from the Rajasthan reactors' spent fuel is, like the reactors, subject to IAEA oversight and, therefore not legally usable for nuclear arms.

The plutonium from the Cirus reactor is not, as just noted, under safeguards, but when Canada transferred the plant under a 1956 agreement, it did require India to pledge that any plutonium produced in the plant's spent fuel would be used only for peaceful purposes. In 1974, when India used Cirus-origin plutonium for its nuclear test, it circumvented this restriction by asserting that it had tested a "peaceful nuclear explosive" of the type the United States and the Soviet Union were investigating for use in canal-building and similar projects. There is, however, no technologically significant difference between a so-called peaceful nuclear explosive and a nuclear weapon. Canada therefore claimed that the peaceful-use pledge prohibited the use of plutonium produced in the Cirus reactor for nuclear explosions of any kind and, charging India with violating this undertaking, terminated all nuclear cooperation.[42]

India however, has never asserted the right to use plutonium from the spent fuel produced in the Cirus reactor for nuclear weapons, as such. Thus, while it is believed to have accumulated about 150 kilograms of Cirus-origin plutonium over the years, and perhaps as much safeguarded plutonium from the Rajasthan plants, only when India separated plutonium from the Madras I reactor's spent fuel did it obtain plutonium that it could use freely for nuclear weapons without the risk of violating any international agreement.[43] While the precise amount of Madras-origin separated plutonium now available to India has not been disclosed, American officials estimate that India has enough for between one and four atomic weapons comparable to that dropped on Nagasaki.[44]

Indian nuclear aides went to considerable lengths to obtain the material. In order for its plutonium to be extracted, the Madras I spent fuel had to be transported in massive radiologically-shielded casks nearly 1000 miles by rail to the Tarapur reprocessing plant near Bombay. The transport was significantly complicated by the fact that the gauge of the railroad lines between the reactor site and the reprocessing plant changes, necessitating the reloading of the hazardous cargo onto a second set of rail cars en route, a costly and potentially dangerous operation.

Moreover, at the time of these activities, which are thought to have begun during the second half of 1985, India already possessed more than enough restricted plutonium from the Rajasthan and Cirus reactors, i.e., plutonium which it had pledged not to use for nuclear weapons, to meet all of its civilian nuclear research and development needs; indeed, India is using Cirus-origin plutonium to fuel its newly commissioned experimental breeder reactor.[45] Indian nuclear aides say they intend to use plutonium from the Madras reactor in future refuelings of the experimental breeder, but such refuelings will not be required for many years.[46] Thus it is difficult to comprehend why Indian nuclear officials would have undertaken this costly and complicated operation to obtain unrestricted plutonium unless they intended to use the material for the one purpose to which India's existing plutonium stocks could not be put—the development of nuclear arms. To be sure, the mere fact that it has reprocessed the Madras I spent fuel does not necessarily mean that the Gandhi government has decided to build nuclear weapons. But the action does provide strong evidence that, at a minimum, Gandhi is taking steps to ensure that India will have the option to do so rapidly if circumstances require.

New Delhi has not publicized the development, possibly to avoid provoking Pakistan. Moreover, highlighting its acquisition of unrestricted nuclear-weapons material would tend to muddy India's claim that Pakistan's ongoing drive to obtain such material is the principal stimulus of the region's incipient nuclear arms race.

As noted earlier, there have also been a number of reports in the press indicating that India has been working on improved nuclear-weapon designs for a number of years.[47] Several American officials have recently concurred in this assessment.[48] If true, India may be working to upgrade what was thought to be the relatively crude atomic-weapon type device tested in 1974 in order to make a nuclear weapon suitable for delivery by aircraft.[49] It is also possible that India is attempting to move up the ladder of nuclearization to develop the more complex and far more powerful hydrogen bomb.[50]

One piece of evidence tending to support the view that India is indeed working on designing nuclear weapons of one type or another is the fact that in 1985 it sought to purchase two Swedish-made "flash X-ray" machines through a British company.[51] Flash X-ray machines are used to take split-second photos through solid materials of very rapid processes and are used in nuclear-weapons development programs to observe dummy nuclear cores as they undergo compression following the detonation of a nuclear-weapon-triggering package. In effect, such machines, which played a key role in the Swedish and French nuclear programs, permit verification that the triggering mechanism is working as designed. They may also play a role in designing hydrogen bombs by simulating X-ray pressure waves of the kind used to trigger such weapons.[52]

The British government reportedly stopped the sale of the machines to India. India then appears to have approached the Swedish manufacturer directly, but the Swedish government also refused to authorize export of the devices.[53] Flash X-ray machines, it should be noted, are also used in developing conventional munitions, and it is possible that India was seeking them for this less controversial purpose. Apparently, however, this possibility did not allay the concerns of British and Swedish officials when they barred the export.

If India has indeed been pursuing the design of nuclear weapons in addition to building up its stocks of unrestricted plutonium, then Prime Minister Gandhi's statement in May 1984 that India could exercise its nuclear-weapon option in "a few weeks or a few months"—at least to the point of having a number of aircraft-deliverable atomic bombs—would appear only too accurate today.[54]

Unfortunately, according to several American sources with access to classified information, in the first half of 1986 Pakistan also apparently made a major advance in its efforts to acquire nuclear arms. The precise nature of this advance was not disclosed.[55] But a later press report citing U.S. intelligence sources, stated that Pakistan had produced weapons-grade uranium at its Kahuta enrichment plant, thereby surmounting the last major obstacle to the manufacture of nuclear arms and apparently violating President Zia's 1984 pledge to President Reagan that the plant would produce only material enriched to the innocuous five-percent level.[56] Senior Pakistani officials denied the charge.[57]

Prospects. As these recent developments in India and Pakistan become more widely appreciated, public outcry in both countries is likely to destroy what little incentive may remain for negotiations on confidence-building measures in the nuclear field. In India, moreover, pressures will inevitably mount for Prime Minister Gandhi to respond more assertively to the Pakistani nuclear challenge, particularly if India's internal situation continues to deteriorate.

In recent years the nuclear policy debate in India has slowly shifted. While as late as 1979 Prime Minister Moraji Desai could respectably oppose Indian nuclear arming as a matter of moral principle, the position is now dismissed as "Gandhian." Today the debate is between what might be called the moderate and hawkish camps. The moderates, who include a number of prominent columnists, editors, academics, and civilian planners in the Defense and Foreign Ministries and in the office of the Prime Minister, recognize that India must respond to the Pakistani nuclear-weapons effort.[58] They hope to avoid nuclear arming as long as possible, however, because it would be extremely costly in economic terms and because it would entail a wrenching shift in India's diplomacy, which for decades has linked the country's non-aligned status with the pursuit of global nuclear disarmament. If Pakistan obtains nuclear weapons or is perceived to have them, the moderates appear to favor an ambiguous response—neither testing a second device nor declaring that India had become a nuclear power—while at the same time creating the strong impression that nuclear arming was in such easy reach that Pakistan could never place India at a serious disadvantage.[59]

Such an ambiguous posture, the moderates argue, could successfully deter a nuclear attack by Pakistan. At the same time, since China would be unlikely to consider India's veiled and limited nuclearization a direct threat, India's nuclear relations with China could remain essentially unchanged, and India would have no need to build a costly deterrent against a nuclear attack from this quarter.

In addition, by not testing or declaring itself a nuclear power, India could avoid the potentially grave diplomatic repercussions of such actions. These repercussions might well include the chilling of India's relations with the Soviet Union; the undermining of its improving ties with the United States; the imposition of economic sanctions (which would be required under U.S. law and might well be implemented by other Western governments);[60] and the loss of stature in the Non-Aligned Movement, which is strongly committed to nuclear disarmament.

The hawkish camp is perhaps more vocal than the moderate one, but appears still to be a minority voice. The hawks, who include opposition politicians, analysts at India's principal defense think-tank, some senior military officers, and top nuclear aides, along with several respected editors and opinion-makers, argue that India, by virtue of its geographic location, physical size, and population is an emerging, but unrecognized, great power.[61] To achieve its destiny, they assert, India must have nuclear weapons since this has become the *sine qua non* for great power status. Only then will India be treated on a par with China, as is its due.

More broadly, the hawks stress that India is encircled by nuclear armed states (including the United States, which they claim has nuclear weapons in the Indian Ocean) and argue that, as long as India lacks such armaments, the superpowers will be able to impose their will on affairs in the region. Besides ameliorating this unpalatable situation, the hawks contend, the addition of India to the handful of nuclear powers would contribute to the evolution of the international order from the present "intrinsically highly tension-prone" bipolar system to a more stable and diffuse global balance of power. This would prevent any one state from accumulating the excessive power that leads to aggression, while, incidentally, guaranteeing India its deserved "place in the sun."[62]

India's nuclear future, they contend, must not, therefore,

be focused on Pakistan (or on maintaining India's current posture in the Non-Aligned Movement), but on achieving parity with China through a program that would entail development of intermediate-range ballistic missiles and possibly sea-launched cruise missiles. The hawks claim that the costs of such a nuclear program would represent only a twenty percent increase in India's defense budget and are therefore acceptable.

So far, Gandhi has adopted the moderates' approach. He appears to be personally committed to non-proliferation and has been a highly visible participant in the "Five Continents" initiative, aimed at ending the superpower nuclear arms race.[63] None of his statements or those of other Indian officials echo the "destiny" argument of the hawks, and his actions, including the unpublicized reprocessing of the Madras I spent fuel, are consistent with the moderates' more cautious policy preferences. This suggests that even if Pakistan did obtain nuclear weapons, Gandhi, at least initially, would be likely to adopt the ambiguous strategy described above. Nevertheless, while this doctrine is gaining acceptance among Indian policymakers, the popular backlash that Pakistan's overt acquisition of nuclear arms would trigger in India is unpredictable. Accordingly, the possibility remains that the Gandhi government might respond in kind.

India, it may be noted, has a range of advanced aircraft capable of delivering nuclear weapons. Its most advanced are Soviet-supplied MiGs, French-supplied Mirages, and the British-French Jaguar. None of these suppliers is known to have required a guarantee from India that its aircraft would not be used for the delivery of nuclear arms.[64]

India also has a sizable space program that could provide it with an intermediate-range ballistic-missile capability in the 1990s.[65] It is possible that India is looking to the development of a missile-based nuclear force over the long term to guarantee its predominance in South Asia and achieve major power status although this seems inconsistent with Rajiv Gandhi's overall nuclear stance. For the time being, Pakistan is India's chief nuclear concern, and it can be addressed with a far less sophisticated deterrent based on aircraft delivery.

Pakistan has proposed a number of arrangements for avoiding regional proliferation. These include an offer to ratify the Non-Proliferation Treaty if India did the same; an offer to place all of its nuclear facilities under IAEA safeguards if India reciprocated; an offer to establish a regional nuclear-weapons-free zone; and an offer to establish a system of bilateral nuclear inspections. Whether these proposals have been advanced in good faith is hard to ascertain, since India, as Pakistan may have predicted, has rejected all of them.

India has long opposed the Non-Proliferation Treaty and the comprehensive application of IAEA safeguards on the grounds that they are discriminatory instruments of the nuclear-weapon powers designed to legitimize their nuclear status while freezing others in permanent inferiority.[66] Citing the potential threat from China's nuclear weapons, it has also rejected the establishment of a regional nuclear-weapons-free zone unless the PRC is included in the arrangement, a condition China is certain to reject.

India has turned down bilateral inspections, since it argues that this would foreclose its nuclear option while leaving a nuclear-armed China on its border. In addition, Gandhi and others have contended that if Pakistan has already produced nuclear-weapons material—which they say cannot be ruled out—India would have no way of verifying that Pakistan had not secretly kept some of this outside the inspection regime.[67] Arguably, these concerns might be resolved through negotiation. A short-term inspection program, for example, might build mutual confidence without permanently foreclosing India's nuclear option and Pakistan, no less than India, would have to be concerned about undeclared nuclear-weapons material. India has declined to enter discussions on the Pakistani proposal, however.

With India by far the stronger of the two nations in conventional military terms and having already demonstrated its nuclear potential, it seems unlikely that the impasse on further nuclear talks can be broken unless India takes the initiative, as it did in December 1985, when it offered the understanding against attacking nuclear sites. Given the present state of Indo-Pakistani relations and new data pointing to Pakistan's continuing pursuit of nuclear arms, however, such new Indian initiatives appear unlikely for the near term, at least.

Pressures from nations outside the region, however, may help contain the Indo-Pakistani nuclear rivalry and push both sides towards accommodation. As covered in greater detail in the section that follows on Pakistan, the United States has long sought to curb Islamabad's nuclear ambitions, though with limited success. New Delhi has tried to prod Washington to act more forcefully in this regard. In mid-1986, New Delhi also reportedly persuaded the Soviet Union to issue a stern warning to Pakistan against nuclear arming.[68]

The United States and the Soviets have also attempted to restrain Indian nuclear activities through diplomatic suasion and, as mentioned above, Washington has threatened to impose economic sanctions if India tests another nuclear device. The United States and the Soviet Union have also promoted a widely adopted set of strict nuclear-supply controls aimed at slowing the progress of both India and Pakistan toward nuclear arming.[69]

Nuclear supply restrictions have appeared to be less valuable in the case of India, which has a considerable indigenous capability to manufacture nuclear hardware and materials. A major study by an American specialist released in 1986, however, revealed that India remains dependent on external sources for one key commodity, heavy water, which is essential to the operation of most of its nuclear reactors, including the Dhruva and Madras plants that are central to India's nuclear-weapons capability. The study concluded that in the early 1980s, India was forced to import over 100 metric tons of heavy water clandestinely—supposedly from China—to meet its requirements.[70] This would suggest that tightened controls on nuclear supplies might have a greater impact on India's nuclear activities than is generally believed.

Unfortunately, U.S.-Soviet competition in South Asia has tended to hamper the superpowers' respective non-proliferation initiatives. The Soviet invasion of Afghanistan, for example, has made it extremely difficult for the United States to withhold aid from Pakistan since this might seriously weaken America's regional ally. Similarly, when the Soviets issued their mid-1986 warning to Pakistan against nuclear arming, the United States felt compelled to remind Moscow of its strong commitment to Pakistan's security, undercutting the impact of the Soviet demarche.[71]

In the case of India, the Soviet Union has been similarly cautious for fear of injuring the two countries' close relations at a time when the United States might exploit such an opening. Washington, in turn, is attempting to build closer links to New Delhi, in part to try to wean it from the Soviet camp, and has apparently sought to avoid friction on the sensitive nuclear issue. Indeed, even as India was moving to obtain unrestricted nuclear-weapons material for the first time, Washington was granting India privileges to import increasingly sophisticated U.S. high technology.[72]

In this setting, with the non-proliferation efforts of the superpowers hamstrung by their own rivalry, hopes for reducing nuclear tensions appear increasingly to lie with some type of Indo-Pakistani accommodation, as urged by the Fortier-Armacost delegation. Unfortunately, as India and Pakistan continue to build up their nuclear capabilities, there is good reason to fear that the pace of nuclearization on the subcontinent will continue to outstrip diplomatic measures aimed at halting this fateful trend.

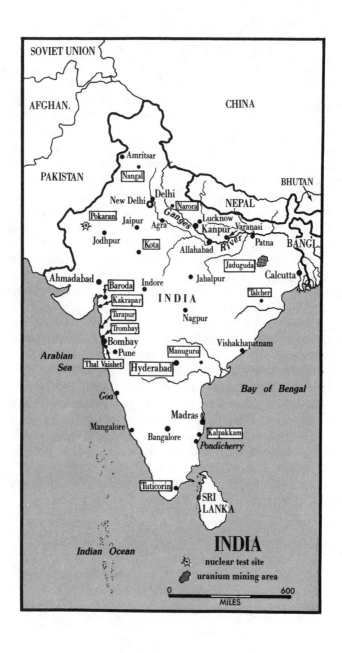

SOVIET UNION

AFGHAN.

CHINA

PAKISTAN

Amritsar

Nangal

New Delhi Delhi

Narora

NEPAL

BHUTAN

Ganges

Lucknow

Pokaran Jaipur Agra Kanpur Varanasi

Jodhpur

Kota

Allahabad River Patna BANGL.

Jaduguda Calcutta

Ahmadabad

Baroda Indore

Jabalpur

INDIA

Talcher

Kakrapar

Tarapur

Nagpur

Trombay

Bombay

Vishakhapatnam

Pune

Manuguru

Arabian
Sea

Thal Vaishet Hyderabad

Goa

Bay of Bengal

Madras

Mangalore

Bangalore Kalpakkam

Pondicherry

Tuticorin

SRI
LANKA

Indian Ocean

INDIA

☼ nuclear test site

uranium mining area

0   600

MILES

India

Power Reactors/Operating or Under Construction

Tarapur I (light-water/low-enriched uranium, 200 MWe)
- supplier: General Electric (U.S.)
- start up: 1969
- fuel source: U.S.; France after 1982
- safeguards: yes

Tarapur II (light-water/low-enriched uranium, 200 MWe)
- supplier: General Electric (U.S.)
- start up: 1969
- fuel source: U.S.; France after 1982
- safeguards: yes

Rajasthan I, Kota (heavy-water/natural-uranium, 200 MWe)
- supplier: Canadian General Electric (Canada)
- start up: 1973[a]
- fuel source: Initial load, half Canadian Westinghouse, half Indian; subsequently all Indian.[a]
- heavy water: 130 metric tons from Canada and U.S.; 80 metric tons from USSR in 1973.[a]
- safeguards: yes

Rajasthan II, Kota (heavy-water/natural-uranium, 200 MWe)
- supplier: Larson and Toubro (India), following termination of Canadian assistance in 1976.
- start up: 1981
- fuel source: India
- heavy water: USSR,[a] India
- safeguards: yes

Madras I, Kalpakkam (heavy-water/natural-uranium, 220 MWe)
- supplier: Larson and Toubro (India)
- start up: 1983[b]
- fuel source: India
- heavy water: India (?)[c]
- safeguards: no

Madras II, Kalpakkam (heavy-water/natural-uranium, 220 MWe)
- supplier: Larson and Toubro (India)
- start up: 1985[d]
- fuel source: India
- heavy water: India (?)[c]
- safeguards: no

Narora I (heavy-water/natural-uranium, 220 MWe)
- supplier: Richardson and Cruddas (India)
- start up: 1987-1988[e]
- fuel source: India
- heavy water: India
- safeguards: no

Narora II (heavy-water/natural-uranium, 220 MWe)
- supplier: Walchandnagar Industries Ltd. (India)
- start up: 1988-1989[e]
- fuel source: India
- heavy water: India
- safeguards: no

Kakrapar I (heavy-water/natural-uranium, 220 MWe)
- supplier: India
- start up: 1990-1991[e]
- fuel source: India
- heavy water: India
- safeguards: no

Kakrapar II (heavy-water/natural-uranium, 220 MWe)
- supplier: India
- start up: 1991-1992[e]
- fuel source: India
- heavy water: India
- safeguards: no

Uranium Resources/Active Mining Sites/Uranium Mills
- reasonably assured
  reserves: 46,090 metric tons[f]
- currently active site: Jaduguda[f]
- mills in operation: Jaduguda[f]

Uranium Purification (UO$_2$)[e]
Hyderabad
- capacity: ?
- supplier: India
- start up: ?
- safeguards: partial (?)

Heavy Water
Nangal
- capacity: 14 metric tons per year[a]
- supplier: Linde Gmbolt (West Germany)[a]
- start up: 1962[a]
- safeguards: no

Baroda
- capacity: 45 metric tons per year[a,j]
- supplier: GELPRA (Swiss-French)[a]
- start up: 1977 (closed 1977-80; intermittent operation thereafter)[k]
- safeguards: no

Tuticorin
- capacity: 49 metric tons per year[a,j]
- supplier: GELPRA (Swiss-French)[a]
- start up: 1978
- safeguards: no

Talcher
- capacity: very little production[a,j]
- supplier: Friedrich Unde Gmbolt (West Germany)[a]
- start up: 1979, but has operated at less than 10% capacity.[k]
- safeguards: no

Kota
- capacity: 85 metric tons per year[a,j]
- supplier: India, Canada (Canadian aid terminated 1974)[l]
- start up: 1984 (est.)[m]
- safeguards: no

Thal-Vaishet
- capacity: 110 metric tons per year[j]
- supplier: Rashtriya Chemicals and Fertilizers (India)[j]
- start up: 1987 (est.)[a]
- safeguards: no

Manuguru
- capacity: 185 metric tons[j]
- supplier: ?
- start up: 1988[v]
- safeguards: no

Fuel Fabrication
Hyderabad
- capacity: 90 metric tons/yr. (for Rajasthan, Madras, Tarapur, Cirus, Dhruva, FTBR blanket assemblies; being expanded to 180 metric tons/yr.)[h]

Trombay
- capacity: ? (for FBTR fuel pins)
- supplier: India
- start up: 1983-4 (?)
- safeguards: no

Reprocessing
Trombay
- capacity: 30 metric tons of spent fuel per year (CIRUS, Dhruva fuel)[r]; has been enlarged[a]
- supplier: India[s]
- start up: 1966; shut down, 1974; restarted late 1983 or early 1984[w]
- safeguards: no

Tarapur
- capacity: 100 metric tons of spent fuel per year (currently for Rajasthan, potentially for Tarapur, Madras I, FBTR[n]); 135-150 kg plutonium per year when at full capacity.[n]
- supplier: India
- start up: trial runs, 1979;[a] full scale operations, 1982[n]
- safeguards: partial (for Tarapur and Rajasthan reactor fuel)

Kalpakkam
- capacity: laboratory scale
- supplier: India
- start up: 1985
- safeguards: no

Kalpakkam
- capacity: 125 metric tons per year (for Madras I, II, and FTBR)[o]
- supplier: India
- start up: 1986 (est.)
- safeguards: no

Research Reactors

Apsara, Trombay (light-water/medium-enriched-uranium, 1 MWt)[p]
- supplier: India
- start up: 1956
- fuel source: United Kingdom
- safeguards: no

Cirus, Trombay (heavy-water/natural-uranium, 40 MWt)[p]
- supplier: Canada
- start up: 1963[q]
- fuel source: Canada, then India
- heavy water: United States
- safeguards: no

Zerlina, Trombay (heavy-water/variable-fuel, 400 Wt)[p]
- supplier: India
- start up: 1961; decommissioned 1983[d]
- fuel source: India?
- safeguards: no

Purnima, Trombay (no moderator/plutonium, 10 MWt)[p]
- supplier: India
- start up: 1972; decommissioned. Modified and recommissioned as Purnima II, 1984.
- fuel source: India
- safeguards: no

Purnima II, Trombay (uranium-233)[d]
- supplier: India
- start up: 1984
- fuel source: India
- safeguards: no

Dhruva (formerly R-5) Trombay (heavy-water/natural-uranium, 100 MWt)[d]
- supplier: India
- start up: 1985[d]
- fuel source: India
- heavy water: India (?)[j]
- safeguards: no

FBTR, Kalpakkam (fast breeder/plutonium & natural uranium, 42 MWt, 15MWe)
- supplier: India, with French assistance[a]
- start up: 1985
- fuel source: India
- safeguards: no

Delivery Systems

India has several lines of advanced combat aircraft able to deliver an atomic bomb (assumed to weigh 1,300 pounds): the Canberra, the Jaguar/GR-1, the MiG-21 Fishbed, the MiG-23BN Flogger H, the MiG-23MF Flogger B, the Mirage 2000, and the SU-7BM Fitter.[x] India's space program couild provide it with intermediate range ballistic missiles by the mid-1990s.

Sources and Notes

a. David Hart, *Nuclear Power in India, A Comparative Analysis* (London: George Allen and Unwin, 1983), pp. 45-54. GELPRA is a consortium of Sulzer Brothers, Cie de Construction Mecaniques (a French licensee of Sulzer Brothers) and Société Air Liquide (France) "India and France," *Nucleonics Week*, July 4, 1985.

b. "Sethna Present as Kalpakkam Reactor Goes Critical," *The Hindu*, reprinted in *Joint Publication Research Service (JPRS)/Nuclear Development and Proliferation (NDP)*, August 3, 1983, p. 30.

c. Judith Miller, "U.S. Is Holding Up Peking Atom Talks," *New York Times*, September 19, 1982. Gary Milhollin, "Dateline New Delhi: India's Nuclear Cover-Up," *Foreign Policy* (Fall 1986): 161. (Both suggest China supplied heavy water that may have been used in these plants.)

d. "India's Plutonium Production Ability to Soar," *Nucleonics Week*, August 15, 1985, p. 1. The Dhruva reactor was shut down shortly after commissioning and was not operating as of fall 1986. Vyvyan Tenorio, "India's Supply of Unsafeguarded Pu Grows," *Nuclear Fuel*, August 11, 1986, p.3.

e. *The Annual Report of the Department of Atomic Energy, 1985-1986*, (New Delhi, 1986.)

f. Reasonably Assured Reserves at less than $130 per kilogram. OECD Nuclear Energy Agency and the International Atomic Energy Agency, *Uranium, Resources, Production and Demand* (Paris: OECD, 1986), pp. 223-225.

g. "Spokesman: Uranium Production to Double," *Delhi Domestic Service*, reprinted in *Foreign Broadcast Information Service (FBIS)/South Asia*, August 8, 1982, p. E-1.

h. David Hart, *Nuclear Power in India*, p. 43; *Nuclear Engineering Int'l*, September 6, 1986, p.6.

i. According to the *Annual Report of the Department of Atomic Energy, 1982-1983*, Hyderabad started up in 1971, but according to David Hart, *Nuclear Power in India*, the facility started up between 1973 and 1975. Fuel fabrication line for Tarapur (light-water reactor) fuel is safeguarded. Line for natural-uranium/heavy-water reactor fuel and research reactor fuel is not. Hyderabad plant includes zirconium sponge, oxide, and fabrication plants. *Annual Report of the Department of Atomic Energy, 1985-1986*.

j. "DAE Official Writes on Heavy Water Production," *The Hindu Survey of Indian Industry*, reprinted in *JPRS/NDP*, April 9, 1984, pp. 18-20. "Commissioning of Vitrification Facility," *Nuclear Fuel*, June 3, 1985, p. 9. In 1983, the capacities of Baroda, Tuticorin, Talcher, and Kota plants were derated from 67, 71, 65, and 100 metric tons per year respectively. Actual production has been below derated capacities. Dpt. Atomic Energy testimony before Consultative Committee of Parliament, May 1986. But see, Gary Milhollin, "Dateline New Delhi: India's Nuclear Cover-Up."

k. Pearl Marshall, "India's Desperate Push for Enough Indigenous Heavy Water to Commission," *Nucleonics Week,* May 27, 1982, p. 12.

l. "Problems in Production of Heavy Water Discussed," Jairam Ramesh, *The Times of India,* reprinted in *JPRS/NDP,* August 18, 1982, p. 11.

m. "AEC Chairman Describes Nuclear Energy Program," *The Hindu Survey of Indian Industry,* reprinted in *JPRS/NDP,* April 9, 1984, p. 14.

n. Milton Benjamin, "India Storing Arms Grade Plutonium," The Washington Post, February 20, 1983. Plant is currently reprocessing fuel from the safeguarded Rajasthan I reactor and from the unsafeguarded Madras I reactor. India is barred by the United States from reprocessing spent fuel from the Tarapur reactors until at least 1993 under the 1963 Indo-U.S. agreement for nuclear cooperation and a follow-up agreement with France. India disputes this view, however.

o. "ISI Gives Details on Nuclear Reprocessing Plant," *ISI Diplomatic Information Service,* reprinted in FBIS/South Asia, December 16, 1982, p. E-1.

p. Albert Wohlstetter, ed., *Swords From Plowshares* (Chicago: University of Chicago Press, 1979), p. 206.

q. Fully operational in 1963; started up in 1960.

r. David Hart, *Nuclear Power in India,* p. 54; but see, sixty metric tons per year, "ERDA: Fuel Reprocessing Capabilities, 1977," *Nuclear Proliferation Factbook,* Subcomm. on Int'l. Trade and Policy of the House Int'l. Relations Comm. and Subcomm. on Energy, Nuclear Proliferation and Federal Services, Senate Comm. on Governmental Affairs (Washington: Gov't. Print'g. Off., 1977), p. 200; one hundred metric tons per year, Wohlstetter, *Swords From Plowshares,* p. 214. Thirty metric ton figure selected because it is the most conservative and may best reflect actual operating experience.

s. India received engineering assistance from Vitro International (U.S.) and from French engineering consultants, Roberta Wohlstetter, *"The Buddha Smiles": Absent-minded Peaceful Aid and the Indian Bomb,* Monograph 3, Energy Research and Development Administration, Contract No. (49-1)-3747, April 30, 1977, p. 63.

t. "Commissioning of Vitrification Facility," *Nuclear Fuel,* June 3, 1985.

u. "Indian Nuclear Industry," *Nucleonics Week,* May 23, 1985, p. 14.

v. "Indians Announce Breakthrough," *Nuclear Fuel,* December 17, 1984.

w. "Trombay Is Ready for Work," *Nuclear Engineering Int'l,* June 1983, p. 6; "Interview, Nuclear Energy," *India Int'l Center Quarterly,* Vol. 10, #4, 1983, p. 379. Some sources state plant was shut down in 1972, not 1974.

x. 1,300 lb. selected as illustrative on basis of Sweden's untested atomic weapon design prepared in the late 1950s. (Christer Larsson, "Build a Bomb!" *Ny Teknik,* April 25, 1985). Source: *The Military Balance 1985-1986 (London: International Institute for Strategic Studies,* 1985).

Pakistan

Assessing the status of Pakistan's nuclear capabilities is difficult because the most sensitive parts of its nuclear program are cloaked in secrecy. Nonetheless, a consensus appears to have emerged that Pakistan is at the nuclear-weapons threshold: it either possesses all of the components needed to manufacture one or several atom bombs or else remains just short of this goal because its uranium enrichment plant at Kahuta has not yet produced a sufficient quantity of nuclear-weapons-usable highly enriched uranium. While opinion on the matter remains divided, as of late 1986 there appeared to be growing support for the "all-components-available" characterization of the Pakistani nuclear program; a year earlier, by contrast, only a minority of observers considered the program to be this advanced.[1] American and Soviet pressure may yet slow Pakistan's further progress toward nuclear arming, however, and may well lead Pakistan to refrain from conducting a nuclear test.

Background. Pakistani leaders have repeatedly denied that the nation is developing nuclear arms.[2] Nevertheless, the available evidence leaves little doubt that Pakistan is indeed pursuing this course, a conclusion shared by the United

States, the Soviet Union, India, and other nations.[3]

Although Pakistan, like India, refused to join the Non-Proliferation Treaty in 1968, thereby leaving itself free to develop nuclear arms, Pakistan's nuclear-weapons program was not initiated until shortly after the country's devastating defeat in the 1971 Indo-Pakistani War. The following year, according to eye-witnesses, then-Prime Minister Zulfikar Ali Bhutto announced his plan to develop nuclear arms at a secret meeting of Pakistan's top scientists and nuclear aides in Multan.[4] The program appears to have been aimed at countering India's substantial conventional military superiority and its significant, but then still untested, nuclear capability.

Initially, it appears that Bhutto intended to pursue nuclear weapons by acquiring a large reprocessing plant from France for extracting plutonium from spent power-reactor fuel. Although France insisted that the facility and any others based on its technology be placed under International Atomic Energy Agency (IAEA) safeguards, the installation would have nonetheless permitted Pakistan to accumulate nuclear-weapons material, material apparently unneeded for its civilian nuclear power program, which then, as now, has only one small nuclear power reactor.[5]

By 1976, American concerns over Pakistan's possible misuse of the plant had intensified to the point that President Gerald Ford dispatched Secretary of State Henry Kissinger to Islamabad and then to Paris in an unsuccessful bid to head off the reprocessing plant sale. In August 1977, France suspended deliveries for the plant after Washington showed Paris intelligence data disclosing Pakistan's intentions. In the interim, to underscore its concern, Washington cut off economic and military aid to Islamabad.[6]

Indeed, Mr. Bhutto himself ultimately acknowledged the veiled purpose behind the French deal, following his fall from power in 1977. In a testament written in 1978 shortly before his execution at the hands of his successor, General Zia ul-Haq, he declared that Pakistan was "on the threshold of a full nuclear capability." "All we needed," he wrote, "was the nuclear reprocessing plant."[7]

Reprocessing, however, was not the only route Pakistan was pursuing to obtain nuclear arms. In 1975, according to a subsequent Dutch government investigation, Pakistan began acquiring hardware and technology for a uranium enrichment plant using ultra-high-speed centrifuges, a plant potentially capable of producing highly enriched uranium, the alternative nuclear-weapons material to plutonium.[8]

A key figure in the effort was Dr. A. Q. Khan, a German-trained metallurgist, who worked intermittently at a classified centrifuge enrichment plant at Almelo, the Netherlands, where he is believed to have gained access to key plans and listings of component suppliers. In 1975, Dr. Khan suddenly returned to Pakistan. "It is reasonable to assume," the Dutch government investigation concluded, "that through Dr. Khan, Pakistan has been able to obtain possession of essential gas centrifuge know-how."[9]

In 1979, Washington made public its own concerns over the Pakistani enrichment program. In announcing that Washington was again terminating aid to Islamabad, Assistant Secretary of State Thomas Pickering declared in congressional testimony that Pakistan's enrichment program was not justified by its nuclear-energy needs. "We are concerned, therefore," he concluded, "that the Pakistani program is not peaceful but related to an effort to develop a nuclear-explosive capability."[10]

Since that time, Pakistan has made a concerted effort to obtain hardware for its enrichment plant, located at Kahuta, and for several related installations from a number of Western nations. The effort, which has involved the use of dummy corporations and transshipments through third countries, has by now been well-documented in the press and has been officially recognized by West Germany, Canada, Britain, the Netherlands, and the United States either in the course of prosecutions or in published government reports.[11] Perhaps the most egregious case involved the smuggling from West Germany between 1977 and 1980 of an entire plant for converting uranium powder into uranium hexafluoride, the easily gasified material that is the feed-stock for the Kahuta enrichment facility. In March 1985 a West German court convicted Albrecht Migule for the deed.[12] The plant, located in the town of Dera Ghazi Khan, is continuing to operate, producing material that is essential for the Pakistani nuclear-weapons effort. Pakistan, it may be noted, has refused to place the Kahuta facility and the Dera Ghazi Khan plant under IAEA inspections.

After the 1979 Soviet invasion of Afghanistan, Washington moved to restore economic and military aid to Islamabad. Although President Zia rejected the $400 million in assistance initially offered by the Carter administration, he ultimately accepted a six-year $3.2 billion aid package subsequently offered by President Reagan. The package included an agreement to sell Pakistan 40 advanced F-16 fighter-bombers. In approving the aid in 1981, Congress granted Pakistan a six-year exemption from the law, familiarly known as the "Symington amendment," that had previously prohibited such assistance because of Pakistan's importation of enrichment equipment. However, it also strengthened a portion of the law prohibiting U.S. aid to any non-nuclear-weapon state that subsequently detonated a nuclear explosive device.[13]

The Reagan administration has argued that the aid package will help slow the Pakistani nuclear-weapons program by providing an alternate means for Pakistan to protect its national security. So far, as detailed below, it has failed to halt the program, although the risk of losing American aid may forestall a Pakistani nuclear test. India, it may be noted, whose concerns over the Pakistani nuclear-weapons effort began to mount in 1979, has seen Pakistan's six-year exemption from the Symington amendment as a sign that the United States is easing its efforts to retard Islamabad's progress towards nuclear arming.[14]

In early 1984, Dr. A. Q. Khan, who had been appointed the head of the Pakistani enrichment program, announced that the Kahuta plant had succeeded in producing enriched uranium.[15] President Zia subsequently confirmed the point but stressed that only low-enriched, non-weapons-grade material had been produced.[16] A June 1984 speech by Senator Alan Cranston, meanwhile, declared that the Pakistani nuclear-weapons program was continuing, and Reagan administration officials at the time privately confirmed that this effort included nuclear-weapon-design work and the acquisition of hardware from abroad.[17]

Also in June, still further evidence of Islamabad's pursuit of nuclear arms surfaced when three Pakistani nationals were indicted for attempting to smuggle parts for atomic weapons—50 high-speed electronic switches, known as krytrons—out of the United States. Two of the three were released after turning state's evidence and the third, Nazir Vaid, ultimately pleaded guilty to a lesser charge, serving a total of three months in jail before being deported to Pakistan.[18] Official Pakistani denials that the defendants were linked to the Pakistani government only made matters look worse when cables, taken from the defendants at the time of their arrest, revealed that the parts were ordered by S. A. Butt, a director of supply and procurement for the Pakistani Atomic Energy Commission.[19] The episode left little doubt about Islamabad's nuclear intentions.

The krytron affair was soon followed by press accounts that quoted Reagan administration officials as saying that the People's Republic of China was assisting Pakistan, its long-time ally, in operating the Kahuta plant and had given Pakistan design information on nuclear weapons.[20] Such data might allow Pakistan to manufacture reliable nuclear arms without the need for a nuclear test. Although China denied the reports that it was aiding Pakistan, the Reagan administration took the extraordinary step of halting for nearly a year formal approval of a highly publicized nuclear trade pact with China, suggesting that the evidence available to the government was persuasive.[21]

Apparently in response to the krytron affair and China's nuclear assistance, in September 1984 President Reagan sent a letter to President Zia expressing strong U.S. concern over Pakistan's continuing nuclear activities and threatening grave consequences—implicitly the termination of U.S. aid—if Zia used the Kahuta enrichment plant to produce uranium enriched to more than the relatively innocuous five percent level. (Ninety percent enriched uranium is used for nuclear weapons.)[22] Such a limitation on the Pakistani nuclear program would keep it an important step short of nuclear arms. Thus the Reagan letter went considerably further than U.S. legislation at the time, which made the detonation of a nuclear device, but not the possession of an untested (though potentially reliable) nuclear arsenal, the trigger for the termination of U.S. assistance.[23]

In mid-November, during a visit to Washington, Pakistani Foreign Minister Yaqub Ali Khan apparently advised the Reagan administration of Pakistan's willingness to limit the output of the Kahuta facility as requested in the Reagan letter.[24] President Zia appeared to confirm this stance several months later, when he announced that the Kahuta plant had been able to produce a small amount of enriched uranium but stressed that "it is less than five percent. . . ."[25]

Pakistan's seeming acquiescence in the American restriction came at a time of its increasing dependence on the United States. In the fall of 1984, some 40,000 additional Soviet troops were deployed in Afghanistan, many close to the Pakistani border, bringing the total to 120,000. At the same time, Soviet planes began repeatedly violating Pakistani air space to bomb Afghan refugee camps in Pakistan. As these incursions continued, in March of 1985, the Reagan administration agreed to supply Pakistan with sophisticated air-to-air missiles, and key congressional committees demonstrated their support by approving another installment of the $3.2 billion in U.S. aid begun in 1981.[26] When it authorized the aid in July, however, Congress tightened the conditions under which it was being provided, requiring that the President certify that Pakistan did not "possesses a nuclear explosive device" before funds under the authorization could be disbursed.[27]

After the assassination of Indian Prime Minister Indira Gandhi in late October 1984, President Zia launched a "peace offensive" aimed at improving ties between the two countries. Though a slight warming of relations ensued, by mid-1985 a decline was again evident. On the nuclear front, in June and July Zia and his top aides accused India of provoking a nuclear arms race by building up its nuclear capabilities and by refusing Pakistan's repeated offers of mutual inspections and bilateral non-proliferation pledges. The effectiveness of this campaign was severely undercut, however, by the report in July 1985 that Pakistan had passed a major milestone in its quest for the bomb by successfully testing the non-nuclear triggering package for a nuclear weapon.[28] In August, moreover, it was revealed that Pakistan had been trying unsuccessfully to obtain flash X-ray machines, described previously.[29] The events appeared to leave little doubt that Pakistan's quest for nuclear status was continuing.

Political Developments. During the fall of 1985, an important new trend emerged, as a number of senior Pakistani political figures began openly advocating the development of a nuclear deterrent. At a November 1985 round-table conducted by a major Pakistani daily, for example, S. M. Zafar, secretary of Prime Minister Muhammad Khan Junejo's ruling Pakistan Muslim League Party, declared:

We have learned to purify uranium. Now we should, with the help of God, produce an explosion. It will stop all danger of war in this region just as the nuclear strength of the two superpowers has eliminated the danger of war between them since World War II.[30]

In the same seminar, the leader of the opposition Pakistan Musawat Party, Mohammad Hanif Ramay, similarly declared, "India's expansionism will make it attack us sooner or later. The only way we can protect ourselves is by developing nuclear weapons."[31] Former Pakistan Air Force chief, Air Marshal Zafar Chaudhary, and another former military figure, Major General Mumtaz Ali, expressed similar views during the discussion.

In December, the chief of the Muslim fundamentalist Jamaat-i-Islami Party, Tufail Mohammad, also demanded that the government use its nuclear capabilities to produce nuclear arms.[32]

Perhaps most startling was a paper, prepared in late 1985 and published in mid-1986, by Dr. A. Q. Khan, the head of Pakistan's enrichment program. In the paper, which most likely had official sanction given Khan's sensitive position, he appeared to depart significantly from Pakistan's public stance on nuclear arming and wrote favorably about a Pakistani nuclear deterrent:

The appreciation by the threshold countries that nuclear weapons confer enormous advantages upon the country having them and can affect the imbalance in manpower, natural resources, industrial potential and military strength, is a very big incentive for nuclear proliferation and has contributed a lot to the desire of these countries to keep all options open. India's persistence [sic] and continuing quest for international recognition as more than a "pawn on a global chessboard" forced it to detonate a nuclear device in 1974. Pakistan's future policy is to remain closely tied to Indian actions. If India openly starts a weapons programme, the deep-rooted Pakistani fears of India, especially after its active role in the dismemberment of Pakistan in 1971, would put tremendous pressure on Pakistan to take appropriate measures to avoid a nuclear Munich at India's hands in the event of an actual conflict, which many Pakistanis think very real.[33]

These pro-bomb pronouncements offer some of the first public indications of what appears to be significant political support for nuclear arming among elements of Pakistan's elite.[34] Given the country's continued pursuit of nuclear arms detailed below, it would appear that this faction is in control of nuclear decision making. Nonetheless, as described in the preceding section on India, the apparent intensification of pro-bomb lobbying did not preclude President Zia from improving ties with New Delhi during late 1985 or from entering into his important December 1985 understanding with Indian Prime Minister Rajiv Gandhi against attacks on nuclear installations.

On December 30, 1985, President Zia ended nine years

of martial law in the country, adding a new complexity to the nation's domestic politics. Among other effects, the step significantly increased the power of Prime Minister Junejo, leader of the nation's civilian parliament, whose members had been elected in non-party elections in February 1985.

The division of responsibilities between Junejo and Zia, who continues to serve as President and Army Chief of Staff, is not yet clear. Junejo is said to be the nation's chief executive officer and handled the important negotiations with the United States in the spring of 1986 that led to an agreement for a six-year, $4.02 billion aid program to begin in October 1987, when the current U.S. assistance program expires.[35] In July, Junejo made a state visit to the United States, further enhancing his stature.

Nevertheless, some observers believe that General Zia remains in control of all major policy decisions, including nuclear affairs, where the military has long played a major role.[36] Whoever has the final say on nuclear matters, there has been no indication of disagreement between the two. Publicly, Junejo has adopted a stance identical to Zia's, denying that Pakistan is developing nuclear arms and stating that only non-weapons-grade enriched uranium will be produced at the Kahuta enrichment plant, as the United States has insisted.[37] Nor is there evidence that behind the scenes Junejo is seeking to change the direction of the program, possibly because he and his Pakistan Muslim League Party—to judge from the comments of the party's secretary noted above—support the nation's secret nuclear-weapons effort.

The domestic political scene has been further complicated by the tumultuous return to Pakistan of Benazir Bhutto, who arrived to two weeks of massive and emotional rallies in April 1986. She is the daughter of Zulfikar Ali Bhutto, whom General Zia ousted in 1977 and executed in 1979 after his conviction on a disputed murder conspiracy charge. Miss Bhutto, who has become the leader of her late father's political organization, the Pakistani People's Party (PPP), has demanded that President Zia hold new elections by the end of 1986, four years ahead of schedule; many observers believe she would easily win any early vote.[38] After President Zia rejected her bid for elections, Miss Bhutto declared the PPP would take to the streets, using massive and possibly violent demonstrations to force the issue, a step that could plunge the country into political turmoil.[39]

Miss Bhutto's nuclear stance is uncertain. Pakistan's nuclear-weapons program was initiated by her father, whose political legacy she is seeking to exploit. Moreover, though there has been little public debate on the issue, Pakistani nuclear arming is presumed to have widespread public support. Both factors make it unlikely that the populist Miss Bhutto will challenge the Zia-Junejo government's nuclear course. Nonetheless, such a step cannot be ruled out, since Miss Bhutto has been quoted as saying that the "nuclear research program" begun by her father—seemingly a veiled reference to nuclear arms—was no longer feasible and had to be assessed anew.[40] She has also stated that, if elected, she would be prepared to "settle all doubts" concerning the possible military use of Pakistan's nuclear program, a possible hint that she might be willing to permit outside inspection of Pakistan's now secret nuclear installations.[41]

Against this background, there seem to be few domestic incentives for the Zia-Junejo government to alter its seemingly popular stance of publicly denying interest in nuclear arming, while at the same time pursuing the development of such weapons in secret. Indeed, with the advent of an increasingly independent parliament and Miss Bhutto's return, a change of nuclear policy that went against public sentiment might be more costly for the government than ever before.

Similarly, the unsettled state of Pakistani domestic politics is likely to make the Zia-Junejo government wary of major new initiatives with India in the field. For several years, Pakistan has offered to enter into a range of non-proliferation arrangements with its neighbor, including mutual adherence to the Non-Proliferation Treaty and bilateral nuclear inspections.[42] Since India is known to oppose such measures, it is not entirely clear whether Pakistan has advanced them in good faith. In the event that India offered to begin negotiations on one of the proposals, Pakistan would no doubt go along, but would probably proceed very cautiously toward reaching an actual agreement. Unfortunately, as described in the preceding section, Indian domestic tensions, its own provocative advances toward nuclear arming, and the downturn in Indo-Pakistani relations have lessened the likelihood of significant progress in this regard, at least in the near term.[43]

The presence of 120,000 Soviet troops in Afghanistan has added to the precariousness of Pakistan's security and undoubtedly contributed to its interest in nuclear arms. While a nuclear face-off with the Soviet Union would be suicidal, Islamabad may reason that a small nuclear force—which might include the possible smuggling of one or two nuclear weapons into the southern Soviet Union[44]—would lessen the likelihood of direct Soviet military intervention in Pakistan by raising the stakes of such an incursion and by helping ensure early U.S. or Chinese political involvement.

On June 21, 1986, the Soviets issued another in a series of warnings to Islamabad demanding it restrict its support for the Afghan rebels. In an unusual departure, however, the note also sternly warned Pakistan against developing nuclear weapons, an issue which had not been a top priority in previous Moscow-Islamabad exchanges. The note charged that Pakistan had achieved the capability to make nuclear weapons and that this poses a threat to "the southern part of the U.S.S.R." to which Moscow "cannot be indifferent."[45] U.S. officials speculated that the note may have been triggered by Indian concerns over the Pakistani nuclear program, pointing out that Indian Foreign Minister P. Shiv Shankar had met with Soviet leader Mikhail Gorbachev in Moscow on June 14. (It is also possible that the Soviets hoped to use the nuclear issue to increase pressure on the Afghan question; indirect talks between Pakistan and Afghanistan on the Afghan situation were scheduled for July 30.)

The United States apparently replied to the Soviet note

by warning the Soviets not to interfere in Pakistani affairs.[46] Although Washington has, itself, been issuing stiff demands that Pakistan desist from its nuclear quest, its regional rivalry with Moscow prevented the two from making common cause on this important issue as they have often done in the past on other proliferation questions.

Whether the Soviet warning will influence Pakistani nuclear policy cannot be predicted. It is worth noting, however, that after the Soviet warning was received, Pakistan suspended the transfer of U.S. Stinger missiles to the Afghan rebels. The missiles, offered to the rebels for the first time by the United States in March as a means for defending against increasingly successful attacks by the Afghan air force, represented a significant escalation in the level of weaponry available to the rebel forces.[47] Pakistan's decision to avoid this further provocation may signal that it will also restrain its nuclear activities rather than risk angering the Soviets on this front.

Over the past decade, Pakistan has built strong ties to other Islamic nations, particularly those in the middle East, giving rise to speculation that its nuclear program is aimed at developing the "Islamic bomb"—nuclear weapons to be shared with those similarly oriented nations in return for their financial contributions to the endeavor. Although U.S. officials do not rule out the possibility that Libya or Saudi Arabia may have helped to fund Pakistan's nuclear efforts, they strongly doubt that Pakistan has agreed to a nuclear *quid pro quo,* which would entail parting with what would be Pakistan's most precious military assets.[48]

There is, however, little question that a Pakistani nuclear capability would be a source of pride for the Moslem world and would enhance Islamabad's prestige among these nations. Indeed, in an unusually candid statement on the topic in March 1986, President Zia appeared to make this very point:

Pakistan has reached a high level of nuclear technology for peaceful uses. . . . We have announced that we have managed to enrich uranium, a very advanced technological operation. There are only five countries which have so far accomplished it. . . . It is ironic that the Soviet bomb is not called the communist bomb, and the U.S. bomb is not called the Christian bomb. India has nuclear reactors but no one calls it the Hindu bomb, or Israel's the Jewish bomb. Why must they call Pakistan's bomb, supposing we have it, an Islamic bomb? You can see the mentality. They are fearful that if an Islamic country such as Pakistan acquires this technology they will spread it. In fact if the Islamic world possessed this technology, it means that 900 million Muslims possess advanced technology. Hence comes the aggressive campaign against Pakistan and the aggressive talk about the Pakistani nuclear bomb. It is our right to obtain the technology. And when we acquire this technology, the entire Islamic world will possess it with us.[49]

Several months earlier, it may be noted, Pakistan apparently sought to cement its non-military nuclear ties with two other Islamic nations by entering into a program of nuclear cooperation with Egypt and Iraq. The program will include the establishment of an experimental nuclear reactor in Egypt and a Cairo-based authority for nuclear safety.[50]

Although Chinese aid for Pakistan's nuclear-weapons efforts have apparently ceased, in mid-September 1986, the two nations signed a comprehensive nuclear cooperation agreement. The agreement provides that all equipment and materials supplied by China will be covered by IAEA safeguards, but the accord does not require as a condition of supply that Pakistan place all of its nuclear installations under the IAEA system. The United States and, at least for the moment, all other Western nuclear supplier countries have made such comprehensive coverage a condition for nuclear trade with Pakistan. It remains possible that China will use the accord as a cover so that it can offer technical assistance—for which safeguards are not apparently required—for more sensitive aspects of Pakistan's nuclear program.[51]

Technical Developments. As noted earlier, in July 1985, Congress enacted legislation making further U.S. economic and military assistance contingent upon a certification by the president that Pakistan did not "possess" a nuclear explosive device.[52] In October, to permit foreign aid funds for fiscal year 1986 to be disbursed to Pakistan, President Reagan made this determination.

At the time, Pakistan had apparently just completed yet another operation to smuggle strictly regulated nuclear hardware out of West Germany. On August 10, according to a detailed account of the operation published in the West German weekly, *Der Stern,* the shipping company Global International Transport shipped 880 kilograms (1,936 pounds) of specially hardened "maraging" steel to a Karachi address.[53] The steel was fabricated into round bars whose diameter exactly matched that of a German-designed uranium-enrichment centrifuge of the type that A. Q. Khan is believed to be building at Kahuta.[54]

Centrifuge components made from maraging steel are on the list established by the Nuclear Suppliers Group of items that require special export licenses to ensure either that the export will be used for non-nuclear purposes or that it will be used only in a nuclear installation—unlike the Kahuta enrichment plant—that is covered by IAEA safeguards.[55] According to the *Stern* article, a small London steel-trading firm, Lizrose Ltd., originally ordered the maraging steel from the Arbed Corporation of Voelklingen, West Germany, in October 1984. Lizrose is run by Inam Ullah Shah, a man of Pakistani descent. Western intelligence agents learned of the order and persuaded Arbed not to go through with the sale. Two weeks afterwards, Arbed received a second order for the same material from Mark Blok, a Cologne steel dealer, who is married to a Pakistani and is said to be a friend of Inam Shah. Blok had the material delivered to a Cologne warehouse, thus avoiding the possible need for Arbed to obtain an export license. The material was then shipped to Hamburg and on to Karachi by Global Transport, presumably under false labeling.

The Pakistani embassy in Bonn, the *Stern* report continues, was involved in the operation from the beginning. A few weeks after the first order was placed with Arbed, Pakistan's military attache visited the steelworks and showed considerable interest in specialized steels. The most damning piece of evidence of Pakistani governmental involvement, however, is that Global International Transport sent the shipping documents and its invoice for shipping the material to the Pakistani embassy in Bonn for payment.[56]

During 1985, through a separate clandestine operation, Pakistan may have also attempted to reactivate its pursuit of a second route to nuclear arming, the production and separation of plutonium. Pakistan is believed to have a nearly completed pilot-scale reprocessing plant, known as the "New Labs," for extracting plutonium from spent nuclear-reactor fuel. At present, however, both of its reactors (a research reactor and a relatively small nuclear power plant) are subject to IAEA safeguards. This would mean that any plutonium extracted from the spent fuel of these reactors would also have to be placed under IAEA oversight and thus would be unavailable for nuclear weapons.

In August 1984, Pakistan announced that it was producing high-quality graphite. If further purified, this could allow it to build a simple unsafeguarded graphite reactor which could be used to produce plutonium for weapons. Although little progress appears to have been made in this regard, Pakistan is said to have attempted to purchase several hundred tons of pure graphite in the United States, Britain, France, and West Germany. Western officials successfully blocked the purchases, however.[57]

The details of the attempted graphite purchase and possibly the maraging steel operation were known to U.S. officials at the time of President Reagan's certification allowing aid to Pakistan, but the United States has been willing to continue aid notwithstanding such activities since 1981. Indeed, earlier in 1985, the Reagan administration, in a decision ultimately supported by Congress, had rejected proposed legislation that would have terminated such assistance unless all Pakistani actions in support of its nuclear-weapons-development effort—including smuggling operations—had ceased.[58]

As of October 1985, it appeared that Pakistan was still

adhering to an understanding, stemming from President Reagan's September 1984 letter to President Zia, that it would restrict the output of the Kahuta enrichment plant to non-weapons-usable uranium enriched to a level of five percent or less.[59] Thus, when a high-level U.S. delegation, led by Under Secretary of State for Political Affairs Michael H. Armacost and senior National Security Council staff member Donald Fortier, visited New Delhi and Islamabad in September to urge a regional solution to the growing nuclear competition between India and Pakistan, there was still a basis for hoping that the situation in Pakistan could be stabilized short of de facto nuclear arming.[60]

In subsequent months, however, further evidence emerged that Pakistan's nuclear-weapons program was not holding at such a plateau but was in fact continuing onward toward its goal. In December, Pakistan, using shell companies to disguise its involvement, apparently purchased six additional flash X-ray machines from the Swedish firm, Scandiflash.[61] More troubling was the late March account in the usually reliable *Foreign Report,* stating that Kahuta had produced uranium enriched to thirty percent.[62] This would be well above the five-percent level supposedly agreed to by Pakistan's leaders, though still short of the ninety-percent enriched material needed for nuclear arms.

While Pakistani officials have denied the report, by the time of Pakistani Prime Minister Junejo's visit to Washington in July 1986, U.S. aides were plainly concerned that Pakistan had made important new progress toward nuclear weapons.[63] The precise nature of the new American concerns remained unclear, but they apparently went well beyond the fear that Pakistan had produced thirty-percent-enriched uranium at Kahuta. A series of press stories in July, citing Reagan administration sources, stated that Pakistan was considered to have the capacity to build nuclear arms or to be on the verge of having that capability, with one account stating that all that remained was for Pakistan to assemble the components. In early November 1986, U.S. intelligence sources were reported to have concluded that

Pakistan had produced weapons-grade uranium and might be able to produce weapons in as little as two weeks—information that was apparently available to President Reagan when, on October 27, he had once again certified that Pakistan did not "possess" a nuclear device.[64] If these reports are accurate, Pakistan has now effectively crossed the nuclear weapons threshold.

A particularly troubling aspect of these new allegations was that they suggested that U.S. diplomacy had been far less effective than hoped. In effect, Pakistan appeared ready to violate clear-cut non-proliferation understandings with the United States even if it meant risking the loss of U.S. aid. Perhaps President Zia and Prime Minister Junejo believed that such aid was not really at risk, in view of the failure of the United States to terminate assistance in previous years, despite the often unambiguous evidence that Pakistan was continuing its pursuit of nuclear arms. Unfortunately, the Reagan administration may have compounded this problem when it agreed, in its late March negotiations with Prime Minister Junejo, to extend U.S. assistance for another six years under terms more generous than ever before.[65] At that time, if the account in the *Foreign Report* is accurate, American officials would have been aware that Pakistan had violated the five-percent limit on enrichment at Kahuta—and possibly that it had taken the further steps, noted above, to advance its nuclear-weapons program. It remains to be seen how Congress will respond to these developments when it takes up the new aid package, probably in early 1987.

Pakistan has several aircraft that could be used for delivering nuclear weapons, the most advanced being its forty U.S.-supplied F-16s. The United States is not known to have obtained explicit assurances from Pakistan that the aircraft will not be used for this purpose. Pakistan also has launched a number of sounding rockets as part of its embryonic space program. Development of a satellite launch vehicle is still a number of years off and long-range missiles only a distant possibility.[66]

Prospects. Though the details remain murky, there seems to be little doubt that Pakistan is continuing its pursuit of nuclear arming. The real question is the point at which Islamabad's efforts will level off.

Washington's attempt to forestall the production of more than five-percent-enriched uranium appears not to have succeeded. President Reagan's September 1984 letter, however, did not state explicitly that U.S. assistance would be cut off if Pakistan exceeded this threshold. In contrast, U.S. law unambiguously specifies that such aid will be terminated if Pakistan fabricates a complete nuclear weapon. Quite possibly, Pakistan will refrain from doing so, since the restriction would not, in any event, prevent Islamabad from obtaining a de facto nuclear deterrent by building all the necessary components and thereby remaining only "a screwdriver away" from nuclear arms. On the other hand, having seen the United States repeatedly back away from terminating assistance because of concerns over the Soviet presence in Afghanistan, Islamabad may reason that if it quietly violates this stricture, U.S. law will be amended to permit aid to continue just as the Symington Amendment was modified in 1981 for this purpose.

Testing a nuclear device, however, would be a far more visible and provocative step, which would leave Washington little choice other than to suspend assistance. It would also be likely to stimulate India to move toward nuclear arming and would trigger a strong international outcry, as well, possibly resulting in additional economic sanctions. For the near term, therefore, it is probable that the Zia-Junejo government will refrain from this action.

Recently intensified Soviet pressure may also play a more important role than previously assumed in slowing the Pakistani nuclear-weapons effort and in deterring a Pakistani test. The United States, by declaring that it would not see Pakistan's security jeopardized, undercut the impact of Moscow's June 1986 warning to Pakistan about its nuclear program. Nonetheless, one scenario Pakistan must consider is the threat of a Soviet or Afghan air strike against Kahuta.

While Pakistani officials have stated that such an attack by India would be considered an act of war (and one that would probably lead to a raid against one of India's equally vulnerable nuclear installations),[67] Islamabad would have few means for replying to a Soviet attack and would also have to question what posture the United States would take in such a situation. U.S. warnings to Moscow notwithstanding, it is extremely unlikely that Washington would respond militarily to a Soviet or Afghan surgical strike against a Pakistani nuclear plant whose construction the United States, itself, has repeatedly sought to block.[68]

Short of such an extraordinary development or a Pakistani test, however, U.S.-Soviet competition in the region will limit the amount of pressure either will be able to apply to curb Pakistan's nuclear ambitions. This leaves regional non-proliferation initiatives as the most likely mechanism for slowing Pakistan's drive for nuclear status. With Pakistan having already offered a range of such proposals and with India by far the stronger regional power with a demonstrated nuclear capability, it appears that New Delhi must make the next move. Unfortunately, the prospects for an accommodation of this kind are dim, in light of domestic political factors in both countries, the current deterioration of Indo-Pakistani relations, and the provocative steps both took between mid-1985 and late 1986 to enhance their respective nuclear capabilities.

Against this background, it is all too likely that the subcontinent will shortly have two de facto nuclear powers—if it does not already have them today.

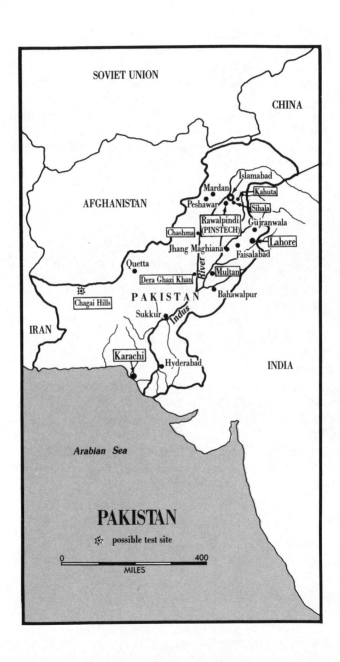

SOVIET UNION

CHINA

AFGHANISTAN

Islamabad

Mardan

Peshawar

Kahuta

Sihala

Rawalpindi
(PINSTECH)

Chashma

Gujranwala

Jhang Maghiana

Lahore

Faisalabad

Quetta

River

Indus

Dera Ghazi Khan

Multan

PAKISTAN

Bahawalpur

☼

Chagai Hills

Sukkur

IRAN

Karachi

Hyderabad

INDIA

Arabian Sea

PAKISTAN

☼ possible test site

0   400

MILES

Pakistan

Power Reactors/Operating or Under Construction
KANUPP, Karachi (heavy-water/natural-uranium,125 MWe[a])
- supplier: Canadian General Electric (Canada)
- start up: 1972
- fuel source: Canada[b], also Pakistan after 1980
- heavy water: United States and Canada[c]
- safeguards: yes[d]

Uranium Resources/Active Mining Sites/Uranium Mills
- reasonably assured   sufficient for Kahuta
  reserves: enrichment plant[e]
- currently active site: Dera Ghazi Khan
- mills in operation: Lahore[f]

Uranium Conversion (UF_6)
Dera Ghazi Khan
- capacity: max. 198 metric tons of hexafluoride per year[g]
- supplier: CES Kalthof G.m.b.H. of Freiburg (West Germany)[h]
- start up: 1980[h]
- safeguards: no

Heavy Water
Multan
- capacity: 13 metric tons[c]
- supplier: Belgonucléaire (Belgium)[f](?)
- start up: 1980 (?)[f]
- safeguards: no

Karachi
- capacity: upgradation unit to serve KANUPP, quantity unknown[f]
- supplier: Canada (?)
- start up: 1976
- safeguards: (?)

Enrichment
Kahuta
- type: ultracentrifuge
- capacity: Currently 1,000-14,000 (?) centrifuges[i]; some highly enriched uranium possibly produced[p]
- supplier: Vakuum Apparat Technik (Switzerland), CORA Engineering (Switzerland), Emerson Electric (Britian), Van Doorne Transmissie (Netherlands), Leybold Heraeus (West Germany), Aluminum Walzwerke (West Germany); items also obtained from U.S. and Canada; plans thought to be obtained from URENCO.[r]
- start up: 1984 (partial)[j]
- safeguards: no

Sihala
- type: ultracentrifuge[f]
- capacity: experimental scale
- supplier: same as Kahuta (presumed)
- start up: prior to 1984 (presumed)
- safeguards: no

Fuel Fabrication
Chashma/Kundian
- capacity: sufficient fuel for KANUPP[c], (currently, probably less).
- supplier: Pakistan, plans from Canada[k]
- start up: 1980[l]
- safeguards: no

Reprocessing
Chashma
- capacity: 100 metric tons of spent fuel; 100 to 200 kg of plutonium per year[g]
- supplier: SGN (France)
- start up: France terminated this project in 1978; construction may be continuing.
- safeguards: uncertain; agreement between Pakistan, France, and IAEA provides for safeguards, but these provisions not yet in force.

New Labs, Rawalpindi
- capacity: capable of extracting 10 to 20 kg of plutonium per year[q]
- supplier: SGN (France), Belgonucléaire (Belgium)[g,m]
- start up: cold tests 1982; uncertain whether plant is running.[n]
- safeguards: no (but might be subject to safeguards as a "replicated" plant under Pakistan-France-IAEA agreement covering Chashma, if safeguards under this agreement are implemented).

PINSTECH, Rawalpindi
- capacity: experimental scale[o]
- supplier: Pakistan (?); plans from Great Britain[o]
- start up: ?
- safeguards: no

Research Reactor
PARR, Rawalpindi (light-water/highly enriched uranium, 5 MWt)[a]
- supplier: United States[a] (through the IAEA)
- start up: 1965[a]
- fuel source: United States
- safeguards: yes[a]

Delivery Systems

Pakistan has two lines of advanced combat aircraft able to deliver an atomic bomb (assumed to weigh 1,300 pounds): the F-16 Falcon and the Mirage 5PA3. In addition, the Mirage 3EP and the Q-5 Fantan A could also serve in this capacity with slight modifications or a modest reduction in weapon weight.[s]

Sources and Notes

a. International Atomic Energy Agency, *The Annual Report for 1981* (IAEA, 1982), pp. 73-76. An enlargement of the research reactor to 10MWt is planned. "LWR's for Pakistan," *Nuclear Engineering Int'l*, April 1986, p.5.

b. Canada terminated fuel supplies in 1976 because of Pakistan's unwillingness to sign the Non-Proliferation Treaty; since 1980, plant has run partly on Pakistani-produced fuel and on remaining Canadian-supplied material.

c. David Hart, *Nuclear Power in India: A Comparative Analysis* (London: George Allen and Unwin), p. 133; "Pakistan AEC Journal Says Nation Has Mastered Front End of Fuel Cycle," *Nuclear Fuel*, March 25, 1985, p.10.

d. From September 1980 until March 1983, IAEA was unable to certify that no diversion of spent fuel occurred. Milton Benjamin, "Pakistan Backs Atomic Safeguards," *Washington Post*, November 17, 1982.

e. "Scientist Affirms Pakistan Capable of Uranium Enrichment, Weapons Production," *Nawa-I-Waqt* (Lahore). February 10, 1984, translated in *Joint Publication Research Service/Nuclear Proliferation and Development*, March 5, 1983, p. 36; "Pakistan AEC Journal . . .," *Nuclear Fuel*.

According to press reports in November 1979, Pakistan had obtained as much as 100 metric tons of uranium concentrate, or "yellowcake," not subject to International Atomic Energy Agency monitoring from Libya. The material had originally been purchased by Libya from Niger and then re-exported to Pakistan, possibly along with material that Pakistan had itself purchased from Niger through normal, above-board channels. John J. Fialka, "West Concerned by Signs of Libyan-Pakistan A-Effort," *Washington Star*, November 25, 1979.

f. P. B. Sinha and R. R. Subramanian, *Nuclear Pakistan* (New Delhi: Vision Books 1980), pp. 35, 121.

g. Weissman and Krosney, *The Islamic Bomb* (New York: Times Books, 1981), p. 219, (UF_6); (pp. 80-84 New Labs); (p. 81, experimental reprocessing unit); "Germans Fostered Climate for Bombs," *Der Stern*, July 2, 1981, pp. 96-99.

h. Weissman and Krosney, *The Islamic Bomb*, p. 219. John M. Geddes, "Bonn Says Firm Illegally Sent Pakistan Gear That Can Be Used for Atomic Bombs," *Wall Street Journal*, July 16, 1981.

i. Senator Alan Cranston, "Nuclear Proliferation and U.S. National Security Interests," *Congressional Record*, June 21, 1984, p. S 7901; "Inside Kahuta," *Foreign Report*, May 1, 1986. Annual capacity of plant 10 (*Foreign Report*) to 45 (Cranston) kilograms of highly enriched uranium.

j. "Scientist Affirms," *Nawa-I-Waqt*, pp. 43-44.

k. "Nuclear Facilities in the Middle East," Department of State, submitted in *Hearings on the Israeli Air Strike*, June 18, 19, and 25, 1981, 97th Congress, 1st Session (Washington, D.C.: Government Printing Office, 1981), p. 40.

l. James Katz and Onkar Marwah, *Nuclear Power in Developing Countries* (Lexington, MA: Lexington Books, 1982), p. 268.

m. According to Weissman and Krosney, *The Islamic Bomb*, France may not have been aware of SGN participation.

n. Cranston, "Nuclear Proliferation and U.S. National Security Interests." Cranston states facility has operated with radioactive material, but U.S. officials deny this. (Personal communication). Seymour M. Hersh, "Pakistani In U.S. Sought to Ship A-Bomb Trigger," *New York Times,* February 25, 1985.

o. Thomas W. Graham, "South Asian Nuclear Proliferation and National Security Chronology," Center for International Affairs, Massachusetts Institute of Technology, 1984, citing Weissman and Krosney, *The Islamic Bomb,* p. 81.

p. See references in note 1 of Pakistan text.

q. Milton R. Benjamin, "Pakistan Building Secret Nuclear Plant," *Washington Post,* September 23, 1980.

r. See Leonard S. Spector, *The New Nuclear Nations* (New York: Vintage Books, 1985) Chapter II, "The Nuclear Netherworld," and accompanying notes, especially note 31.

s. 1,300 lb. selected as illustrative on basis of Sweden's untested atomic weapon design prepared in the late 1950s. (Christer Larsson, "Build a Bomb!" *Ny Teknik,* April 25, 1985). Source: *The Military Balance 1985-1986 (London: International Institute for Strategic Studies, 1985).*

Chapter IV:
The Middle East

"Plutonium production rates amount to 40 kilograms a year, enough to build 10 bombs. In the past six years Israel has added further equipment to make components for thermonuclear devices."

London *Sunday Times* "Insight" report on the Israeli nuclear program, based on photos and data from a former Israeli nuclear technician, October 1986

Israel remains the only Middle Eastern nation thought to possess nuclear weapons or the capability to produce them. A detailed exposé of Israel's nuclear program published in October 1986 indicates, however, that the program is far more advanced than previously believed and that, accordingly, the pace of proliferation in the region in recent years has been more rapid than generally acknowledged. The exposé, based on information and photos supplied by a technician formerly employed at Israel's classified Dimona nuclear complex, indicates that Israel may now possess more than 100 nuclear weapons—not the twenty to twenty-five previously thought—and that some of them may employ nuclear fusion, the principle of the H-bomb, which would make them tens of times more powerful than the atom bombs used in World War II.[1] Israel is not an NPT party.

New evidence also appears to confirm that Israel in the early 1980s deployed the short-range (400-mile) Jericho II missile, capable of carrying a nuclear warhead. If these various reports are accurate, as they appear to be, since 1980 Israel has vastly increased its nuclear might.

Three other regional states—Libya, Iraq, and Iran—are

thought to harbor an interest in acquiring nuclear arms and at one time or another have taken steps toward this goal, despite their status as parties to the Non-Proliferation Treaty. All, however, are far from possessing the necessary nuclear infrastructure. Libya and, it appears, Iraq have made unsuccessful attempts to purchase nuclear weapons or nuclear-weapons material from other nations or on the international black market; fortunately such commodities do not appear to be available from either source. Published here for the first time, however, are the details of a 1981 would-be black-market nuclear arms deal between top Libyan nuclear aides and former CIA agent Edwin P. Wilson—testimony to Libya's keen desire for nuclear weapons.

Syria must also be factored into the Middle East nuclear equation. In two interviews, one in September 1984 and the second in October 1985, Syrian Defense Minister Mustafa Tlas declared that the Soviet Union had "guaranteed" it would give Damascus nuclear weapons if Israel employed nuclear arms against Syria.[2] A Soviet spokesman claimed Tlas's statement was untrue, but other Soviet officials have reportedly told Western visitors that if Israel were to attack Syria itself—even if only with conventional armaments—Moscow would assist its ally with military force, including tactical nuclear weapons if necessary.[3] It seems most unlikely that Moscow would place nuclear arms under Syrian control; nevertheless, these reports together with the presence of several thousand Soviet military advisers in Syria leave little question that Israeli planners have to weigh seriously the risk of a Soviet response. These developments recall reports that Moscow may have taken steps toward bringing nuclear weapons to Egypt during the 1973 October War.[4]

Syria's reported development of chemical weapons, which might be used in warheads on its Soviet-supplied surface-to-surface missiles, raises another concern of relevance to the issue of nuclear proliferation in the region.[5] With Iraq having repeatedly used chemical munitions in its six-year war with Iran both against combatants and against the Iranian city of Abadan, the taboo against the use of such arms in the Middle East context, if not elsewhere, has been seriously weakened.[6] Although Israel is believed to possess a chemical weapons capability of its own, its presumed nuclear arsenal can also be considered as serving in part as a deterrent against a possible Syrian chemical attack on its population centers. In effect, though Syria lacks nuclear weapons, its access to chemical arms—the "poor man's A-bomb"—may increase the risk of nuclear escalation in a future regional conflict.

One additional development has been the absence of attacks on nuclear installations in this volatile area since mid-1985. At least five such attacks are known to have taken place: an unsuccessful bombing raid by Iranian aircraft against Iraq's large Osiraq research reactor outside Baghdad on September 30, 1980; Israel's June 7, 1981, air strike against Osiraq, which destroyed the unit; and three Iraqi attacks against the two partially completed Iranian nuclear power plants at Bushehr, on March 24, 1984, and February 12 and March 4, 1985.[7] Although no new attacks have taken place, at the August 1986 annual summit meeting of the Non-Aligned Movement, Libyan President Muammer Khadafi renewed his threat to destroy Israel's Dimona complex, denouncing Egypt and Jordan for failing to offer him the use of air bases from which he could mount the attack.[8] Thus the issue remains a source of concern.

Despite the fact that no new Middle East state seems likely to acquire nuclear arms in the foreseeable future, new information about Israel's nuclear-weapons program shows that nuclear dangers in the area have continued to grow.

Israel

During the past year, Israel appears to have continued the steady build-up of a nuclear arsenal that is thought to date from the late 1960s. Using past analyses of the Israeli program, which assumed the arsenal consisted of relatively crude, aircraft-deliverable atomic bombs and had grown at a rate of one or two weapons a year, the Israeli arsenal would now contain about twenty to twenty-five weapons with yields similar to the Nagasaki bomb. In light of several recent reports—including detailed revelations in October 1986 by a former employee at Israel's classified Dimona nuclear complex—it now appears, that these estimates must be significantly revised. The reports state that Israel's nuclear weapons number between 100 and 200; this would indicate a growth rate of perhaps five to ten weapons annually. These reports also claim that the Israeli nuclear arsenal is far more sophisticated than previously believed and contains weapons of advanced design, some of which rely partly on nuclear fusion and are thus many times more powerful than the atomic bombs used in World War II.[1] New evidence has also come to light that Israel has deployed a short-range (400 mile) missile capable of carrying a nuclear warhead.[2] While many questions remain, it appears that the newer estimates of Israeli nuclear capabilities are the more accurate.[3]

Background. Israel is not known to have tested a nuclear weapon and has never declared it has crossed the nuclear-weapons threshold. Its official posture, adopted in the early 1960s, is the highly ambiguous formula that it will not be the "first to introduce nuclear weapons" into the Middle East.[4] Nonetheless, it is widely believed that Jerusalem has developed a nuclear arsenal using the Dimona research reactor supplied by France in the late 1950s and a reprocessing installation thought to have been completed at the same site in the latter half of the 1960s. As noted above, together these facilities have been thought capable of producing the plutonium needed for one or, possibly, two weapons annually.[5]

In addition, during the mid-1960s, Israel is believed to have illegally diverted about 100 kilograms (220 pounds) of highly enriched uranium from a privately owned uranium fabrication plant, the Nuclear Materials and Equipment Corporation (NUMEC) facility, at Apollo, Pennsylvania. The material would be sufficient for four to six additional weapons (assuming the standard fifteen to twenty-five kilograms of highly enriched uranium per weapon).[6] Israel is also alleged to have obtained an unknown quantity of plutonium from France in the 1960s.[7]

Although one 1981 report stated that Israel possessed over one hundred nuclear devices, it was not until 1985 that this estimate began to gain support in other published analyses.[8] In May of that year, two reports in the usually reliable *Aerospace Daily,* citing unnamed "U.S. sources," stated that Israel might possess as many as 200 nuclear weapons and that since 1981 it had deployed nuclear-armed Jericho II missiles, with a range of 400 miles.[9] The reports described the Jericho II as a solid-fuel rocket with an inertial guidance system developed in the mid to late 1970s that make it far more accurate than an earlier version, the Jericho I.

The author of the reports, Richard Sale, subsequently provided additional details during a July 1985 interview on

NBC "Nightly News." He said that Israel's warhead for the Jericho II was developed at the Weizman Institute near Tel Aviv, a program in which U.S. scientists were involved. One of the American scentists told Sale that he had seen the warhead, describing it as about 2 feet long, 20 to 22 inches in diameter, and weighing 226 pounds.[10] On the same broadcast, Anthony Cordesman, a recognized expert on Middle Eastern military affairs, appeared partially to confirm Sale's assertions by declaring that there are "at least 100 nuclear weapons in the Israeli inventory, possibly over 140."

Sale's and Cordesman's estimates, however, left one key question unanswered: how had Israel amassed such an arsenal, given the limitations of its known nuclear resources? For their estimates to be valid, it had to be assumed that some additional source of nuclear-weapons material was available other than Dimona, NUMEC, or France, or that Israel needed less material per weapon than previously estimated.

Technical and Political Developments. A detailed exposé on the Israeli nuclear program published by the London *Sunday Times* in October 1986 sheds additional light on this question and lends credence to the higher estimates of Israel's nuclear capabilities, although the report still leaves a number of questions unanswered.[11]

The *Sunday Times* story is based on details provided by a 31-year-old technician, Mordechai Vanunu, who had worked in the plutonium separation facility at the Dimona complex for nine years, beginning in 1977. Vanunu was laid off in early 1986 after Israeli authorities apparently became concerned about his growing contacts with a number of West Bank Arab students. Before leaving his position, Vanunu reportedly took sixty color photographs of the building in which he worked, "Machon 2," a handful of which were published in the *Sunday Times* report. Interviewed by reporters for the paper in Sydney, Australia, Vanunu also provided extensive technical details on the facility and its operations. American and British nuclear specialists consulted by the *Sunday Times* have attested to the technical validity of Vanunu's evidence, although questions as to how he could have circumvented Israeli security to obtain the photographs have led some to doubt whether the pictures are in fact of Dimona.[12] The Israeli government has acknowledged that Vanunu worked for the Israeli Atomic Energy Commission at Dimona, but did not indicate what his responsibilities were. In an unexpected twist, Vanunu disappeared from his London hotel room two days prior to the publication of the *Sunday Times* story. Reportedly he was taken to Israel by Israeli intelligence agents, where he will face charges of treason at a secret trial.[13]

Perhaps the most critical piece of information in the *Sunday Times* article is its confirmation of the existence of a reprocessing (plutonium extraction) plant at the Dimona site. The existence of this essential facility has long been assumed, but it has never been acknowledged by Israel, and only the sketchiest data on the unit has ever been reported.

According to Vanunu, Machon 2, which houses the facility, has two stories above ground and six below-grade levels. The reprocessing line—where plutonium is extracted from a nitric acid solution in which spent fuel from the Dimona research reactor has been dissolved—is three stories tall, rising from underground level four through level two. The control room for the unit occupies the floor above it, the first underground level, while the machining of weapon parts takes place under the reprocessing hall, on the fifth subterranean level. Emergency radioactive waste storage tanks are below this, at the bottom of the building. The two above-ground floors contain an air filtration plant, a receiving area for spent fuel (which is then carried by elevator down to the reprocessing hall), offices, a canteen, and dressing areas.[14]

The *Sunday Times* states that despite French President de Gaulle's claim that France had terminated aid for the facility in 1960, the unit was built with French technology and engineering assistance—a conclusion consistent with previous analyses and confirmed by Francis Perrin, a former senior French nuclear official, in a subsequent *Sunday Times* report.[15] Excavation for the underground plant—an eighty-foot deep crater—began in 1957, at the same time as construction on the then-secret Dimona reactor got under way. The article, which states that Israel has been building nuclear arms for twenty years, implies the reprocessing facility started up around 1966. This is a bit earlier than some estimates, but consistent with a detailed 1982 study by a French journalist.[16] According to Vanunu, false walls were built to hide the service elevators to the underground floors from U.S. inspectors who visited the Dimona site annually from late 1963 or early 1964 until 1969. Washington had insisted on such visits, after discovering the Dimona reactor in 1960, apparently by means of a U-2 surveillance aircraft photo. (Unanswered in the *Sunday Times* report is how U.S. reconnaisance planes could subsequently have failed to observe several years of continued construction on the reprocessing plant within the excavated area or how the U.S. inspectors could have failed to detect radioactive emissions from the unit. In fact, the Johnson administration had suspicions that Israel was building a reprocessing capability.)[17]

The second key finding in the *Sunday Times* exposé is that the reprocessing facility has an annual output of forty kilograms (88 pounds) of plutonium—more than five times the output previously assumed. Based on data from Vanunu, the article precisely details the plutonium extraction process from the number of fuel rods brought into the unit (100 large and 40 smaller ones) to the molding of plutonium "buttons," each weighing 130 grams, at a rate of 9 buttons per week, resulting in a total output of approximately 40 kilograms (88 pounds) over 34 weeks of operations annually. As discussed below, this could be enough for five to ten weapons per year, depending on what assumptions are made concerning Israeli weapon designs.

The Dimona reactor is usually rated at twenty-six megawatts. Such a facility, however, could produce only seven or eight kilograms of plutonium annually, not the forty specified by Vanunu. This discrepancy led the authors of the *Sunday Times* article to speculate that the reactor had been enlarged, "probably" to 150-megawatts, sometime after the last U.S. inspection in 1969.[18] Two earlier reports had also indicated that the reactor was enlarged beyond its original specifications, although only to about seventy-five megawatts. One report suggests this occurred during the initial construction of the reactor between 1957 and 1963; the other places the enlargement around 1980.[19] While questions remain, Vanunu's testimony and photos concerning the plutonium extraction operations and Israel's nuclear-weapon designs (discussed below) appear to be so persuasive that it does not seem unreasonable to posit a commensurate expansion of the Dimona reactor.

The third critical conclusion in the *Sunday Times* investigation is that Israel's nuclear weapons are far more sophisticated than previously believed: they apparently require less than the standard eight kilograms (17.6 pounds) of plutonium generally presumed necessary and are far more powerful than the weapons used in World War II.

Several of Vanunu's photos—not published by the *Sunday Times*—were said to show full-scale models of bomb components, and one shows an actual component. Based on an examination of the photos and Vanunu's testimony, Dr. Theodore Taylor, a former U.S. nuclear-weapons designer, told the *Sunday Times* investigative team:

Assuming that the photographs were taken at Dimona, the models of the interior components of a nuclear weapon are genuine and Vanunu's identification of the nature and purpose of the various facilities and of the materials corresponding to the "models" are generally correct.

The information obtained from Vanunu's statements and photographs as presented to me are entirely consistent with a present Israeli capacity to produce at least five to ten nuclear weapons a year that are significantly smaller, lighter, and more efficient than the first types of nuclear weapons developed by the U.S., U.S.S.R., U.K., France, and China.

If, as Taylor states, Israel can make five to ten weapons annually from forty kilograms of plutonium, it is not implausible that Israel could have acquired between 100 and 200 weapons over the past two decades.   At least as significant is Vanunu's evidence that Israel has produced weapons relying on nuclear fusion—the principle of the H-bomb—in addition to nuclear fission, the process used in atomic weapons. This advanced concept can greatly increase the power of nuclear arms. As explained more fully in Appendix B, fusion weapons contain an atom-bomb style nuclear core (relying on the principle of nuclear fission), which when detonated, instantaneously ignites "fusion material"—usually lithium-6 deuteride and tritium—that has also been packed within the weapon's shell. By this means, the yields of fission weapons can be "boosted" ten-fold or more to hundreds of kilotons. In hydrogen bombs, in which yields hundreds to thousands of times greater than those of simple atomic bombs can be achieved, a third ignition is triggered, as the powerful primary and secondary reactions cause a casing of natural uranium to fission.

The *Sunday Times* quotes Dr. Taylor as stating that Vanunu's photos of the weapon models and single component show a bomb that uses the fusion principle and, indeed, that the component appears to be made of lithium-deuteride, the fusion material. A second expert to whom the *Sunday Times* showed the photos, Dr. Frank Barnaby, a nuclear physicist who worked in the British nuclear weapons program, was quoted as concurring in this view. (Barnaby, who conducted extensive interviews with Vanunu, said that overall he found Vanunu's testimony to be "totally convincing.")

Historically, the five nuclear-weapon states have graduated from atomic bombs to hydrogen bombs and along the way have applied the principles learned to develop "boosted weapons." But the key to this progression has been an extensive atomic-weapons testing program, which has permitted them to experiment with the fission trigger needed for the more advanced designs. Israel is not known to have conducted a nuclear test.[20] Although the photos do not provide evidence that Israel has developed a full-fledged hydrogen bomb—which Taylor in a separate interview stated would almost certainly require an extensive testing program—they indicate that Israel has been able to advance to boosted weapons, using a simplified design to help ensure the reliability of the devices. Presumably Israel relied on computer simulations and the testing of non-nuclear sub-components to achieve this result.[21]

Vanunu also provided details on Israel's production of lithium-6, deuterium, and tritium. All of these, he said, were manufactured in units built in Machon 2 between 1980 and 1982, alongside the plutonium production line.

Apart from revealing a far more powerful Israeli nuclear arsenal than previously imagined, Vanunu's testimony could have far-reaching significance. Heretofore, nuclear testing has been seen as a critically important proliferation threshold. But before the revelations in the *Sunday Times* article, there was increasing concern that nations like Pakistan or South Africa could develop reliable atomic bombs without testing—indeed, revelations in 1985 showed that Sweden's nuclear-weapons program of the 1950s had made considerable advances in nuclear-weapons design without testing. Nonetheless, it was believed that emerging nuclear states would not be able to move beyond relatively inefficient designs without testing programs. Now it appears that nuclear testing may not be essential for the development of more advanced weapon designs, assuming a nation has scientific and technical capabilities comparable to those of Israel.

Although not mentioned in the *Sunday Times* article, Vanunu's revelations support the proposition that Israel has been able to progress up the proliferation ladder in a second respect. The small size and relatively light weight of the nuclear devices examined by Taylor and Barnaby indicate that Israel would have little difficulty building nuclear warheads for missiles. Since, as discussed further below, there is increasing evidence that Israel possesses a sophisticated short-range missile, the Jericho II, it appears reasonable to assume that it now possesses not only aircraft-deliverable nuclear bombs, but—as reported by the *Aerospace Daily* in 1985—

also missiles that either have or can be rapidly equipped with nuclear warheads.

Many questions remain about Vanunu's evidence. Some are technical: Could the Dimona reactor have been expanded six-fold within its existing structure? How long has Israel produced plutonium at the forty-kilograms-per-year rate? How many weapons has it actually built? What proportion incorporate the fusion principle?

Questions as to Vanunu's credibility are also unresolved. What were Vanunu's motives for giving away Israel's nuclear secrets? Could he have really smuggled a camera into Israel's best protected installation? Why would he take the risk, particularly if, as the *Sunday Times* claims, he did not even bother to develop his film for months until he happened to meet a Colombian reporter in Sydney, who tried to hawk his story to the European press? What led to Vanunu's disappearance in London?

Although the Israeli government appeared distressed by Vanunu's disclosures, the possibility remains that it deliberately planted the story. Israeli military planners have become increasingly concerned recently about Syria's highly accurate Soviet-supplied SS-21 missiles and the possibility that Syria might use them with chemical warheads.[22] Israel may have hoped to chill Syrian adventurism by means of Vanunu's revelations, issuing a reminder of Israel's overwhelming military strength. Or, outgoing Labour Prime Minister Shimon Peres, about to hand over office to the conservative Yitzak Shamir, may have hoped to sustain momentum toward Middle Eastern peace negotiations by showing the Israeli public that the nation was so strong that it could safely offer future concessions.[23]

An important related development is that as Israel was advancing its nuclear-weapon capabilities, it appears that the country was also developing a surface-to-surface missile, known as the Jericho II, able to carry a nuclear warhead weighing up to 750 kilograms (1,650 pounds).[24] Given Israel's accomplishments in nuclear-weapons design, described above, and the fact that Sweden, in the late 1950s, designed (and tested the components of) atomic weapons weighing 600 kilograms (1,300 pounds) in which it had high confidence without conducting a full-scale nuclear test, there is little doubt that Israel could equip the Jericho II with a nuclear warhead.[25]

According to documents said to have been abandoned at the Israeli trade mission in Tehran soon after the Shah fell in early 1979, the Israeli military fully appreciated the nuclear potential of the missile. One of the documents, part of some fifty-five paperback volumes that have subsequently been published by the Iranians who seized the American Embassy in November 1979, contains the minutes of a 1977 conversation in Tel Aviv between then Israeli Foreign Minister Moshe Dayan and Iranian General Hassan Toufanian in which the missile was discussed.[26] Toufanian subsequently authenticated the description of the conversation, which covered a proposed Israeli-Iranian project, known as Operation Flower, for the joint production of the missile.[27] The summary of the talks states:

General Dayan raised the problem of the Americans' sensitivity to the introduction of the kind of missiles envisaged in the joint project. He added that the ground-to-ground missile that is part of the joint project can be regarded also as a missile with a nuclear head, because with a head of 750 kg. it can be a double-purpose one.[28]

At the time of the talks, the missile was sufficiently advanced that Toufanian was able to witness a test firing. U.S. officials were apparently aware of the missile development program at the time, but not of Iran's participation.[29] The Jericho II is believed to have been deployed in the early 1980s. It is possible that some carry nuclear warheads, although the more likely case is that the warheads are stored separately and could be mated with the missile rapidly in time of crisis.[30]

If the London *Sunday Times* article is accurate, the deployment of the Jericho IIs roughly coincided with the start-up at Dimona of the unit in Machon 2 for producing fusion material. Thus, by the mid-1980s, it appears that Israel had acquired both nuclear-capable missiles and fusion-based nuclear weapons probably ten times or more as powerful as the previous generation of Israeli nuclear arms. If these have been mated, Israel in effect would have acquired what specialists term a major new "strategic system," comparable at its lower level of destructiveness to the deployment by the United States of a new generation of nuclear arms, such as the MX missile.

Nuclear matters are a forbidden topic for public discussion in Israel, where there is virtually no press coverage of the issue because of governmental censorship. Thus while there is an extensive public debate today in India, Argentina, and Brazil over the direction of those nations' nuclear policies—as there is in the United States, Great Britain, and France—Israel, despite its strong democratic traditions, appears to have implemented a major expansion of its nuclear force structure in complete secrecy.

The role of the United States must also be questioned. The Carter administration made non-proliferation a foreign policy priority. Though it was apparently aware that the Jericho II was under development, however, it is not known to have objected to Israel's pursuit of the project. Nor has the Reagan administration, which apparently considered the missile in its conventional mode to be an appropriate addition to Israel's arsenal; U.S. policy has long supported Israel's maintenance of a qualitative military edge in the Middle East. Whether either administration was aware of the new unit Vanunu says was built at Dimona for the production of lithium-6 and tritium is unclear, but construction activity at the site might have been telltale signs for U.S. intelligence agencies. One former high-ranking Reagan administration official whose responsibilities included Middle Eastern security issues has stated, however, that the United States was unaware of Israel's advance into the realm of fusion weapons and that this would have been a matter of considerable concern. After the revelations in the *Sunday Times,* it may be noted, a State Department spokesman responded only with the *pro forma* statement that the United States continues to oppose proliferation wherever it may take place.

In sum, while a number of uncertainties remain, there is reason to believe that, during the early 1980s, Israel acquired a nuclear arsenal so diverse and numerous that it became the sixth nuclear power, without the knowledge of its citizenry and while the U.S. government, at least partially aware of the direction of events, turned a blind eye.[31]

LEBANON

SYRIA

Mediterranean Sea

Sea of Galilee

Haifa

Tel Aviv
Rehovot
WEST BANK
Nahal Soreq
Jerusalem
Amman

Gaza Strip I S R A E L
Dead Sea

Beersheba

Dimona

JORDAN

Negev Desert

EGYPT

ISRAEL

phosphate/uranium
mining area

0   50

MILES

Gulf of Aqaba

Israel

Research Reactors
IRR I Nahal Soreq (light-water/highly enriched uranium, 5MWt)[a]
- supplier: United States
- start up: 1960
- fuel source: United States, through 1977 (expiration of U.S. agreement).
- safeguards: yes

IRR 2, Dimona (heavy-water/natural-uranium, probably 70-150 MWt)[b,c]
- supplier: France
- start up: 1963
- fuel source: Israel, Argentina, South Africa(?), Belgium(?), France(?), Niger(?), Central African Republic(?), Gabon(?)[d]
- heavy water: Norway[a], Israel(?)[a], France [f]
- safeguards: no

Uranium Resources/Active Mining Sites/Uranium Mills
- reasonably assured reserves: 30-60,000 tons is available from processing phosphate ores.[a]
- currently active site: phosphate deposits in the Negev near Beersheba.[e]
- mills in operation: phosphoric acid plants producing yellowcake as by-product, two in Haifa, one in southern Israel. Combined output, 100 tons.[a]

Uranium Purification (UO_2)
- capacity: sufficient to supply Dimona reactor (presumed)
- supplier: Israel(?)
- start up: ?
- safeguards: no

Heavy Water Production
Rehovot
- capacity: pilot scale[a]; sufficient to supply Dimona reactor (presumed).
- supplier: Israel
- start up: 1954(?)[a]
- safeguards: no

Fuel Fabrication
Dimona(?)[i]
- capacity: sufficient to supply Dimona reactor (presumed)
- supplier: Israel(?)
- start up: mid-1960s(?)
- safeguards: no

Reprocessing
Dimona[c,f,l]
- capacity: Probably 15^f - 40^c kilograms of plutonium per year
- supplier: Israel and France[c,f,h]
- start up: probably 1966[c,f]
- safeguards: no

Nahal Soreq
- capacity: laboratory-scale[j]
- supplier: Great Britain; some U.S. equipment(?).[j]
- start up: 1960(?)
- safeguards: no[k]

Enrichment
- type: laser(?)[g]
- capacity: 2-3 kilograms highly enriched uranium per year(?)[g]
- supplier: Israel
- start up: 1974(?)
- safeguards: no

Uranium Conversion (UF_6)
- capacity: Small capacity to permit enrichment activities (presumed).
- supplier: Israel (?)
- start up: 1974(?)
- safeguards: no

Delivery Systems
Israel has several lines of advanced combat aircraft able to deliver an atomic bomb (assumed to weigh 1,300 pounds): the A-4 Skyhawk, the F-15 Eagle, the F-16 Falcon, and the F-4 Phantom II. In addition, the Kfir could also serve in this capacity with slight modifications or a modest reduction in weapon weight.[m]

In addition, Israel is believed to have deployed the Jericho II missile (range, 400 miles; payload, 1650 pounds) during the early 1980s. The missile is considered nuclear capable.[n]

Sources and Notes

a. *Israeli Nuclear Armament,* Report of the Secretary General, United Nations General Assembly A/36/431, September 18, 1981, pp. 8-11, 15-18.

b. Pierre Péan, *Les Deux Bombes* (Paris: Fayard, 1982), p. 96 (75 megawatts); "The Middle East's Nuclear Arms Race," *Foreign Report,* August 13, 1980 (reactor upgraded from 26 megawatts to 70 megawatts in 1980). Traditional estimate of size is 24-26 megawatts; see reference a. Estimate of 150 megawatts given in reference c.

c. "Revealed: The Secrets of Israel's Nuclear Arsenal," *Sunday Times* (London), October 5, 1986.

d. John R. Redick, *The Military Potential of Latin American Nuclear Energy Programs* (Beverly Hills, CA: Sage Publications, 1972) p. 13 (Argentina); personal communication with informed former U.S. official (Argentina); Richard Kessler, "Argentine Officials Deny Rumors of Trade With Israel," *Nucleonics Week,* May

29, 1986, p. 6. Bertrand Goldschmidt, *Le Défi Atomique* (Paris: Fayard, 1980) pp. 205-206 (initially, uranium bought on world market from a number of sources, mainly Western and African); Fuad Jabber, *Israel and Nuclear Weapons* (London: Chatto and Windus, 1971) p. 89 (first load of Dimona reportedly comprised of 10 tons from South Africa, 10 tons from Dead Sea phosphates, 4 tons from French sources); Christopher Raj, "Israel and Nuclear Weapons," in K. Subrahmanyam, ed. *Nuclear Myths and Realities* (ABC: New Delhi, 1981) p. 105 (South Africa, France, French-controlled uranium mines in Gabon, Central African Republic, and Niger); William Drozdiak "Uranium Loss is Admitted," *Washington Post*, May 3, 1977 (200 tons of yellowcake diverted on Mediterranean Sea from Belgium thought to wind up in Israel.)

e. "Yellowcake from Phosphates," *Business Review and Economic News from Israel* (Tel Aviv), reprinted in *Joint Publication Research Service/Nuclear Development and Proliferation,* March 14, 1983, p. 28.

f. Pierre Péan, *Les Deux Bombes*.

g. Robert Gillette, "Uranium Enrichment: Rumors of Israeli Progress with Lasers", *Science,* No. 183, March 22, 1974, p. 1172; U.N., *Israeli Nuclear Armament,* p. 15.

CIA officials were convinced that Israel diverted approximately 100 kilograms of highly enriched uranium from the NUMEC plant in Apollo, Pennsylvania, between 1964 and 1966. Transcript of "Near Armageddon: The Spread of Nuclear Weapons in the Middle East," ABC News Close-Up, April 27, 1981, pp. 13-14 (Statement by former CIA official Carl Duckett). No concrete evidence that the material was diverted has come to light, however.

h. Weissmann and Krosney, *The Islamic Bomb,* (New York: Times Books, 1981) p. 113, citing Charles de Gaulle, *Memoirs of Hope: Renewal and Endeavor* (New York: Simon and Schuster, 1971), p. 266.

i. Fuad Jabber, *Israel and Nuclear Weapons* (London: Chatto and Windus, 1971), p. 45.

j. Ibid. p. 43.

k. Not listed in 1985 IAEA Annual Report among safeguarded installations.

l. IAEA Bulletin, Vol. 19, No. 5, p. 2; Weissman and Krosney, *The Islamic Bomb,* p. 110.

m. 1,300 lb. selected as illustrative on basis of Sweden's untested atomic weapon design prepared in the late 1950s. (Christer Larsson, "Build a Bomb!" *Ny Teknik*, April 25, 1985). Source: *The Military Balance 1985-1986* (London: International Institute for Strategic Studies, 1985).

n. Communications with informed U.S. officials; "Israel Said to Deploy Jericho Missile," *Aerospace Daily*, May 1, 1985.

Photo, taken by former Israeli nuclear technician Mordechai Vanunu, said to be Israel's classified Dimona nuclear complex viewed from the roof of the building (Machon 2) where Vanunu worked.
© *The Sunday Times*, London.

Photo, taken by Mordechai Vanunu, said to be the control room of Israel's secret underground plutonium separation plant, housed in Machon 2 at the Dimona site. © *The Sunday Times*, London.

Photo, taken by Mordechai Vanunu, said to be a cutaway model of an Israeli atomic bomb. Dark outer casing represents high explosives, which would implode when the weapon is detonated and instantaneously crush the smaller sphere, triggering the nuclear explosion. (See next photo.)

© *The Sunday Times*, London.

Model, said to be an Israeli nuclear weapon, seen in previous photograph, with the core disassembled. Open sphere (at rear right) is thought to represent a beryllium reflector/tamper, which would help compress the smaller sphere of plutonium (front) during detonation. The object between the two spheres is part of the reflector/tamper, which can be unscrewed to permit insertion or removal of plutonium.

© *The Sunday Times*, London.

Libya

The image of a nuclear-armed Muammar Khadafi, contemptuous of world opinion and the value of innocent lives, has become a symbol of the dangers posed by unrestrained proliferation. Libya has made little progress toward this goal, however, as an international embargo of nuclear transfers to Tripoli has gained strength over the years. New details of Libya's negotiations to obtain nuclear weapons—which in fact did not exist—from former CIA agent Edwin Wilson in 1981, however, provide a chilling reminder of the country's interest in nuclear arming.

Background. During the 1970s, after its attempt to purchase nuclear arms from China was rebuffed,[1] Libya established a network of nuclear trade relations through which it hoped to gain rapid access to nuclear-weapons related technologies and assistance in developing an indigenous nuclear infrastructure. Today, many of these relationships are being either curtailed or terminated.

Libya seems to have received few if any benefits from its reported 1973 accord with Pakistan, under which Tripoli is said to have agreed to finance Pakistan's nuclear-weapons effort in return for access to technology for producing nuclear-weapons material or possibly nuclear weapons themselves.[2] Between 1978 and 1980, Libya is believed to have supplied Pakistan with significant quantities of uranium concentrate, or yellowcake, not subject to IAEA monitoring. The material, originally purchased from Niger, was apparently intended for use in Pakistan's clandestine uranium-enrichment program. (See Chapter III, Pakistan.) Although Libya ratified the Non-Proliferation Treaty in 1975, it did not enter into a formal safeguards agreement with the Agency until 1980 and thus was able to import and export uranium concentrate without having to list the transactions on an IAEA-monitored inventory.[3] Since 1980, however, all Libyan yellowcake purchases have been covered by the IAEA, depriving Tripoli of additional unrestricted material that it might barter for the bomb. Presumably all of Libya's previously stocks of yellowcake in Libya's were disclosed to the Agency when it established its initial inventory, although it is possible that Libya has secretly set aside some of the material.[4]

Similarly, Libya appears to have garnered little from its open nuclear-cooperation agreement with India. When he was in New Delhi in July 1978 to sign the accord, Libyan Prime Minister Abdul Salam Jalloud is said to have pressed Indian nuclear officials for a commitment to assist Libya in obtaining an "independent nuclear capability"—a veiled reference to plutonium extraction and nuclear explosives technology.[5] India, over the course of the following year, limited nuclear cooperation to strictly innocuous areas, and Libya abruptly terminated its oil shipments to New Delhi—expected to amount to one million tons per year—in an attempt to force India to share more sensitive nuclear technology. India refused and recalled its ambassador from Tripoli for consultation.[6]

In August 1984, then Indian Prime Minister Indira Gandhi, in response to a parliamentary question, revealed that she had had "some reservations" about the Indo-Libyan accord, which had been negotiated by former Prime Minister Moraji Desai without consulting senior Indian nuclear aides. Accordingly, she stated, she had confined activities to the exchange of scientists before allowing the agreement to lapse. This has foreclosed further Indo-Libyan cooperation of any kind.[7]

Tripoli's gains from its nuclear dealings with Moscow have also been modest. In 1975, the two signed a nuclear trade pact under which the Russians agreed to provide a small research reactor and help Libya build an associated atomic research center.[8] The reactor, located at Tajoura, is believed to have begun operating in 1981.[9] In 1977 Tripoli and Moscow signed a second accord for construction of two 440-megawatt nuclear-power reactors.[10] In early 1986, after years of inconclusive negotiations, however, the deal appeared to have been shelved indefinitely, only to be rekindled in May. Nonetheless, it seems that Russia, like India, is wary of extensive nuclear trade with Colonel Khadafi.[11]

The United States has not made any sales to Libya of nuclear equipment or materials. In 1983 Washington prohibited the training of Libyan nationals in nuclear sciences at U.S. universities and placed Libya on a list of states subject to especially strict nuclear export controls.[12]

During the early 1980s Libya received extensive technical assistance from two Belgian firms, Belgatom and Belgonucléaire, on the Tajoura Research Center, the then pending Soviet nuclear-power reactor sale, and the development of a number of Libyan uranium deposits.[13] In 1982, Libya began negotiations with Belgonucléaire for the purchase of a plant for producing uranium tetrafluoride. The material itself is not usable for nuclear weapons or as nuclear fuel; however, both uranium metal, which can be irradiated to produce plutonium, and uranium hexafluoride, which can be enriched to produce highly enriched uranium, are made from uranium tetrafluoride.[14]

In 1984, Belgian nuclear officials announced that the two countries would shortly sign an agreement for nuclear cooperation. This would have provided the legal framework for the sale not only of the uranium tetrafluoride plant but also for a $1 billion contract under which Belgium was to sell Libya non-nuclear equipment and architect-engineering services for the twin Soviet nuclear power plants.[15] Concerned that there appeared to be no logical use for the tetra-fluoride plant's output within Libya's nuclear energy and research program, Washington pressed Brussels to cancel the pending accord.[16] Belgium ultimately rejected the Libyan nuclear trade pact in early 1985.[17]

Argentina and Libya have also had a long-standing nuclear relationship, which Tripoli may have hoped to strengthen by its reported sale of $100 million worth of arms to Buenos Aires during the 1982 Falklands/Malvinas War.[18] In mid-1983 an Argentine nuclear trade delegation reportedly visited Tripoli, and at approximately this time Libya tried unsuccessfully to purchase an Argentine research reactor.[19] There have been no reports of continuing Libyan-Argentine nuclear trade, however, since the civilian government of Raul Alfonsín took power in late 1983.

Nuclear relations with Brazil may run counter to this overall trend. In late 1984, Brazil began negotiations to supply Libya, a major purchaser of Brazilian armaments, with uranium prospecting and development services.[20] Whether Brazil's new civilian government will pursue these discussions remains to be seen. Given Libya's long-standing interest in acquiring sensitive enrichment and reprocessing technology and Brazil's emerging capabilities in these fields, nuclear cooperation between the two could pose significant proliferation dangers in the years ahead. Overall trade with Brazil was expected to reach $1 billion in 1986.

Political and Technical Developments. The April 15, 1986 U.S. air raid against Libya and a subsequent controversial American disinformation campaign aimed at unsettling Colonel Khadafi kept Libya in the headlines during much of 1986. In addition to retaliating against specific acts of Libyan-sponsored terrorism, these U.S. actions have sought to bring pressure against Khadafi to moderate his radical, anti-Western stance and, it seems, to encourage other Libyan elements to remove him as leader.[21] Should these efforts ultimately prove successful in dislodging Khadafi, Libya's quest for nuclear arms might well taper off, since this effort appears to have been motivated primarily by Khadafi's personal animus toward Israel and the West and by his preoccupation with attaining international status. Although for the time being, Khadafi appears to remain firmly in control, he continues to lack the means to attain his nuclear objectives.

During 1986, new information—published here for the first time—became available on Libya's 1981 negotiations to purchase nuclear weapons on the black market from former CIA employee Edwin Wilson. Wilson's offer was plainly a hoax; nevertheless, the seriousness with which Libya approached the negotiations is testimony to Khadafi's desire to acquire such arms.[22]

The lurid history of Wilson's dealings with Libya throughout the mid- and late 1970s is extensively discussed elsewhere.[23] By the time of the 1981 nuclear negotiations, Wilson had supplied Khadafi with more than 20 tons of C-4 plastique explosive, notorious for its use in terrorist bombings; a thousand miniature timer/detonators for use with the C-4; training by former Green Berets in producing and disarming explosives; and, reportedly, embargoed spare parts for Libya's C-130 air transports. Wilson had also signed a multi-million dollar contract for the complete arming of a 3,500-man Libyan infantry strike force.[24]

The nuclear scam was reportedly initiated in February or March 1981, when Wilson was contacted by a Belgian associate, Armand Donnay, who claimed to have access to enough "fissionable material" to build a nuclear weapon.[25] It was decided that a formal proposal would be made to Wilson's contacts in Libya, and soon afterwards, Donnay went there with a stack of documents containing the details of the deal.[26]

John Heath, an associate of Wilson's, was present at the first of the meetings with the Libyans at which Wilson and Donnay discussed the sale of nuclear weapons. According to Heath's testimony at Wilson's 1983 trial for illegally exporting the C-4 explosive, the meeting was held with top Libyan nuclear officials—the "Libyan nuclear committee," in Heath's words—and Wilson and the others were introduced to the group by a senior military aide.[27] The Libyans quickly rejected Donnay's presentation as incomplete. One account—apparently based on Heath's recollections—states that the Libyans wanted to know the quality of the fissionable material Donnay had to offer. When he told them it was "twenty percent"—presumably twenty-percent enriched uranium, unsuitable for weapons—the group's chairman stated, "That's no good for us. We need eighty percent. If you can't do better than this, we have no business."[28]

Donnay then offered to rework and expand his offer and one or more additional meetings were held with the Libyans to discuss the nuclear-weapons deal. The Libyans rejected the revised proposal, however, because of its incompleteness and technical defects.[29] Though the deal did not go through, the episode provides strong evidence—the seniority of the Libyan officials involved, the explicit request for weapons-grade material, and the willingness to extend negotiations over two or more meetings—that the Libyans were seriously interested in acquiring nuclear arms by clandestine means.

At this point, Wilson, already under indictment in the United States for solicitation-to-commit-murder of a Libyan defector and the shipment of weaponry to a terrorist training camp, decided to try to use the nuclear documents in a different way—to work a deal with the prosecutors in Washington. Through intermediaries, he advised the federal officials that Khadafi was about to make a purchase of nuclear arms through the blackmarket; Wilson offered to help U.S. authorities block the transfer if the prosecutors would meet with him outside the country and discuss reducing the charges against him. To demonstrate that a nuclear sale was under way, Wilson, pretending he had no role in the affair, had a copy of Donnay's initial proposal delivered to senior prosecutor Lawrence Barcella.

Barcella forwarded the documents to the Central Intelligence Agency for review and was promptly told they were so deficient as to be worthless to the Libyans. Wilson then tried again, apparently with Donnay's second, considerably expanded version of the proposal, but again the CIA advised Barcella that the documents did not add up to anything and were, in effect, a hoax. Barcella refused to deal with Wilson, who was subsequently brought to trial and convicted on the gun-running charge and under a subsequent indictment for the illegal export of explosives from Houston.[30]

What, in fact, did Donnay and Wilson offer Khadafi? Donnay's second proposal has been obtained under the Freedom of Information Act; it was nothing if not grandiose. Known as the "Mickey Project," it specified that by May 1, 1987, Donnay and Wilson would provide Libya "nuclear active forces for 38.500 kiloton [sic] of power." Included in this was the sale of a five-to-ten-megawatt research reactor for training Libyan students; two other units for producing medical isotopes (a synchrotron and a calutron); a complete "fire test field"—apparently a nuclear test site; a factory for producing weapons-grade material, some of which would also be supplied via "export black agreements [sic]"; and a nuclear warhead production facility to be built in a converted factory in the Tripoli area. Training for troops in the use and handling of nuclear weapons would also be offered. No price was given in the document for these goods and services.

Appendices, written in the Belgian Donnay's imperfect English, provided additional details. A decoy contract, covering the sale of the research reactor, sychrotron, and related medical facilities, would be prepared: "This part of the contract is official part, for protect displacement of technicians and export license for some material." There would be a second, secret, contract for the delivery of highly enriched uranium and plutonium, which would "start from the international black market and [would come] progressively from the [isotopes] factory," which would extract plutonium from "the nuclear fuels from European nuclear power stations." A third, also secret, contract would cover test firings and the actual production of weapons.

The planned output from the warhead factory, given in appendices 4 and 5 of the proposal, was staggering. Between July 1986 and May 1987, the facility would produce 8 1-megaton and 25 .5-megaton aircraft-deliverable bombs. Each of these would be vastly more powerful than the Hiroshima bomb, which had a yield of only .012 megatons, or 12 kilotons. (A megaton is equivalent to 1 million tons of TNT, a kiloton equivalent to 1,000 tons of TNT.) In addition, the factory would turn out 35 250-kiloton warheads for Libya's Soviet-supplied, short-range (40 to 150 kilometer) Frog-7 missiles and 155 100-kiloton warheads for Tripoli's Soviet-supplied Frog-3 tactical missiles (with a range of 10 to 40 kilometers). Several units in each category would be used in tests.

Even the smallest of the weapons Wilson and Donnay were proposing to manufacture would have required considerable sophistication and, as the illustrations accompanying the proposal reveal, the larger weapons, at least, were to be hydrogen bombs—exceedingly complex weapons that are considered virtually impossible to build without numerous preliminary tests with simpler, and less powerful, atomic weapons. (Israel's advanced nuclear weapons described in the previous chapter are not true hydrogen bombs and even so, undoubtedly required many years to develop.) Moreover, developing missile warheads of the correct weight and size to match the Soviet-supplied Frog rockets would take years of work. In effect, Donnay and Wilson were promising the moon—as the Libyans must have rapidly discerned.

The only detailed sketch of a nuclear device included in the proposal—a document two-inches thick, but mostly taken up by a listing of subsystems for the research reactor—shows a supposed .5 megaton hydrogen bomb. Its exterior, cigar-shaped, with fins on one end, is realistic enough. The nuclear portion of the device shows a sphere of plutonium, weighing .5 kilograms (1.1 pounds), centered in a cylinder of highly enriched uranium, weighing 17.2 pounds. The cylinder appears to rest within a slightly larger cylinder, containing hydrogen. At the opposite ends of this cylinder and having the same diameter as it are two squat conical "reflexion covers," and attached to the outwardly pointing ends of these are tapering cones of high explosives (178 kilograms or 392 pounds). Though the sketch contains one or two design elements frequently seen in unclassified illustrations, it includes virtually no detail in key areas. Thus the sketch is by no means a blueprint for the final device and displays no specific knowledge of nuclear-weapons design. (See illustration on p. 159.)

Leaving aside the requirements for the missile warheads and the 1-megaton bombs, the 25 .5-megaton bombs alone would have called for 450 kilograms (990 pounds) of highly enriched uranium and 15 kilograms (33 pounds) of plutonium (including some extra material for "safety"). Donnay and Wilson appeared to make no provision for producing the former material, nor did they explain in the proposal how they hoped to obtain the strictly controlled plutonium-bearing spent fuel from European power reactors.

Donnay included one important touch of realism to his prospectus, however, a means for preventing unauthorized use of the nuclear arsenal he was proposing to place at Khadafi's disposal:

For safety, each nuclear bomb or missile have a safety key lock, only the president and the chief of staff control the 2 keys for release the safety. In other case it is impossible use the nuclear projectiles.

We have also possibilities for adapted radio safety key, in this case only one radio transmiter using microprocessors systeme, can release the safety trought radio impulsion. But the last systeme is more dangerous, any body that know radio code can release the safaty.

In case of Nuclear alrm, The President and chief of staff can send security oficer on evry nuclear place, with both safety keys and can use, in plus, the radio safety systeme.

Our preference go to the complete safety systeme, turn key lock + radio code impulsions. [Spelling as in original.]

By these means Donnay would have ensured that the weapons remained safely under the control of one of the world's most erratic leaders.

In some respects, the Donnay/Wilson proposals are reassuring. They show that even one of the most accomplished black-market arms merchants of recent years had trouble putting together a credible clandestine deal for nuclear weapons or nuclear-weapons material. Still, as noted earlier, Libya's interest in pursuing the transaction is troubling.[31]

Prospects. For the foreseeable future, nuclear weapons are likely to remain beyond Colonel Khadafi's grasp. His indigenous nuclear capabilities remain too rudimentary to permit the production of nuclear-weapons material, and a global embargo on nuclear transfers to Libya is likely to prevent further advances. Although Tripoli has turned to clandestine nuclear dealings in the past, it remains unlikely that Libya will be able to obtain nuclear arms or nuclear-weapons material by that means because such commodities remain unavailable. In short, although Khadafi's nuclear ambitions appear strong, there is little reason to fear that they will soon be realized.

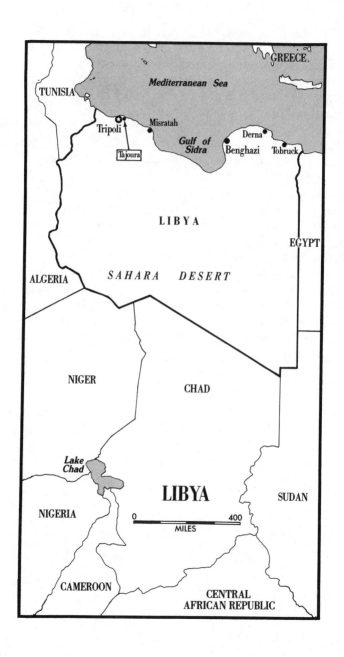

Libya

Research Reactor

Tajoura (light-water/highly-enriched uranium, 10 MWt)[a]
- supplier: Soviet Union[a]
- fuel source: Soviet Union[a]
- start up 1981[b]
- safeguards: yes[c]

Power Reactor Planned

Gulf of Sidra (light-water/low-enriched uranium, 440 MWe)[d]
- supplier: Atomenergoexport (USSR)[e]
- fuel source: Soviet Union?
- start up: (?)
- safeguards: yes

Uranium Resources/Active Mining Sites/Uranium Mills

- reasonably assured
  reserves: none assessed, four active exploration projects.[f]
- currently active sites: none
- mills in operation: none

Uranium Tetrafluoride (UF$_4$)

Tripoli
- capacity: ?
- supplier: Belgonucléaire (Belgium)[g]
- start up: negotiations for purchase of plant suspended[g]
- safeguards: uncertain

Delivery Systems

Libya has several lines of advanced combat aircraft able to deliver an atomic bomb (assumed to weigh 1,300 pounds): the MiG-23 Flogger E/F, the MiG-25 Foxbat A/U, the Mirage 5D/DD/DE, the Mirage F-1A/B/E, the Su-20/22 Fitter, and the TU-22 Blinder A. In addition, the MiG-21 Fishbed could also serve in this capacity with slight modifications or a modest reduction in weapon weight.[h]

Sources and Notes

a. Senate Foreign Relations committee, *Hearings on the Israeli Air Strike,* June 18, 19, and 25, 1981, 97th Congress, 1st Session (Washington, D.C.: Government Printing Office, 1981) p. 40.

b. Claudia Wright, "Libya's Nuclear Program," *The Middle East,* February 1982, p. 47; *Hearings on the Israeli Air Strike,* p. 50.

c. International Atomic Energy Agency, *The Annual Report, 1985,* (Vienna, Austria: International Atomic Energy Agency, 1986), p. 81.

d. Claudia Wright, "Libya's Nuclear Program," p. 50; "Envoy Says Soviets May Build Nuclear Plant in Libya," Associated Press, May 10, 1986, AM cycle.

e. Robin Miller, "Nuclear Power Plans Outlined," *Jamahiriyah Review, Joint Publication Research Service/Nuclear Development and Proliferation,* March 22, 1982, p. 17.

f. OECD Nuclear Energy Agency and the International Atomic Energy Agency, *Uranium Resources, Production, and Demand* (Paris: OECD, 1983), p. 208. Libya reportedly purchased several hundred tons of uranium concentrate from Niger between 1978 and 1980. Steve Weissman and Herbert Krosney, *The Islamic Bomb,* (New York: Times Books, 1981), p. 210.

g. "Libya and Belgonucléaire of Belgium Are In Detailed Negotiation," *Nucleonics Week,* December 2, 1982, p. 4; "Government Stopping Libyan Deal," *Nuclear News,* (January 1985).

h. 1,300 lb. selected as illustrative on basis of Sweden's untested atomic weapon design prepared in the late 1950s. (Christer Larsson, "Build a Bomb!," *Ny Teknik,* April 25, 1985). Source: *The Military Balance 1985-1986* (London: International Institute for Strategic Studies, 1985).

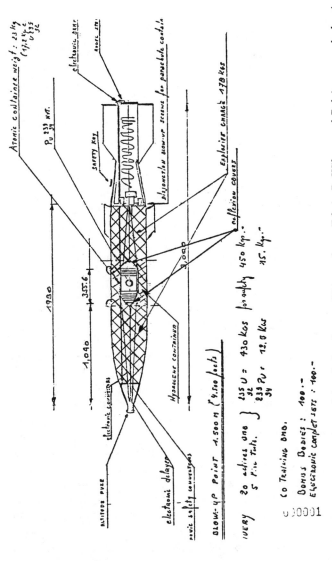

Sketch of a 500-kiloton "hydrogen" bomb that former CIA employee Edwin P. Wilson and Belgian arms dealer Armand Donnay offered to build for Libya during discussions with senior Libyan nuclear officials in early 1981. The proposal was determined to be a hoax. See pp. 150-155 and accompanying notes.

Iraq

Iraq's nuclear program has been dormant since Israel's 1981 bombing raid destroyed its centerpiece, the large French-supplied Osiraq research reactor outside Baghdad. Although France agreed in principle to help rebuild the facility under strict non-proliferation controls, no steps toward implementing this commitment are known to have been taken.[1] Similarly, implementation of the Soviet Union's offer to build a nuclear power plant in Iraq is still at the site-selection stage.[2]

Iraq's continued possession of 12.5 kilograms (27.5 pounds) of French-supplied highly enriched uranium fuel, possibly enough for one carefully designed nuclear weapon, however, presents a proliferation threat whose danger could increase if Iran continues to make advances in the six-year Iran-Iraq war.[3] Indeed, Iraq appears to have remained interested in acquiring nuclear arms. In 1982, according to evidence obtained in an ongoing Italian prosecution, it expressed interest in purchasing plutonium from an Italian arms smuggling ring.[4] Iraq is a party to the Non-Proliferation Treaty (NPT), but its continuing violations of the 1925 Geneva Protocol against using lethal chemical weapons, to which it had agreed, raise fundamental questions as to the strength of its other arms-control commitments.[5]

Background. There is a growing consensus, based on strong circumstantial evidence, that the hidden objective behind Iraq's expansion of its nuclear sector in the mid-1970s was the gradual acquisition of a nuclear-weapons capability—a capability intended to serve as a deterrent against Israel's presumed nuclear arms and to advance Iraq's claim to Arab leadership.[6] First, the Osiraq research reactor, purchased from France in 1976, was unusually large and capable of irradiating uranium specimens to produce significant quantities of plutonium. Iraq had simultaneously acquired from Italy three radiologically shielded "hot cells," in which at least small quantities of plutonium could be extracted from irradiated uranium specimens—possibly enough over a period of years for a single weapon—and a model of a larger reprocessing unit that might have permitted a subsequent expansion. In 1981 Baghdad was also negotiating with Italian vendors to buy a larger heavy-water power reactor (an efficient plutonium producer) and a sizable reprocessing facility, which would have been a highly premature addition to Baghdad's nascent nuclear-energy program, but an essential part of a nuclear-weapons effort. All of these negotiations were conducted in secret, or at least outside of public view.[7]

In 1980 and 1981, Iraq also bought inexplicably large amounts of natural uranium from Brazil, Portugal, Niger, and Italy, suggesting a secret intention to irradiate the material in Osiraq to produce plutonium. (The natural uranium could not be used to fuel Osiraq because the reactor required enriched uranium fuel.) And a number of statements by Iraqi officials strongly suggested that Baghdad had a deep interest in acquiring nuclear arms.[8]

Perhaps most revealing of Iraq's intentions to use Osiraq to produce plutonium was that in early 1980 Baghdad placed an order with a West German firm, NUKEM, for 25,000 pounds of depleted-uranium-metal fuel pins.[9] The pins were sized to fit into Osiraq, where they could be irradiated to produce plutonium, and were unsuited to any other nuclear purpose—including use in a lab-scale "subcritical assembly," which was the stated end-use for the NUKEM pins. The deal, which could have netted Iraq ten to twelve kilograms (twenty-two to twenty-six pounds) of plutonium, was ultimately aborted when NUKEM's subcontractors in the United States and Canada were told by regulatory officials that they could not get export licenses for the material.

Whatever its covert intentions, Iraq, as a party to the NPT, had to place all of its nuclear installations under IAEA inspection, and as Osiraq neared completion, the Agency was preparing plans to apply to apply stringent controls to the facility.[10] In 1978, Iraq had also agreed to permit French technicians to remain at the Osiraq plant until 1989; so it seems almost impossible that by the time of the Israeli raid in 1981 Osiraq could have secretly produced plutonium in the quantities needed for a clandestine nuclear-weapons program. It is more likely that Iraq intended to pursue a plan, similar to Sweden's in the 1960s, of mastering plutonium-production technology in the open and building a nuclear infrastructure, perhaps with a stockpile of plutonium, which could later be turned into nuclear armaments, if such a decision were taken.[11] (The NPT allows parties to withdraw from the pact on ninety days' notice if their "supreme interests" are threatened.)

When it appeared that the Osiraq reactor would shortly go into operation, despite a series of temporary setbacks to the Iraqi nuclear program and extensive Israeli lobbying for the imposition of additional controls by Iraq's European suppliers, Israel mounted its highly controversial June 7, 1981 air attack.[12] Caught up in its deadly war with Iran, Iraq was unable to respond militarily to the Israeli raid, but Baghdad subsequently mounted an aggressive campaign against Israel at the United Nations and the International Atomic Energy Agency, seeking to impose sanctions against Jerusalem for its refusal to rule out future military action against nuclear installations in the middle East. When the 1982 IAEA General Conference, at Iraqi instigation, refused to accept Israel's credentials, the United States temporarily withdrew from the Agency. This precipitated a crisis that was not finally resolved until the 1985 General Conference, when Israel's assurance that it would not "attack or threaten to attack any nuclear facilities devoted to peaceful purposes either in the middle East or anywhere else" was accepted as a basis for its continued participation.[13]

After Osiraq was destroyed, it is possible that Baghdad pursued a separate track for obtaining a nuclear-weapons capability. According to evidence obtained in a 1984 Italian prosecution, senior Iraqi military figures expressed interest in obtaining 33.9 kilograms (74.6 pounds) of plutonium—enough for several weapons—from an Italian arms smuggling ring purporting to have such material for sale.[14] One member of the ring, interviewed in 1985, claimed that he met first in Baghdad and then in Rome with members of the Iraqi military to discuss the sale; 1982 telexes between members of the smuggling ring contained in the prosecution file are consistent with this claim.[15] The deal fell through when, after a third meeting in Baghdad, the smugglers were unable to produce samples of the nuclear material. Although it is virtually certain that the plutonium offer was a hoax, possibly intended as a come-on to pave the way for sales of conventional arms, the episode suggests that through mid-1982, when negotiations on the matter ended, at least some in the Iraqi government remained interested in nuclear arming.

Political and Technical Developments. Iraq's nuclear program is now at a virtual standstill, both because of the Osiraq raid and because of a lack of funds resulting from Iraq's declining oil revenues and the demands of its war with Iran. This situation appears unlikely to change any time soon.

Similarly there have been no new indications of Iraqi attempts to obtain nuclear materials clandestinely for the purpose of developing nuclear arms. The trial of the Italian arms smugglers is now scheduled for October 1987, and no new evidence on this episode has emerged.

Iraq has suffered a number of serious reverses in its war with Iran. In February 1986, Iranian troops overran the strategic Faw Peninsula on the Persian Gulf, placing Iraq's second largest city, Basra, in jeopardy, and Iranian forces made significant advances on other fronts.[16] Iraq's past setbacks and the risk of still more serious defeats ahead have undoubtedly been a major spur to its repeated use of chemical weapons in the course of the conflict—a development that raises questions about Iraq's non-proliferation commitments and about the effectiveness of such commitments more generally.

In March 1986, a team of U.N.-appointed experts found that Iraq had used chemical weapons "on many occasions" against Iranian forces. The agent most commonly used was mustard gas, but nerve gas was also deployed on "some occasions." The investigation also found that "the use of chemical weapons appears to be more extensive than in 1984," when the organization conducted its last inquiry into the matter.[17] The most shocking finding of the U.N. team's report, however, was that Iraq had used chemical weapons against a major civilian target, the city of Abadan, in southern Iran. Such use against a major urban center appears to be unprecedented.[18]

Baghdad's actions, as noted earlier, violated the 1925 Geneva Protocol, which Iraq ratified in 1931, prohibiting "the use in war of asphyxiating, poisonous, or other gases." They also defy the long-standing moral taboo against using these inhuman weapons that has prevailed, with a handful of exceptions, since World War I.

Nonetheless, Iraq has suffered only *pro forma* condemnation for its ongoing resort to chemical arms.[19] Baghdad continues to receive vitally needed arms from the Soviet Union, still committed to its long-standing ally, and from France, eager for military sales and access to Arab oil.[20] Although the United States has refused to supply arms to Iraq and has pressed for tightened export restrictions on the substances used to manufacture chemical agents, Washington has made clear that it favors the Iraqi side, largely out of fear that an Iranian victory might lead to the destabilization of more moderate states on the Persian Gulf.[21]

As a test of the effectiveness of arms control agreements

and norms in restraining the use of unconventional armaments during war, the episode is, to say the least, unsettling.
Engaged in an all-out conflict against a seemingly stronger
enemy, Iraq has brushed aside a long-standing, widely accepted arms control accord and moral standard, while the
major powers with the greatest influence over Iraqi behavior
have tolerated this breach to avoid damaging other interests
deemed to be of greater importance. These events raise serious questions as to whether Iraq would stand by its commitment to the NPT if the country possessed the capability to
manufacture nuclear arms and as to how the international
community would react if Baghdad withdrew from or violated the pact and built such arms.[22]

Indeed, the episode would seem to have wider significance: the example of Iraq so baldly placing self-preserva-
tion over adherence to an international code of conduct
forces one to acknowledge that few states would be likely to
behave differently, and that, in the end, the Geneva Protocol or the NPT — which by its own terms allows parties to
withdraw from the pact if their "supreme interests" are
threatened—may be far less potent in forestalling the deployment of unconventional weapons than their universality
would suggest. And, sadly, the response of the international
community to Iraq's conduct may not be atypical. If unconventional arms were brought into play during a conflict elsewhere in the middle East, in South Asia, or in another region of tension, it is all too likely that the major powers,
because of competing interests, would oppose the punitive
measures necessary to vindicate the relevant norm of
behavior.

One further development of importance with respect to
Iraq's nuclear activities is the establishment of a nuclear cooperation program between Iraq, Pakistan, and Egypt. The
focus of the program will be the construction of an experimental nuclear reactor in Al-Wadi Al-Jadid, Egypt and the
establishment of a Cairo-based nuclear safety authority with
offices in all three countries.[23] The announcement of the tri-
partite accord did not suggest that the three Islamic states

might cooperate in the more sensitive areas of nuclear technology, but this possibility cannot be ruled out.

Iraq, finally, has several lines of aircraft capable of delivering a nuclear device, including the Soviet-supplied TU-22, TU-16, and MiG-23, and the French-supplied Mirage F-1.

Prospects. In the near term, there is little risk that Iraq's now dormant nuclear program could lead to the production of nuclear arms or that Iraq could obtain nuclear-weapons material clandestinely, because such material does not appear to be available for sale. Baghdad's continued possession of 12.5 kilograms (27.5 pounds) of highly enriched uranium, which is subject to periodic IAEA inspections, however, must remain a source of concern.

Iraq is threatened with a crushing defeat at the hands of Iran; it has shown itself ready to disregard international arms control agreements and norms by its repeated use of chemical weapons; and it is possible that Baghdad seriously considered trying to obtain plutonium by clandestine means in 1982. Although it would be an extraordinary step for Iraq to terminate IAEA inspections and appropriate the French-supplied uranium, the action would be an effective way of signaling to Iran that Baghdad was readying a nuclear device as a last resort deterrent against an overwhelming Iranian offensive. If faced with an all-out Iranian invasion, the Baghdad regime might believe it had few other options for ensuring its survival.[24]

In the longer term, Iraq's increasing alignment with moderate Arab states and its reestablishment of full diplomatic relations with Washington in 1984 may be harbingers of an increasing willingness on the part of President Saddam Hussein to adopt a more conciliatory stance vis-à-vis Israel in the years ahead.[25] If hostilities with Iran could be ended, this could ultimately reduce Iraqi motivations for developing nuclear arms. With Iran's Ayatollah Khomeini declaring that Hussein's ouster is one of his nation's principal war goals, however, predictions about future Iraqi nuclear policy can be little more than speculation until the denouement of that conflict or a change in the complexion of the Iranian regime.

IRAQ

0   300

MILES

Iraq

Research Reactors
Osiraq, Tammuz I (light-water/highly enriched uranium, 40 MWt)
- supplier: France
- start up: Destroyed by Israel June 1981, prior to start up; future status uncertain.
- fuel source: France
- safeguards: yes

Isis, Tammuz II (light-water/highly enriched uranium, 800 KWt)[a]
- supplier: France
- start up: 1980 (?)
- fuel source: France
- safeguards: yes

IRT-2000 (light-water/highly enriched uranium, 5 MWt)[b]
- supplier: Soviet Union
- start up: 1968
- fuel source: Soviet Union[b]
- safeguards: yes

Uranium Resources/Active Mining Sites/Uranium Mills
- reasonably assured
  reserves: none
- currently active site: none
- mills in operation: none[c]

Uranium Purification (UO$_2$)
Tuwaitha (laboratory scale)
- capacity: ?
- supplier: Italy
- start up: not operating (?)
- safeguards: yes

Fuel Fabrication
Tuwaitha
- capacity: ?
- supplier: Italy
- start up: not operating (?)
- safeguards: yes

Reprocessing
- capacity: 8 kg plutonium per year(?)[d]
- supplier: Italy
- start up: not operating (?)
- safeguards: yes

Delivery Systems

Iraq has several lines of advanced combat aircraft able to deliver an atomic bomb (assumed to weigh 1,300 pounds): the MiG-23 BM Flogger F, the Mirage F-1EQ/BQ, the Su-7 Fitter A, the Su-7 Fitter C, the TU-16 Badger A, and the TU-22 Blinder. In addition, the MiG-21 Fishbed could also serve in this capacity with sight modifications or a modest reduction in weapon weight.[e]

Sources and Notes

a. Steve Weissman and Herbert Krosney, *The Islamic Bomb* (New York: Times Books, 1981), pp. 94, 100, 266. See also, Congressional Research Service, *Analysis of Six Issues About Nuclear Capabilities of India, Iraq, Libya, and Pakistan,* prepared for the Subcommittee of Arms Control, Oceans, and International Operations and Environment of the Senate Foreign Relations Committee (1982).

b. Jed C. Snyder, "The Road to Osiraq: Baghdad's Quest for the Bomb," *The Middle East Journal,* (Autumn 1983), p. 1.

c. Yellowcake supplied from Portugal, Brazil, and Niger, Italy. *Congressional Research Service, Six Issues,* p. 46; see notes 5, 6, 7 of this section.

d. Richard Burt, "U.S. Says Italy Sells Iraq Atomic Bomb Technology," *New York Times,* March 18, 1980, p. 1. Five to ten kg of plutonium per year. Weissman and Krosney, *The Islamic Bomb,* p. 268; Italian and U.S. officials state only hot cells, not reprocessing equipment, supplied.

e. 1,300 lb. selected as illustrative on basis of Sweden's untested atomic weapon design prepared in the late 1950s. (Christer Larsson, "Build a Bomb!" *Ny Teknik,* April 25, 1985). Source: *The Military Balance 1985-1986* (London: International Institute for Strategic Studies, 1985).

Iran

The history and current status of Iran's nuclear program is discussed in detail in Chapter II.[1] A brief section on the country is included here for the purpose of underscoring the potential interest of the Khomeini regime in nuclear arming and highlighting the capabilities that it would have available to advance such a program. In essence, Iran is a nation whose nuclear activities pose a future proliferation threat and deserve to be monitored.

The Khomeini government inherited extensive nuclear hardware, materials, and technology that had been built up during the Shah's reign, which ended in January 1979, although some of the former regime's accomplishments were dissipated during the turmoil of the revolution. Construction of two partially completed, West German-supplied nuclear-power plants at Bushehr, was halted by the end of 1979, as was a French project to build at Darkhouin.[2] In addition, many of the Iranian technicians involved in the projects fled the country. Although Tehran sought to restart work at Bushehr in 1984, Germany has stated it will not participate until hostilities in the Iran-Iraq war have ended.[3]

The nuclear research activities inherited from the Shah,

however, suffered less upheaval, and work at the Tehran Research Center has apparently continued without major interruption since Khomeini took power.[4] This means that Iran has been able to train specialists and perform experiments using a small U.S.-supplied research reactor, which remains under IAEA safeguards.

In addition, researchers at the center have presumably had access to the know-how obtained during the years of work under the Shah, which included investigations concerning plutonium extraction and, according to some sources, nuclear-weapons design.[5] The Khomeini regime has apparently pursued the research side of its nuclear program with some vigor, and in 1984, opened a new research center at Isfahan, for which ground had been broken under the Shah.[6] For now, however, there have been no published reports to indicate that Iran has or will soon have the capability to produce nuclear-weapons material.

Although in 1979 some elements of Iran's revolutionary government expressed an interest in acquiring nuclear arms, there have been no reports in recent years of Khomeini regime officials manifesting a similar interest. Nonetheless, Iran might be motivated to move in this direction in the future.

Should the war with Iraq drag on, for example, nuclear weapons would give Iran a means for meeting Baghdad's superiority in conventional armaments and would undoubtedly make Iraq more cautious in continuing to use unconventional weapons, i.e., chemical arms, particularly against civilian targets.[7] Nuclear arms would also strengthen the Khomeini government's ability to advance its brand of messianic Muslim fundamentalism by enhancing the regime's status and allowing it to intimidate neighboring states. Similarly, such weapons would support Iran's claims to leadership in the Muslim world and offset the prestige Pakistan is likely to enjoy for attaining nuclear status. Finally, although the modest nuclear arsenal Iran might build would have only limited military utility against the superpowers, it could at least serve as a symbolic shield behind which Khomeini could vent his hostility toward the "twin satans" of East and West and might conceivably be used to blackmail them into granting political concessions.[8]

For now, there is no evidence to indicate that Tehran possesses the capability to manufacture nuclear arms or the necessary nuclear material. The nation, however, has maintained and expanded its costly nuclear research program at a time of considerable economic hardship, stemming from the worldwide slump in crude oil prices and the massive costs of the war with Iraq. In such circumstances, it seems fair to speculate that, as appears to have been true under the Shah, at least a portion of these activities have a military purpose. Given the available evidence, however, there is little reason to fear that Iran is making substantial progress toward nuclear arming.

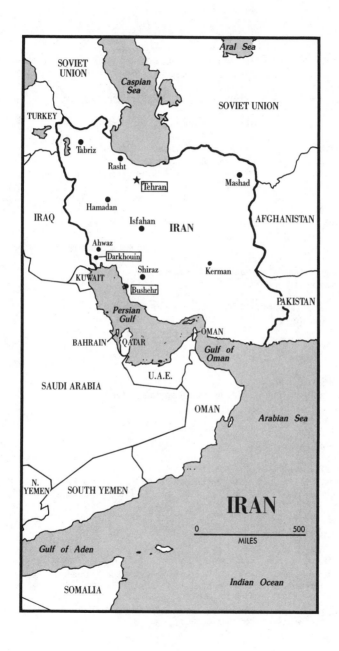

Iran

Power Reactors/Operating or Under Construction

Bushehr I (light-water/low-enriched uranium, 1300 MWe)[a]
- supplier: Kraftwerk Union (West Germany)
- start up: Presumed at least 75% complete. Construction suspended in 1979[b]
- fuel source: West Germany (no fuel supplied)
- safeguards: yes

Bushehr II (light-water/low-enriched uranium, 1300 MWe)[a]
- supplier: Kraftwerk Union (West Germany)
- start up: Presumed at least 50% complete. Construction suspended in 1979[b]
- fuel source: West Germany (no fuel supplied)
- safeguards: yes

Darkhouin (light-water/low-enriched uranium, 935 MWe)[c]
- supplier: Framatome (France)
- start up: Only minimal site work completed before termination in 1979[b]
- fuel source: France (no fuel supplied)
- safeguards: yes

Uranium Resources/Active Mining Sites/Uranium Mills

- reasonably assured reserves: 5,000 tons discovered in Yazd Province.[d]
- currently active sites: none
- mills in operation: none

Research Reactor

Tehran (light-water/highly-enriched uranium, 5 MWt)[e]
- supplier: United States
- start up: 1967[f]
- fuel source: United States
- safeguards: yes

Delivery Systems

Iran has two lines of advanced combat aircraft able to deliver an atomic bomb (assumed to weigh 1,300 pounds): F-4D/E Phantom II and the F-5E/F Tiger II.[g]

Sources and Notes

a. Office of Technology Assessment, *Technology Transfer to the Middle East*, (Washington, D.C.: U.S. Congress, Office of Technology Assessment, 1984) p. 353.

b. Daniel Poneman, *Nuclear Power in the Developing World*, (London: George Allen & Unwin Ltd., 1982) p. 96. Since 1984, Iran has unsuccessfully sought outside assistance to restart construction.

c. James Katz and Onkar Marwah, *Nuclear Power in Developing Countries*, (Lexington, MA: Lexington Books, 1982) p. 206.

d. "Briefly . . . Iran," *Nuclear Fuel*, January 28, 1985, p.11.

e. Office of Technology Assessment, *Technology Transfer to the Middle East*, p. 355.

f. International Atomic Energy Agency, *Nuclear Research Reactors in the Third World*, (Vienna: International Atomic Energy Agency, 1986) p.11.

g. 1,300 lb. selected as illustrative on basis of Sweden's untested atomic weapon design prepared in the late 1950s. (Christer Larsson, "Build a Bomb!" *Ny Teknik*, April 25, 1985). Source: *The Military Balance 1985-1986* (London: International Institute for Strategic Studies, 1985).

Chapter V:
Latin America

"If it was up to me to decide, I would make an atomic bomb and detonate it in front of international observers to demonstrate the extent of national technical know-how. . . . One hates to see the big powers developing and detonating atomic, cobalt and neutron bombs without being able to do the same ourselves."

Former Brazilian Navy Minister
Maximiano Fonseca, September 1986

The advent of civilian governments in Argentina and Brazil in late 1983 and early 1985, respectively, and a series of subsequent bilateral initiatives aimed at easing the countries' long-simmering nuclear rivalry hold the promise of substantially reducing the threat that either will build nuclear weapons. These two are the only nations in the region with programs that might lead to the development of nuclear arms before the end of the century. Both have refused to accept binding non-proliferation pledges under the Non-Proliferation or Tlatelolco treaties.

Neither Argentina nor Brazil faces an external security threat that might arguably call for the development of a nuclear deterrent. Rather, the risk of a nuclear arms race between them has arisen largely because both have viewed nuclear development as a potentially important factor in their enduring competition for regional preeminence and, at a minimum, an area in which neither could afford to fall behind. Over the years, nationalistic desires for nuclear mastery, combined with concerns over their neighbor's nuclear activities, have led to a process of action and reaction that has gradually propelled the two countries ever closer to nuclear-weapons capabilities. In the early 1980s, as military regimes in both countries pursued projects that could provide access to nuclear-weapons material, mutual suspicions intensified, and advocates of nuclear arming in each appeared to become more outspoken.

Despite the change to civilian leadership in Buenos Aires

and Brasilia, elements in both nations supportive of open-ended nuclear development continue to wield significant political power and have won further funding for previously initiated, sensitive nuclear projects, while slowing the adoption of added non-proliferation restraints. Given these dynamics and the history of instability in both Argentina and Brazil, the long-term possibility of proliferation in Latin America cannot be ruled out, despite highly favorable recent trends.

Argentina

Since Raul Alfonsín took office in December 1983 as Argentina's first democratically elected president in over a decade, the threat that Argentina might develop nuclear weapons appears to have steadily declined.[1] Between mid-1985 and mid-1986, Alfonsín pursued a series of promising non-proliferation initiatives with Brazilian President José Sarney, including negotiations on a system of mutual inspections, that could go far toward ensuring that the long-standing nuclear rivalry between the two nations does not lead to a regional nuclear arms race.

At the same time, however, Alfonsín has pledged to complete all the elements of the nuclear program initiated by Argentina's former military regime, including two facilities that will be capable of producing significant quantities of nuclear-weapons material. It is unlikely that these facilities will contribute to proliferation during Alfonsín's tenure, but they might play such a role in the future, should another right-wing military government or one motivated by nationalistic populism come to power—an eventuality that cannot be ruled out given the country's history of instability and continuing right-wing and labor agitation.

Background. Argentina's nuclear program has long been a symbol of the nation's technological prowess and its aspirations for continental leadership. When Alfonsín took office, that program was the most successful in Latin America and included two operating nuclear power plants,[2] along with uranium-production and nuclear-fuel manufacturing facilities, which gave Argentina increasing independence from outside nuclear supplies.[3]

Two nuclear projects initiated by Argentina's former military leaders, the Ezeiza reprocessing plant and the Pilcaniyeu (pronounced PIL-CAN-EE-JAY-OO) enrichment plant, triggered fears that Argentina might have launched a program to develop a nuclear-weapons capability. The decision to build the Ezeiza reprocessing plant, which will provide Buenos Aires with direct access to weapons-usable plutonium, was announced by Argentina's military leaders in 1978. The facility will be under IAEA safeguards for the foreseeable future, although Argentina has reserved the right to operate it without IAEA oversight whenever it processes fuel from unsafeguarded reactors—which Argentina now lacks.[4] The plant is now scheduled for completion in 1989.[5]

The Pilcaniyeu plant was also begun in 1978, but the project was kept secret for five years and announced by the military government only weeks before Alfonsín's inauguration. Although Argentine nuclear aides asserted at the time that it had been built to produce only reactor fuel that would not be usable in nuclear weapons, there are strong grounds for believing that the secret project, which is not subject to IAEA safeguards and was begun at a time of growing Argentine militarism, was initiated to provide Argentina with a nuclear-weapons option.[6] Indeed, revelation of the plant led several top officials of Brazil's military government to declare in December 1983 that it would acquire a nuclear-weapons capability of its own by 1990.[7] The Pilcaniyeu plant has already produced small quantities of very slightly enriched uranium and is expected to begin full operation in 1987, but will produce only non-weapons-grade material.[8]

Shortly after taking office, Alfonsín, in a seeming attempt to end the military overtones of the nation's nuclear program, ousted the former head of the Argentine Atomic Energy Commission (CNEA), an admiral, and replaced him with a civilian, Alberto Constantini. From this point on, however, Alfonsín's efforts to change the direction of the Argentine nuclear program seemed to founder. During 1984 and the first half of 1985, Constantini, backed by nationalistic parliamentarians from the opposition Peronist Party,[9] successfully challenged the President's efforts to cut the nation's nuclear budget and, specifically, to kill funding for the Ezeiza and Pilcaniyeu plants.[10] Similarly, Alfonsín, apparently fearing a divisive fight with these same elements, refrained from pursuing legislation to reorganize the CNEA and make it strictly accountable for materials under its control.[11] The lack of consensus on nuclear policy also appeared to preclude Argentina's ratification of the Treaty of Tlatelolco, a step said to be favored by Alfonsín, which would bring the country an important step closer to placing all of its nuclear plants under IAEA inspection.[12]

During this period, Alfonsín confronted a series of pressing domestic issues, including Argentina's continuing economic crisis and the prosecution of Argentina's former military leaders for human-rights abuses. Undoubtedly, he feared that a pitched political battle over the highly charged question of the country's nuclear future, in which he would be accused of weakening Argentina's long-term strategic potential, would have undermined his ability to rally public support to deal with these other urgent challenges.

Despite this seeming paralysis over nuclear policy, in mid-March 1985 Argentine sources revealed that Alfonsín and Brazilian President-elect Tancredo Neves had agreed in principle to open their countries' nuclear installations to mutual inspections.[13] According to Argentine sources, the confidence-building proposal specifically envisaged reciprocal visits to the Pilcaniyeu facility and to Brazil's unsafeguarded laboratories where enrichment research is being conducted.[14] The two leaders were said to have agreed to this in principle at a meeting on February 7, 1985 in Buenos Aires.

Neves' tragic death prior to taking office cast the proposal into limbo, and it appeared unclear whether his successor, José Sarney, whose political mandate was highly uncertain, would have the power or the inclination to make the proposal a reality. Moreover, Brazilian spokesmen at the time seemed to back away from the proposal, claiming that Neves had never committed himself to mutual inspections, but only to further discussions.

If successfully implemented, the historic proposal could go far toward eliminating the risk of proliferation in Latin America, which as noted earlier, appears to arise from competition for regional status rather than vital security concerns.[15] Alfonsín's 1985 mutual inspection proposal could reverse this trend, allowing both countries to follow the other's progress in sensitive areas of nuclear technology and to verify that the output of facilities potentially capable of producing weapons-grade material was being devoted exclusively to peaceful purposes. At a more fundamental level, the opening of the two countries' nuclear programs would gradually reduce the competitiveness that has surrounded them and the tendency to dramatize their strategic potential.

Political Developments. During the summer and fall of 1985, Alfonsín slowly consolidated his political power. In June, he announced a set of draconian economic reforms, including wage and price controls and the issuance of a new currency, which gained widespread support and brought the country's staggering inflation at least temporarily under control.[16] In October, after a wave of bombings by right-wing terrorists, he ordered the arrest of twelve army officers and civilians on charges that they were attempting to destabilize the government. To ensure the legal validity of the arrests, Alfonsín imposed a limited "state of siege," and again received strong popular backing.[17] Similarly, Alfonsín's Radical Civic Union Party increased its parliamentary majority in Argentina's November 3 elections, while its principal opposition, the Peronists, suffering from internal divisions, lost ground.[18]

Against this background, on November 29 and 30,

Alfonsín met with Brazilian President Sarney at the adjacent cities of Puerto Iguazu, Argentina, and Foz de Iguacu, Brazil. Among a number of initiatives aimed at improving bilateral economic ties and enhancing the coordination of foreign policies, the leaders signed a joint declaration on nuclear policy, reiterating the commitment of both nations to develop nuclear energy solely for peaceful purposes.

The statement also established a bilateral commission to further nuclear cooperation between them and to "create mechanisms to insure the supreme interests of peace, security and development in the region, without detriment to the technical aspects of nuclear cooperation, which will continue to be governed by the regulations in force [viz., a nuclear cooperation agreement the two countries signed in 1980]."[19] Although this part of the declaration did not refer explicitly to mutual nuclear inspections, apparently because of Sarney's reluctance to embrace this measure publicly, it was understood that inspections would be on the agenda of the commission, which was to report its recommendations in six months.[20] Despite Sarney's caution, the declaration, by addressing the nuclear issue openly, was an important step toward reducing nuclear tensions between the countries and seemed to signal that the two leaders were intent on ending the suspicions built up during the years of military rule.[21]

The joint nuclear commission met in late March 1986 and again in mid-July. At their first meeting, the participants appear to have endorsed the mutual inspection concept, but decided that any such system would operate in parallel with the safeguards regime of the IAEA and that data obtained in the course of mutual inspections would not be shared with the Agency.[22] A separate internal Brazilian nuclear-policy review, completed in April, also supported the reciprocal inspection concept, a finding welcomed in Argentina.[23]

The mid-July joint commission meeting, coming in the wake of the April 28 accident at the Chernobyl reactor in the Soviet Union, focused on nuclear safety issues. When President Sarney visited Buenos Aires on July 29, he and President Alfonsín agreed to create an early warning system to notify each other promptly in the case of a nuclear accident—a step toward further cooperation in the nuclear sector, though not directly relevant to the mutual inspection issue.[24] At the July meeting, the two leaders also signed additional protocols to eliminate customs barriers between the countries and to establish balanced bilateral trade. These steps testified to the historic shift in relations under way between the two states.[25]

During May and June, it may be noted, Alfonsín had confronted a new wave of right-wing violence at home. The terrorism had included an apparent attempt on his life and led to rumors, which proved unfounded, that a military coup might be imminent.[26] Although the military's long-standing distrust of Brazil was a well-known fact of Argentine life, these developments did not deter Alfonsín from pursuing his opening with President Sarney. Nor did an August 1986 report in the Brazilian press that a nuclear test site was being built on a Brazilian military reservation at Cachimbo derail the on-going nuclear talks, as Alfonsín accepted President Sarney's assurances that the site was for testing conventional munitions.[27]

By September, detailed planning for the mutual inspection scheme was under way. One proposal envisioned the use of non-intrusive electronic monitoring devices and the exchange of technicians to work at sensitive plants in both countries.[28] These measures would differ from IAEA safeguards, which rely on the systematic tracking of nuclear materials. Nonetheless, the steps would go far toward building confidence that nuclear activities in the two countries were not being used to further military ends.

The most effective confidence-building measure, however, would be the extension of IAEA safeguards to all the nuclear activities in both nations; some activities in each are currently under the IAEA system. Such comprehensive IAEA coverage is the key verification mechanism under both the Non-Proliferation and Tlatelolco Treaties; it is a standardized approach that has been widely implemented, and, backed by a multilateral institution, it is a system with legitimacy and permanence. Ad hoc bilateral Argentine-Brazilian measures will be more provisional and, perhaps, less likely to survive future changes in government.

Historically, both Argentina and Brazil have rejected full-scope IAEA safeguards. Although they have framed their objections more circumspectly in public, undoubtedly the underlying reason for this stance has been that neither nation has been prepared to relinquish the option of developing nuclear arms.[29] As a result, nationalistic elements in both countries have repeatedly denounced comprehensive IAEA inspections as an unacceptable intrusion on national sovereignty, a characterization that has become ingrained over the years. The bilateral inspection approach permits Alfonsín and Sarney to sidestep this long-standing opposition to the IAEA system, while obtaining many of its benefits. Unfortunately, in building a rationale for bilateral inspections, there has been a tendency to denounce the IAEA system and the Tlatelolco Treaty as instruments of the advanced nuclear-supplier countries aimed at restricting the autonomy of other states, a characterization that may unnecessarily abet opponents of these institutions.[30]

The joint nuclear commission was expected to meet once more during 1986. Argentine sources are hopeful that the joint inspection arrangement will be worked out by the time of a planned trip by President Alfonsín to Brasilia at the end of the year.[31]

One important related development during 1986 was Argentina's decision in February to place restrictions on possible future sales of enrichment and reprocessing technology and equipment to foreign governments. Such commodities, according to the new policy, would not be sold unless they were part of a larger sale of nuclear equipment, presumably because this would demonstrate the intent of the purchaser to use the items solely for nuclear energy. IAEA safeguards would also be required, consistent with Argentina's April 1985 decision to insist on such coverage for all of its nuclear exports.[32] The United States has traditionally opposed the sale of enrichment and (since 1974) reprocessing equipment and technology, although in the case of enrichment, it has on occasion indicated a willingness to make limited exceptions for some of its allies after determining that the sales would not increase the risk of proliferation. Whether Argentina's export policy will be as stringent remains to be seen.

Argentina has important nuclear trade relations with Brazil, and since 1980 has entered into contracts to sell small research reactors to Peru, Colombia, and Algeria.[33] It has also entered into some sixteen agreements for nuclear cooperation, including those with India and Libya—both now dormant—and China.[34] In addition to the importation of nuclear power plants from West Germany and Canada, Argentina has imported significant nuclear materials and equipment from Switzerland, the Soviet Union, France, and China; in 1983, China supplied Argentina with heavy water without requiring the application of IAEA safeguards.[35]

In 1986, Argentina reportedly received a nuclear delegation from Iran seeking to explore whether Buenos Aires might be able to assist it in completing two West German-supplied nuclear-power plants at Bushehr.[36] Some Argentine nuclear specialists had helped with the project when it was initiated in the mid-1970s by the Shah. There are no indications that these recent talks between the two nations involve more sensitive areas, such as reprocessing or enrichment.

During the past year, U.S. non-proliferation diplomacy with respect to Argentina has been conducted out of public view and has apparently focused on quietly encouraging Argentina to pursue its nuclear initiatives with Brazil and to adopt responsible nuclear export policies. A U.S. embargo of nuclear fuel and reactors for Argentina remains in effect because of the latter's refusal to place all of its nuclear plants under IAEA safeguards.[37]

Technical Developments. On May 30, 1986, in a major address celebrating the anniversary of Argentina's Nuclear Energy Commission, President Alfonsín agreed to support the continuation of every major nuclear project initiated by Argentina's former military regime.[38] The speech represented a major defeat for elements in the Alfonsín government that had hoped to curtail the nation's costly nuclear program and a victory for Argentine Atomic Energy Commission Chairman Constantini and his allies in the Peronist Party. The most controversial elements of the program, which had been the subject of protracted budgetary battles over the preceding two years, were five partially constructed facilities: the West German-supplied Atucha II nuclear-power plant, a Swiss-supplied industrial-scale heavy-water production plant at Arroyito, an indigenous experimental heavy-water production plant at Atucha, the indigenous Ezeiza reprocessing plant, and the previously secret, indigenous Pilcaniyeu enrichment facility. All of them would be completed, Alfonsín declared.[39]

Only ten months earlier, Jorge Lapena, a top Alfonsín energy aide, had declared that "nuclear energy will not play a major role in the production of electricity in the next twenty years," noting that electricity demand had dropped dramatically and that natural gas would be the future fuel of choice for electricity production.[40] By December, however, Alfonsín was said to have approved completion of the Atucha II nuclear-power reactor and, in February he authorized major funding increases for the nuclear program as a whole.[41] The May 30 speech thus confirmed that the nation's nuclear program was on firm political and financial footing, although Alfonsín again underscored that the program was dedicated exclusively to peaceful purposes.

The reasons for Alfonsín's decision are not clear. Quite possibly, however, this was the *quid pro quo* he had to accept to ensure support by backers of the nuclear program for his opening to Brazil and his pursuit of the reciprocal inspection program described above.

Completion of the Ezeiza and Pilcaniyeu facilities as envisioned in the May 30 address, it may be added, will place significant quantities of nuclear-weapon materials within Argentina's grasp. The Ezeiza plan will produce plutonium, albeit subject to IAEA safeguards, as noted earlier. The Pilcaniyeu plant is expected to produce only uranium enriched to 20 percent, or less, and therefore unusable for weapons.[42] The facility, which is not subject to IAEA oversight, could be reconfigured at some later time to produce highly enriched uranium. If Argentina opens the site to Brazilian technicians or inspectors in an effort to dispel suspicions about the plant, however, this scenario would appear less likely, since even if disclosed, the production of weapons-grade material might be seen as a provocation.

Argentina has a number of lines of aircraft able to deliver nuclear weapons, including the U.S.-supplied A-4G Skyhawk and French-built Mirage 3EBR. It has also reportedly participated in cooperative sounding rocket programs, building the Castor rocket with West Germany and the Orion II with the United States.[43] In 1985, Argentina was developing the Condor C1-A3 rocket, a solid-fuel rocket with a range of 100 kilometers (66 miles) and a 400 kilogram (880 pounds) payload, probably too small for use with a first generation nuclear weapon.[44]

Prospects. For the near term, it seems highly unlikely that Argentina would consider developing nuclear arms. The nation is now led by an individual with a seeming personal commitment to non-proliferation,[45] and a major element of recent Argentine diplomacy has been to establish close ties in the nuclear area and in many other fields with its erstwhile rival. With Brazil reciprocating these initiatives, any conceivable rationale for Argentine nuclear arming is fast evaporating.

Argentina's development of facilities capable of producing nuclear-weapons material, however, remains a cause for concern over the longer term. The country has had a long history of instability—and even today is experiencing right-wing terrorism and significant Peronist/Labor agitation.[46] Once these facilities are completed, they will become part of the infrastructure inherited by any future regime.

Such regimes might well include intensely nationalist governments, which, like Argentina's recent military leaders, might be opposed to détente with Brazil and prone to adventurism. Under such leadership, renewed interest in nuclear arming could not be ruled out. With Alfonsín's term expiring in 1989 and with the deep divisions in Argentine society still unhealed, the nation's nuclear activities will continue to bear close watching in the years ahead.

BOLIVIA

PARAGUAY

• Salta

• Tucuman

Resistencia •

Corrientes •

BRAZIL

Parana

Los Gigantes

Córdoba

Santa Fe

Río Tercero
(Embalse)

Rosario

URUGUAY

Pacific
Ocean

• Mendoza

La Estela

Atucha

San Rafael

Sierra Pintada

Malargüe

Buenos Aires
(Constituyentes)
(Ezeiza)

Río de
la Plata

A R G E N T I N A

Mar del Plata •

CHILE

Arroyito

Bahia Blanca •

Neuquén

Atlantic
Ocean

Pilcaniyeu •

San Carlos
de Bariloche

Rawson •

Comodoro
Rivadavia •

ARGENTINA

uranium mining area

0   400

MILES

Río Gallegos

Argentina

Power Reactors/Operating or Under Construction

Atucha I (heavy-water/natural-uranium, 320 MWe)
- supplier: Siemens AG (West Germany)
- start up: 1974
- fuel source: Argentina and West Germany (for some process steps); Argentina, principally, after 1984.[a,z]
- heavy water: initial charge, U.S., West Germany.[b]
- safeguards: yes

Embalse (heavy-water/natural-uranium, 600 MWe)
- supplier: Atomic Energy of Canada Ltd. (Canada) and Italimpianti (Italy)
- start up: 1983
- fuel source: Canada and Argentina through 1985; Argentina, principally, after 1985.[a,z]
- heavy water: initial charge, Canada[e]
- safeguards: yes

Atucha II (heavy-water/natural-uranium, 745 MWe)
- supplier: Kraftwerk Union (West Germany)
- start up: 1992[v]
- fuel source: Argentina
- heavy water: Argentina and West Germany[r]
- safeguards: yes

Uranium Resources/Active Mining Sites/Uranium Mills

- reasonably assured reserves: 18,900 metric tons[f]
- currently active sites: Los Gigantes, La Estella, Sierra Pintada[g]
- mills in operation: San Rafael, Los Gigantes, Don Otto, Marlagüe[f]

Uranium Purification (UO$_2$)

Córdoba
- capacity: 50 metric tons per year, planned 330 metric tons per year[h]
- supplier: Kraftwerk Union (West Germany) and Argentina
- start up: 1982 (West German line), 1983 (?) (Argentinian line; full operation, 1987)[c,v]
- safeguards: One of two production lines is safeguarded because of West German equipment.

Córdoba[s]
- capacity: unknown; 180 tons UO$_2$ produced to mid-1984
- supplier: Argentina
- start up: ?
- safeguards: no

Uranium Conversion (UF$_6$)

- Capacity presumed (to serve pilot enrichment plant)(unsafeguarded)

Heavy Water

Arroyito (industrial scale)
- capacity: 250 metric tons per year
- supplier: Sulzer Brothers (Switzerland)
- start up: 1988[v]
- safeguards: yes

Atucha (pilot scale)
- capacity: 2-4 metric tons per year[t]
- supplier: Argentina (with possible foreign aid)[d]
- start up: late 1987[t,v]
- safeguards: no

Enrichment

Pilcaniyeu
- type: gaseous diffusion
- capacity: experimental; as announced, 500 kg. per year of 20% enriched uranium by 1985; reduced to 250kg. per year.[j]
- supplier: Argentina
- start up: 1983 (experimental unit); 1987 (full operation)[j,v]
- safeguards: no

Fuel Fabrication

Ezeiza
- capacity: Substantial part of requirements for Atucha I, 1984[z]; substantial part of requirements for Embalse, 1985 (est.)[z].
- supplier: Atucha I line, West Germany; Embalse line, Argentina.[j]
- start up: 1982 (Atucha I line)[a]; 1985 (Embalse line)[z]
- safeguards: Atucha line safeguarded, Embalse line safeguarded only when fabricating safeguarded UO_2.[k]

Constituyentes
- capacity: Pilot plant for enriched uranium research reactor fuel
- supplier: Argentina
- start up: 1976[x]
- safeguards: only when safeguarded uranium is processed

Reprocessing

Ezeiza
- capacity: 15 kg plutonium, 5 metric tons spent fuel per year [e]
- supplier: Argentina (possible Italian aid)[m]
- start up: 1989[v]
- safeguards: only when safeguarded fuel is processed.[n]

Ezeiza
- capacity: laboratory scale
- supplier: Argentina
- start up: 1969; operated intermittently until dismantled in 1973.[e]
- safeguards: no

Research Reactors [l,o]

RA-0, Córdoba (tank/medium-enriched uranium, 1 Wt)
- supplier: Argentina
- start up: 1965
- safeguards: no

RA-1, Constituyentes (tank/medium-enriched uranium, less than 1 MWt)
- supplier: Argentina
- start up: 1958
- safeguards: yes

RA-2, Constituyentes (tank/highly enriched uranium, less than 1 MWt)
- supplier: Argentina
- start up: 1966
- safeguards: yes

RA-3, Ezeiza (pool/highly enriched uranium, 5 MWt)[u]
- supplier: Argentina
- start up: 1967
- safeguards: yes

RA-4, Rosario (homogeneous, medium-enriched uranium, less that 1 MWt)
- supplier: West Germany
- start up: 1972
- safeguards: yes

RA-6, San Rafael de Bariloche (MTR, highly enriched uranium, 500 KWt[p, u]
- supplier: Argentina
- start up: 1982
- safeguards: only when safeguarded fuel is present.

RA-7, cancelled (heavy-water/natural-uranium 40-100 MWt)[q]
- supplier: Argentina
- start up: development suspended, 1985 [aa]
- safeguards: no

Delivery Systems

Argentina has several lines of advanced combat aircraft able to deliver and atomic bomb assumed to weigh 1,300 pounds): the A-4P/Q Skyhawk, the Canberra B-62, the IA 58 Pucara, and the Mirage 5P. In addition, the Mirage 3EA/CJ and the Dagger (Nesher) could also serve in this capacity with slight modifications or a modest reduction in weapon weight.[bb] Argentina is developing a short range, solid-fueled missile with an 880 pound payload, the Condor Cl-A3.[cc]

Sources and Notes

a. "Fuel Fabrication Factory Opened," *Nuclear Engineering International*, May 1982, p. 8; "Nuclear Firms Advance Level of Technology to Meet Objectives," *Energia Nuclear 1983*, translated in *Joint Publication Research Service/Nuclear Development and Proliferation*, hereafter *JPRS/TND*, February 28, 1984, pp. 15-17; "Nuclear Institute's Financial Problems Reported," *Noticias Argentinas*, 1935 GMT February 5, 1985, *JPRS/TND* February 26, 1985, p. 36. Argentina also possesses a significant but not yet completely autonomous zirconium alloy and tube manufacturing capability for sheathing reactor fuels. See ref. x and "Argentina Closer to Fuel Independence," *Nuclear Fuel*, May 20, 1985, p. 5.

b. John Redick, "The Military Potential of Latin American Nuclear Programs," International Studies Series, Sage Publications, 1972, p. 13; personal communication. Between 1980 and 1982, Argentina imported 6 metric tons of heavy water each from the USSR and the People's Republic of China to make up for losses at Atucha I. Richard Kessler, "U.S. Approval for West Germany to Sell 143 Tonnes of Heavy Water to Argentina," *Nucleonics Week*, August 25, 1983, p. 7; Judith Miller, "U.S. Is Holding Up Peking Atom Talks," *New York Times*, September 19, 1982; Richard Kessler, "Argentina to Tender for Heavy Water After June Purchase from China," *Nucleonics Week*, September 25, 1986, p. 5. Additional heavy water was obtained from West Germany (with U.S. permission) in 1983. Kessler, "U.S. Approval."

c. Carlos Castro Madero, "Argentina's Nuclear Energy Program," *Nuclear Europe*, July-August 1983, pp. 31-33.

d. Burt Solomon, "Argentina Bent on Home-Grown Nuclear Program," *Energy Daily*, November 9, 1982, p. 3.

e. Powell A. Moore, Assistant Secretary of State for Congressional Relations, to Senator Gary Hart, August 19, 1982.

f. Reasonably Assured Reserves at less than $130 per kilogram. OECD Nuclear Energy Agency and the International Atomic Energy Agency, *Uranium, Resources Production and Demand* (Paris: OECD, 1986), pp. 84-99.

g. "Uranium Concentrate Plant," *TELAM, Noticias Argentinas* (Buenos Aires), November 16, 1982, translated in Foreign Broadcast Information Service (FBIS)/Latin America, December 9, 1982, p. B4; "CNEA Resumes Uranium Excavation," DYN, 2311 GMT, December 13, 1984, FBIS/Latin America, December 17, 1984, p. B-3.

h. "Argentina to Start Producing U0$_2$ This Year," *Nuclear Fuel*, September 13, 1982, p. 15.

j. "CNEA Chairman Makes Announcement," *TELAM* (Buenos Aires) 2102 GMT, November 18, 1983, translated in *JPRS/TND*, December 12, 1983, p. 7; Milton R. Benjamin, "Argentina Seen Capable of 4 A-Bombs a Year," *Washington Post*, December 9, 1983; Richard Kessler, "Argentina to Delay Production," *Nucleonics Week*, February 14, 1985. See also reference v (capacity in 1987 will be 20,000 separate work units, to be expanded to 100,000.)

k. Personal communication with informed U.S. official.

l. International Atomic Energy Agency, *Annual Report for 1982*, p. 84.

m. Robert Laufer, "Argentina Looks to Reprocessing to Fill Its Own Needs Plus Plutonium Sales," *Nuclear Fuel*, November 8, 1982, p. 3; Leonard S. Spector, *The New Nuclear Nations* (New York: Vintage Books, 1985) pp. 61-63; Richard Kessler, "Argentina's Alfonsín Pledges Funding for Fuel Projects," *Nucleonics Week*, June 5, 1986, p. 3.

n. Currently only safeguarded spent fuel is available.

o. Pilat and Donnelly, "An Analysis of Argentina's Nuclear Power Program and Its Closeness to Nuclear Weapons," December 2, 1982. Reactors may be operating at reduced levels. See reference x.

p. "Research Reactor Inaugurated," *Nuclear Engineering International*, June 1983, p. 10.

q. Sometimes referred to as *RA-5*.

r. Some of the 143 metric tons of heavy water sold to Argentina by West Germany in 1983 (with U.S. permission) was to be available for Atucha II. Personal communication with U.S. and West German officials.

s. Reportedly this is a second facility in Cordoba; scheduled to be closed after domestic line at larger Cordoba plant is opened; personal communication with knowledgeable U.S. official.

t. May not be capable of producing reactor-grade heavy water.

u. Currently being converted to 20 percent enriched uranium.

v. Speech by President Raul Alfonsin, Central Atomic Energy Day Ceremony, Embalse Rio Tecero, May 30, 1986.

x. Jozef Goldblat, ed., *Non-Proliferation, The Why and Wherefore,* (Philadelphia: Taylor and Francis, 1985), p. 295.

y. Richard Kessler, "Argentina Denies Receiving West German, Italian Reprocessing Aid," *Nucleonics Week,* May 30, 1985, p. 4.

z. Richard Kessler, "Argentina Moving Ahead with Plans for Fuel Fabrication Independence," *Nuclear Fuel,* July 15, 1985, p. 6; fabrication of Atucha II fuel, planned.

aa. Richard Kessler, "Argentina Denies It Plans Large Unsafeguarded Research Reactor," *Nucleonics Week,* August 8, 1985, p. 5.

bb. 1,300 lb. selected as illustrative on basis of Sweden's untested atomic weapon design prepared in late 1950s. (Christer Larsson, "Build a Bomb!" *Ny Teknik,* April 25, 1985). Source: *The Military Balance 1985-1986 (London: International Institute for Strategic Studies, 1985).*

cc. "Ballistic Missile Proliferation Potential in the Third World," (Washington: Congressional Research Service, 1986), p. 17.

Brazil

The possibility that Brazil might develop nuclear weapons appears to have decreased since March 1985, when José Sarney took office as the nation's first civilian president in more than two decades. Sarney's growing political stature, his seeming commitment to non-proliferation, and his success in improving relations with Argentina, including possible progress toward the establishment of a mutual nuclear inspection system described in the preceding section, all promise to reduce the risk that Brazil's nuclear program might eventually be used for nuclear arming.

Background. In recent years, Brazil's nuclear affairs have followed two parallel tracks. The first, controlled by the state-owned Brazilian Nuclear Corporation (Nuclebras), has been aimed at implementing a grandiose nuclear-energy program that relies heavily on imported equipment and technology and is subject to strict IAEA safeguards and other non-proliferation controls.[1] Its cornerstones are Brazil's first nuclear power plant (Angra I), a 626-megawatt U.S.-supplied reactor, which entered commercial service in January 1985, and a mammoth nuclear transfer agreement signed with West Germany in 1975.[2] The agreement provided for the sale to Brazil of up to eight 1300-megawatt nuclear power reactors, a pilot reprocessing plant, and a large-scale enrichment plant using the jet-nozzle technique.

Germany's sale of the last two plants was highly controversial because they could provide Brazil with significant quantities of weapons-usable plutonium[3] and, theoretically, highly enriched uranium.[4] But major construction delays and cost overruns, followed by severe budget cuts imposed by the International Monetary Fund, have derailed implementation of the West German agreement, as detailed below, and it is unlikely to contribute directly to a Brazilian nuclear-weapons program.

The second track of Brazil's nuclear activities, sometimes referred to as the "parallel program," is of greater concern. Directed by various arms of the Brazilian military and the National Nuclear Energy Commission (CNEN), Brazil's nuclear research-and-development organization, it relies on indigenously developed technology, is not covered by IAEA safeguards, and is conducted largely in secret. Brazil has refused to ratify the Non-Proliferation Treaty, which would require it to place all of its nuclear activities under the IAEA system, and although it has ratified the Treaty of Tlatelolco, which contains a similar requirement, it has not waived certain conditions that must be satisified before the pact becomes binding on it.[5]

Activities under the parallel program seem to have progressed furthest at the Institute of Nuclear and Energy Research (IPEN), a federally funded research unit at the University of São Paulo. Substantial portions of the work there, including a program to develop nuclear propulsion systems for submarines, are under the control of the Brazilian Navy.[6]

Most troubling from the standpoint of proliferation is a joint Nuclear Energy Commission/Navy program at IPEN for the construction of an unsafeguarded uranium enrichment plant using the gas-centrifuge method. The plant could eventually produce weapons-usable, highly enriched uranium, but so far progress on the installation has been slow.

Brazil now produces its own natural uranium and has unsafeguarded facilities for refining it and converting it into uranium hexafluoride—the form of uranium needed in the enrichment process. Thus if the IPEN centrifuge unit is completed, Brazil would have a completely autonomous capability for manufacturing highly enriched uranium free from any non-proliferation controls.[7] Brazilian nuclear officials have justified the IPEN centrifuge program as providing a far more efficient technology for producing low-enriched uranium for power reactor fuel than the jet-nozzle system supplied by West Germany. With the cutback in Brazil's nuclear power program and a worldwide glut of low-enriched uranium, however, there seems to be little economic justification for the centrifuge development effort.

Work on uranium enrichment using lasers is also said to be under way at IPEN and at the Institute for Advanced Studies at the Brazilian Air Force's Aerospace Technology Center in São José dos Campos, the principal site of Brazil's rocket research-and-development effort.[8] It is unlikely, given the difficulties that other nations have experienced in pursuing this technology, that Brazil has yet mastered it.

According to the Brazilian press, federal workers at IPEN are also working to obtain plutonium, the alternative nuclear-weapons material. IPEN is believed to have a laboratory-scale reprocessing capability, but at most, only miniscule quantities of plutonium have been separated to date, and this would be subject to IAEA oversight. The unit is said to have first operated in 1985.[9]

Whatever their status, the activities at IPEN and the Aerospace Technology Center are widely perceived to have a military purpose.[10] Indeed, in late 1983 and early 1984, responding to Argentina's surprise disclosure of its uranium-enrichment plant, a number of Brazilian military figures openly pointed to the military potential of the parallel program and declared that it would provide Brazil with the ability to produce nuclear arms by 1990.[11]

The program, it should be added, had the visible support of Brazil's last military President, João Figueiredo, who visited IPEN to observe a demonstration of the centrifuge enrichment process in October 1984.[12] Tancredo Neves, who resoundingly defeated the military's preferred candidate, Paulo Maluf, in Brazil's January 15, 1985 indirect elections, also appeared to support the nation's pursuit of technologies with the potential for producing nuclear-weapons material. During his election campaign, he declared that "it is important for Brazil to master the entire fuel cycle"—a term that is usually taken to refer to uranium enrichment and reprocessing—and that "Brazil cannot abandon its policy of mastering the atom in all its phases."[13]

Political Developments. Neves, a figure of immense popularity because of his long-standing opposition to military rule, died before he could assume office. José Sarney, his running mate, succeeded to the post of president and was inaugurated in March 1985. Sarney had switched parties to join Neves only in the closing months of the election campaign, however; until mid-1984, he had been the leader of the military government's Social Democrat Party. As a result, Sarney took office with an extremely uncertain mandate.

For much of his first year in office, Sarney depended heavily on the political support of the military, which unlike its counterpart in Argentina, was not tainted by a recent defeat and retained considerable political influence. To help ensure its cooperation, Sarney supported its position on a number of controversial issues, including land reform and amnesty for officers cashiered for disloyalty by the former government.[14] Only in late February 1986, when he imposed his sweeping program of economic reforms to contain Brazil's skyrocketing inflation, did Sarney acquire a base of popular support.[15]

During the intervening months, Brazilian military figures were unusually outspoken on the subject of nuclear arming and made clear that, at the least, they wanted to keep the Brazilian nuclear-weapons option alive by continuing to develop the necessary enrichment and reprocessing technologies—euphemistically referred to as the "nuclear fuel cycle." In June 1985, for example, Admiral José Maria do Amaral Oliveira, chief of the Armed Forces General Staff, publicly opposed a draft amendment to the Brazilian constitution prohibiting the development of nuclear arms, declaring that, "we must not restrict ourselves in the future."[16] Two months later, Brigadier General Hugo de Oliveira Piva, director of the Air Force's Aerospace Technology Center declared that "Brazil will be able to make the atomic bomb within five years" and that a decision on taking this step "is being discussed by the National Security Council."[17]

In September, Army Minister Leonidas Pires Goncalves was said to have made a still more direct call for Brazilian nuclear arming. According to a detailed press report, he openly urged the development of a Brazilian nuclear bomb during a meeting with senior members of the Brazilian congress, and solicited their support for further nuclear technology development. Asserting that Brazilian intelligence services had learned that at the time of the 1982 Falklands crisis Argentina's military regime had intended to invade southern Brazil to recover disputed territory in Rio Grande do Sul province, Pires Goncalves told the parliamentarians, in the words of the news account, "that Brazil should develop its nuclear industry only for deterrence and to prevent the Brazilian Armed Forces from remaining at a disadvantage in case of a military conflict."[18] The report, acutely embarrassing to the Sarney government, was quickly denied, but Pires Goncalves' views reportedly "received positive reaction" in other military quarters.[19]

Moreover, just days after denying the comments attributed to him, the general appeared to belie his disclaimer. "Countries that do not complete the nuclear fuel cycle," he declared, "in the 21st century will not be considered a [world] power," a none-too-subtle call for developing a nuclear-weapons option, though the general asserted the technologies involved were sought solely for peaceful uses.[20] Navy Minister Enrique Saboya took a similar stance ten days later, urging support, in one Brazilian newspaper's paraphrase, for "mastering the cycle of studies for manufacturing the atomic bomb."[21]

These various efforts to ensure continued support for Brazil's parallel nuclear program were apparently successful, because it appears to have continued without interruption.[22] The military's stance may also have dictated Sarney's cautious response to Argentine President Raul Alfonsín's call for the adoption of a system of mutual nuclear inspections.

Although Tancredo Neves, as president-elect, was said by Argentinian sources to have supported the concept at a February 1985 meeting with Alfonsín in Buenos Aires, Sarney appeared to be a more reluctant partner.[23] When he met with Alfonsín at Foz de Iguacu in late November 1985, the two signed a joint declaration on nuclear policy pledging their countries to develop nuclear energy solely for peaceful purposes and to increase cooperation in the field. The pledge seemed to reflect Sarney's fundamental commitment to non-proliferation. But on the subject of nuclear inspections, Sarney agreed only to the establishment of a bilateral commission to "create mechanisms to insure the supreme interests of peace, security and development in the region, without detriment to the technical aspects of nuclear cooperation"—a formulation that avoided even using the term "inspection."[24]

Less than a week later, Armed Forces Chief of Staff Amaral Oliveira again underscored his opposition to premature foreclosure of Brazil's nuclear options. In an interview, he stressed his support for research aimed at developing facilities that could produce nuclear-weapons material, while declaring, rather disingenuously, given the military's continuing influence, that a decision on nuclear arming was strictly a civilian matter:

We must master the complete fuel cycle in order to produce energy and all other possibilities that this technology may grant us, such as its use for genetic purposes in the agricultural field and other similar benefits. . . . We must remember that the technology can be used for producing anything from electricity to nuclear arms. . . . It all depends on a political decision that is not in the hands of the military ministries. It falls within the jurisdiction of the president of the republic and congress. . . . [25]

Despite this call for an open-ended nuclear program, the Brazilian delegation backed the mutual inspection concept in principle at the first meeting of the joint Argentine-Brazilian nuclear commission in late March.[26] By this point, support for the idea was growing among non-military elements of the government, as became clear in April, when a special inter-ministerial committee reviewing Brazil's troubled nuclear accord with West Germany released its final report. The committee, established the previous September and made up of industrialists and officials from a range of government departments, strongly endorsed the reciprocal inspection idea.[27]

Nonetheless, in July, Sarney was still unready to accept an Argentine proposal that a provision establishing such an inspection system be included among a series of major protocols he and Alfonsín signed in Buenos Aires to increase bilateral trade and lay a foundation for the future integration of the two nations' economies.[28] A Brazilian foreign ministry official crystalized Sarney's cautious support for reciprocal safeguards when he stated in September that eventually they would be established—but that the concept was going to be refined over a period of time in future twice-yearly talks with Buenos Aires.[29]

Whatever hesitancy Sarney may have on this particular course, however, the overall improvement in relations with Argentina is in itself an important positive step that can reduce the mistrust and competitiveness that have fueled the two states' nuclear rivalry. These improving ties were dealt a momentary set back in early August, when the astonishing report appeared in the Brazilian press that the Armed Forces General Staff and the Air Force's Institute for Advanced Studies were building a nuclear-weapon test site at a remote military reservation in Cachimbo in southern Para state.[30] The article claimed that a shaft, one meter (3 feet) in diameter and 320 meters (over 1,000 feet) deep, had been completed in July and implied that it had been built for an underground nuclear test.

The Sarney government quickly issued a denial, stating that "Brazil has no projects for the fabrication of nuclear weapons, neither does it have sufficient technological development for this nor a program for testing to this end."[31] The denial continued that the shafts had been sunk at the site during the 1960s and 1970s as part of unsuccessful mineral exploration projects and that the site had been turned over to the military for rocket testing to take advantage of its partial development.[32]

U.S. non-proliferation officials claim that the shaft is not intended for a nuclear test because it is of too small diameter to accommodate a test device and the test monitoring equipment that would be involved. They also point out that Brazil is a number of years away from possessing the necessary nuclear material for a test device.[33]

According to a non-government U.S. expert familiar with the design and testing of nuclear devices, however, the shaft would indeed be suitable for testing, if the yield of the test device were similar to that of the Hiroshima bomb. Such a test would need only rudimentary instrumentation within the shaft itself; this would be augmented by seismic data from nearby pick-ups and after-the-fact analysis of radioactive debris in the shaft. The original Hiroshima bomb was less than a meter in diameter and the nuclear device designed by Sweden in the late 1950s was only .6 of a meter in diameter.[34] It may be added that the mere fact that the shaft was drilled prematurely does not preclude the possibility that it was test-related; South Africa's Kalahari test site was discovered several years before that nation apparently possessed the material necessary for a nuclear device.[35]

Argentina, after urgently seeking a clarification of the situation, accepted Brazil's denial of the press allegation.[36] In less than a month, it appears, the issue had been laid to rest, and the two countries were again discussing options for non-intrusive reciprocal inspections and looking forward to

Alfonsín's visit to Brasilia, scheduled for December.[37]

Whatever the accuracy of the report of the supposed nuclear site, a statement released by former Navy Minister Admiral Maximiano Fonseca in early September left no doubt that interest in nuclear arms among elements of the Brazilian military continued to smoulder. In an unusually explicit statement, he declared, "If it was up to me to decide, I would make an atomic bomb and detonate it in front of international observers to demonstrate the extent of national technical know-how. . . . One hates to see the big powers developing and detonating atomic, cobalt and neutron bombs without being able to do the same ourselves."[38] Maximiano Fonseca is said to be notorious for his inflammatory statements, and thus his views may not be widely shared. Nonetheless, his open enthusiasm for nuclear explosives is cause for concern and suggests that debate over the issue will continue for some time to come.

On a separate issue, Brazil has yet to develop into a significant nuclear exporter, but has considerable potential in this field. In August 1985, for example, it bid on an Algerian uranium exploration project and, until China scaled back its nuclear power program in April 1986, Brasilia had hoped to serve as a subcontractor to West Germany on the latter's anticipated power-reactor sales to Beijing.[39] Brazil signed a nuclear cooperation accord with Egypt in 1986 which contemplated Brazilian sales of power reactor components.[40] A nuclear cooperation agreement with Colombia was also expected to be ratified in 1986.[41] Unlike Argentina, however, Brazil has not announced the non-proliferation controls that it will require on its nuclear transfers. A 1985 nuclear trade pact with China required that all exports be placed under IAEA safeguards, but it is not known whether Brazil will adopt this condition across-the-board.[42]

It may be noted that Brazil has made major arms sales to several nations of proliferation concern. In December 1985, it concluded a major arms deal with Libya, as part of its $1 billion dollars in annual trade with Tripoli, and in June 1986, Brazil contracted to supply Iraq 250 Cascavel tanks.[43] The possibility that this commerce in conventional arms might someday broaden into nuclear trade will be an issue of potential concern in the years ahead.

U.S. efforts to curb possible proliferation in Brazil were relatively low-key during 1985-86, in part because of the view that Brazil still remained a number of years away from the possible development of a nuclear-weapons capability. In addition, the United States has kept its distance from the ongoing discussions between Brasilia and Buenos Aires on non-proliferation measures to avoid any appearance that such measures are being dictated from the North, a factor which could lessen their political acceptability in the two Latin American states. A U.S. embargo of nuclear fuel and reactor sales to Brazil remains in effect, however, because the latter has refused to place some of its nuclear installations under IAEA safeguards; some transfers of lesser non-prohibited nuclear goods and services may be allowed.[44]

Technical Developments. Brazil's parallel nuclear program, though a cause for long-term concern, appears to be making little progress, having suffered serious budget cuts like much of Brazil's public sector. The status of the IPEN centrifuge enrichment project has changed little since late 1984, when it was reported that only 20 of 1,000 planned centrifuges had been completed.[45] It appears that uranium hexafluoride—the gaseous feedstock of the enrichment process—has yet to be introduced into any centrifuge units.[46] Nor have more than milligram quantities of plutonium apparently been extracted at IPEN's laboratory-scale reprocessing unit, said to be a series of radiologically shielded rooms, known as "hot cells." Similarly, no significant progress is known to have been made on the laser enrichment process at the Institute for Advanced Studies at the Air Force's Aerospace Technolgy Center.[47]

In August, President Sarney issued a major policy statement on the Brazilian nuclear program, outlining the future implementation of the 1975 nuclear transfer agreement with West Germany and other decisions. Continuing what had been de facto policy for several years, Sarney announced that for the time being, Brazil would complete only two of the eight nuclear power plants contemplated by the 1975 deal (Angra II and III); that the planned commercial-scale reprocessing plant would be indefinitely postponed; and that only the first stage of the jet-nozzle uranium enrichment plant at Resende would be completed.[48] The last facility will be subject to IAEA safeguards, which will effectively preclude its being used to produce highly enriched uranium. In effect, the proliferation threat arising from the West German agreement appears to be quite limited for the foreseeable future.

These decisions echoed the recommendations issued the previous April by Sarney's inter-ministerial committee set up to reevaluate the Brazilian nuclear program. The August policy statement departed from the committee's recommendations regarding other aspects of the Brazilian nuclear program in two important respects, however. First, whereas the committee had recommended that the Brazilian Nuclear Energy Commission continue its work on uranium enrichment at IPEN, the August policy statement was broader. It called for research and development of all areas of the nuclear fuel cycle, which would include reprocessing as well as enrichment, and it did not specify which government units were to be involved—thereby apparently authorizing continued work by the military at the Aerospace Technology Center. Secondly, the August policy statement dropped the inter-ministerial panel's call for the adoption of a mutual inspection system with Argentina, again reflecting Sarney's hesitancy in openly embracing these controls.

Brazil's rocket program, by far the most advanced in Latin America, may pose future dangers. Since November 1984, Brazil has had five successful launches of its Sonda IV sounding rocket. The two-stage, solid-fuel rocket can travel 1,000 miles into space with a payload of 1,100 pounds.[49] By 1989, Brazil expects to develop a multi-stage satellite launch vehicle based on the Sonda IV that may be controlled by an on-board, inertial guidance system and carry a 440-pound payload, still probably too small to carry an early generation nuclear warhead.[50]

Finally, the Sonda IV has an overland range of under 200 miles and lacks the accuracy necessary to destroy hard targets. Other rockets in the Sonda series, however, have been adapted for military purposes and sold abroad, reportedly to, among others, both sides in the Iran-Iraq war.[51] The planned satellite launch vehicle could have even greater military implications by taking Brazil an important step forward toward the development of an intermediate-range nuclear-missile capability. NASA, the European Space Agency, Canada, and West Germany have all assisted the Brazilian rocket program.[52] Under an agreement with China, Brazil is reportedly to receive advanced technology on liquid-fuels and rocket guidance systems in return for providing Beijing solid-fuel technology.[53]

Currently, Brazil possesses two types of aircraft able to deliver early-generation nuclear weapons, the U.S.-supplied A-4G Skyhawk and the French-supplied Mirage 3EBR.[54]

Prospects. Brazil's continued pursuit of technologies that can lead to the production of unsafeguarded nuclear-weapons material remains a cause for concern, although it is improbable that the country could develop a nuclear-weapons capability for a number of years. Given the military's strong backing for the program, President Sarney appears unlikely to terminate it for the time being and will also proceed cautiously on the question of bilateral nuclear inspections with Argentina. Sarney's domestic successes have steadily increased his authority vis-à-vis the military, however, and his improvement of relations with Argentina will help defuse the two nations' long-standing nuclear rivalry. These are positive trends that are likely to reduce the threat of Brazilian nuclear arming, even if some doubts remain as to the direction of the country's nuclear program over the long term.

Caribbean Sea

VENEZUELA

COLOMBIA

GUYANA

SURINAME

FR. GUIANA

Atlantic Ocean

Macapa

Manaus

Amazon River

Belem

BRAZIL

Fortaleza

Natal

Recife

Cachimbo

Salvador

PERU

BOLIVIA

Brasilia

Poços de Caldas

São Paulo (IPEN)

Belo Horizonte

Resende

Rio de Janeiro

PARAGUAY

Santos

Angra dos Reis

Curitiba

São José dos Campos

Porto Alegre

URUGUAY

Pacific Ocean

ARGENTINA

CHILE

BRAZIL

uranium mining area

0   800

MILES

Atlantic Ocean

Brazil

Power Reactors/Operating or Under Construction

Angra I (light-water/low-enriched uranium, 626 MWe)
- supplier: Westinghouse (U.S.)
- start up: 1982 (commercial operation, 1985)
- fuel source: Initial load, U.S.; current reloads URENCO (W. German, British, Dutch)[a]; Brazilian enriched uranium after 1989. (est.).[b]
- safeguards: yes

Angra II (light-water/low-enriched uranium, 1300 MWe)
- supplier: Kraftwerk Union (West Germany)
- start up: 1992 (est.)[c]
- fuel source: Initial load, URENCO (W. German, British, Dutch); subsequent loads, Brazilian enriched uranium.[b].
- safeguards: yes

Angra III (light-water/low-enriched uranium, 1300 MWe)
- supplier: Kraftwerk Union (West Germany)
- start up: 1995 (est.)[c]
- fuel source: Initial load, URENCO (W. German, British, Dutch), subsequent loads, Brazilian enriched uranium.[b]
- safeguards: yes

Uranium Resources/Active Mining Sites/Uranium Mills
- reasonably assured reserves: 163,276 metric tons[d]
- currently active site: Poços de Caldas[d]
- mills in operation: Poços de Caldas[d]

Uranium Purification (UO_2)

IPEN, São Paulo
- capacity: more than 10 metric tons per year[e]
- supplier: Brazil, with some W. German equipment.[f]
- start up: 1981 (?)[e]
- safeguards: no

Uranium Conversion (UF_6)

Resende
- capacity: planned 500 metric tons per year (eventually 2000 metric tons per year)[g]
- supplier: P.U.K. (France)[h]
- start up: indefinitely postponed[j]
- safeguards: yes (planned)

IPEN, São Paulo (pilot scale)
- capacity: 90 metric tons UF_6 per yr.[i]
- supplier: Brazil[l]
- start up: 1984[l]
- safeguards: no

IPEN, São Paulo (laboratory scale)
- capacity: (?) (50 kg. UF_6 produced by 1982).[i]
- supplier: Brazil (with some foreign assistance)[i]
- start up: 1981-1982[i]
- safeguards: no

Enrichment
Resende
- type: jet-nozzle
- capacity: 64 metric tons low-enriched uranium in 1988-89.[k]
- supplier: Kraftwerk Union (West Germany)[l]
- start up: first cascade 1987 (est.)[m]
- safeguards: yes

Belo Horizonte
- type: jet-nozzle
- capacity: laboratory scale
- supplier: Kraftwerk Union (West Germany)
- start up: 1980[n]
- safeguards: yes

IPEN, São Paulo
- type: ultracentrifuge
- capacity: lab scale until 1990, semi-industrial capacity thereafter
- supplier: Brazil
- start up: 1986-1987 (?), lab scale; 1990 semi-industrial unit, indefinitely postponed[j,o]
- safeguards: no

Fuel Fabrication
Resende
- capacity: Planned 100 tons per year for Angra I, II, III[p]
- supplier: West Germany
- start up: 1982 (initial phase)[q]; additional stages, 1990, 1991[m]
- safeguards: yes

IPEN, São Paulo (pilot plant)

Reprocessing
Resende
- capacity: pilot scale, 10 kg spent fuel per day[r,s]
- supplier: West Germany
- start up: indefinitely postponed[m]
- safeguards: yes[t]

IPEN, São Paulo (laboratory scale)
- capacity: varying estimates[u]
- supplier: Brazil with some West German equipment[f]
- start up: 1985 (?)[u]
- safeguards: only when safeguarded fuel is processed[w]

Principal Research Reactors[x,y]

IEAR-1, São Paulo (Pool/highly-enriched uranium[v] , 5 MWt)
- supplier: United States
- start up: 1957
- safeguards: yes

RIEN-1, Rio de Janeiro (Argonaut/medium-enriched uranium, 10 KWt)
- supplier: Brazil
- start up: 1965
- safeguards: yes

Triga-UMG, Belo Horizonte (Triga I/medium-enriched uranium 100 KWt)
- supplier: United States
- start up: 1960
- safeguards: yes

Delivery Systems

Brazil's Mirage 3EBR advanced combat aircraft would be able to deliver an atomic bomb (assumed to weigh 1,300 pounds) given slight modifications or a modest reduction in weapon weight.[z] Under similar conditions, Brazil's latest research rocket, the Sonda IV, would be capable of delivering an atomic bomb over short ranges if adapted for military use. Brazil's active space program, however, seems unlikely to yield an intermediate range ballistic missile before the turn of the century.[aa]

Sources and Notes

a. "German Uranium for Angra," *Jornal do Brasil,* translated in *Joint Publication Research Service/Nuclear Development and Proliferation,* hereafter *JPRS/NDP,* January 18, 1982, p. 28.

b. Assis Mendonca, "Germany Denies Having Negotiated Another Process," *O Estado de São Paulo,* translated in *JPRS/NPD,* May 13, 1982, p. 21; Charles Thurston, "Brazil Readies Enrichment Plant," *Nuclear Fuel,* December 3, 1984, p. 8.

c. Ivo Dawney, "Brazilian Dream Fades," *Financial Times,* September 11, 1986.

d. Reasonably Assured Reserves at less than $130 per kilogram. OECD Nuclear Agency and the International Atomic Energy Agency, *Uranium: Resources, Production, and Demand,* (Paris: OECD, 1986).

e. Personal communication with informed U.S. official, 1985.

f. Bernardo Kucinski, "Argentine Boast Spurs Brazil into Race for Bomb," *The Guardian,* reprinted in *JPRS/NPD,* February 19, 1982, pp. 6-8.

g. "Researchers Developing Brazil's Know-how on UF-6 Beyond the Plant Now Being Built," *Nuclear Fuel,* September 27, 1982, p. 13.

h. "Uranium Enrichment Plant in Itataia Confirmed," *O Estado de São Paulo,* translated in *JPRS/NPD,* January 25, 1982, p. 22.

i. "IPEN Produces Uranium Hexafluoride on Laboratory Scale," *Jornal do Brasil,* translated in *JPRS/NPD,* July 28, 1982, p. 18.

j. Charles Thurston, "Brazil's First Enrichment Cascade," *Nuclear Fuel,* November 26, 1984, p. 6. "Specifications of IPEN Uranium Enrichment Facility Noted," *Jornal do Brasil,* October 8, 1984. Expansion beyond lab-scale postponed. See reference m.

k. "Unfavorable Aspects of Nuclear Accord Coming to Light," *Estado de São Paulo,* April 1, 1982 translated in *JPRS/NPD,* May 3, 1982, p. 11. Expansion beyond demonstration phase indefinitely postponed. See reference m.

l. "KWU Recommends Development of Jet-Nozzle Enrichment Process Here," *O Estado de São Paulo,* translated in *JPRS/NPD,* June 3, 1982, p. 22.

m. Rik Turner, "Brazil's Sarney Defines Emphasis for National Fuel Cycle Development," *Nuclear Fuel,* August 11, 1986, p. 10. First cascade of enrichment plant 81% complete. Ibid.

n. Charles Thurston, "Critics See Brazil as Taken For a Ride on Its 'Last Train' to SWU Technology," *Nuclear Fuel,* April 26, 1982, p. 3.

o. Eneas Filho, "Ten Billion Cruzeiros to be Allocated for Nuclear Research," *Jornal do Brasil,* translated in *JPRS/NPD,* March 21, 1983, p. 28. According to U.S. officials, no enrichment had taken place as of August 1986.

p. "Operation of Fuel Elements Factory in Resende Discussed," *Manchete,* (Rio de Janeiro), translated in *JPRS/NPD,* December 6, 1982, pp. 18-21.

q. Juan de Onis, "Brazil's Crash Program Slows to Realistic Pace," *International Herald Tribune,* October 1982.

r. William W. Lowrance, "Nuclear Futures For Sale: To Brazil From West Germany, 1975," *International Security,* Fall 1976, p. 152.

s. "Resende Site of Uranium Reprocessing Plant Confirmed," *O Estado de São Paulo,* translated in *JPRS/NPD,* May 10, 1983, p. 21. Later start-up date probable; reportedly little construction to date, (personal communication with informed U.S. official.)

t. International storage also required for any plutonium reprocessed from URENCO fuel.

u. "Brazil Says It Now Produces Small Amounts of Plutonium," *Washington Post,* December 18, 1986. Only milligram quantities of plutonium have been produced, if that, according to Brazilian Embassy officials in Washington. See also, Leonard S. Spector, *Nuclear Proliferation Today* (New York: Vintage Books, 1984), pp. 247-252 (possible startup in 1983). Capacity estimates range from minute quantities (scientist Roberto Hukay in "Report on IPEN Reactor," *Jornal do Brasil,* translated in *JPRS/NPD,* February 18, 1983, p. 5) to five kg plutonium per year (Kucinski, "Argentine Boast Spurs Brazil into Race for the Bomb.")

v. Currently 90 percent enriched uranium, soon to be converted to 20 percent enriched uranium.

w. Currently, only safeguarded fuel is available.

x. James Katz and Onkar Marwah, *Nuclear Power in Developing Countries* (Lexington: Lexington Books, 1982), p. 100.

y. International Atomic Energy Agency, *The Annual Report for 1981,* p. 70.

z. 1,300 lb. selected as illustrative on basis of Sweden's untested atomic weapon design prepared in the late 1950s. (Christer Larsson, "Build a Bomb!" *Ny Teknik,* April 25, 1985). Source: *The Military Balance 1985-1986* (London: International Institute for Strategic Studies, 1985).

aa. "Ballistic Missile Proliferation Potential in the Third World," (Washington: Congressional Research Service, 1986), p. 14.

Chapter VI:
Africa

"I myself actually fear that in the end, because they [South Africa's whites] are so irrational, they seem to have a Samson complex . . . They are going to pull down the pillars and everybody must go down with them. . . . If as most of us believe, they do have a nuclear capability, I don't put it past them to have their own version of a scorched earth policy."

Bishop Desmond Tutu
January 9, 1986

The only sub-Saharan African nation posing a significant proliferation risk today is South Africa, whose ability to produce nuclear arms and apparent interest in acquiring them may have led it to build a small, slowly expanding nuclear arsenal of perhaps 15 atomic weapons. No other country in the region has more than the most rudimentary nuclear program.

Other African nations have, however, begun to discuss the desirability of obtaining nuclear arms. In April 1986, for example, Nigerian Foreign Minister Bolaji Akinyemi, when asked whether Nigeria should develop nuclear weapons, declared, "I can't give a direct answer but I'll say that a country the size of Nigeria, with its role and status in the world, cannot rule out any option."[1] Nigerian President Ibrahim Babangida echoed these sentiments in a contemporaneous statement, rejecting the principle of non-proliferation—despite the fact that Nigeria is a party to the Non-Proliferation Treaty—by stating that "the argument about the non-proliferation of nuclear weapons, besides its social overtones, now seems to border on the irresponsibility of [sic] weaker nations."[2]

Similarly, in June 1983, the secretary-general of the Organization of African Unity, Edem Kodjo of Togo, said at the nineteenth summit meeting of black African states, "Let us not be told especially about denuclearizing Africa when South Africa already has a nuclear arsenal. Against whom is it manufacturing its atomic bomb? Against us, of course, and the duty of the African states that can is to resolutely embark on the nuclear path. Such will be easily done within the framework of a community."[3]

Notwithstanding these statements of intent, no steps appear to have been taken toward achieving this objective. Indeed, if South Africa's is excluded, nuclear programs in sub-Saharan Africa are virtually non-existent. No other state in the region possesses a nuclear power plant, and only Zaire has a research reactor, a one-megawatt, U.S.-supplied unit. Uranium mines and ore-processing mills in Gabon, Niger, and Namibia (under South African control) are the only other significant nuclear installations. While the long-term potential for further proliferation in Africa remains, it is hard to imagine a second nation obtaining a nuclear-weapons capability for decades to come.

One additional African nuclear risk, discussed in detail in Chapter II and in the following section, must be borne in mind, however. That is the risk that nuclear weapons or nuclear-weapons material produced by South Africa's current regime might, for example, fall into the hands of a radical ruling faction—black or white—which might use or threaten to use them to advance extremist objectives.[4] Indeed, should domestic order crumble, governmental authorities could lose positive control over nuclear weapons or highly enriched uranium, which a non-governmental group might seize to create domestic or international turmoil, or possibly sell or take into exile in order to lay the base for a return to power.

While these risks are present in every country possessing nuclear weapons or the potential to produce them, the South African case appears to have an element of concreteness lacking in others because of the widespread view that sooner or later there will be a violent revolution in the country. In a 1985 television series on Africa to be aired in the United States in 1986-87, the author and narrator, Dr. Ali A. Mazrui, a prominent African intellectual, publicly declares his expectation that the successor regime in Pretoria will take control of South Africa's presumed nuclear arsenal.

In the final racial conflict, nuclear weapons could not be used internally without endangering the whites themselves. When the war does end, blacks will inherit the most advanced infrastructure on the continent. Out of the ashes of apartheid will emerge a black-ruled republic with convincing nuclear credentials.[5]

Such open anticipation of a nuclear "inheritance" has rarely, if ever, been seen in other settings.

South Africa

For a number of years, South Africa has had the capability to produce enough highly enriched uranium not subject to international non-proliferation controls to manufacture up to several nuclear weapons annually. In view of past South African activities indicating an intent to develop nuclear arms, there is reason for concern that between mid-1985 and mid-1986 Pretoria used this capability either to add to its stocks of nuclear-weapons material or, if it has indeed decided to build nuclear arms, to add several weapons to an undeclared nuclear arsenal of perhaps a dozen atomic bombs.

It is difficult to imagine the government of Prime Minister Pieter W. Botha using its nuclear capability against any external threat that it is likely to confront in the foreseeable future, and nuclear arms would be even less useful in dealing with internal civil strife. Rather, South Africa's white minority government has probably maintained its nuclear status despite its lack of military utility to intimidate regional adversaries and lend the minority regime an aura of permanence and inviolability. It has been widely assumed that Prime Minister Botha will not conduct a nuclear test for fear of complicating his relations with the West,[1] but in view of events during 1986, the premises underlying this assumption may need to be reexamined. With South Africa's Western ties already under serious strain because of Botha's unwillingness to share power with the nation's black majority, the added diplomatic costs of a test—which would give a major boost to white morale—may not loom as large in Botha's calculations as they once did.

Such a step would have serious consequences for global non-proliferation efforts. But another grave danger inherent in Pretoria's nuclear capability, as suggested in the introduction to this chapter, is the risk that a radical faction within the country may gain control over nuclear weapons or nuclear-weapons material and blackmail other elements in the nation or outside states to advance its political goals.

Background. South Africa's strong interest in developing nuclear weapons was unambiguously revealed in early August 1977, when both Soviet and U.S. satellites determined that Pretoria was preparing a nuclear-test site in the Kalahari Desert.[2] Indeed, according to a former Ford administration non-proliferation official, Washington had intelligence data at least as early as 1976 indicating that South Africa was embarked on a nuclear weapons effort.[3] At the time the Kalahari site was discovered, U.S. officials assumed that South Africa had obtained weapons-usable highly enriched uranium from a pilot-scale uranium enrichment plant at Valindaba, which began operating in 1975.[4] After strong diplomatic intervention by the United States, France, West Germany, and Britain, said to include the threat to break relations with Pretoria, South African Prime Minister John Vorster agreed to dismantle the test site and apparently pledged to the United States that South Africa would not build nuclear arms.[5]

In 1980, as further data on the Valindaba plant emerged, U.S. analysts concluded that Pretoria had not, in fact, been able to produce the highly enriched uranium needed for a test in 1977 and that South African nuclear planners had apparently prepared the test site at that juncture on the basis of over-optimistic projections. In April 1981, however, South

Africa announced that it had produced uranium enriched to forty-five percent, which it intended to use to fuel the U.S.-supplied SAFARI research reactor.[6] Since it is relatively easy to improve forty-five percent enriched uranium to the ninety-percent level needed for weapons, U.S. analysts now date South Africa's status as a state capable of producing nuclear weapons from 1981.[7] Nevertheless, the Kalahari test-site episode remains important, since it provides compelling evidence of South Africa's interest in nuclear arming.[8] (There has also been speculation that a flash observed by a U.S. satellite in September 1979 was that of a South African nuclear test; a panel of experts convened by the Carter White House Office of Science and Technology Policy determined that the event "probably" was not a nuclear detonation, however.)[9]

Whether South Africa has, in fact, developed nuclear arms, or merely stockpiled nuclear-weapons material, remains unclear. Although it has declared that it will not produce nuclear weapons, Pretoria has steadfastly refused to permit verification of this pledge, rejecting repeated demands that it place the Valindaba pilot enrichment plant under IAEA safeguards. As a result, U.S. officials and others remain concerned that highly enriched uranium from the facility is being used for weapons purposes.[10]

Since 1977, the political and military pressures that presumably prompted Pretoria to pursue nuclear explosives in the first place—its isolation in world affairs, the perceived threat from neighboring, black-governed African states, and the need for political symbols of legitimacy and permanence—have not abated. Its March 1984 ceasefire with Angola and a similar agreement a month later with Mozambique seemed to reflect improving regional security for South Africa. But Pretoria's continuing military forays into these and other near-by states made clear that South Africa's white rulers continue to see themselves locked in conflict with their neighbors and the anti-South African guerrilla groups these states have supported.[11] Moreover, as discussed further below, anti-government agitation within the country has seriously intensified, triggering repressive measures that in turn have increased South Africa's estrangement from the West.[12]

At the same time, despite South Africa's general record of success on the battlefield, its margin of overall military superiority vis-à-vis some of the front-line states may be declining. According to a number of analysts, the longstanding conventional arms embargo against South Africa, adopted by most Western governments in 1963 and made mandatory by the UN Security Council in 1977, has prevented the country from obtaining advanced weaponry, especially aircraft, tanks, and naval equipment. While the embargo has been far from airtight and while South Africa has also built up significant domestic conventional-arms-production capabilities, evidenced by the recently unveiled Cheetah jet fighter, some of its adversaries have apparently been able to obtain at least comparable weaponry from the Soviet Union, slowly reducing Pretoria's equipment advantage.[13]

These factors and the evidence of Pretoria's active pursuit of nuclear explosives in the mid-1970s are good reason to fear that South Africa has indeed built nuclear arms.

Pretoria has suffered considerable diplomatic and economic costs to maintain its nuclear option. In June 1977, for example, South Africa was ousted from its permanent position on the IAEA Board of Governors and it has not participated in the IAEA General Conference since 1977 when its credentials were rejected there. Moreover, its nuclear posture has exposed it to repeated attacks by various African and other non-aligned states in the United Nations General Assembly, the IAEA, and related international fora, such as the 1985 Review Conference on the Non-Proliferation Treaty.[14] Although opposition to Pretoria's racial policies underlie many of these assaults, the country's nuclear stance has provided an additional focus for international opprobrium.

Pretoria's refusal to place its entire nuclear program under IAEA safeguards also led to the formal termination in 1980 of U.S. nuclear reactor and fuel exports under the

Nuclear Non-Proliferation Act.[15] This not only codified a *de facto* 1975 embargo on U.S. highly-enriched-uranium fuel for the SAFARI research reactor, but also meant that South Africa was unable to take delivery of low-enriched-uranium fuel it had contracted to buy from the United States for its two French-supplied nuclear-power reactors at Koeberg, which were due to come on line in the early 1980s.

In 1981, the Reagan administration sought to open a dialogue with the Botha government on nuclear matters by holding out the promise that Washington would authorize lesser nuclear exports to Pretoria that were not prohibited by law. The 1980 U.S. fuel embargo, for example, had confronted Pretoria with the problem of finding an alternative source of fuel for the Koeberg reactors. Despite advance knowledge, the Reagan administration turned a blind eye when two U.S. uranium brokering firms arranged for South Africa to purchase a significant portion of the needed fuel from European sellers. Washington also authorized American companies to provide technical services for the Koeberg plants and granted export licenses for a number of dual-use commodities destined for the installations.[16]

This policy—a direct parallel to Washington's "constructive engagement" strategy for dealing with South Africa's racial stance—appeared to have a modest success in early 1984 when the Botha government declared that its own nuclear exports would be made only under strict controls, comparable to those adopted by the Nuclear Suppliers Group, and when it agreed to reopen negotiations with the IAEA on the application of the Agency's safeguards to the semi-industrial-scale enrichment plant it is building at Valindaba. However, the Botha government explicitly rejected placing the smaller Valindaba pilot-scale enrichment plant under comparable controls, thereby retaining its nuclear-weapons option. Moreover, Pretoria appeared to betray the Reagan administration's conciliatory non-proliferation stand in 1983 and 1984 by quietly hiring twenty-five U.S. reactor operators and technicians to work at the Koeberg nuclear-power station in disregard of U.S. regulations prohibiting such activities without special authorization.[17] The Americans have since returned to the United States or have been assigned to non-prohibited duties.

Western European states have also reacted mildly to South Africa's nuclear stance. South Africa bypassed the U.S. nuclear-fuel embargo by obtaining a substantial quantity of bulk low-enriched uranium from Swiss and Belgian sources, for example, and France willingly agreed to fabricate the material into fuel rods so that it could be used in the French-supplied Koeberg plants.

Political Developments. By the summer of 1985, however, a new pattern began to emerge, albeit as a result of growing Western concerns over intensifying cycles of South African racial violence and government repression. On July 24, France imposed a prospective nuclear trade embargo, directly triggered by the Botha government's declaration days earlier of a state of emergency giving South African security forces broad new powers to crack down on black dissidents.[18]

In September, in response to congressional pressure President Reagan also implemented a series of anti-South Africa trade sanctions by executive order that included an embargo on all classes of nuclear exports to Pretoria, including those still permitted by the Non-Proliferation Act.[19] Like the French nuclear trade sanctions, the U.S. embargo was imposed exclusively as an expression of American disapproval of apartheid and, indeed, the Reagan executive order made no provision for the embargo's repeal in the event that South Africa accepted stronger non-proliferation controls. In effect, American concerns over apartheid had superseded concerns over South African nuclear policy in triggering nuclear trade sanctions.[20]

During the fall of 1985 racial violence in South Africa intensified.[21] A notable incident took place in November, when South Africa's strategic Sasol 2 complex near Pretoria for producing oil from coal was hit by rockets. The three men responsible for the attack, later arrested by South African authorities, were said to be members of the outlawed

African National Congress (ANC), which has been waging a guerrilla war against the South African regime for over two decades. In June 1985, the ANC had announced plans to step up its acts of anti-government violence.[22]

The Sasol 2 complex, one of the most advanced of its kind in the world, has become a symbol of the ruling white minority's technological prowess and of its determination to "go it alone," if need be, in order to maintain South Africa's current political order. In 1980, the ANC had blown up part of the original Sasol 1 plant using limpet mines.[23] Two years later, the group had caused severe damage to another technological showpiece of the white regime by setting off four bombs at the Koeberg reactor construction site.[24] This history provides ample reason for concern that the ANC may soon attack a South African nuclear installation once again. The two Valindaba enrichment plants, which represent the very pinnacle of white technical accomplishment and military power, would be very inviting targets, indeed. Moreover, compared to the Koeberg reactors, which are protected by massive concrete safety containments, the enrichment installations are relatively vulnerable, especially to a rocket attack that could be carried out from some distance away.

The seizure of highly enriched uranium or actual nuclear weapons (assuming they have been manufactured and that their location could be ascertained) would be far more difficult, since a sizable frontal assault would probably be necessary. An operation of this scale cannot be ruled out, however, inasmuch as ANC guerillas armed with hand-held automatic weapons and grenades have attacked security targets, such as police stations.[25] If successful, a raid to seize nuclear weapons or significant quantities of weapons material would deal the Botha government a stunning political blow.

Despite Botha's announcement of a series of carefully limited reforms of apartheid, pressure on the South African government from the British Commonwealth nations, the European Community, and the United States continued to mount during 1985-86, as these powers pressed Botha to begin substantive negotiations on a transition to majority rule.[26] Botha's response to these efforts throughout the spring and summer of 1986 was one of bitter defiance—and sometimes outright provocation—as he attempted to demonstrate that he would not allow adjustments in South Africa's racial policies to be dictated from outside.

In May, the British Commonwealth nations sent a six-member "Eminent Persons Group" to South Africa to explore the possibilities for black-white negotiations and to make recommendations on whether the Commonwealth should impose economic sanctions. On May 19, while the group was in South Africa, Botha launched a series of military attacks against alleged ANC outposts in Botswana, Zambia, and Zimbabwe—all three Commonwealth states.[27] As Botha no doubt intended, the raids scuttled the Commonwealth initiative when the delegation cut short its visit in protest. In June, in a further blow to black-white reconciliation, Botha reimposed a state of emergency, a step that led to the detention of thousands of black dissidents.[28]

The following month British Foreign Minister, Sir Geoffrey Howe, undertook a similar special mission to South Africa as a representative of the European Community, which, like the Commonwealth, was hoping to facilitate power-sharing talks in South Africa, while continuing to review the possible imposition of sanctions on the country. Although Britain was known to be arguing against sanctions in both organizations, Botha declined to make any gesture recognizing Britain's support and flatly rejected Howe's plea for the legalization of the ANC and release of its jailed leader, Nelson Mandela. Responding to the implicit threat of European Community economic sanctions, Botha declared, "If we are forced until our backs are against the wall, we will have no alternative but to stand up in self-respect and say to the world, 'You won't force South Africans to commit national suicide.' "[29]

At the time, the U.S. Senate Foreign Relations Committee was also considering legislation to extend the sanctions imposed by President Reagan in 1985 and to add a number of tough new restrictions. The legislation was enacted in October 1986, Congress overriding President Reagan's veto of the legislation.[30]

In early August, responding to the recommendations of the Eminent Persons Group, the leaders of six Commonwealth member states voted to impose sanctions on South Africa (despite the opposition of Great Britain, which refused to take this step).[31] In response, Botha defiantly declared that "our standard of living will be lowered but we are prepared to make sacrifices for the principles we believe in." He went on to threaten to impose a retaliatory tax on all imports from Zimbabwe and Zambia; the economies of the two states are highly dependent on trade and transportation links with Pretoria.[32]

The imposition of moderately harsh sanctions by the Commonwealth, the United States, and the European Community (which adopted them in September), could have an impact on South African nuclear policy. To date, the threat of sanctions has been seen as one of the principal factors deterring Pretoria from conducting a nuclear test or otherwise declaring itself a nuclear power. How long this threat will retain its force as a nuclear restraint is less clear.

On the one hand, a test or declaration of nuclear-weapon-state status might be the final blow that would force those few outside actors who still voice their opposition to sanctions—principally the Reagan and Thatcher administrations—to change their stance, which in turn could precipitate harsher sanctions than those now being implemented, such as a total trade embargo or the severing of diplomatic ties.[33] Yet, as just described, where apartheid is concerned, Botha has shown himself relatively impervious to the threat of sanctions. Moreover, he may consider the imposition of tougher sanctions unlikely, irrespective of his nuclear stance, given the difficulty pro-sanctions forces experienced in gaining the adoption of even moderate sanctions in the United States and elsewhere. In this context, Botha might well believe that the political benefits of a test or a declaration of nuclear-weapon possession, in terms of rallying white support and demonstrating national resolve, would outweigh the possible costs.

It should be added that even Botha's limited reforms of apartheid have triggered a growing backlash from the extreme right—a grouping that includes the Conservative Party, the Herstigte Nasionale Party, the neofascist, extraparliamentary Afrikaner Resistance Movement, and elements within the state security apparatus.[34]

The Conservative Party, which broke away from Botha's National Party in 1982 and has been seeking to displace the liberal Progressive Federal Party as the country's largest opposition party, has directly challenged Botha's leadership in a bitter white-against-white rift that has been compared to the split that occurred during World War II, when right-wing Afrikaners opposed the government's backing of the anti-German allies. The Afrikaner Resistance Movement is said to be even more extreme. Its leader, Eugene Terre Blanche, is reported to have declared that if Botha's policies result in black-white civil strife, "true nationalists will retake control of the government by force."[35]

The political power of the ultra-conservatives was seen in May, when the Botha government attempted to placate these critics with the military raids on ANC camps in Botswana, Zambia, and Zimbabwe. The raids came in the wake of a series of land-mine explosions near South Africa's northern border and shortly after South African police announced the discovery of the largest arms cache in the nation's history.

Although the extreme right has said little publicly about South Africa's nuclear posture, it is hard to imagine that these interests would favor any step, such as the application of IAEA safeguards to the Valindaba pilot-scale enrichment plant, which might curtail South Africa's nuclear-weapons option. With Botha struggling to maintain a white consensus for his program of incremental reforms of apartheid, it seems highly unlikely that he would risk further antagonizing his growing right-wing opposition by accepting comprehensive non-proliferation controls over South Africa's nuclear program. Moreover, making such a concession to outside pressures might be taken as a sign of weakness that would run counter to Botha's own hard-line stance in rejecting external demands to soften the nation's racial policies.

In short, South Africa, at best, can be expected to continue its current course of slowly enlarging its undeclared nuclear-weapons capability. At worst, it may perceive some incentive to declare its status openly, conceivably with a test. Its acceptance of comprehensive non-proliferation controls appears highly unlikely.

Technical Developments. As noted earlier, South Africa is believed to have had the ability since 1981 to produce approximately 50 kilograms (110 pounds) of highly enriched uranium annually.[36] Using the standard assumptions that 15 to 25 kilograms of the material is needed to manufacture a 20 kiloton device of approximately the size used on Hiroshima, this, in principle, would give Pretoria a potential nuclear arsenal of 11 to 18 weapons as of mid-1986, assuming that 275 kilograms of highly enriched uranium had been produced in the interim. Because this would require that South Africa had operated the plants at full capacity throughout this period, however, in all likelihood the South African stockpile is somewhat smaller. Still, this represents continuing growth in South Africa's nuclear potential.

South Africa is currently negotiating with the International Atomic Energy Agency regarding the application of safeguards to the semi-industrial-scale enrichment plant at Valindaba, but the talks appear to have stalled.[37] Pretoria is planning to use the output of the plant to fuel the twin Koeberg reactors, which are themselves under IAEA coverage. Bringing the larger Valindaba enrichment plant under the IAEA system is critically important, because if it remains outside of safeguards it could greatly augment South Africa's ability to produce highly enriched uranium for weapons. Pretoria could, for example, more than triple the amount of highly enriched uranium the smaller, pilot-scale plant could produce if low-enriched uranium from the larger enrichment plant were used as feed, rather than the natural uranium that is now used.[38]

It is also possible that in the early 1980s, when it was trying to obtain fuel for the Koeberg reactors, South Africa was able to obtain a significant amount of low-enriched uranium from the People's Republic of China without safeguards. If Pretoria did obtain this material, this low-enriched uranium could also be used as feed for the pilot-scale enrichment plant, allowing the output of the facility to be tripled for a number of years. China has denied making the sale, but there is still something of a mystery over the source of the Koeberg fuel.[39] Pretoria is known to have obtained 130 tons of the material from Belgian and Swiss sellers in 1981, but each of the two Koeberg plants requires 75 tons to start up and 30 tons for each annual refueling.[40] Since Koeberg I went on-line in 1984 and Koeberg II in 1985, Pretoria apparently obtained additional supplies from some outside source, and American officials remain concerned that China may have been involved.

One additional technical development of importance is the possibility that in late 1985 South Africa obtained two 600-kilovolt flash X-ray machines from Sweden through a clandestine purchasing network.[41] The devices are used in nuclear-weapon-development programs to test the weapon's non-nuclear triggering package, a step that can significantly increase confidence in the reliability of an untested nuclear device. If correct, the story would support other circumstantial evidence discussed earlier suggesting that Pretoria is, indeed, preparing nuclear arms.

Prospects. As suggested above, Prime Minister Botha no doubt perceives that there are strong incentives to maintain South Africa's nuclear option, despite the lack of any identifiable security threat that nuclear weapons might redress. To give up this option in response to external prodding would further antagonize right-wing nationalist factions and would tend to undercut Botha's overall posture of implacable resistance to outside pressure. Whether South Africa might conduct a nuclear test or announce the possession of a nuclear arsenal raises more complicated questions. Developments discussed earlier suggest that in the future the risk of such occurrences will have to be taken more seriously than in the recent past.

Even if Pretoria were to maintain its current nuclear stance, however, this would not necessarily mean that South Africa had frozen its *de facto* nuclear potential. If, as many fear, Pretoria has either been stockpiling highly enriched uranium at a rate of approximately fifty kilograms per year since 1981, or if it has been building complete nuclear weapons at a rate of two or three per year since that time, in 1986 Pretoria's nuclear strength would have increased by twenty percent, and in 1987 it would increase by another fifteen percent.

Moreover, while South Africa's nuclear policy may be static, its domestic political situation is not. As unrest increases, nuclear dangers for the nation, the region, and perhaps beyond will intensify. The threat of nuclear terrorism has already been noted. Moreover, if the South African government were to move its carefully circumscribed reforms of South Africa's race laws toward actual power-sharing with the nation's black majority, the possibility of a right-wing coup, supported by elements of South Africa's security establishment must also be recognized. Were such forces to take power, the new government might seek to demonstrate its absolute power and indominability by conducting a nuclear test or even making nuclear threats against nearby states harboring anti-South Africa guerrillas. It is also possible that in the course of a coup attempt or in behind-the-scenes maneuvering between moderate and right-wing groups, nuclear weapons or nuclear-weapons material could come under the control of rightist elements, who might use this incomparable military and political prize to extract concessions.

If there is no negotiated settlement, it is possible that after years of struggle a revolutionary black government, deeply alienated from the West, will come to power and inherit the nation's current nuclear capabilities in the process. With the June 1986 report of the Commonwealth Eminent Persons

Group predicting that Pretoria's current racial policies could lead to "the worst bloodbath since the second World War," and moderate South African black leader Bishop Desmond Tutu declaring in July that as long as it remains unwilling to impose stiff economic sanctions on Pretoria, "the West can go to hell," this scenario seems increasingly plausible.[42] If the country's new leaders were bitterly antipathetic (in the manner of Iran's Khomeini government) toward supporters of the former regime, the new government could lead an anti-Western coalition of unprecedented power, and even nuclear blackmail through the infiltration of a nuclear weapon into a Western city could not be ruled out.

It is also possible that South Africa's white leaders might be able to take steps to deprive such a government of the nation's nuclear treasure. This might entail secretly shipping nuclear weapons or nuclear-weapons material out of the country, possibly to provide a basis for a subsequent return to power; giving them to a nuclear-weapon state or possibly Israel (with whom Pretoria is reported to have close military ties) for long-term safekeeping; permanently placing their nuclear-weapons material under IAEA safeguards before turning over power to the new leadership; dismantling any nuclear weapons and diluting stocks of highly enriched uranium to make the material unusable for nuclear explosives; or, simply destroying these nuclear goods, possibly as Bishop Tutu envisioned in the apocalyptic epigraph to this chapter, along with other highly valued assets.

Finally, there is the risk that during the tumult of a contested transfer of power from white to black, a subnational group might gain control of nuclear arms or highly enriched uranium. In such circumstances, the danger of nuclear blackmail for political ends would be very grave, and the possibility that the weapons might be offered for sale to other national governments or subnational groups would pose a serious added threat.[43]

None of these troubling scenarios, apart from the risk of a terrorist attack against a nuclear facility, is likely to transpire in the immediate future. On the other hand, unless current apprehensions are proven wrong and an orderly transition from minority to majority rule is achieved, there is reason for concern that sooner or later one of these scenarios will, in fact, take place. Thus the inheritance factor adds considerably to the dangers posed by South Africa's nuclear-weapons capability. It is likely to be a source of increasing concern in the years ahead.

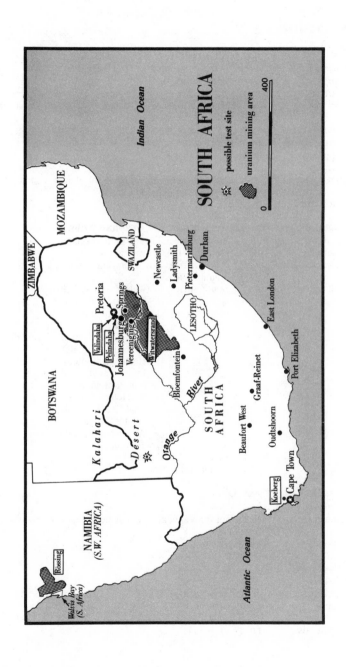

Indian Ocean

SOUTH AFRICA

☼ possible test site

⬛ uranium mining area

0   400

MOZAMBIQUE

ZIMBABWE

SWAZILAND

Newcastle
Ladysmith
Pietermaritzburg
Durban

BOTSWANA

Pretoria
Valindaba
Pelindaba
Johannesburg Springs
Vereeniging
Witwatersrand
Bloemfontein

East London

LESOTHO

K a l a h a r i

D e s e r t

Orange
River

SOUTH
AFRICA

Port Elizabeth

Graaf-Reinet

Beaufort West

Oudtshoorn

NAMIBIA
(S.W. AFRICA)

Rossing

Koeberg
Cape Town

Walvis Bay
(S. Africa)

Atlantic Ocean

South Africa

Power Reactors/Operating or Under Construction

Koeberg I (light-water/low-enriched uranium, 922 MWe)
- supplier: Framatome (France)
- start up: 1984[a]
- fuel source: Switzerland, France, W. Germany, Belgium, China (?) for initial loads; S. Africa after 1987.[b]
- safeguards: yes

Koeberg II (light-water/low-enriched uranium, 922 MWe)
- supplier: Framatome (France)
- start up: 1985
- fuel source: Switzerland, France, W. Germany, Belgium, China (?) for initial loads; S. Africa after 1987.[b]
- safeguards: yes

Uranium Resources/Active Mining Sites/Uranium Mills

- reasonably assured reserves:
  South Africa: 385,700 metric tons[c]
  Namibia: 120,000 metric tons[d]
- currently active sites:
  South Africa: Witwatersrand Basin, Palabora
  Namibia: Rössing
- mills in operation:
  South Africa: Witwatersrand and Group
          Blyvooruitzicht
          Buffelsfontein
          Chemwes
          East Rand Gold and Uranium
          Harmony (3 mills)
          Hartebeestfontein
          Joint Metallurgical Scheme
          Randfontein
          St. Helena-Beisa
          Vaal Reefs (3 mills)
          Western Areas
          Western Deep Levels
       Driefontein
       Palabora
  Namibia: Rössing

Uranium Conversion (UF_6)

Valindaba
- capacity: Sufficient for Valindaba pilot-scale enrichment plant (presumed).
- supplier: Great Britain (?)[e]
- start up: prior to 1975
- safeguards: no

Valindaba
- capacity: commercial scale
- supplier: South Africa (?)
- start-up: 1986[j]
- safeguards: no

Reprocessing[n]

Pelindaba[n]

- capacity: hot cell complex; size unknown; able to handle Koeberg, SAFARI fuel[n]
- supplier: South Africa (?)
- start-up: after 1985 (under construction)
- safeguards: only when safeguarded fuel present[n]

Enrichment

Valindaba (pilot plant)[n]

- type: stationary-wall centrifuge/jet-nozzle[f]
- capacity: 50 kg high-enriched uranium per year[g]
- supplier: Siemens AG (West Germany), Messerschmidt-Boelkow-Bloem GmbH (West Germany), GHH-Sterkrade (West Germany), Hispano-Suiza (France), and Sulzer Brothers (Switzerland), Foxboro Corporation (U.S.), and Leybold-Heraus (West Germany).[h]
- start up: 1975; full operation in 1977[i] (sufficient material for nuclear weapon probably not available until 1980-1981).
- safeguards: no

Valindaba (semi-commercial plant)

- type: stationary-wall centrifuge/jet-nozzle[f]
- capacity: 50 metric tons of low-enriched uranium per year[g]
- supplier: South Africa
- start up: 1987 (est.)[j]
- safeguards: no

Fuel Fabrication

Elprod (Pelindaba)[n]

- capacity: sufficient to fuel SAFARI I reactor (development of line for Koeberg fuel probably under way)
- supplier: South Africa (?)
- start-up: 1981[n]
- safeguards: no

Research Reactors

SAFARI I, Pelindaba (light-water/high-enriched uranium, 20 MWt)

- supplier: Allis Chalmers Corporation (U.S.)
- start up: 1965
- fuel source: United States;[k] after 1981, South Africa.
- safeguards: yes

Pelinduna Zero (SAFARI II) (heavy-water/low-enriched uranium, 0 MWt)

- supplier: South Africa
- start up: 1967[l] (now decommissioned)
- fuel source: United States
- heavy water: United States
- safeguards: yes

Delivery Systems

South Africa has several lines of advanced combat aircraft able to deliver an atomic bomb (assumed to weigh 1,300 pounds): the Buccaneer, the Canberra B(I)12, and the Mirage F-1. In addition, the mirage 3CZ/EZ could also serve in this capacity with slight modifications or a modest reduction in weapon weight.[p]

Sources and Notes

a. "Koeberg Ups Power," *Rand Daily Mail, Joint Publication Research Service/ Nuclear Development and Proliferation (JPRS/NDP)*, April 17, 1984, p. 36.

b. Ann MacLachlan, "U.S. Firm Plays Role in South Africa Purchase of Uranium," *Energy Daily*, December 10, 1981. George Lardner,Jr., and Don Oberdorfer, "China Was Source of Atomic Fuel for South Africa, U.S. Believes," *Washington Post*, November 18, 1981. The fuel obtained from the Belgian nuclear fuel supply company and the Swiss, French, W. German, Kaiseraugst utility consortium was enriched and fabricated in France; U.S. uranium brokers helped arrange the sale with the knowledge of the U.S. State Department. The United States was to supply fuel for the plant, but U.S. fuel exports to South Africa have been prohibited by law since 1980.

c. Reserves at less than $130 per kg; *Uranium Resources, Production, and Demand,* A Joint Report of the OECD Nuclear Energy Agency and the International Atomic Energy Agency (Paris: OECD, 1986), pp. 299-305.

d. Reserves at less than $130 per kg; *Uranium Resources, Production, and Demand,* A Joint Report of the OECD Nuclear Energy Agency and the International Atomic Energy Agency (OECD: Paris, 1986), pp. 264-268.

e. J. E. Spence, "The Republic of South Africa: Proliferation and the Politics of 'Outward Movement,' " in Lawrence and Larus, eds., *Nuclear Proliferation Phase II.* (Lawrence, KA: University Press of Kansas), p. 217.

f. Possibly based on German jet-nozzle process, degree of similarity uncertain.

g. Department of Political and Security Council Affairs, United Nations Centre for Disarmament, Report of the Secretary General, *South Africa's Plan and Capability in the Nuclear Field,* Report A/35/402 (New York: United Nations, 1981), p. 22.

h. C. Raja Mohan, "Atomic Teeth to Apartheid: South Africa and Nuclear Weapons," in K. Subrahmanyam, *Nuclear Myths and Realities* (ABC, New Delhi, 1981), p. 123.

i. David Fishlock, "The South African Nuclear Weapons Scare," prepared for Congressional Research Service, December 1977, p. CRS-5. Communications with informed U.S. officials.

j. "SWU's For Sale," *Nuclear Engineering Int'l*, April 1986, p.11.

k. U.S. exports ceased in 1975.

l. J. E. Spence, "South Africa: the Nuclear Option," *African Affairs*, October 1981, p. 441. The reactor is presently decommissioned; (Robert Jaster, "Politics and the Afrikaner Bomb," *Orbis*, Winter 1984, p. 827.)

m. "South Africa," *Nucleonics Week*, March 21, 1985, p. 15; "Koeberg Reaches Full Capacity," *The Citizen, JPRS/NDP*, July 16, 1984.

n. Jozef Goldblat, ed., *Non-Proliferation: The Why and the Wherefore*, (Philadelphia: Taylor and Francis, 1985), p. 315; *Report by the Board of Governors and the Director General to the General Conference, South Africa's Nuclear Capabilities*, GC (XXVIII)/724, September 24, 1984, Annex 1, Attachment 2, p. 2.

o. Jozef Goldblat, ed., *Non-Proliferation: The Why and Wherefore*, p. 314; communications with informed U.S. officials.

p. 1,300 lb. selected as illustrative on basis of Sweden's untested atomic weapon design prepared in late 1950s. (Christer Larsson, "Build a Bomb!" *Ny Teknik*, April 25, 1985). Source: *The Military Balance 1985-1986* (London: International Institute for Strategic Studies, 1985).

Chapter VII:
Controls and Safeguards

The nuclear non-proliferation regime—a constellation of international treaties, institutions, codes, and bilateral nuclear-trade arrangements—is a major restraint on the spread of nuclear arms. Although the year ending in early October 1986 was a relatively uneventful one for the regime, a number of developments added to its vitality. Several others, however, underscored its continuing limitations. Most are discussed elsewhere in this book and will be summarized here only briefly.

The International Atomic Energy Agency. The value of the IAEA as a forum for addressing issues relating to nuclear energy and as a repository of knowledge on the subject was emphatically demonstrated in the aftermath of the April 1986 accident at the Soviet Union's Chernobyl-4 nuclear power plant. Although the accident itself and the issues it raised concerning trans-border radioactive pollution are beyond the scope of this volume, it may be said that the Agency played a unique role in gathering and disseminating information on the incident and in developing two international conventions within a very short time span for improving timely notification and emergency assistance in the event of future nuclear accidents.[1] Unquestionably, these accomplishments strengthened the organization and enhanced its credibility and prestige in the international community.

The cohesiveness evidenced by the adoption of the two nuclear safety conventions at a special IAEA session in mid-September carried over to the organization's regular General Conference later that month. Since Israel's destruction of Iraq's Osiraq reactor in 1981, Arab-sponsored resolutions have sought to punish Israel for its refusal to rule out future attacks against nuclear installations that it considers threatening.[2] After Israel's credentials were rejected at the 1982 General Conference, the United States briefly withdrew from the Agency. This precipitated a crisis that was not finally resolved until the 1985 General Conference, when Israel's assurances that it would not "attack or threaten to attack any nuclear facilities devoted to peaceful purposes either in the Middle East or anywhere else" were accepted as a basis for laying the issue to rest. Prior to the 1986 annual session, the United States—as it had for the past several years—threatened to withdraw from the IAEA if anti-Israel sanctions were adopted, but so little support for the proposal was manifest that its Arab sponsors withdrew the measure without putting it to a vote.

Although the outcome appears to indicate that the politicization of the Agency is waning, it must be noted that the startling *Sunday Times* revelations that Israel's nuclear arsenal was far larger and more powerful than previously believed were published two days after the 1986 session ended. (The *Sunday Times* story is discussed in the section on Israel.) Had the story appeared a week earlier, it could well have increased the support for the anti-Israel measure, raising the risk of a second U.S. withdrawal and renewed disarray within the organization.

A separate positive development was China's late-1985 announcement that it would voluntarily place some of its civilian nuclear installations under IAEA safeguards, a symbolic step that matches "voluntary offers" by all of the other nuclear-weapon states.[3]

According to the 1985 edition of the Agency's annual Safeguards Implementation Report, during 1985 the Agency "did not detect any anomaly which would indicate the diversion of a significant amount of safeguarded material—or the misuse of facilities or equipment subject to safeguards under certain agreements—for the manufacture of any nuclear weapon, or for any other military purpose, or for the manufacture of any other nuclear explosive."[4]

The IAEA conducted 1,980 inspections at 514 installations in 51 non-nuclear weapon states during the year, up slightly from its activities in l984. In addition, the Agency operated more than 290 automatic photo and television cameras at nuclear installations around the world; verified that there had been no tampering with some 9,000 seals on nuclear materials and equipment; and analyzed 1,270 uranium and plutonium samples. The Agency found some 150 mostly minor discrepancies, all of which were resolved.

During 1985, 9 metric tons (nearly 10 short tons) of separated plutonium (enough for more than 1,100 weapons using the Agency's standard of 8 kilograms per device) were under Agency safeguards, up from 7.7 tons in 1984, and 2 tons in 1975. Agency safeguards also covered 12.3 metric tons of highly enriched uranium (defined by the Agency to be uranium enriched to more than 20 percent), possibly enough for several hundred weapons depending on the level of enrichment, along with far larger quantities of less sensitive material.[5]

The Non-Proliferation Treaty. The treaty, which was unanimously endorsed by its members at the Third Review Conference on the accord held in September 1985, was further strengthened by the subsequent accession of several additional nations, most significantly North Korea.[6] North Korea was one of perhaps a dozen important industrializing nations that had refused to join the pact, and Pyongyang's adherence, apparently at the encouragement of the Soviet Union, thus brings the treaty a major step closer to universality.

It may be noted that concerns had been raised in 1985 that

North Korea was building a large unsafeguarded research reactor, which some feared might possibly be the first step toward the development of a nuclear weapons capability. Adherence to the treaty, with its requirement that all nuclear activities be placed under IAEA oversight, will significantly reduce the possible risk from the unit.[7]

The Nuclear Suppliers and the Nuclear Netherworld. Since the mid-1970s, the nuclear-supplier countries, principally the industrialized countries of the West and the Soviet bloc, have applied a set of uniform export controls over their nuclear transfers to ensure that they are not used by recipients for military purposes. Central to these controls are periodically updated lists of nuclear commodities whose export is permitted only if the recipient nation agrees to place the article in question under IAEA safeguards. (The lists are known as "trigger" lists because they trigger the application of IAEA oversight.) Export licensing programs in the supplier countries implement this regime.

Argentina, South Africa, and China, though not formal members of the groups implementing these standards, have voluntarily adopted them, and Brazil has agreed to require IAEA safeguards on its exports to China under their 1984 nuclear cooperation agreement. Indeed, the requirement that all nuclear transfers be made only under IAEA safeguards is gradually becoming an international norm, and no nation has expressly adopted a contrary policy, despite the fact that several non-nuclear-weapon states—in particular, Argentina, Brazil, India, Israel, Pakistan, and South Africa—have reserved the right to keep indigenously developed facilities and materials outside the IAEA system.

Comprehensive though they may be, supplier controls have been repeatedly circumvented over the years by nations that, seeking to build or expand nuclear-weapons capabilities, have exploited loopholes in the trigger lists or, in some instances, engaged in outright smuggling to obtain nuclear commodities free from IAEA safeguards. A detailed 1985 analysis of eight prosecutions in Western Europe and North America for nuclear smuggling to Pakistan and

Israel, moreover, revealed that convictions were rare and that those found guilty were treated with surprising leniency.[8] Of the eight cases reviewed, the total penalties meted out were $16,000 in fines and fifteen months' imprisonment. In 1986, however, a one-year prison sentence included in this total was suspended by a Dutch appeals court; the sentence had been given to a Dutch businessman, Henk Slebos, for the illegal export of a wide-band oscilloscope to Pakistan in 1983.[9] Thus, only one of those indicted has actually served time in prison, Nazir Vaid, the Pakistani national who was held for three months and then deported from the United States in 1984 after pleading guilty to attempting to illegally export 50 high-speed electronic switches, known as "krytrons," used in nuclear weapons.[10]

Several important new reports of clandestine nuclear trade—the "nuclear netherworld"—appeared during the past year. These include the episodes discussed above in the relevant country sections involving Pakistan's acquisition of specially hardened "maraging" steel from West Germany; Pakistani and Indian efforts to Swedish-made flash X-ray machines useful in testing dummy nuclear weapons; India's undisclosed importation of heavy water; and China's sale, in the early 1980s, of unsafeguarded heavy water to Argentina.[11] None of these cases, however, involves the transfer of nuclear weapons or nuclear-weapons material, and it appears that such items remain unobtainable in the clandestine nuclear marketplace.

The reports of underground nuclear trade, of course, highlight the shortcomings of international nuclear controls, whose far more numerous behind-the-scenes successes all too often go unreported. Nonetheless, these exposés are a reminder that the nuclear netherworld continues to pose a serious threat to global efforts to curb the spread of nuclear arms.

* * *

Despite occasional bright spots, the events detailed in this volume are discouraging, indeed. Nuclear tensions in South

Asia are on the rise and show little prospect of soon abating, given the advances in India's and Pakistan's nuclear programs, the deterioration of overall Indo-Pakistani relations, and domestic political unrest in both countries. In the Middle East, Israel, it now appears, has significantly expanded its nuclear forces in the recent past, without objection from those most able to influence its behavior—the United States and the other Western democracies— while Iraq has repeatedly violated arms-control norms with seeming impunity. South Africa's increasing isolation because of its despised racial policies has increased the risk that it may conduct a nuclear test, and the danger that its nuclear assets may fall into the hands of radical forces in the years ahead is also growing. The trend in Latin America is certainly more positive, but even here nationalistic elements, clinging doggedly to hopes for nuclear status, have been able to maintain the momentum behind the development of sensitive nuclear technologies.

In region after region, moreover, superpower rivalries have blunted their respective non-proliferation efforts and made joint initiatives on the issue virtually impossible. Nor have international institutions, such as the United Nations or the International Atomic Energy Agency, been able to deal constructively with the threat of further proliferation by the countries whose activities are discussed in this volume. If the dangerous trends noted above are to be reversed, greatly intensified international non-proliferation efforts will be required; current policies, unfortunately, appear unequal to the task.

Notes

Chapter II:
The Nuclear Inheritors

1. Among the émigré nuclear scientists were Enrico Fermi from Italy; the Hungarians Leo Szilard, Eugene Wigner, and Edward Teller, who had been working in Berlin when Hitler took power; and the German-born Albert Einstein and Rudolf Peierls.
2. Martin J. Sherwin, *A World Destroyed* (New York: Vintage, 1977), p. 37.
3. Apparently when France fell several months later, the Vemork heavy water was again evacuated, this time to England. Richard G. Hewlett and Oscar E. Anderson, Jr., *The New World, 1939/ 1946: A History of the United States Atomic Energy Commission, I* (University Park: Pennsylvania State University Press, 1962), p. 29.
4. David Irving, *The German Atomic Bomb* (New York: Simon and Schuster, 1967), chapters 6-8. A number of eminent nuclear scientists working in Nazi-occupied countries were able to escape to the Allies, including Neils Bohr of Denmark in 1943.
5. Daniel Yergin, *Shattered Peace* (Boston: Houghton Mifflin Company, 1977), p. 344 note.
6. Gregg Herken, *The Winning Weapon* (New York: Alfred A. Knopf, 1980), pp. 101-102.
7. Irving, *The German Atomic Bomb*, chapters 10 and 11.
8. British Prime Minister Winston Churchill concurred with American desire to deprive the Russians and the French of German nu-

clear know-how, as was evidenced by his observation to Foreign Secretary Anthony Eden that the Anglo-Americans "had better get a hold of" the area south of Stuttgart, because "in this region are the main German installations connected with their atomic research." But the British themselves were not exempt from American maneuverings. As part of their roundup of German atomic specialists, two Alsos officers smuggled the eminent scientist Paul Harteck out of the British zone without British approval. Irving, *The German Atomic Bomb*, p. 281.

9. This section is based on: Jean Planchais, "Le Putsch des Généraux d'Alger," *Le Monde*, April 4, 1986; D.G. Brennan, "The Risks of Spreading Weapons: A Historical Case," *Arms Control and Disarmament*, Volume 1, (1968), p. 59; Keesing's *Contemporary Archives*, April 29-May 6, 1961; contemporaneous reports in the *New York Times*; and communications with two former French nuclear aides, spring 1986. Former Prime Minister Michel Debré declined to confirm the episode.

10. Under de Gaulle's proposal, four years after the cessation of hostilities between French and Muslim nationalist forces, Algerians would vote to decide whether Algeria would become a completely independent state, an integral part of France, or an independent state loosely associated with France. Opponents of the plan included civilian politicians of the French right, elements of the French military, and Algerians of European ancestry—settlers known as "pieds noirs." France had occupied Algeria in 1830; in 1961 it was administered as a province of France.

11. Jean Planchais, "Le Putsch. . . ." Salan, based in Spain, had recently formed the ultra-rightest Secret Army Organization, whose motto was "French Algeria or Death." Like Challe, Zeller, and Jouhaud, his retirement from the French military had been actively encouraged by de Gaulle because of previous plotting incidents. Roy C. Macridis and Bernard E. Brown, *The de Gaulle Republic: Quest for Unity* (Homewood, Illinois: Dorsey Press, 1960), chapters 4 and 5.

12. Roy C. Macridis and Bernard E. Brown, *The de Gaulle Republic: Quest for Unity*, chapters 4 and 5.

13. The device detonated in France's first atomic test, conducted on February 13, 1960, had a yield of 60 to 70 kilotons, equivalent to 60,000 to 70,000 tons of TNT. The devices detonated in France's two subsequent tests, on April 1 and December 27, 1960, had yields of 10 to 15 kilotons, equivalent to 10,000 to 15,000 tons of TNT, in the same general range as the Hiroshima bomb.

14. Brenner's implicit conclusion that the insurgents were unaware of the existence of the test device now appears incorrect. See, Jean Planchais, "Le Putsch . . ."; Keesing's *Contemporary Archives*, pp. 18511-18524.

15. Keesing's *Contemporary Archives*, p. 18524. At his subsequent trial, Mentre denied he had sided with the rebels, claiming that the word "his" had been erroneously included in his order and that he had thus never intended to tell his troops to obey Challe. Mentre's testimony was apparently disbelieved, because he was convicted for his insurrectionist activities and given a five-year suspended sentence. Ibid.
16. The precise date of this order is not clear, but as explained below, it most likely was given between April 22 and 24.
17. Robert C. Doty, "Algiers is Seized By Rebel Forces of French Army," *New York Times*, April 22, 1961; Robert C. Doty, "France in State of Alert After Coup in Algiers," *New York Times*, April 23, 1961.
18. Robert C. Doty, "Debre Warns France to Prepare for Air Invasion from Algeria; de Gaulle Assumes Full Powers," *New York Times*, April 24, 1961.
19. Ibid.
20. Ibid.
21. Ibid.
22. Ibid.
23. Robert C. Doty, "Paris Orders Algeria Blockade; Calls Troops, Renews Air Alert; Rebel Generals Remain Defiant," *New York Times*, April 25, 1961.
24. Jean Planchais, "Le Putsch . . ."; Henry Giniger, "Millions in France Stop Work to Back de Gaulle," *New York Times*, April 25, 1961; Robert C. Doty, "Paris Orders Algeria Blockade. . . ."
25. Robert C. Doty, "Paris Orders Algeria Blockade . . ."; Jean Planchais, "Le Putsch. . . ."
26. "France Explodes Nuclear Bomb at Sahara Test Site in Algeria," *New York Times*, April 25, 1961; Robert C. Doty, "Mutiny in Algeria Ends," *New York Times*, April 26, 1961.
27. Jean Planchais, "Le Putsch . . ."; "Four Generals Slip Away as Algiers Coup Collapses," *New York Times*, April 26, 1961.
28. "France Explodes Nuclear Bomb . . ."; see e.g. D.G. Brennan, "The Risks of Spreading Weapons."
29. Jean Planchais, "Le Putsch . . ."; D.G. Brennan, "The Risks of Spreading Weapons"; communication with former French nuclear official.
30. Jean Planchais, "Le Putsch. . . ." French Atomic Energy Commission officials at the site presumably reported directly to their superiors in Paris through a separate chain of command, and there has been nothing to suggest that the Reganne nuclear officials sided with the rebel cause. The military at the site, however, could undoubtedly have blocked them from carrying out a test, if necessary by taking them into custody, just as other loyalist civilian officials had been detained.

31. Keesing's *Contemporary Archives,* p. 18523.
32. Robert C. Doty, "Paris Orders Algeria Blockade. . . ."
33. Donald H. McMillen, *Chinese Communist Power and Policy in Xinjiang, 1949-1977* (Boulder, Colo.: Westview Press, 1979), chapter 12.
34. Tsao Ching, "An Analysis of the Situation in Sinkiang," *Issues and Studies,* November 1968, pp. 14-15. According to Soviet reports and refugee sources, the number of border incidents reached 5,000 per year. Ibid.
35. Donald H. McMillen, *Chinese Communist Power and Policy,* chapter 12.
36. "A Chance for Chiang To Invade Now," *World Journal Tribune,* January 10, 1967. The article states that it is based on Wang's statement as originally quoted in a right-wing Hong Kong newspaper, which may raise questions about its authenticity. See also, H.M. Jones, "Autonomous Wang," *Far Eastern Economic Review,* December 28, 1967, p. 570; Tsao Ching, "An Analysis of the Situation in Sinkiang."
37. Tsao Ching, "An Analysis of the Situation in Sinkiang," p. 13.
38. Donald H. McMillen, *Chinese Communist Power and Policy,* p. 205; "What's News: The Anti-Mao Leader of Sinkiang Province," *Wall Street Journal,* February 1, 1967. See also C. L. Sulzberger, "Foreign Affairs: The Nuclear Pawn," *New York Times,* February 9, 1967.
39. H. M. Jones, "Autonomous Wang." Whether Beijing may have feared that Wang might actually use an appropriated nuclear weapon against it is uncertain, but at a minimum, the central authorities could not afford to lose control over part of their nuclear-weapons program at a time when the nation was particularly vulnerable because of internal turmoil.
40. Donald H. McMillen, *Chinese Communist Power and Policy,* p. 216, citing, *inter alia,* Richard Hughes, "Mao Calls Truce with Rebel General in Bomb Province," *London Sunday Times,* July 2, 1967; H. M. Jones, "Autonomous Wang."
41. One report, however, states that the test of the hydrogen device did not, in fact, take place at Lop Nor, but was conducted at Chiuchuan outside Xinjiang Province. Richard Hughes, "Mao Calls Truce with Rebel General." If accurate, this might indicate that Beijing lacked confidence in its ability to guarantee the security of the Lop Nor site. Other sources uniformly give Lop Nor as the location of the test.
42. H. M. Jones, "Autonomous Wang"; Donald H. McMillen, *Chinese Communist Power and Policy,* chapter 14; see also Tsao Ching, "An Analysis of the Situation in Sinkiang," p. 12-13.
43. John W. Finney, "U.S. Evidence Indicates Failure of Latest Chinese Nuclear Test," *New York Times,* January 4, 1968. The

low yield suggests that the fission portion of the test device detonated but failed to ignite the fusion part of the bomb.

44. Ibid.

45. John W. Finney, "U.S. Says Chinese Have Conducted 7th Atomic Test," *New York Times,* December 25, 1967.

46. Tsao Ching, "An Analysis of the Situation in Sinkiang," p. 14.

47. Tillman Durdin, "Nuclear Program Slowed in China," *New York Times,* October 28, 1968.

48. Donald H. McMillen, *Chinese Communist Power and Policy,* chapter 16.

49. For convenience, the Democratic Republic of Vietnam will be referred to as North Vietnam and the Republic of Vietnam will be referred to as South Vietnam in describing events through late April of 1975, when the Hanoi government unified the country.

50. "Vietnam Has Rebuilt its Old TRIGA Research Reactor," *Nucleonics Week,* September 27, 1984, p. 6.

51. A.S. Friedman, Director of International Programs, Energy Research and Development Administration, to Congressman Bob Wilson, June 19, 1975, obtained under the Freedom of Information Act.

52. In theory, over many years the plant could have been used to irradiate small amounts of uranium until enough plutonium for a weapon—five to eight kilograms (eleven to eighteen pounds)—was accumulated. U.S.-Republic of Vietnam Agreement for Cooperation in the Civil Uses of Atomic Energy, 10 U.S.T. 1150, T.I.A.S. 4251 (1959); 15 U.S.T. 1463, T.I.A.S. 5622 (1964); 25 U.S.T. 1170, T.I.A.S. 7846 (1974). The agreement expired June 30, 1979.

53. U.S.-IAEA-Republic of Vietnam Agreement on the Application of Safeguards, 16 U.S.T. 1629, T.I.A.S. 5884 (1965). The agreement was suspended when the Republic of Vietnam signed an agreement with the IAEA for the application of safeguards under the Non-Proliferation Treaty in 1974. 25 U.S.T. 178, T.I.A.S. 7780 (1974).

54. Stanley Karnow, *Vietnam: A History* (Viking: New York, 1983), p. 685.

55. Ibid.

56. Interviews with knowledgeable U.S. officials, spring 1986. ERDA was the successor agency to the Atomic Energy Commission and at the time the principal U.S. agency responsible for U.S. nuclear export policy. In a subsequent reorganization, ERDA was abolished and its functions transferred to the Department of Energy.

57. U.S. Embassy, Saigon, Cable 19677, February 17, 1968.

58. Communication with former U.S. official, summer 1986; Joint Chiefs of Staff cable 2158, "Removal of Nuclear Reactor Material from South Vietnam," March 27, 1975, obtained under Freedom

of Information Act.

59. State Department cable 066714, "Vietnam Research Reactor Security," March 25, 1975, obtained under Freedom of Information Act. Despite the assertion in the cable as to the "real" purpose for removing the fuel, a senior official who ordered the mission and cleared the cable has stated that the underlying rationale for the effort was, as noted above, concern over the political impact in the United States of losing the fuel to North Vietnam.

60. Ibid.

61. U.S. Mission to the IAEA, cable 2536, "Viet Nam Reactor Security," March 25, 1975, obtained under Freedom of Information Act.

62. U.S. Mission to the IAEA, cable 2801, "Removal from Vietnam of Nuclear Reactor Fuel," April 3, 1975, obtained under Freedom of Information Act.

63. Interview with knowledgeable U.S. official, spring 1986; US Embassy Saigon cable 3625, "Vietnam Research Reactor," March 27, 1975; Department of State cable 69248, "Abandonment of Viet Nam Research Reactor," March 27, 1975; both obtained under Freedom of Information Act.

64. FCJN Johnston Atoll, cable RUHHJIA0604, "Removal of Nuclear Reactor Fuel RVN [Republic of Viet Nam]," April 1, 1975, obtained under Freedom of Information Act.

65. Department of State cable 71723, "Abandonment of Vietnam Research Reactor," March 29, 1975, obtained under Freedom of Information Act. The cable advises the two ERDA specialists, "In event contingency plan to concrete reactor were implemented, plan should include the following: (1) Remove water from tank or if that is not possible, (2) consider pouring cement through tube to bottom of tank to displace water upward. (3) Remove the six central elements . . . from core lattice and place elements on bottom of tank. (4) Fully insert control rods and disconnect control rod drives."

66. Department of State cable 073460, "Removal of Nuclear Reactor Fuel from South Vietnam," April 1, 1975, obtained under Freedom of Information Act.

67. Le Van Thoi to John Horan and Wally Hendrickson, April 19, 1975, obtained from Department of Energy under the Freedom of Information Act. Le Van Thoi had also sent a formal notification to ERDA on the transfer of the Da Lat fuel to the United States. ERDA specialist Neil Moore's official acknowledgement of the notification on May 8, however, had to be in the form of a "memorandum to files," since Saigon had fallen a week earlier. Memorandum entitled, "Files: Return of Fuel from South Vietnam," May 8, 1975, signed R. Neil Moore, obtained from Department of Energy under Freedom of Information Act.

68. Department of State cable 086860, "Removal From Vietnam of Nuclear Reactor Fuel," April 16, 1975.

69. U.S. Mission to the IAEA cable 4059, "Removal from Viet Nam of Nuclear Reactor Fuel," May 12, 1975.

70. In contrast to the situation in Vietnam, outside forces had little opportunity to react to the inheritance of a nuclear research reactor during the early 1960s crisis in the Belgian Congo. In this instance, the suddenness of an anti-Belgian insurgency, which rapidly led Belgium to grant the country independence, resulted in a small Belgian-supplied research reactor in Leopoldville unexpectedly falling into the hands of the Congo's new government before any steps could have been taken to ensure its security. According to former U.S. nuclear aides interviewed in 1986, however, the reactor—and its U.S.-supplied fuel—were fully accounted for after the change of regime and have remained under IAEA supervision.

The United States was also concerned in the mid-1960s that an American-supplied research reactor and its fuel might fall into the hands of communist insurgents in Indonesia. In September of 1965, the year following Indonesia's acquisition of the reactor, pro-communist elements of the military launched an unsuccessful coup against the government of President Sukarno. The violence of the failed coup, however, provoked a powerful conservative backlash. This led to the entrenchment of General Suharto as Sukarno's successor and continuity of a non-Communist government.

71. Daniel Poneman, *Nuclear Power in the Developing World* (London: George Allen and Unwin, 1982), chapter 5.

72. Zalmay Khalilzad, *Iran: The Nuclear Option* (Los Angeles: Pan Heuristics, 1977), p. 8, quoted in David Blair, *Nuclear Proliferation Prospects For the Middle East and South Asia* (Marina Del Rey: Pan Heuristics, 1981), p. A-17.

73. Daniel Poneman, *Nuclear Power in the Developing World,* pp. 89, 92; U.S. Energy Research and Development Administration, *U.S. Nuclear Power Export Activities: Final Environmental Impact Statement,* ERDA 1542 (April 1976), vol. 1, 3-52.

74. It is possible that some of these initiatives were undertaken without the Shah's knowledge. See note 79.

75. Robert Gillette, "Iran's Deal with L.A. Firm Widens Nuclear Capability," *Los Angeles Times,* August 22, 1979; General Accounting Office, *Circumstance Surrounding the Government's Approval of Nuclear-related Exports to Iran* (Washington, D.C.: General Accounting Office, March 17, 1980).

76. The General Accounting Office quoted the Department of Energy classification office as objecting to Eerkens' discussions because it thought "it probable that additional work on the process

would soon reveal where the key deficiencies of the process are and how to circumvent them. Such a development may very well result in a process that would have reasonable potential of separating practical quantities of special nuclear material [i.e. enriched uranium]." General Accounting Office, *Circumstances Surrounding the Government's Approval,* p. 7.

77. Robert Gillette, "Iran's Deal with L.A. Firm."

78. Ibid. Producing lasers to generate light at this wave-length has subsequently proven far more difficult to achieve than Eerkens believed at the time. Other wavelengths can also be used, however. Telephone communication with Dr. Jeffrey Eerkens, October 1986.

79. Robert Gillette, "Iran's Deal with L.A. Firm." There is some evidence suggesting that Taherzadeh may have been pursuing acquisition of the lasers without specific authorization from more senior officials, possibly in the hopes of impressing the Shah.

80. Ibid.

81. General Accounting Office, *Circumstances Surrounding the Government's Approval,* p. 4. The approval of the export license appears to be inconsistent with ERDA's prior refusal to authorize Eerkens' discussions with Iran on his laser process. Energy Department officials reviewing the export license application were apparently unaware of the earlier decision because it was filed under Eerkens, while the export license application was requested by Lischem. Not appreciating the connection between the two, Energy Department officials did not call for the Eerkens file. Ibid.

82. Daniel Poneman, *Nuclear Power in the Developing World,* pp. 95-96.

83. Akbar Etemad, "Iran," in Harald Müller, ed., *European Non-Proliferation Policies* (Oxford: Oxford University Press, forthcoming). Etemad goes on to state that after the revolution any experimentation in this area ceased "for the obvious reason that the nuclear power programme itself came to a halt." This does not necessarily follow, however, since the Revolutionary Government may have chosen to pursue these activities for weapons purposes.

84. Tehran had long been interested in acquiring a reprocessing capability, which it invariably justified as a needed part of its nuclear-energy program. By 1978, Iran had seemingly deferred its pursuit of this technology, however, agreeing during negotiations on a nuclear cooperation agreement with the United States that it would pursue other options, such as having its spent power-reactor fuel reprocessed abroad, before turning to development of an indigenous capability. The research activities mentioned in the text suggest the Shah was pursuing the reprocessing option more vigorously than he was admitting to outsiders. "Iran Wants An Option on a

German-Made Fuel Reprocessing Plant," *Nucleonics Week,* April 22, 1976, p. 6; Edward Cowan, "U.S. Says Iran Must Share Atomic Fuel Plant Control," *New York Times,* May 17, 1976; "Iran Was Expected to Ask France for Nuclear Fuel Reprocessing Technology," *Nucleonics Week,* May 27, 1976, p. 6; James F. Clarity, "Iran Devises Plans to Use Atom Plant for Nuclear Arms," *New York Times,* May 29, 1976.

85. Interviews with knowledgeable former and current U.S. officials, spring 1986.
86. See section on Iraq.
87. "Monarch Sees Persian Gulf as Center of Big Power Rivalry," *Journal of Tehran,* September 16, 1975, cited in Lewis A. Dunn, *Controlling the Bomb* (New Haven, Conn.: Yale University Press, 1982). Shortly after the Indian test, the Shah had also boasted, when asked whether he would possess nuclear weapons in the future, "Without any doubt, and sooner than one would think." "Report Says India Plans H-Bomb Test," *New York Times,* June 24, 1974. Through the years, however, Iran issued numerous official denials of any intent to develop nuclear arms.
88. Application for License to Export Byproduct, Source, or Special Nuclear Material, XSNM 1088, obtained under the Freedom of Information Act.
89. U.S. Embassy Tehran cable 4198, "Highly Enriched Uranium (HEU) Export to Iran," May 12, 1977, obtained under the Freedom of Information Act.
90. U.S. State Department cable, 115011, "HEU Exports to Iran," May 19, 1977, obtained under the Freedom of Information Act.
91. Ann MacLachlan, "France, Iran to Keep Talking About Dispute Over EURODIF Loan," *Nuclear Fuel,* January 13, 1986, p.9.
92. See e.g. Thomas Stauffer, "Ayatollah Rediscovers Nuclear Power, With Kraftwerk Union's Aid," *Energy Daily,* October 2, 1984; Bernard Gwertzman, "U.S. Urges Ban on Atom Sales to Iran," *New York Times,* April 26, 1984.
93. Akbar Etemad, "Iran." Etemad's paper does not acknowledge that nuclear-weapons research was being conducted under the Shah, although as noted in the text, research teams were given considerable leeway in their activities and some, apparently, were engaged in analyses relevant to plutonium extraction.

The Khomeini government has recently attempted to attract nuclear specialists back to Iran, ostensibly to work on a reinvigorated nuclear-power program, but with little success. Ibid.
94. According to Eerkens and other knowledgeable sources interviewed by the author in the fall of 1986, after the lasers arrived in Iran, they remained at Iranian customs until at least the summer of 1979. After the Iranian Claims Commission was established to settle debts contracted under the Shah, Eerkens sued to obtain

payment for the devices. In late 1983, agents of a shipping company involved in the proceeding determined that the lasers had been taken to the Tehran Research Center, but that they were still in their original crates. Thus, whatever other steps the Khomeini government may have taken to pursue the nuclear-weapons research initiated by the Shah, up to this time, at least, it did not choose to pursue the laser option. Indeed, to settle Eerkens' claim, the Iranian government offered to return the devices to him in lieu of payment. Eerkens refused the offer and ultimately obtained a partial settlement of his claim.

In the meantime, Eerkens pursued his research on laser enrichment in the United States with private financing, but has been unable to demonstrate the commercial viability of his technique.

It is possible that with the revitalization of the Iranian nuclear program in 1984, Iranian scientists are using the devices for research purposes. Eerkens now believes that it is highly unlikely that the lasers could produce significant quantitites of enriched uranium.

95. The reactor itself was provided to Iran under an IAEA project agreement; procedurally, the United States supplied the reactor to the Agency which then transferred it to Iran under a separate agreement.

96. Articles IV and VIII, U.S.-Iran Agreement for Cooperation in the Civil Uses of Atomic Energy, as amended, 10 U.S.T. 733, T.I.A.S. 4207, (1957); 18 U.S.T. 205, T.I.A.S. 6219 (1967); 20 U.S.T. 2677, T.I.A.S. 6726 (1969).

97. Washington, it may be added, had a similar problem with the Revolutionary Government's inheritance of Iran's advanced U.S.-supplied F-14 fighters. Here the United States persuaded Iran to permit it to remove sensitive electronic equipment to prevent its possibly falling into Soviet hands and in October 1979 resumed the shipment of spare parts for the aircraft. In effect, the policy was again one of making the best of a difficult situation.

98. Interview with knowledgeable former Iranian energy official, spring 1986.

Another danger that must be considered is that which would arise if Iran defeats Iraq in their ongoing war. In that case, Iran—by conquest—might gain access to Iraq's nuclear assets, which include radiologically shielded units potentially capable of separating small quantities of plutonium from irradiated uranium; twelve and one-half kilograms of highly enriched uranium, provided to Iraq by France in the late 1970s and now under IAEA safeguards (potentially sufficient for a carefully designed nuclear weapon using design principles described in published sources); considerable quantities of natural uranium; and trained scientific manpower.

99. Had nuclear weapons or nuclear-weapons material been avail-

able, it may be added, these might well have become a bargaining chip in the hands of one of the many factions vying for power, with dangerous and unpredictable consequences for Iran and the outside world.

100. In addition, the new government would inherit significant uranium deposits, mines, and mills.

101. Based on entry in *Facts-on-File,* January 6, 1978.

Chapter III:
Asia – Introduction

1. Shin Ho-Chul, "North Korea Signs NPT and Soviets Agree to Supply Nuclear Plant," *Nucleonics Week,* January 2, 1986.
2. Michael Gordon, "North Korea Joins Pact to Prevent the Spread of Nuclear Weapons," *New York Times,* December 27, 1985; see Office of Technology Assessment, *Nuclear Proliferation and Safeguards* (Washington, D.C.: U.S. Government Printing Office, 1977), p. 176.
3. According to the report of the House International Relations Committee on its 1978 investigation into Korean-American relations ("Koreagate"):

> There are indications in the early 1970's some steps were taken which appeared designed to pave the way for an ROK [Republic of Korea] nuclear-weapons program. Specifics on this matter came from a subcommittee staff interview (on February 28, 1978) with a former high-ranking Korean Government official who was a member of the WEC [the secret Weapons Exploitation Committee of senior Korean officials]. He told the subcommittee that the WEC voted unanimously to proceed with the development of nuclear weapons. Subsequently, the Korean Government discussed purchase of a nuclear fuel reprocessing facility from France and a mixed-oxide fuel reprocessing lab from Belgium. The explosion of an Indian nuclear device in April 1974 using fissionable material produced with the assistance of a Canadian NRX research reactor led to greater caution by nuclear technology suppliers, however, and the Belgians and the Canadians withdrew offers for certain technology. Negotiations between the ROK and France continued for some time over a reprocessing facility. Ultimately, it appears that by some time in 1975, any ROK nuclear weapons program had been canceled and the negotiations for purchase of a fuel reprocessing facility also ended. U.S. Congress, (House Committee on International Relations, Subcommittee on International Organizations, *Investigation of Korean-American Relations,* 95th Cong., 2nd Sess., 1978, p. 80).

According to former U.S. officials involved in U.S.-Korean nuclear affairs at the time, the contract for the French plant was in fact concluded and subsequently canceled by Korea.

A lengthy news report following up the House investigation of these matters suggested that Korea, in addition to negotiating the purchase of the reprocessing plant, had acquired numerous other components needed for nuclear weapons. The report quotes a "government arms-control analyst" as saying that the reprocessing plant was "practically the last thing on the list of things they needed, from special machine tools to the non-nuclear components of weapons . . . They were running all over the world picking up material and equipment." According to the report:

> Shortly after the Indian test, a small group of intelligence and technical

experts, including one from the U.S. Atomic Energy Commission, is said to have begun canvassing U.S. embassies for signs of similar activities on the part of governments considered likely to seek nuclear weapons. The basic approach was to search embassy files for requests by foreign governments to import materials and equipment on a "critical list" of items considered indicative of an interest in atomic weapons. Among these items, sources said, were such things as equipment for machining plutonium metal, bulk orders of beryllium and boron, and exotic, explosive chemicals and shaped-charge technology needed to detonate fission weapons.

"When they got to Korea, everything snapped into place," the analyst said. Simply by rummaging through embassy files for references to material and equipment that the Korean government had sought to import from U.S. industry and through military channels, a "substantial number" of items on the critical list came to light. (Robert Gillette, "U.S. Squelched Apparent S. Korea A-Bomb Drive," *Los Angeles Times,* November 4, 1978.)

In 1984-85, South Korea and Canada held discussions on possible reprocessing of Korean spent fuel, but these were abandoned. See David Albright, "World Inventories of Plutonium" (Working Paper), Federation of American Scientists, citing T. Shorrock and O. Gadacz, "U.S. Intervention in Nuclear Fuel Project Still a Mystery," *Business Korea* (April 1985): 47.

4. In March, for example, South Korean President Chun Doo Hwan cautioned that another Korean war may be on the horizon. Defense Minister Lee Ki Baek pointed out that such a conflict might be precipitated by North Korea's military buildup, an augmentation that included Soviet-supplied MiG-23 aircraft and Scud-B ground-to-ground missiles. A September bomb explosion at Seoul's international airport further heightened tensions, as South Korea immediately associated the detonation with North Korean attempts to disrupt the Asian Games to be held in Seoul. "South Korean President Warns of War Risk," *Washington Times,* March 19, 1986; Steven Butler, "Seoul Warns That North Korea Is Readying for War," *Financial Times,* March 21, 1986; John Burgess, "Games Seen Target of S. Korean Attack," *Washington Post,* September 15, 1986.

5. Michael Weisskopf, "Taiwan, Nearing Limits of U.S. Arms Supply, To Build Own Jets," *Washington Post,* March 3, 1984. In the late 1960s and particularly during the mid-1970s, when the United States was opening friendly relations with mainland China, Taiwan made repeated attempts, some apparently secret, to develop a reprocessing capability. Because of Taiwan's precarious security situation and the lack of any clear need for this capability as part of Taiwan's nuclear energy program, U.S. officials came to believe that these efforts were aimed at eventually producing plutonium for nuclear weapons.

In 1969, for example, Taiwan sought to buy a reprocessing plant from the United States, but the Nixon administration denied this request and barred U.S. firms from selling key components for such plants. Edward Schumacher, "Taiwan Seen Reprocessing Nuclear Fuel," *Washington Post,* August 29, 1976. Taiwan then turned to other possible suppliers—in particular, France, from whom it sought to purchase a large reprocessing facility. When the United States intervened, discussions on the sales were broken off. France, however, apparently supplied a number of component parts useful for a reprocessing facility, Steven R. Weisman and Herbert Krosney, *The Islamic Bomb* (New York: Times Books, 1981), pp. 152-153.

From 1974 to 1976, Taiwan tried to negotiate an agreement with the British for the reprocessing of Taiwanese spent fuel in England and the return of the plutonium to Taiwan. Once again, the United States stepped in, this time to insist that any plutonium produced under this arrangement be shipped to the United States instead. Melinda Liu, "Accounting for the N-Factor," *Far Eastern Economic Review,* December 17, 1976, p. 33.

By 1974, the U.S. CIA had concluded:

Taipei conducts its small nuclear program with a weapon option in mind, and it will be in a position to fabricate a nuclear device after five years or so. Taipei's role in the world is changing radically, and concern over the possibility of complete isolation is mounting. Its decisions will be much influenced by U.S. policies in two key areas—support for the island's security and attitudes about the possibility of a nuclear-armed Taiwan. Taipei's present course probably is leading it toward development of nuclear weapons (CIA, "Prospects for Further Proliferation of Nuclear Weapons," DCI NIO 1945/74, Sanitized Copy, September 4, 1974.)

Despite U.S. interventions, by 1975 Taiwan was constructing a hot cell (a laboratory-scale reprocessing unit) on its own. The facility was apparently constructed with components purchased from around the world, including some from France. Schumacher, "Taiwan Seen Reprocessing." Although the facility was capable of producing only tiny amounts of plutonium, it would have provided Taiwan with valuable experience in this field. Ibid. In that year, Taiwan asked the United States for permission to reprocess a small amount of spent fuel from a U.S.-supplied research reactor in Taiwan, but the United States did not reply to the inquiry. Don Oberdorfer, "Taiwan to Curb A-Role," *Washington Post,* September 23, 1976.

In 1976, reports surfaced that Taiwan may have been secretly extracting plutonium from spent fuel at a clandestine reprocessing facility of some kind. Schumacher, "Taiwan Seen Reprocessing"; Oberdorfer, "Taiwan to Curb A-Role." Although in congressional hearings U.S. officials stated that no reprocessing had actually taken place and that such a facility had not, in fact, been built, U.S.

suspicions over Taiwan's activities in this area became so intense that the Ford administration insisted Taiwan cease all activities in the reprocessing field, dismantle the hot-cell laboratory, and pledge not to engage in any activities related to reprocessing. U.S. Congress, Senate Subcommittee on Arms Control, International Organizations, and Security Agreements, *Hearings on Non-Proliferation Issues,* September 22, 1976 (Washington, D.C.: U.S. Government Printing Office, 1976), pp. 346-371.

6. Nayan Chanda, "New Planes for Old," *Far East Economic Review,* January 2, 1986, p. 11.

7. See generally John A. Barnes, "Taiwan's Aging Arsenal Could Invite Attack by China," *Wall Street Journal,* January 21, 1985; Gus Constantine, "Taipei Calls U.S. on Commitment on Defense," *Washington Times,* February 21, 1985.

8. "Taiwan Makes Nuclear Arms Claim," *Washington Post,* May 15, 1983.

9. "Cabinet Rules Out Developing Nuclear Weapons," *Chung Yang Jih Pao* (Taipei), November 19, 1983, translated in *Joint Publication and Research Service (JPRS)/Nuclear Development and Proliferation (TND),* December 20, 1983, p. 25.

10. The Non-Proliferation Treaty, for example, requires all parties to ensure that their nuclear exports will be placed under IAEA safeguards in the recipient state, and this is also required under the Nuclear Supplier Group Guidelines. China has not adhered to either.

Reportedly, China sold, without requiring IAEA safeguards, 3-percent-enriched uranium to South Africa (possibly through intermediaries); 20-percent-enriched uranium to Argentina; and heavy water to Argentina and possibly to South Africa and India as well. Jack Anderson, "CIA Says China Has Sent A-Fuel to South Africa," *Washington Post,* July 23, 1981; Judith Miller, "U.S. is Holding Up Peking Atom Talks," *New York Times,* September 19, 1982; Rob Laufer, "Interview With Malone: Defense of Policy and Assessment of 'Hot Spots,' " *Nucleonics Week,* August 19, 1982, p. 1; Richard Kessler, "Argentina to Tender for Heavy Water after June Purchase from China," *Nucleonics Week,* September 25, 1986, p. 5.China has denied making the uranium sales. Christopher S. Wren, "China Denies Selling Uranium to South Africa," *New York Times,* September 26, 1982. However, it has acknowledged exporting "a limited quantity of nuclear materials," for which it required recipients to pledge that they would "never transfer the nuclear materials to a third country, particularly South Africa and Israel, or use the same for non-peaceful purposes." Warren Donnelly and Carol Eberhard, "U.S. Nuclear Cooperation with the People's Republic of China," Issue Brief IB83149, Congressional Research Service, December 27, 1983, p. CRS-4, citing China News Service.

The statement did not mention that China had required IAEA safe-guards on these transfers, seeming to confirm at least this part of the press accounts. China recently acknowledged selling heavy water to Argentina without safeguards. See note 15, below.

Regarding China's prior non-proliferation policies, see Kenneth Adelman, Director, Arms Control and Disarmament Agency, "Non-Proliferation Assessment Statement for the Peaceful Nuclear Cooperation Agreement Between the United States and China," July 19, 1985.

See also Gary Milhollin, "Dateline New Delhi: India's Nuclear Cover-up," *Foreign Policy*, (Fall 1986): 161, pointing to China as the source of unsafeguarded Indian heavy-water imports.

11. Milton R. Benjamin, "China Aids Pakistan on A-Weapons," *Washington Post*, February 28, 1983; Leslie H. Gelb, "Pakistan Link Perils U.S.-China Nuclear Pact," *New York Times*, June 22, 1984; Miller, "U.S. is Holding Up Peking Atom Talks"; Simon Henderson, "Why Pakistan May Not Need to Test a Nuclear Device,"
Financial Times, August 14, 1984.

See also testimony of Richard T. Kennedy, *Hearings on Review of 1985 U.S. Government Non-proliferation Activities*, U.S. Senate Subcommittee on Energy, Nuclear Proliferation, and Government Processes, Committee on Governmental Affairs, April 10, 1986 (Washington: Government Printing Office, 1986), p. 17 (China and Pakistan have engaged in nuclear cooperation for years; only non-military cooperation may be continuing.)

12. Adelman, "Non-Proliferation Assessment Statement," p. I-5. Premier Zhao's statement was endorsed by the Congress, the Chinese government's highest vehicle for the pronouncement of public policy.

13. Gelb, "Pakistan Link Perils U.S.-China Nuclear Pact;" communications with U.S. officials.

14. Adelman, "Non-Proliferation Assessment Statement," p. I-5. The details of the U.S.-Chinese understanding on the matter are contained in a classified note submitted by the Reagan administration to Congress along with the agreement. The document is said to contain a U.S.-prepared summary of oral understandings reached between U.S. and Chinese negotiators. China has not apparently signed the document but has not objected to its being used by U.S. officials to characterize China's position.

15. Daniel Southerland, "U.S., China Sign Accords," *Washington Post*, August 28, 1985.

It appears that some unsafeguarded transfers of Chinese nuclear materials to Argentina and possibly South Africa continued into 1985, although these were supposedly based on pre-existing contracts. China also apparently held talks with Iran on nuclear trade, although these appear to have been limited to providing possible assistance in the construction of two partially completed nuclear power plants in Iran. Patrick Tyler, "Hill Panels Add Conditions to U.S.-China Nuclear Pact," *Washington Post*, November 14, 1985. In an unusual twist, in November 1985, China acknowledged that it had supplied unsafeguarded heavy water to Argentina, a charge Argentina had denied the previous month. Richard Kessler, "Premier Zhao Ziyang Appeared to Confirm that China," *Nucleonics Week*, November 14, 1985; Richard Kessler, "Argentina Officials Deny Any Purchases of Chinese Heavy Water," *Nucleonics Week*, October 31, 1985, p. 5.

16. Atomic Energy Act of 1954, Sections 123 and 130 (1985).
17. S.J. Res. 238 (99th Cong. 1st Sess.) (1985)
18. The provision was added as an amendment to the fiscal year 1986 continuing appropriations bill introduced by Senator John Glenn; it was adopted by the Senate on December 9, 1985, but later dropped from the legislation by the House-Senate conference on the bill. See *Congressional Record*, 99th Cong., 2nd Sess., December 9, 1985, pp. S17141-17163.
19. James P. Sterba, "China's Great Leap Backward?: China Dashes Sales Hopes of Foreign Nuclear Firms," *Wall Street Journal*, April 25, 1986.
20. "Pakistan and China Signed a Comprehensive Agreement for Co-operation," *Nucleonics Week*, September 25, 1986, p. 3; Simon Henderson, "China May Help Build Pakistan's N-Bomb," *Financial Times*, September 29, 1986 (A.Q. Khan in interview says pact covers "all nuclear activities.")

India

1. During a recent interview, for example, a senior aide to Pakistani President Zia ul-Haq described his Indian counterparts as "devious Hindus."
2. This historical summary of the Indian nuclear program is based on a more detailed review found in Leonard S. Spector, *Nuclear Proliferation Today* (New York: Vintage Books, 1984), pp. 23-48.
3. The shift in India's stance began during Charan Singh's six-month tenure as prime minister which began in July 1979. In August of that year he stated, "We do not want to join the race to make a bomb, but if Pakistan sticks to its plans to assemble a bomb, we will perhaps have to reconsider the whole question." Michael T. Kaufman, "India Gives Warning of Atom-Arms Race," *New York Times*, August 16, 1979. Other top officials of his government made similar statements during this period.
4. Steven R. Weisman and Herbert Krosney, *The Islamic Bomb* (New York: Times Books, 1981), pp. 43-46. The authors' information

comes from two participants in the key meeting, held in Multan, at which Bhutto announced that Pakistan would develop nuclear weapons.

5. For a detailed discussion of some of these activities, including a review of a number of prosecutions for the smuggling of nuclear goods to Pakistan, see Leonard S. Spector, *The New Nuclear Nations* (New York: Vintage Books, 1985), pp. 22-41.

6. See testimony of Thomas R. Pickering, Assistant Secretary of State for Oceans and International Environmental and Scientific Affairs, *Hearings on Nuclear Proliferation: The Situation in India and Pakistan,* Senate Subcommittee on Energy, Nuclear Proliferation, and Federal Services of the Committee on Governmental Affairs, May 1, 1979 (Washington, D.C.: U.S. Government Printing Office, 1979) p. 10; K.K. Sharma, "Pakistan Nuclear Pledge to India," *Financial Times,* April 9, 1979.

7. For example see testimony of Thomas R. Pickering; "India Not to Make Nuclear Arms," Delhi Domestic Service, 0240 GMT, November 20, 1985, reprinted in *Foreign Broadcast Information Service (FBIS)/South Asia,* December 2, 1985, p. C-5; "Kuwaiti Paper Interviews Prime Minister Gandhi," *Arab Times,* September 2, 1985, pp. 8-9, translated in *FBIS/South Asia,* September 4, 1985, p. E-3.

8. Spector, *The New Nuclear Nations,* pp. 92-98.

9. "Gandhi Says National Interest May Require Nuclear Blasts," *Washington Post,* March 14, 1980. Judith Miller, "Cranston Says India and Pakistan Are Preparing for Nuclear Testing," *New York Times,* April 28, 1981; Roger Gale, "India to Press 'Start Button' on Nuclear Fuel Reprocessing Plant," *Energy Daily,* February 5, 1981; Yogi Aggarwal, "India Makes Another Bomb," *Sunday Observer* (Bombay), August 30, 1981 (government had one atomic bomb ready in April, could prepare another one in weeks); K. Subrahmanyam, "Bomb—The Only Answer," *Times of India,* April 26, 1981, p. 1; Milton R. Benjamin, "U.S. Is Delaying Nuclear Exports to India," *Washington Post,* June 23, 1983.

10. This apparently is the view of the Pakistani army. Stephen P. Cohen, *The Pakistan Army* (Berkeley: University of California Press, 1984), p. 153; "Shadow of An Indian H-Bomb," *Foreign Report,* December 13, 1984, p.1. In a 1985 interview with the author, K. Subrahmanyam, director of the Indian Institute for Defence Studies and Analyses, indicated that he assumed Mrs. Gandhi had pursued such activities because not to have done so would have been "irresponsible."

11. See chart at end of chapter. The Cirus research reactor is also unsafeguarded. India, however, is legally precluded from using its output for nuclear weapons, as discussed in the text below.

12. The Cirus reactor is believed capable of producing 9 kilograms of

plutonium per year in its spent fuel. The Dhruva reactor, which is two and one-half times larger than Cirus, is thought to be able to produce approximately 25 kilograms of plutonium in its spent fuel per year. The two Madras reactors each have an estimated annual plutonium output of 50-60 kilograms. Thus the combined plutonium output from these facilities each year is between 134 and 154 kilograms, assuming that they operate steadily, an amount 14-17 times larger than that available from the Cirus reactor, alone, in 1974.

As discussed below, plutonium from the Cirus reactor may be used only for peaceful purposes, leaving an annual plutonium output of 125 to 145 kilograms potentially available for weapons. Using the standard 5 to 8 kilograms of plutonium per weapon, this would mean that in theory, India could manufacture between 15 and 29 devices annually. India has four other nuclear power reactors that have not been included in this estimate, the two U.S.-supplied Tarapur power plants and the two Canadian-supplied Rajasthan power plants. All four of these installations are subject to International Atomic Energy Agency (IAEA) inspections and audits to insure that their output is not used for nuclear weapons.

The Trombay reprocessing plant is designed to extract plutonium from the metallic uranium fuel used in the Cirus and Dhruva reactors. The considerably larger Tarapur reprocessing plant has the capability of extracting plutonium from both metallic fuel and from the oxide fuels used in India's nuclear power reactors. It is currently reprocessing power-reactor fuel from the Rajasthan reactors and from the Madras I reactor. IAEA inspectors are present when fuel from the former reactors is processed to ensure that plutonium from it is not diverted to military purposes. However, India does not permit IAEA oversight of the reprocessing of the Madras I fuel, and as discussed below, plutonium from this fuel is thus available for use in nuclear weapons.

13. Rick Atkinson, "3 Pakistanis Indicted on A-Arms Charges," *Washington Post,* July 17, 1984; Leslie Gelb, "Peking Said to Balk at Atom Pledges," *New York Times,* June 23, 1984.

14. The accounts were based on a U.S. intelligence briefing to a congressional committee. The report was originally carried by ABC News; "U.S. Sees India-Pakistan Rifts Not as Signals of Imminent War," Don Oberdorfer, *Washington Post,* September 15, 1984; Oberdorfer, "Pakistan Concerned About Attack on Atomic Plants," *Washington Post,* October 12, 1984. India was reportedly considering such a raid as early as 1982. Milton R. Benjamin, "India Said to Eye Raid on Pakistani A-Plants," *Washington Post,* December 20, 1982.

15. "Paper Assesses Pakistani Umbrella Proposal," *Indian Express,* October 15, 1984, reprinted in *FBIS/South Asia,* October 29, 1984,

p. E-3; William K. Stevens, "India Worried By U.S. Links to Pakistan," *New York Times,* October 21, 1984.

16. " 'People's Expectations Are Scary,' " *India Today,* February 15, 1985, p. 8. "Gandhi on Nuclear Weapons, Sri Lanka, Punjab," Delhi Domestic Service, 0240 GMT, January 31, 1985, reprinted in *FBIS/South Asia,* January 31, 1985, p. E-1; John Elliot, "We've Got Five Years," *Financial Times,* April 4, 1985; "Defense Ministry Security Report Raps Pakistan," Delhi Domestic Service, 1530 GMT April 16, 1985, reprinted in *FBIS/South Asia,* April 17, 1985, p. G-1; "India to Review Nuclear Policy, Gandhi Says," *Washington Post,* May 5, 1985; "Congress-I Party Meets in New Delhi," *FBIS/South Asia,* May 6, 1985.

17. "*Le Monde* Interview," *Le Monde,* June 4, 1985, translated in *FBIS/South Asia,* June 5, 1985, p. E-1, emphasis added. Gandhi's subsequent statements through the fall did not repeat this incautious assertion.

18. John Scali, "Good Morning America," American Broadcasting Company, July 11, 1985.

19. Rone Tempest, "India Starts Up New Reactor That Can Make Arms-Grade Plutonium," *Los Angeles Times,* August 9, 1985; "New Delhi Says It Can Make Plutonium From Indian Fuel," *New York Times,* August 9, 1985; Swaminathan S. Aiyar, "Dhruva Reactor an N-Bomb Spinner," *Indian Express,* August 10, 1985. Earlier official descriptions of the reactor, in contrast, had stressed its use for medical isotope production and engineering research. "New Reactor Capable of Producing Plutonium," AFP 0905 GMT, August 8, 1985, reprinted in *FBIS/South Asia,* August 9, 1985, p. E-1.

20. Mohamed Aftab, "Pakistan Concern Over India's Nuclear Move," *Financial Times,* August 8, 1985; "India Can Make 30 N-Bombs a Year," *Pakistan Times Overseas Weekly,* August 18, 1985; "Karachi Raps India's Nuclear Plans, 'Propaganda,' " Karachi Domestic Service, 1715 GMT, August 11, 1985, reprinted in *FBIS/South Asia,* August 13, 1985, p. F-1; "*The Muslim* on India's Nuclear Capabilities," August 13, 1985 (editorial) reprinted in *FBIS/South Asia,* August 21, 1985, p. F-1.

21. In an interview with *The Guardian* (London) on October 10th, Gandhi stated, "Pakistan has either already got the bomb or will get one in a matter of months and may not even need to test it." "Delhi Reports Gandhi Interview with UK Paper," *Delhi Domestic Service,* 0830 GMT, October 9, 1985, reprinted in *FBIS/South Asia,* October 10, 1985, p. E-1. The following day, Gandhi was reported as stating that "our information is that Pakistan is fairly advanced in its efforts to produce a nuclear bomb." "Gandhi on Pakistani Bomb; US; Other Topics," *Delhi Domestic Service,* 1330 GMT, October 11, 1985, reprinted in *FBIS/South Asia,* October 15, 1985, p. E-3.

22. Steven R. Weisman, "India Is Hopeful on Coming U.S. Visit," *New York Times,* September 15, 1985; "The South Asia Two-Step," *Newsweek* (European Edition), November 4, 1985, p. 42; "Papers Report U.S. Regional Nuclear Policy Developments, Armacost-Fortier Delhi Visit," *Times of India,* September 18, 1985, reprinted in *Joint Publication Research Service (JPRS)/Nuclear Development and Proliferation(TND),* November 25, 1985, p. 22.

23. "Papers Report U.S. Regional Nuclear Policy Developments; Commentary on Pakistan Nuclear Program, U.S. Role," Delhi General Overseas Service, 1340 GMT, September 20, 1985, reprinted in *FBIS/South Asia,* September 27, 1985, p. E-3. Pakistan's arms control initiatives are discussed below.

24. On July 22 a convention of India's leading right-wing opposition party (the Bharatiya Janata Party) adopted a resolution demanding that the Gandhi government "take immediate steps to develop our own nuclear bomb." Narenda Sharma, "BJP's Turn-about?" *Mainstream,* July 27, 1985, p. 34.

    On August 8, parliamentarians from the ruling Congress(I) Party and opposition parties called for a firm decision to be made on India's response to Pakistan's acquisition of nuclear weapons. "MP's 'Urged' Possession of Nuclear Weapons," Delhi Domestic Service, August 8, 1985, reprinted in *FBIS/South Asia,* August 8, 1985, p. E-2.

25. Don Oberdorfer, "Gandhi, Zia Said to Agree on Opening Nuclear Talks," *Washington Post,* October 24, 1985; Elaine Sciolino, "Gandhi and Zia Set Talks on Border and Other Issues," *New York Times,* October 24, 1985.

26. Elaine Sciolino, "Gandhi and Zia Set Talks;" "No Talks With Pak on N-Issue: P.M.," *Times of India,* October 28, 1985.

27. Kirit Bhaumik, "Rajiv Invites Zia to Inauguration of Breeder Reactor," *Times of India,* December 1, 1985; "Reportage on Fast Breeder Reactor at Kalpakkam, Dedication, Rajiv Speaks," *Statesman,* December 17, 1985, reprinted in *JPRS/TND,* February 7, 1986, p. 35.

    The fast breeder test reactor is fueled with a mixed plutonium-uranium carbide fuel. In principle, once it becomes fully operational, it will be able to produce slightly more plutonium than is required to fuel it, hence the term "breeder." However, probably for several years until the plant is fully operational, more Indian plutonium will be required to fuel it than will be produced. Thus, broadly speaking, for some time it will diminish India's overall nuclear-weapons capability.

    Plutonium to fuel the Fast Breeder Test Reactor was produced in the Canadian-supplied Cirus reactor. Under the terms of the agreement transferring the reactor to India, plutonium from the facility can be used only for "peaceful purposes." Use of the plutonium in the Fast Breeder Test Reactor appears to be consistent with this requirement. The question arises, however, whether plutonium that is subsequently produced in the Fast Breeder Test Reactor itself, *i.e.*, plutonium produced through the use of plutonium coming from the Cirus reactor, will also be subject to the peaceful-use guarantee.

If subsequent generations of plutonium produced in the Fast Breeder Test Reactor are not subject to the guarantee, India can use the Fast Breeder Test Reactor to "launder" Cirus-origin plutonium, placing plutonium restricted to peaceful uses into the test reactor, but removing plutonium that is not subject to this restriction and therefore available for nuclear weapons. (Analysis suggested to author by Mr. Gary Milhollin.)

28. "India, Pakistan Set Limited Accord," *Washington Post,* December 18, 1985; Steven R. Weisman, "Gandhi-Zia Talks Said to Bear Fruit," *New York Times,* December 18, 1985.

29. "Report on Kahuta Denied," Karachi Domestic Service, 1703 GMT, September 30, 1985, reprinted in *JPRS/TND,* October 21, 1985, p. 37; "Minister Talks About India's Alleged Attack Plans," Karachi Domestic Service, 1500 GMT, October 16, 1985, reprinted in *JPRS/TND,* November 4, 1985, p. 42; "Plans to Attack Pakistan Nuclear Complex Denied," Delhi Domestic Service, 1540 GMT, November 6, 1985, reprinted in *FBIS/South Asia,* November 6, 1985, p. E-1.

30. "India, Pakistan Set Limited Accord;" Steven R. Weisman, "Gandhi-Zia Talks;" Vyvyan Tenorio, "Gandhi the Troubleshooter," *Christian Science Monitor,* December 20, 1985.

31. In June 1984, former Prime Minister Indira Gandhi ordered an army attack on the Golden Temple in Amritsar to oust Sikh radicals, an action that ultimately led to her assassination in October by two of her Sikh bodyguards seeking to avenge what they considered a desecration of their holiest shrine. Since then, thousands have been killed in the anti-Sikh rioting that followed the assassination and by further Sikh terrorist acts.

32. In January 1986, for example, Sikh militants occupied the Golden Temple for a second time. They were again expelled in May. Vyvyan Tenorio, "Violence in Punjab Raises Concerns About Finding Lasting Peace," *Christian Science Monitor,* December 26, 1985; Steve R. Weisman, "Indian Policemen Raid Sikh Temple," *The New York Times,* May 1, 1986. On a related issue, Gandhi was repeatedly forced to postpone the adjustment of the Punjab's borders because of objections by the neighboring state of Haryana.

33. One additional source of tension between the two countries at this time was the comment by Pakistan Minister of State for Foreign Affairs, Zain Noorani, that Pakistan could not remain indifferent

to the plight of Muslims in India, who were being attacked in a series of communal riots. Relations were also strained by Pakistan's continued insistence on a plebiscite to determine the future of the former princely state of Jammu and Kashmir which, though made up predominantly of Muslims, became part of India in 1947 and has been the subject of two wars between India and Pakistan. In addition, former agreements between the two nations did not demarcate a portion of the border in the area of the Siachen Glacier, which has become the site of increasingly violent clashes between Indian and Pakistani troops. Vyvyan Tenorio, "Gandhi Under Fire As Political and Economic Troubles Deepen," *Christian Science Monitor,* February 26, 1986; John Eliot, "Pakistan's Relations with India Deteriorate," *Financial Times,* March 19, 1986; Vyvyan Tenorio, "Gandhi's Regional Initiatives Bog Down," *Christian Science Monitor,* March 21, 1986; Mohan Ram, "The Warmth Wears Off," *Far East Economic Review,* March 27, 1986; Matt Miller, "India and Pakistan Are So Busy Squabbling They Ignore Their Languishing Trade," *Wall Street Journal,* May 2, 1986.

"*Nawa-I-Waqt* On Postponement of Gandhi's Visit," *Nawa-I-Waqt,* February 11, 1986, translated in *FBIS/South Asia,* February 20, 1986. "Gandhi May Delay Pakistan Trip; Comments on Sri Lanka," AFP, 0633 GMT, March 12, 1986, reprinted in *FBIS/South Asia,* March 14, 1986.

These headlines stand in stark contrast to those of January: "Memorandum of Understanding Signed with India," Karachi Domestic Service, 0600 GMT, January 10, 1986, reprinted in *FBIS/South Asia,* January 10, 1986, p. G-1; "Pak-India Ties Improving," *The Muslim,* January 8, 1986; John Eliot and Mohammed Aftab, "Trade Between India and Pakistan to Double This Year," *Financial Times,* January 13, 1986.

34. Information on the status of nuclear agreement obtained during interviews with Indian and Pakistani officials, June 1986.

35. Indeed, some analysts have suggested that India's portrayal of Pakistan at this juncture as the party fomenting regional turmoil was a deliberate attempt to make it appear a less worthy aid recipient in U.S. eyes. According to this view, India was concerned about the supply of American arms to Pakistan, since previous U.S. military assistance to Islamabad had been used against India in the 1965 and 1971 Indo-Pakistani Wars. Mohan Ram, "The Warmth Wears Off."

36. Government of India, Ministry of Defence, *Annual Report* for 1985-1986.

37. "Gandhi Comments on Pakistani Nuclear Arms, Sri Lanka," Delhi Domestic Service, 1230 GMT, April 8, 1986, reprinted in *FBIS/South Asia,* April 9, 1986.

38. With 50 million Tamils living in India's southern state of Tamil

Nadu, India, in the past, has supported the Tamil minority in Sri Lanka by accepting thousands of refugees and by tolerating private training camps for Tamil insurgents in south India. Gandhi's attempt to shift India's role toward mediating the conflict between the Government of Sri Lanka, dominated by the mostly Buddhist Sinhalese, and the Tamil guerrilla groups has not been successful, as fighting in Sri Lanka has escalated and talks between the two factions have broken off. Steven R. Weisman, "India Role Grows in Sri Lanka Talks," *The New York Times,* July 15, 1985; Robert N. Kearney, "Tension and Conflict in Sri Lanka," *Current History,* March 1986, p. 109. Mohan Ram, "The Honeymoon Is Over," *Far East Economic Review,* March 13, 1986. Gandhi also faced a major challenge to his leadership within the Congress (I) Party during this period. Salamat Ali, "Gandhi Strikes Back," *Far East Economic Review,* May 8, 1986.

39. This information was provided by a senior Indian official during a June 1986 interview with the author in Bombay. See also, Vyvyan Tenorio, "India's Supply of Unsafeguarded Pu Grows As Reprocessing of MAPS Fuel Begins," *Nuclear Fuel,* August 11, 1986, p. 3.

40. Vyvyan Tenorio, "India's Supply of Unsafeguarded Pu."

41. It is sometimes asserted that plutonium produced in power reactors is less desirable for nuclear arms than that produced in reactors that have been specially designed for the manufacture of weapons-quality material. The critical factor, however, is not the kind of reactor used, but the length of time uranium fuel is irradiated in the reactor. The longer the period of irradiation, the greater the build-up of isotopes of plutonium considered to be less desirable for nuclear arms. American specialists believe that the uranium fuel from Madras I that has been reprocessed was fuel that was subjected to relatively short periods of irradiation during the initial start-up period of the reactor. The reprocessing of the fuel, it may be noted, is taking place at the PREFERE reprocessing plant located at Tarapur, near Bombay.

The Madras I reactor (and also its twin, the Madras II reactor) is fueled continuously, i.e. fresh fuel elements are inserted at one side of the reactor daily and an equivalent number of used elements are removed from the other side after residing within the reactor for a given time. To obtain weapons-quality plutonium, the reactor operator need only accelerate the rate of fueling of the reactor so as to ensure that the residence time of the uranium fuel elements involved is not so long as to permit the build-up of the undesirable isotopes of plutonium. Thus, while it is correct that power-reactor plutonium is normally less desirable for nuclear weapons, power reactors like Madras I and Madras II can be operated in a manner to avoid this problem.

42. Indo-Canadian nuclear relations during this period are discussed in Leonard S. Spector, *Nuclear Proliferation Today,* pp. 31-35.

43. The estimate in the text of the amount of Cirus-origin plutonium now available is based on the following assumptions. The Cirus reactor can produce about 9 kilograms of plutonium per year and began full operations in 1964. Assuming that all plutonium was extracted through 1974 when the Trombay plant was closed, some 90 kilograms would have been produced and separated. Fifteen kilograms were reportedly used in the 1974 explosion and twenty used to fuel the Purnima reactor in 1972. N. Seshagiri, *The Bomb!* (Delhi: Vikas, 1975), p. 6. Thereafter, assuming Cirus continued to operate at capacity, unreprocessed spent fuel would have accumulated for a number of years. In 1979, India began test runs at the Tarapur reprocessing plant—without IAEA safeguards — conducting three separate campaigns with research reactor fuel, presumably from Cirus. Government of India, Department of Atomic Energy, *Annual Report,* 1980-1981, pp. 4, 31; *Annual Report* 1981-1982, p. 26; *Annual Report* 1982-1983, pp. 6, 31. Presumably this cleared most of the Cirus spent-fuel backlog. Additional unsafeguarded reprocessing of Cirus spent fuel could then have been conducted at the refurbished Trombay plant, which was reopened after enlargement in late 1983 or early 1984. Thus most of the plutonium produced in Cirus from 1964 to 1985 could have been recovered. Subtracting the 35 kilograms used for the 1974 test and in the Purnima plant provides an estimate of about 150 kilograms of material, an amount that will be increasing at a rate of 9 kilograms annually. (The author wishes to thank David Albright for his assistance in developing this analysis.)

44. The plutonium from Madras I is being extracted at the PREFERE reprocessing plant located at Tarapur near Bombay. That facility also reprocesses safeguarded spent fuel from the Rajasthan reactors. International Atomic Energy Agency inspectors are present during the reprocessing of fuel from the latter plants and apply safeguards to the resulting plutonium. Reprocessing at the installation is performed in batches, however, and the IAEA inspectors are called in only when reprocessing of the Rajasthan material is taking place. Four batches or "campaigns" of Madras I spent fuel are believed to have taken place as of the summer of 1986. The size of each such campaign is not known, but given the size of the PREFERE plant and other data, American officials developed the estimate reported in the text.

45. Fifty kilograms of plutonium has been required to test and start the reactor, but perhaps as much as 150 kilograms will be needed in the next several years to operate it at full capacity. "India's FBTR Set for World First with Mixed Carbide Fuel," *Nuclear Europe* (June

1985):39; communications with informed U.S. officials. Apparently, India has decided to use plutonium from the Cirus reactor in the plant because the material is not subject to IAEA safeguards, thus allowing New Delhi to avoid the application of IAEA monitoring to the experimental breeder facility. Such monitoring would be required if safeguarded plutonium currently available from the Rajasthan reactors were used. Pearl Marshall, "India Bets on Carbide-Fueled Breeders to Power its 21st Century," *Nucleonics Week,* July 11, 1985, p. 7.

India has been experimenting with combined plutonium-uranium fuel ("mixed-oxide fuel") for possible use in the U.S.-supplied Tarapur power plants. These facilities now require low-enriched uranium for their fuel, instead of the natural uranium used in India's other nuclear power and research reactors. Mixing a small percentage of plutonium with natural uranium, however, could give India an indigenous substitute for the imported low- enriched uranium fuel now being used in Tarapur. Since the Tarapur reactors are subject to IAEA safeguards, however, India could use safeguarded plutonium, which it had extracted from the spent fuel of the Rajasthan reactor, for its mixed-oxide fuel experiments without incurring additional non-proliferation controls.

46. Vyvyan Tenorio, "India's Supply of Unsafeguarded Plutonium." The article quotes India's top nuclear official Raja Ramanna as stating that use of the experimental breeder will proceed slowly and that there is no lack of available plutonium to fuel it.

47. See note 10. See also *"Le Monde* Interview."

48. Interviews with the author, Spring 1986.

49. The 1974 test took place underground. To develop an aircraft-deliverable nuclear gravity bomb, India would need to design fuses to make sure the weapon would go off at the proper height. It would also need to refine the aerodynamics of the device so that its behavior in flight could be predicted, and it might also want to miniaturize the device to make it more easily carried. During its clandestine nuclear-weapons-development program in the 1950s and early 1960s, Sweden performed nuclear-weapons-design work of this kind. Leonard S. Spector, *The New Nuclear Nations,* pp. 65-79. See also section on Israel, below, discussing new information on that country's advances in the field of nuclear-weapon design.

50. "Shadow of an Indian H-Bomb." Israel is reported to have taken important steps in this direction. See discussion in Israel section.

51. "Inside Kahuta," *Foreign Report,* May 1, 1986, p. 2.

52. Ibid.

53. "Briefs; India X-Ray Request Rejected," Stockholm Domestic Service, 1000 GMT, November 1, 1985, reprinted in *FBIS/Western Europe,* November 8, 1985, p. P-3. "Third World Countries Buy

Swedish Nuclear Weapons Technology," *Ny Teknik,* May 2, 1986, translated in *JPRS/TND,* July 30, 1986, p. 1.

54. *"Le Monde* Interview."
55. Interviews with the author, Spring 1986. Don Oberdorfer, "Pakistani Spurns Soviets' Afghan Pullout Plan," *Washington Post,* July 18, 1986.
56. "Inside Kahuta," *Foreign Report,* May 1, 1986.
57. Don Oberdorfer, "Pakistani Spurns."
58. This analysis is based on interviews conducted by the author in New Delhi and Bombay, June 1986. *The Indian Express* has adopted the moderate position in its editorials; the stance is supported by a number of senior academics at the Center for Policy Research, New Delhi; and it appears to have support among the civilian officials interviewed by the author in the Prime Minister's Secretariat and in the Indian Foreign Ministry and Defense Ministry. See G.S. Bhargava, "Pakistan Problem," *Indian Express,* June 22, 1985; "Don't Go Nuclear," (editorial) *Indian Express,* May 15, 1985; A.G. Noorani, "Rajiv Gandhi's Nuclear Policy," *Indian Express,* July 7, 1985. See also references in next footnote.
59. This option is receiving increasing attention among Indian strategic analysts. P.R. Chari, "How to Prevent a Nuclear Arms Race Between India and Pakistan," in *Regional Cooperation and Development in South Asia,* Bhabani Sen Gupta, Ed., (New Delhi: South Asian Publishers, 1986) Vol. 1, p. 120 [Chari is now Joint Secretary (Air) in the Indian Defence Ministry]; Lt. General E.A. Vas, "India's Nuclear Options in the 1990's and Its Effect on India's Armed Forces," *Indian Defence Review,* January 1986, p. 11.
60. Both bilateral and multilateral economic aid could be jeopardized. Foreign Assistance Act of 1961, 22 U.S.C. 2429a(b)(2); Export-Import Bank Act, 12 U.S.C. 635(b)(4); International Financial Institutions Act 22 U.S.C. Sec. 262g(b)(3). It should be noted that India receives only a modest amount of U.S. economic aid. Thus the impact of this particular component of future economic sanctions would be limited.
61. The principal opposition party urging that India develop nuclear weapons is the Bharatiya Janata Party. India's principal defense think-tank, the Institute for Defence Studies and Analyses (IDSA) in New Delhi, is also generally supportive of this stand, of which IDSA's director, Dr. K. Subrahmanyam, is the foremost advocate. Two major English language dailies, *The Times of India* and *The Hindu,* have also taken a pro-bomb stand in their editorials. See K. Subrahmanyam, ed., *India and the Nuclear Challenge* (New Delhi: Lancer Int'l, 1986).
62. Jasit Singh, "The Challenge of Our Times," in *India and the Nuclear Challenge.*

63. See e.g., Don Oberdorfer, "Six Nonaligned Countries Offer to Monitor a Nuclear Test Ban," *Washington Post,* October 29, 1985; "Commentary on Nonaligned View of Nuclear Testing," Delhi Overseas Service, 1340 GMT, January 20, 1986, reprinted in *FBIS/South Asia,* January 23, 1986, p. E-2.

64. Regarding aircraft delivery systems, see chart at end of this section. See generally Leonard S. Spector, "Imported High-Performance Combat Aircraft: Will They Drop the Third World Bomb?," *Columbia Journal of International Affairs,* Summer 1986.

65. Mohan Ram, "Options In Outer Space," *Far East Economic Review,* September 11, 1986, p. 48. India's 1970 long-term research and develoment plan called for the manufacture, at an unspecified future time, of "advanced rocket systems capable of putting 1,200-kilogram payloads into synchronous orbits," launch vehicles that could be readily converted into medium-range nuclear missiles. (Roberta Wohlstetter, " 'The Buddha Smiles': Absent-Minded Peaceful Aid and the Indian Bomb," Monograph 3, Energy Research and Development Administration, Contract No. (49-1)-3747, April 30, 1977, p. 114.) In 1980 India launched its first satellite, weighing thirty kilograms, making it the sixth country to achieve that feat. Although the launch, which used a four-stage solid-fuel rocket, was described as a peaceful experiment, Satish Dhawhan, head of India's space research organization, declared that it demonstrated India's capability to develop nuclear missiles. "Any country which can place a satellite in orbit can develop an IRBM [intermediate-range ballistic missile]," he stated. Dhawhan also declared that liquid-fuel rockets capable of carrying up to 1300-pound payloads were planned. (Stuart Auerbach, "India Becomes 6th Country to Put Satellite in Orbit," *Washington Post,* July 19, 1980.) U.S. analysts noted, however, that India was still far from developing a militarily useful nuclear missile. According to one Western observer, the four-stage rocket is poorly suited to military uses since it is unreliable. (But see "India's Rocket Could Meet Military Ambitions," *New Scientist,* August 26, 1982, p. 555 [solid propellant in satellite rocket "ideally suited for missiles;" rocket could be converted to military uses "in six months".])

A major milestone now scheduled for 1986 is the launch of the Augmented Satellite Launch Vehicle, a 39-ton, 23-meter rocket with a 150-kilogram payload. See generally, "India Seeking Site for New Facility To Launch Multipurpose Satellites," *Aviation Week and Space Technology,* May 12, 1986, p. 58; Arthur F. Manfredi, et al., "Ballistic Missile Proliferation in the Third World," *Congressional Research Service Report* (Washington: Congressional Research Service, l986) pp. 11-13; David C. Morrison, "Regional Runners in the Space Race," *Pacific Defence Reporter* (February

1985) pp.16-18; Jerrold F. Elkin and Brian Fredericks, "India's Space Program: Accomplishments, Goals, Politico-Military Implications," *Journal Of South Asian And Middle Eastern Studies* (Spring 1984) pp.46-57.

66. K.V. Narain, "India Won't Sign NPT: PM," *The Hindu,* December 1, 1985.

67. H.K. Dua, "US Asked to Scrap Symington Waiver," *Indian Express,* November 2, 1985.

68. Bob Woodward and Don Oberdorfer, "Pakistani A-Project Upsets Superpowers," *Washington Post,* July 15, 1986.

69. See discussion of Nuclear Suppliers Group, Appendix F. In addition, the United States has sought to gain agreement on a global embargo of major new nuclear sales to India and Pakistan unless these states place all of their nuclear installations under IAEA safeguards.

70. Gary Milhollin, "Dateline New Delhi: India's Nuclear Cover-up," *Foreign Policy* (Fall 1986): p. 161.

Most of India's power reactors (including the unsafeguarded Madras I and II plants) and both of its large research reactors (Cirus and Dhruva) require heavy water to operate. Thus a shortage of the material could severely impinge on India's nuclear power program and on its nuclear-weapons potential.

The Milhollin study found that as of mid-1985 the amount of heavy water required to operate these facilities was considerably larger than the total amount of the material which India had produced indigenously and publicly acknowledged importing. The analysis therefore concluded that India had secretly imported between 100 and 200 metric tons of heavy water, a very substantial quantity. The study speculated that the material had come from China, since the only other suppliers (the United States, Soviet Union, and Canada) have rigid export controls and would have required India to declare the material and place it under IAEA safeguards; China, on the other hand is believed to have made a number of undeclared nuclear exports during the early 1980s, a practice that would have been consistent with an unannounced sale to India. Except for citing China's urgent need for foreign exchange, the study did not explain why China would provide India a commodity essential for its nuclear-weapons program, especially at a time of increasing nuclear tensions between India and China's regional ally, Pakistan.

Indian nuclear officials, while dismissing the study's conclusions, have not offered a detailed rebuttal of the study's assertion that the nation has had a substantial heavy water deficit requiring clandestine imports. Various official Indian reports on its nuclear program have, however, acknowledged the considerable difficul-

ties India has had in operating its indigenous heavy-water production plants. See e.g. comments of Dr. M.R. Srinivasan, Chairman,
Indian Nuclear Power Board, *Times of India,* August 31, 1986.
71. Woodward and Oberdorfer, "Pakistani A-Project."
72. Stuart Auerbach, "India to Get High-Tech U.S. Goods," *Washington Post,* October 10, 1985; Stuart Auerbach, "India Agrees to Buy
U.S. Computers," *Washington Post,* February 7, l986; "U.S. Permits GE to Sell F404 Engines to India," *Aviation Week and Space
Technology,* April 14, 1986.

Pakistan

1. Communications with informed U.S. sources; Bob Woodward and
Don Oberdorfer, "Pakistan A-Project Upsets Superpowers,"
Washington Post, July 15, 1986; Don Oberdorfer, "U.S., Pakistan
Puzzled Over Soviet Move," *Washington Post,* July 21, 1986; Bob
Woodward, "Pakistan Reported Near Atom-Arms Production,"
Washington Post, November 4, 1986; "Bhagat on Pakistan's Nucle-
ar Program, Sri Lanka," Delhi Domestic Service, 0830 GMT, De-
cember 5, 1985, reprinted in *Foreign Broadcast Information Service
(FBIS)/ South Asia,* December 5, 1985, p. E-1.
   For earlier assessments suggesting that Pakistan possesses the
ability to manufacture nuclear arms, see Russell Warren Howe,
"Pakistanis Are Closer to Producing Nuclear Weapon," *Washington Times,* July 26, 1984 (Pakistan secretly producing weapons-
grade uranium says senior administration official); Seymour M.
Hersh, "Pakistani in U.S. Sought to Ship A-Bomb Trigger," *New
York Times,* February 25, 1985 (American intelligence officials
confirm Pakistan now has enough plutonium and highly enriched
uranium to manufacture nuclear weapons); "Pakistan Goes Slow
on the Bomb," *Foreign Report,* March 21, 1985 (Pakistan has
enough highly enriched uranium for one bomb); Simon Henderson,
"Why Pakistan May Not Need to Test a Nuclear Device," *Financial
Times,* August 14, 1984 (unconfirmed report that China handed
over to Pakistan a quantity of highly enriched uranium); Rodney
Jones, interviewed on "ABC World News Tonight," (Pakistan can
build a bomb any time it wants); "Writer [P.K.S. Namboodiri]
speculates on State of Pakistani Nuclear Program," *Times of India,*
May 11, 1985, reprinted in *Joint Publication Research Service
(JPRS)/Nuclear Development and Proliferation (TND),* July 15,
1985 (Pakistan has produced weapons-grade uranium and must be
assumed to have developed other elements for the bomb.) In addition, during the first half of 1985, Indian Prime Minister Rajiv
Gandhi made repeated statements declaring that Pakistan either
has nuclear weapons or is very close. See *"Le Monde* Interview,"

Le Monde, June 4, 1985, translated in *Foreign Broadcast Information Service (FBIS)/Western Europe,* June 5, 1985, p. E-2.

At the time of these earlier statements, however, the consensus of U.S. administration and congressional sources was that Pakistan still lacked the necessary nuclear-weapons material. See also, John Scali, "Good Morning America," July 11, 1985 (U.S. experts say Pakistan still one or two years away from nuclear arming). Pakistan denies it is building nuclear weapons.

2. See e.g., "Pakistan Will Not Make Nuclear Bomb—Zia," *Pakistan Times Overseas Weekly,* August 4, 1985; "Zia Reiterates Peaceful Use of Nuclear Energy," Karachi Domestic Service, 1500 GMT, March 31, 1986, translated in *FBIS/South Asia,* April 1, 1986, p. F-1; "Junejo Says Nuclear Program for Peaceful Purposes," Karachi Domestic Service, 1500 GMT, February 10, 1986, translated in *FBIS/South Asia,* February 11, 1986, p. F-1; Gerald M. Boyd, "Pakistan Denies Developing Bomb," *New York Times,* July 17, 1986.

3. Regarding U.S. and Soviet views, see note 2. India's concerns over the Pakistani nuclear program are described in the preceding section on India. Canadian and West German officials also see Pakistan as moving to acquire nuclear arms. Interviews with author, Islamabad, June 1986.

4. Steven R. Weisman and Herbert Krosney, *The Islamic Bomb,* (New York: Times Books, 1981), pp. 43-46.

5. Leonard S. Spector, *Nuclear Proliferation Today* (New York: Vintage Books, 1984), pp. 74-81.

6. Ibid. Possible renewed Pakistani interest in reprocessing is discussed below.

7. Zulfikar Ali Bhutto, *If I Am Assassinated . . .* (New Delhi: Vikas, 1979), p. 138.

8. "Report of the Interministerial Working Party Responsible for Investigating the 'Khan Affair,' " Foreign Ministry of the Netherlands, October 1979 (mimeo, English version).

9. Ibid. Dr. Khan has repeatedly denied that he has engaged in any illegal conduct, pointing out that no criminal charges were ever brought against him for the activities alleged in the Dutch government report. See e.g., A.Q. Khan, "Letter to the Editor," *International Herald Tribune,* July 1, 1986. Dutch officials state Khan was not prosecuted because it was impossible to prove what information he may have taken. Interviews with the author, Amsterdam and The Hague, May 1985.

10. Testimony of Assistant Secretary of State Thomas R. Pickering, *Hearings on Nuclear Proliferation: The Situation in India and Pakistan,* U.S. Senate Subcommittee on Energy, Nuclear Proliferation, and Federal Services of the Committee on Governmental Affairs,

May 1, 1979 (Washington, D.C.: U.S. Government Printing Office, 1979) p. 10.

11. Leonard S. Spector, *The New Nuclear Nations* (New York: Vintage Books, 1985), pp. 22-41.

12. Ibid, p. 31. Migule was given a $10,000 fine and a six-month suspended sentence for the deed.

13. Spector, *Nuclear Proliferation Today,* pp. 91-93; Foreign Assistance Act of 1961, Section 670(b)(2) (1981). Under the 1981 amendment, U.S. aid would be cut off automatically, although the president could continue assistance for thirty days of "continuous session" (i.e. thirty days when both Houses of Congress were in session) if he determined that termination of assistance would be detrimental to the national security of the United States. After that time, however, aid would cease unless restored by majority vote of both houses of Congress.

   Under section 670 of the Foreign Assistance Act, prior to its amendment in 1981, Pakistan was ineligible for assistance because of its importation of enrichment equipment. In 1981, Congress removed this restriction for Pakistan for six years to permit the $3.2 billion in aid to be authorized.

14. Interviews with Indian officials, academics, and journalists, New Delhi and Bombay, June 1986.

15. "Scientist Affirms Pakistan Capable of Uranium Enrichment, Weapons Production," *Nawa-I-Waqt,* February 10, 1984, translated in *JPRS/TND,* March 5, 1984, p. 32.

16. "Zia Chastises Western Media for Accounts of Khan's Remarks on Weapons Capability," *Nuclear Fuel,* February 27, 1984, p. 11.

17. Senator Alan Cranston, "Nuclear Proliferation and U.S. National Security Interests," *Congressional Record,* June 21, 1984, p. S 7901. Indeed, in early April 1984, the Reagan administration publicly opposed legislation that would have cut off U.S. aid unless the president certified that such activities had ceased. Reagan aides claimed that they could not make the necessary certification and that the aid cutoff, which the legislation would trigger, was unacceptable, given the continuing Soviet presence in Afghanistan. See "United States Security Interests in South Asia: A Staff Report," prepared for the U.S. Senate Foreign Relations Committee (Washington: Government Printing Office, April 1984).

18. Seymour M. Hersh, "Pakistani in U.S. Sought to Ship A-Bomb Trigger," *New York Times,* February 25, 1985.

19. Ibid.

20. Leslie H. Gelb, "Pakistan Links Peril U.S.-China Nuclear Pact," *New York Times,* June 22, 1984; Leslie H. Gelb, "Peking Said to Balk at Nuclear Pledges," *New York Times,* June 23, 1984. Apparently, the United States had evidence as early as 1981 that Pakistan was working on nuclear-weapon triggers. Barry Schweid, "Turks

Ship U.S. A-Tools to Pakistan," *Washington Post*, June 28, 1981.
21. Gelb, "Pakistan Links Peril;" Gelb, "Peking Said to Balk." Chinese assistance apparently ended during late 1984 and the administration submitted the pact for congressional review in July 1985. The agreement entered into force in December of that year. "U.S. and China Exchange Notes," *Nuclear Engineering International*, February 1986, p. 4.
22. David Ignatius, "U.S. Pressuring Pakistan to Abandon Controversial Nuclear-Arms Program," *Wall Street Journal*, October 25, 1984; "Shadow of an Indian H-Bomb," *Foreign Report*, December 13, 1984; Don Oberdorfer, "Pakistani Spurns Soviets' Afghan Pullout Plan," *Washington Post*, July 18, 1986.
23. It is generally believed that reliable first-generation nuclear weapons can be built without testing. If Pakistan, as reported, had obtained a previously tested nuclear-weapon design from China, it would have added reason to have confidence in any untested devices it might build using this data. In the 1950s, Sweden is believed to have developed highly reliable nuclear-weapon designs without testing. See Leonard S. Spector, *The New Nuclear Nations*, pp. 65-77. See also discussion of this issue in the section on Israel, below.
24. "Shadow of an Indian H-Bomb."
25. "A Step Nearer the Bomb . . ." *Observer* (London), February 24, 1985. In the past, Pakistani officials have asserted that Pakistan developed its uranium-enrichment capability in order to produce fuel for the low-enriched-uranium/light-water reactors that it is planning to build, although few observers find the justification credible. Pakistan has yet to order its first power reactor and could not have one on line for at least a decade. Even with several reactors, moreover, domestic production of enriched uranium would be highly uneconomical. In addition, the nuclear-supplier nations have imposed a de facto embargo on nuclear-power-plant sales to Pakistan until it agrees to place all of its nuclear installations, including the Kahuta plant, under IAEA safeguards, making justification of Kahuta on nuclear energy grounds even less persuasive. Mary Ann Weaver, "Pakistan 'Over the Hump'—Zia Interview," *Christian Science Monitor*, March 1, 1985.
26. "Pakistan to Get U.S. Air-to-air Missiles," *Financial Times*, March 14, 1985; Dusko Doder, "Gorbachev Warns on Afghan War," *Washington Post*, March 16, 1985; Joanne Omang, "Lawmakers Exercise Foreign Aid Initiative," *Washington Post*, March 21, 1985.
27. Foreign Assistance Act of 1961, Section 620E(e), (1985).
28. John Scali, "Good Morning America," American Broadcasting Company, July 11, 1985. In nuclear weapons of the kind Pakistan is believed to be making, a hollow sphere of highly enriched uranium is surrounded by conventional high explosives, which is specially shaped so that when it is detonated, it crashes inward (or "im-

plodes") symetrically, instantaneously compressing the highly enriched uranium core to form a solid, explosive "critical mass" of the
material. Additional hollow spheres of metal, such as natural uranium and beryllium, are typically placed between the core and the
high explosives. These smash into the core during the implosion
and reflect neutrons back into it to improve the efficiency of the
nuclear reaction. The parts of the weapon apart from the core are
known as the "triggering package." Any nation developing nuclear
arms would want to be confident it had fully mastered the implosion technique before building or testing a nuclear device in order
to gain confidence that it would work as planned. India detonated
similar dummy nuclear weapons in preparing for its 1974 test. "Reports, Comment on Pakistan Nuclear Development," *Times of
India,* July 14, 1986, reprinted in *JPRS/TND,* September 23, 1985,
p. 63.

29. Simon Henderson, "U.S. Halts High-Tech Camera Sale to Pakistan," *Financial Times,* August 17, 1985. According to U.S. officials, the Pakistani Army had been attempting to purchase small
U.S.-made flash X-ray machines from the Hewlett-Packard company. Flash X-ray machines are used to take split-second photos
through solid materials of very rapid processes and are used in
nuclear-weapons development programs to observe dummy nuclear cores as they undergo compression following the detonation of a
nuclear-weapon triggering package.

   The machine being sought by Pakistan was too small to be used
for this purpose and was intended to calibrate artillery pieces.
Nevertheless U.S. officials became concerned because the training
to be provided for the small machine was the same as that needed to
operate a larger flash X-ray apparatus, such as that Pakistan had
obtained from Sweden in 1982. Washington had intervened in that
instance and persuaded Sweden not to supply the operating man-
uals and spare parts needed to run the larger machine, which was
apparently sitting idle. U.S. officials became suspicious of Pakistan's purpose when they learned that two individuals who were
scheduled to come to the United States for instruction were em-
ployees of the Pakistan Atomic Energy Commission. (It may be
noted that there are alternatives to using a flash X-ray machine for
verifying the effectiveness of nuclear-weapons triggering packages.
Thus Pakistan's lack of this equipment does not mean that it could
not have conducted the triggering package test revealed in July and
judged it a success.)

30. "Panel Supports Pakistan Becoming a Nuclear Power," *Nawa-I-
Waqt,* November 15, 1985, translated in *JPRS/TND,* February 7,
1986. In October, one press account had stated that despite dis-
claimers of any interest in nuclear weapons by top officials, "lower
down in the official echelons, different noises are made, claiming

that Pakistan can produce the Bomb at short notice, and also that it should do so in view of the threat posed by India's proven nuclear capacity. What is more unusual, in recent weeks, at least two politicians—who have so far not been known for any wild ideas—have avowedly reacted to the Indian propaganda [against the Pakistani nuclear program] by declaring that Pakistan should go ahead with production of an atom bomb." "Nuclear Ambitions in Subcontinent Denounced," *Viewpoint,* October 31, 1985, pp. 5-6, reprinted in *JPRS/TND,* December 13, 1985. (The article did not name the two officials to which it referred.)

31. Ibid. Ramay reiterated this open call for nuclear arming in March in addressing a group of lawyers. "Party Urges Nuclear Device," *Dawn,* March 4, 1986, reprinted in *JPRS/TND,* April 10, 1986, p. 37.

32. "Leader Urges 'Full Use of Nuclear Capabilities,' " *The Muslim,* December 2, 1985, reprinted in *JPRS/TND,* January 9, 1986, p. 70.

33. Dr. A. Q. Khan, "The Spread of Nuclear Weapons Among Nations: Militarization or Development," in Sadruddin Aga Khan, ed., *Nuclear War, Nuclear Proliferation and Their Consequences* (Oxford: Clarendon Press, 1986), p. 423.

34. Indeed, one October 1985 editorial in the admittedly nationalistic daily, *The Muslim,* declared that anyone opposed to the Kahuta enrichment plant "must be treated as a traitor to Pakistan," and that "the national consensus in favor of Kahuta is irrevocable and irreversible and no referendum is needed to ascertain it." "Government Stand on Kahuta Defended," *The Muslim,* October 2, 1985, reprinted in *JPRS/TND,* November 4, 1985, p. 48.

35. Communications with knowledgeable U.S. officials; U.S. Department of State, Press Guidance, "Pakistan: Post FY 1987 Assistance," March 24, 1986.

36. The Kahuta enrichment plant, for example, is said to be under military oversight, as is the Wah munitions factory, where nuclear-weapon components are said to be fabricated and tested. See, "Zia's Road to the Bomb," *Foreign Report,* August 26, 1982; Cranston, "Nuclear Proliferation and U.S. National Security Interests."

37. Oberdorfer, "Pakistani Spurns Soviets' Afghan Pullout Plan."

38. James Rupert, "Bhutto's Return Tests Pakistan's New Political Era," *Washington Post,* April 14, 1986. Miss Bhutto claims that the parliament elected in February 1985 lacks legitimacy because its members were not permitted to run as members of political parties. The PPP had boycotted the 1985 elections for this reason. President Zia has stressed the sizable turn-out in the February 1985 balloting as proof that the current parliament has widespread backing.

39. June Kronholz, "Bhutto Daughter Clouds Pakistani Politics," *Wall Street Journal,* June 23, 1986. After a series of often violent demonstrations in late July and early August 1986, Miss Bhutto and other

PPP leaders were arrested. They were held until early September, by which time anti-government rioting by their supporters had subsided.

40. "Benazir for Recognising Karmal and Abandoning Nuclear Research," *Pakistan Times Overseas Weekly*, April 20, 1986.

An additional question is whether Miss Bhutto would be able to wield power effectively after the PPP took power; some observers fear that although she is the political symbol of the PPP, once the current government were ousted, she might lose control of the party to other more radical elements. As discussed in Chapter 2, this scenario could be particularly dangerous if the new leadership inherited nuclear weapons or the capability to build them. There is also the risk that during a period of domestic upheaval brought on by PPP agitation, nuclear-weapons material or nuclear weapons (if either had been produced) might be seized by a faction that did not exercise national political power, a development with potentially grave consequences.

41. "*Indian Express* Interviews Benazir Bhutto," *Indian Express*, July 30, 1986, reprinted in *FBIS/South Asia*, August 14, 1986, p. F2.

42. Prime Minister Junejo, for example, during his July 1986 visit to Washington, reiterated Pakistan's offer to accept binding non-proliferation restraints, if India reciprocated. "Pakistan Says 'No' to Bomb, 'Yes' to Non-Proliferation," *Christian Science Monitor*, July 18, 1986.

43. The partial opening of the Pakistani political system has already contributed to the post-December 1985 downturn in overall Indo-Pakistan relations. Shortly after martial law was lifted, for example, Junejo, under parliamentary pressure, backed away from an understanding with India to expand trade that President Zia had endorsed in his December meeting with Rajiv Gandhi. It is not clear whether Pakistan is, in fact, aiding Sikh militants in India's Punjab state or fomenting unrest in Kashmir, as New Delhi charges. Accommodation on these and other sensitive bilateral issues seems less likely, however, now that the Zia-Junejo government could be accused of selling out Pakistani interests by Miss Bhutto or nationalistic elements in parliament. Interviews with Pakistani officials and journalists, Islamabad, June 1986.

44. This scenario has been suggested by Rodney W. Jones, a Washington-based specialist in Pakistani affairs.

45. Woodward and Oberdorfer, "Pakistan A-Project Upsets Superpowers"; Oberdorfer, "U.S., Pakistan Puzzled Over Soviet Move."

46. Ibid.

47. Charles Waterman, "Making Covert Aid to Rebels Overt," *Christian Science Monitor*, April 21, 1986; James Rupert, "Worried

Pakistan Limits U.S. Arms to Afghan Rebels," *Washington Post,* July 23, 1986.
48. Communications with current and former U.S. officials.
49. "Zia-ul Haq Discusses UN 242, Gulf War, Opposition," *Akhbar Al-Khalij,* March 13, 1986, translated in *FBIS/South Asia,* March 19, 1986 p. F-1. (These comments appear to refer to a symbolic sharing of uranium enrichment technology, rather than to the actual sharing of this technology or of nuclear weapons.)
50. "Nuclear Reactor To Be Built with Iraq, Pakistan," KUNA (Kuwait) 1002 GMT, December 9, 1985, reprinted in *FBIS/Near East & Africa,* December 9, 1986, p. D-1.
51. "Pakistan and China Signed a Comprehensive Agreement for Cooperation," *Nucleonics Week,* September 25, 1986, p. 3; Simon Henderson, "China May Help Build Pakistan's N-Bomb," *Financial Times,* September 29, 1986 (A.Q. Khan in interview says pact covers "all nuclear activities.")
52. Foreign Assistance Act of 1961 Section 620E(e) (1985). Congress, however, did not require a certification that all Pakistani efforts to develop nuclear arms had ceased, a provision that a number of lawmakers had sought.

   A further amendment to the Foreign Assistance Act during the summer of 1985 provides for the termination of U.S. assistance to any nation that violates U.S. export laws in order to obtain equipment that the president determines would materially assist it to make nuclear weapons. Foreign Assistance Act of 1961, Section 670, (1985). The provision permits the president to waive this requirement if he determines that the termination of assistance would be seriously prejudicial to U.S. non-proliferation objectives or would otherwise jeopardize the common defense and security.
53. Egmont Koch and Simon Henderson, "Auf dunken Wegen zur Atommacht" ("Secret Routes to the Bomb"), *Der Stern,* April 30, 1986, p. 52.
54. "Report of the Interministerial Working Party Responsible for Investigating the 'Khan Affair,' " Foreign Ministry of the Netherlands. Khan is thought to have had obtained classified information on this design in the course of his work in 1975 for the Dutch enrichment program at Almelo, where the German design was being vetted.
55. See Appendix F describing the activities and regulations of the Nuclear Suppliers Group.
56. According to a short note dated August 20, which Koch and Henderson apparently obtained in the course of their investigation, the shipping documents and the invoice, numbered 12240 in the amount of DM 1,373.78 (about $400), were sent to embassy counselor Azmat Ullah, "per telephone conversation with Mr. Shaw"— an alias of Inam Shah.

57. "Pakistan Persists," *Foreign Report,* March 27, 1986.
58. See note 52.
59. This was not a unanimous view, however. In December 1985, for example, Indian External Affairs Minister S. Bhagat stated that there were indications that Pakistan might have accumulated weapons-grade uranium for a few devices although he acknowledged that there was no certainty on the issue. "Bhagat on Pakistan's Nuclear Program, Sri Lanka," Delhi Domestic Service, 0830 GMT, December 5, 1985, reprinted in *FBIS/South Asia,* December 5, 1985, p. E-1. See also references in the second paragraph of note 1 (listing those who in mid-1985 thought Pakistan had all it needed for nuclear weapons).
60. Steven R. Weisman, "India Is Hopeful on Coming U.S. Visit," *New York Times,* September 15, 1985; "The South Asia Two-Step," *Newsweek* (European Edition), November 4, 1985, p. 42; "Papers Report U.S. Regional Nuclear Policy Developments, Armacost-Fortier Delhi Visit," *Times of India,* September 18, 1985, reprinted in *Joint Publication Research Service (JPRS)/Nuclear Development and Proliferation(TND),* November 25, 1985, p. 22.

  The October 21 accusation by Indian Army Chief of Staff General A. S. Vaidya that Pakistan was about to conduct its first nuclear test in China briefly called this judgment into doubt. "Haidar Editorial," *Haidar,* October 21, 1985, translated in *FBIS/South Asia,* October 28, 1985, p. F-2; "Paper on Pakistan's Plan for Nuclear Testing in PRC," *Hindustan Times,* October 21, 1985, reprinted in *FBIS/South Asia,* November 1, 1985. The charge was quickly echoed in the Soviet press. "Pakistan Said Ready to Test Nuclear Device in PRC," Tass, 1865 GMT, October 30, 1985, reprinted in *JPRS/TND,* November 25, 1985, p. 43; "Radio Cites Pravda on Pakistani Nuclear Test," Delhi Overseas Service, 1359 GMT, October 22, 1985, reprinted in *FBIS/South Asia,* October 23, 1985, p. E1.

  The timing of the charges, however, was suspicious since they appeared to coincide with a U.S. congressional debate over passage of a pending nuclear trade pact with China. See, e.g., Bernard Gwertzman, "Cranston Assails U.S.-China Accord," *New York Times,* October 22, 1985. In support of the agreement, the Reagan administration was pointing out that China had ceased all of its prior assistance to the Pakistani nuclear program. The charges of a Pakistani nuclear test in China—which faded from the scene in less than a week—appeared to be an attempt to belie the administration's claims that Chinese conduct had improved.

  The October 1985 accusation echoed earlier charges that such a test might have actually occurred on May 16, 1983, the date of an unexpected visit to China by Pakistani Foreign Minister Yaqub

Khan, when an ambiguous seismic event near the Chinese test site was detected in the West. The fact that the 1985 charges spoke of a prospective first Pakistani test seemed to throw cold water on these earlier allegations. See "Information Pertaining to Possible Chinese Test of a Pakistani Nuclear Device," Nuclear Control Institute, September 17, 1985.

61. Christer Larsson and Jan Melin, "Third World Countries Buy Swedish Nuclear Weapons Technology," *Ny Teknik,* May 2, 1986, p. 1, translated in *JPRS/TND,* July 30, 1986, p. 1. See note 29.
62. "Pakistan Persists," *Foreign Reports,* March 27, 1986.
63. Oberdorfer, "Pakistani Spurns Soviets' Afghan Pullout Plan," *Washington Post,* July 18, 1986; Simon Henderson, "Netherlands Drops Proceedings Against Nuclear Scientist," *Financial Times,* July 16, 1986.
64. Woodward and Oberdorfer, "Pakistan A-Project Upsets Superpowers;" Boyd, "Pakistan Denies Developing Bomb," *New York Times,* July 17, 1986; Don Oberdorfer, "Nuclear Issue Clouds Junejo Visit," Washington Post, July 17, 1986; communications with knowledgeable U.S. officials; Bob Woodward, "Pakistan Reported Near Atom Arms Production."
65. Under the new aid package, the proportion of grants to loans will be increased and the loans will be offered at concessional rates, rather than the commercial rates of the 1981 package.
66. Arthur F. Manfredi, et al., "Ballistic Missile Proliferation Potential in the Third World," (Washington: Congressional Research Service, l986), p. CRS-15.
67. "Government Stand on Kahuta Defended," *Muslim,* October 2, 1985, reprinted in *JPRS/TND,* November 4, 1985, p. 48.
68. It may be recalled that immediately prior to the U.S. air raid against Libya in April l986, the Soviets withdrew their naval vessels from the area, in effect signaling that such an attack would not lead to a major East-West confrontation. Nor did the Soviets retaliate when Israel destroyed their ally Iraq's large research reactor outside Baghdad in 1981.

Chapter IV:
The Middle East – Introduction

1. "Revealed: The Secrets of Israel's Nuclear Arsenal," *Sunday Times* (London), October 5, 1986.
2. "War of Liberation," *New York Review of Books,* November 22, 1984, p. 36; Neil Roland, "Soviets Reportedly Offer Nuclear Help to Syria," UPI wire story, November 28, 1985, citing an interview with Tlas in *Al-Ittihad,* October 4, 1985, translated in *Foreign Broadcast Information Service (FBIS)/Middle East and Africa,* October 7, 1985.
3. Neil Roland, "Soviets Reportedly Offer Nuclear Help"; Ze'ev Schiff, "Dealing With Syria," *Foreign Policy* (Summer 1984):94. See also "Defense Minister Interview on Parity With Israel," Al-Majallah, December 11-17, 1985, translated in *FBIS/Middle East and Africa,* December 12, 1985, p. H-1 (Tlas states, "We are capable of acquiring a nuclear option in order to achieve strategic balance with the Zionist enemy"); "USSR Reportedly To Train Syrians on Nuclear Weapons," KUNA 1315 GMT, October 12, 1985, translated in *Joint Publication Research Service (JPRS)/Nuclear Development and Proliferation (TND),* November 25, 1985, p. 66 (citing a Lebanese magazine, *Al-Nahar Al-Arabi Wa Al-Dawli);* "Secret Nuclear Weapons Talks with USSR Reported," Salalah (Syrian) Domestic Service, 1600 GMT, March 21, 1986, translated in *FBIS/ Middle East and Africa,* March 25, 1986, p. H-1.
4. Walter Pincus, "Nuclear Diplomacy Losing Its Edge," *Washington Post,* July 26, 1985; "Revealed: The Secrets of Israel's Nuclear Arsenal," *Sunday Times* (claiming to have new confirmation of this story from a U.S. source).
5. "Syria, Arab Countries Acquiring Chemical Weapons," Jerusalem Domestic Service, 1000 GMT, August 18, 1986, reprinted in *FBIS/ Middle East and Africa,* August 19, 1986, p. I-6.
6. Elaine Sciolino, "Iraq Cited on Chemical Weapons," *New York Times,* March 15, 1986; "Reportage on Combat Operations in War with Iraq; Iraq Deploys Chemical Weapons," Tehran Radio 1930 GMT, April 3, 1986, reprinted in *FBIS/Middle East and Africa,* April 4, 1986, p. I-3.
7. Richard L. Holman, "Iran Again Bombs Baghdad as Diplomatic Efforts Stall," *Washington Post,* October 1, 1980; William Claiborne, "Israeli Planes Bomb Major Iraqi Nuclear Facility," *Washington Post,* June 9, 1981; "Iranian Site Is Attacked By Iraqis," *New York Times,* February 14, 1985; "Iran," *Nucleonics Week,* March 7, 1985, p. 13.

   In the wake of the Osiraq raid, Israel had announced the "Begin doctrine"—that Israel would not tolerate any enemy, Arab or non-Arab, acquiring nuclear weapons or the ability to produce them, a not-so-veiled threat to attack additional plants, possibly including Pakistan's sensitive nuclear installations. Israel has gradually moderated this stance, declaring in 1985 that it "will not attack or threaten to attack any nuclear facility devoted to peaceful purposes either in the Middle East or anywhere else." See Paul F. Power, "The Baghdad Raid: Retrospect and Prospect," *Third World Quarterly* (July 1986):845; Leonard S. Spector, *The New Nuclear Nations* (New York: Vintage Books, 1985), p. 146 (quoting letter of Israeli representative circulated to IAEA members at 1985 IAEA General Conference, September 23, 1985).

8. Allister Sparks, "Gadhafi Denounces Nonaligned; Vows to Lead Anti-Imperialist Army," *Washington Post,* September 5, 1986. A little more than a year earlier, it may be noted, a Libyan official announced that Tripoli had approached Iraq to join in a raid against Israel's Dimona nuclear complex, but Iraq, the official said, had declined. "Iraq Said to Decline Libyan Scheme," *Washington Post,* July 11, 1985.

Israel

1. Leonard S. Spector, *Nuclear Proliferation Today* (New York: Vintage Books, 1984), p. 117 ff.; Peter Pry, *Israel's Nuclear Arsenal* (Boulder, Colo: Westview, 1984), collecting and analyzing various published sources; Secretary General of the United Nations, *Israeli Nuclear Armament,* U.N. General Assembly document A/36/431, 36th Session, September 18, 1981, p. 20 (estimate in text based in part on extrapolation of analyses in report).

    For the view that Israel's nuclear arsenal is larger and more diverse than previously believed, see, "Revealed: The Secrets of Israel's Nuclear Arsenal," *Sunday Times* (London), October 5, 1986; "Israel Said to Deploy Jericho Missile," *Aerospace Daily,* May 1, 1985; "Nuclear Efforts of Israel, Pakistan Prompt Meeting of U.S. Group," *Aerospace Daily,* May 17, 1985; "America's Nuclear Pledge to Israel," *Foreign Report,* January 21, 1981. See also, Pierre Péan, *Les Deux Bombes* (Paris: Fayard, 1982) (analysis of capability of Dimona reactor implies a larger arsenal).

2. Elaine Sciolino, "Documents Detail Israeli Missile Deal with the Shah," *New York Times,* April 1, 1986.

3. Based on communication with informed U.S. official and evidence discussed in text, below.

4. Simha Flapan, "Nuclear Power in the Middle East (Part I)," *New Outlook,* July 1974, p. 51; "Peres Attacks Report on Israeli A-Arms," *New York Times,* October 7, 1986.

5. See sources in note 1 and references therein. The conclusion that Israel possesses nuclear weapons has been supported by various CIA analyses of the Israeli program that have come to light over the

years, by statements of French officials with close ties to the program, and by veiled statements by Israeli officials, themselves. Ibid.

Nuclear testing is not thought to be essential for the production of early generation atomic bombs, permitting Israel to develop a reliable deterrent without this step—and indeed, judging from information discussed in the text below, the development of high-confidence, advanced designs may also be possible without testing, at least for a country such as Israel, with many highly qualified nuclear scientists and the benefits of previous associations with several nuclear-weapon states. It has been alleged that France shared data from its first nuclear test with Israel. Steve Weissman and Herbert Krosney, *The Islamic Bomb* (New York: Times Books, 1981), p. 113. On September 22, 1979, a U.S. VELA satellite detected a signal while over the South Atlantic that had the appearance of a nuclear test. A panel of experts convened by the White House Office of Science and Technology Policy determined that the signal "probably" was not a test, but other government bodies disputed the conclusion and questions over the incident have never been fully laid to rest. Some have suggested that if the incident was a test, it may have been conducted by Israel. If the signal was a nuclear test, it would have been from a very small, two to four kiloton explosion of the type that might be used to trigger a fusion bomb. As noted below, there is now evidence that Israel mya have begun building weapons of this type in the early 1980s.

Uranium fuel for Dimona is thought to have been obtained from various foreign sources, some Israeli domestic production, and at least one illicit smuggling operation, known as the Plumbat affair, involving the 1968 diversion of 200 tons of uranium concentrate while in transit on the Mediterranean between Antwerp and Genoa.(The Plumbat affair was brought to public attention in 1977 by Paul Leventhal, a former Senate staffer then working on a book on nuclear proliferation.)

Former Argentine nuclear officials recently acknowledged that in 1960 the government of Arturo Frondizi supplied one metric ton (2200 pounds) of uranium concentrate to Israel for the Dimona reactor, then under construction. (The amount would represent only a portion of the reactor's annual fueling requirements). Richard Kessler, "Argentine Officials Deny Rumors of [Current] Nuclear Trade with Israel," *Nucleonics Week*, May 29, 1986, p. 6. According to a former U.S. official, however, Argentina subsequently acknowledged export of about fifteen tons of uranium to Israel. (Communication with author, fall 1986).

6. The U.S. Atomic Energy Commission determined the material was missing from the plant in 1966 and, according to former senior CIA official, Carl Duckett, by 1968 the agency had concluded that the

"most likely case" was that the "NUMEC material had been diverted and had been used by the Israelis in fabricating weapons." Transcript of ABC News "Closeup," April 27, 1981, "Near Armageddon: The Spread of Nuclear Weapons in the Middle East," pp.
13-14.

Duckett has stated that the CIA finding was a closely guarded
secret within the Johnson administration and, although his statements have been widely accepted, no other official involved at the
time has publicly confirmed his analysis. In a June 1985 interview,
however, Spurgeon Keeny, a former Johnson administration White
House staff member with responsibility for nuclear issues, who subsequently served as Deputy Director of the Arms Control and Disarmament Agency, stated that key Johnson White House security
advisers appeared to share the assessment that a diversion had occurred. See also Lori Santos, "Government Reveals Top Secret,"
United Press International (wire service story), August 18, 1985,
(AM cycle).

7. Hedrick Smith, "U.S. Assumes the Israelis Have A-Bomb or Its
Parts," *New York Times,* July 18, 1970; Steve Weissman and Herbert Krosney, *The Islamic Bomb,* p.118.
8. "America's Nuclear Pledge to Israel."
9. "Israel Said to Deploy Jericho Missile," *Aerospace Daily;* "Nuclear
Efforts of Israel, Pakistan Prompt Meeting of U.S. Group," *Aerospace Daily.*
10. NBC "Nightly News," July 30, 1985. In a private interview, Sale
stated that his reports had been verified by a number of official and
private sources in the United States who were familiar with Israeli
military programs. Interview with author, May-June 1985.
11. "Revealed: The Secrets of Israel's Nuclear Arsenal," *Sunday
Times.*
12. Responding to how he circumvented Israeli security, Vanunu, in
essence, claimed that security at the plant's perimeter was relatively
lax and that, as a control-room technician, he had the run of the
building—a practice that is relatively common, according to British
control room technicians cited by the *Times,* since such operators
need to be able to follow up irregularities showing up on their
monitors.

Nonetheless, some questions remain about Vanunu—among
others, his motives for revealing some of Israel's most sensitive secrets and how, in Australia, he met with a Colombian reporter who
hawked his story in Europe and first made contact with the *Times*
investigative team that wrote the report. See discussion in text
below.
13. "A Mossad Caper," *Newsweek,* October 27, 1986 (Vanunu lured to
yacht in Mediterranean and arrested in international waters);
Thomas L. Friedman, "Israel Said to Abduct Seller of A-Bomb

Secrets," *New York Times,* October 27, 1986.

14. The existence of this secret underground plant may help explain Israeli concerns over Iraq's Tuwaitha research center near Baghdad which housed the Osiraq reactor. Israeli Premier Menachem Begin claimed shortly after Israeli jets destroyed the Osiraq reactor there, that the facility housed a secret underground chamber for producing nuclear weapons.

15. Former French President Charles de Gaulle states in his memoirs that French assistance for the Dimona reprocessing plant ceased in 1960, but French nuclear aides have disclosed that private French companies continued to work on the project while the government turned a blind eye. Charles de Gaulle, *Memoirs of Hope, Renewal and Endeavor* (New York: Simon and Schuster, 1971), p. 266; Peter Pringle and James Spigelman, *The Nuclear Barons* (New York: Holt Rinehart and Winston, 1981) p. 296; Pierre Péan, *Les Deux Bombes,* chapters VII and VIII; "France Admits It Gave Israel A-Bomb," *Sunday Times,* October 12, 1986.

16. Pierre Péan, *Les Deux Bombes,* p. 120.

17. Leonard S. Spector, *Nuclear Proliferation Today* (New York: Vintage Books, 1984), pp. 120-125.

    Péan, in *Les Deux Bombes,* states that Israeli technicians also disguised the operation of the Dimona reactor itself from the American inspectors. To give the impression that it was operating at low power, rather than at the higher levels needed to produce plutonium, a dummy control room was created, he states, and data fed into it from simulators to complete the ruse. Pierre Péan, *Les Deux Bombes,* p. 104-105.

    Statement regarding Johnson administration suspicions of Israeli activities based on interviews with former State Department and Atomic Energy Commission officials, spring and summer 1985.

18. The *Sunday Times* reporters claim that the six-fold enlargement would have been possible (including a greatly augmented cooling system) without altering the exterior of the plant, but some British officials with whom they discussed Vanunu's evidence were skeptical.

19. Péan states that as originally built the reactor's cooling system was three times larger than normal and implies that from the outset it was operated at the higher level. Pierre Péan, *Les Deux Bombes,* p. 96. "The Middle East's Nuclear Arms Race," *Foreign Report,* August 13, 1980 (reactor recently expanded to 70 megawatts).

20. See note 5.

21. Vanunu was not involved in the weapons fabrication process itself and did not claim to have direct knowledge of the mix of nuclear weapons in the Israeli arsenal, nor of the nature of the weapons it contained. It is therefore possible that the fusion components he photographed are experimental weapons and that simple atomic

arms of more certain reliability form the backbone of the Israeli nuclear arsenal.

22. Thomas L. Friedman, "Israel and Syria Believed to Face Risk of Conflict," May 19, 1986; Leslie H. Gelb, "Israelis Say Syria Might Seek War," *New York Times,* July 20, 1986; "Syria, Arab Countries Acquiring Chemical Weapons," Jerusalem Domestic Service, 1000 GMT, August 18, 1986, reprinted in *FBIS/Middle East and Africa,* August 19, 1986, p. I-6.

23. See Mary Curtius, "Peres: Peace Process Will Top Summit Agenda," *Christian Science Monitor,* September 2, 1986.

24. Elaine Sciolino, "Documents Detail Israeli Missile Deal with the Shah."

25. Leonard S. Spector, *The New Nuclear Nations* (New York: Vintage Books, 1985), pp. 65-77.

26. Elaine Sciolino, "Documents Detail Israeli Missile Deal."

27. Ibid.

28. Ibid.

29. Ibid. Under the joint program, Iran made a down payment on the missiles it was going to purchase of $260 million in oil, in 1978. A team of Iranian specialists then began work on the site of the missile assembly plant near Sirjan, in central Iran. A test range was to be built at Rafsanjan. Iranian participation ended with the fall of the Shah in January 1979.

30. "Israel Said to Deploy Jericho Missile," *Aerospace Daily;* "Nuclear Efforts of Israel, Pakistan Prompt Meeting of U.S. Group," *Aerospace Daily.*

31. Several additional developments deserve brief mention. In December 1985, the Soviet Union appears to have briefly accused Israel of conducting an underground nuclear test in the Negev Desert, but the charge was not repeated and appears to have had no substance. Ihsan H. Hijazi, "Moscow Backs Syria in Missile Feud with Israel," *New York Times,* December 26, 1985; "SANA Quotes NOVOSTI in Israeli Nuclear Test," SANA 1300 GMT December 26, 1985, translated in *FBIS/Middle East and Africa,* December 27, 1985, p. H-1.

On a separate matter, Israel's negotiations with France for the possible purchase of a nuclear power reactor reached an impasse in 1986 because of concerns on the part of French business interests of adverse Arab reactions. Neal Sandler, "Negotiations Between Israel and France Over a Possible Reactor Sale . . ." *Nucleonics Week,* June 12, 1986, p. 6. Despite these setbacks, the Israeli Atomic Energy Commission has chosen a proposed site for a nuclear power plant at Shivta, in the Negev. "Israel Site Selected," *Nuclear Engineering International,* March 1986, p. 12.

At the October 1986 International Atomic Energy Agency General Conference, Israel was once again the subject of an Arab-sponsored condemnatory resolution, but the measure was withdrawn when it became clear that it would not obtain the two-thirds vote needed to carry. The United States had threatened to withdraw from the IAEA if anti-Israel sanctions were adopted, a stance it has taken since 1982 when Israel's credentials to the IAEA General Conference were rejected. The London *Sunday Times* article, it may be noted, appeared two days after the Arab resolution was withdrawn at the 1986 IAEA General Conference.

Libya

1. The story has been reported by Mohamed Heikel, confidant of then Egyptian President Gamal Abdel Nasser, whose assistance Khadafi sought in approaching China. Mohamed Heikel, *The Road to Ramadan* (New York: Quadrangle/The New York Times Book Co., 1975), pp. 76-77. The story was later confirmed by Mohammed al-Mougariaf, the former Libyan ambassador to India. ABC "News Closeup," Monday, April 27, 1981, "Near Armageddon: The Spread of Nuclear Weapons in the middle East," Transcript p. 43. The story is widely accepted by U.S. non-proliferation officials.
2. Steve Weissman and Herbert Krosney, *The Islamic Bomb* (New York: Times Books, 1981), p. 60. Among other elements of the arrangement, according to knowledgeable Pakistani and Libyan officials interviewed by Western journalists, Libya specifically requested training in the operation of hot cells, the radiologically shielded units in which plutonium can be extracted from spent reactor fuel.
3. Weissman and Krosney, *The Islamic Bomb,* pp. 211-212; "Niger Says It Sold Uranium to Libya, Use for Nuclear Weaponry Feared," *Washington Star,* April 14, 1981. Niger has agreed to make future yellowcake sales exclusively to Non-Proliferation Treaty parties with valid safeguards agreements. Pakistan has not ratified the Non-Proliferation Treaty and is under no similar obligation, although most yellowcake suppliers (including Niger) require exports to be placed on IAEA inventories in recipient states. Niger reportedly believed this standard was satisfied in the case of Libya between 1978 and 1980 because the country was a Non-Proliferation Treaty party.
4. U.S. Congress, Office of Technology Assessment, *Technology Transfer to the middle East* (Washington, D.C.: U.S. Government Printing Office, 1985), pp. 385-386. This analysis states that Libya is known to have purchased 788 tons of uranium from Niger and may have purchased about 2,000 tons. See also, "Uranium Exports for First Six Months Given," Agence France Press, 0859 GMT, August 27, 1981, translated in *Joint Publication Research Service (JPRS)/Nuclear Development and Proliferation (TND),* September

24, 1981, p. 17, giving slightly lower figures.

5. "Libya Presses India on Nuclear Technology," *Nuclear Engineering International* (November 1979): 7.

6. Ibid. See also "Libya Charged with Using Oil to Obtain Nuclear Technology," *Business Times* (Kuala Lumpur), August 30, 1979, (quoting from stories in the *Times of India* and the *Hindu*), translated in *JPRS/TND*, October 31, 1979, p. 7.

7. "Indo-Libyan Nuclear Accord," *:he Telegraph* (Calcutta), August 8, 1984, reprinted in *JPRS/TND*, September 24, 1984, p. 69. India's stance provides further evidence of the caution exhibited by "second tier" nuclear-supplier countries in sharing nuclear technology.

8. Congressional Research Service, *Analysis of Six Issues About Nuclear Capabilities of India, Iraq, Libya and Pakistan,* report prepared for the Subcommittee on Arms Control, Oceans, International Operations, and Environment of the Senate Foreign Relations Committee, 1982, p. 11; Joseph V.R. Micallef, "A Nuclear Bomb for Libya?" *Bulletin of the Atomic Scientists* (August-September 1981): 14.

9. Senate Foreign Relations Committee, *Hearings on the Israeli Air Strike*, June 18, 19, and 25, 1981, 97th Cong., 1st Sess. (Washington, D.C.: U.S. Government Printing Office, 1981) p. 50; Claudia Wright, "Libya's Nuclear Program," *The middle East* (February 1982): 47.

10. In 1976, Libya also signed a nuclear cooperation agreement with France for the purchase of a 600-megawatt nuclear power plant, but France later barred the deal because of concerns over Libyan-Pakistani cooperation. "France Is To Build Libyan Atomic Plant," *New York Times*, March 23, 1976; Office of Technology Assessment, *Technology Transfer to the middle East*, p. 385. Thomas O'Toole, "Libya Said to Buy Soviet A-Power Plant," *Washington Post*, December 12, 1977.

11. "Envoy Says Soviets May Build Nuclear Plant in Egypt," Associated Press, May 10, 1986, AM cycle; "Libya Abandons Plans for First Unit," *Nuclear Engineering International,* April 1986, p. 6; "On-Again, Off-Again Libyan Nuclear Power Plant Surfaced Once More," *Nucleonics Week*, March 31, 1983, p. 11; Ann MacLachlan, "Libyans Are Seeking Broad International Cooperation in Nuclear Area," *Nucleonics Week,* September 27, 1984, p. 1.

12. "U.S. Bans Libyans from Some Studies," *Washington Post*, March 11, 1983.

13. Guy Duplat, "Possible Breakthrough in Belgian Nuclear Cooperation with Arab Countries," *Le Soir,* August 8, 1981, translated in *JPRS/TND,* September 8, 1981, p. 2; "US Presses Belgians to Cut Libya Ties," *Nuclear Fuel,* April 26, 1982, p.11.

14. Some U.S. officials feared that Libya could use uranium metal as

fuel in a crude natural-uranium/graphite reactor to produce plutonium. A crude reprocessing plant for extracting the plutonium
might be within the range of Libyan capabilities, especially with
assistance from Pakistan or, possibly, Argentina.

Uranium hexafluoride might serve as feedstock if Libya were to
build an enrichment plant under its supposed arrangement with Pakistan, or the material could be sent to Pakistan for enrichment to
weapons grade.

The Belgonucleaire facility might not have been subject to
IAEA inspections despite Libya's adherence to the Non-Proliferation Treaty, since IAEA rules may exempt such plants. The issue
has, apparently, never been decided by the Agency.

15. "Belgium, Libya Reportedly Ready to Sign Nuclear Pact," *Wall
    Street Journal,* May 18, 1984; Ann MacLachlan, "Belgians Fail To
    Get Guarantees From Neighbors on Libyan Aid," *Nucleonics
    Week,* December 6, 1984, p. 7.
16. Fred Hiatt, "Belgium Urged to Reject Pact With Libyans," *Wash-
    ington Post,* October 9, 1984.
17. Ann MacLachlan, "Belgians Fail to Get Guarantees From Neigh-
    bors on Libyan Aid," *Nucleonics Week,* December 6, 1984; "Gov-
    ernment Stopping Libyan Deal," *Nuclear News* (January 1985); in-
    terviews with Western European officials, May 1985.
18. "Libya Aided Argentina in War," *New York Times,* May 14, 1984.
19. "Brazilian Military Concern Over Argentine Talks with Libya,"
    Correio Braziliense, May 24, 1983, translated in *JPRS/TND,* June
    30, 1983, p. 8; unpublished interview with Carlos Castro Madero,
    former head of the Argentine Atomic Energy Commission, by John
    Cooley, ABC News, fall 1984. The events suggest the possibility
    that Tripoli was seeking a nuclear quid pro quo for its earlier mili-
    tary assistance.
20. "Uranium Mining Aid to Libya," *Correio Braziliense,* November
    8, 1984, translated in *JPRS/TND* January 14, 1985, p. 42; "Negotia-
    tions Begin on Building Warships for Libya," AFP 1624 GMT, Oc-
    tober 5, 1984, translated in *FBIS/Latin America,* October 9, 1984,
    p. D-1; "Libya Seeks Military Cooperation," *O Estado de São
    Paulo,* December 23, 1984, translated in *FBIS/Latin America,* De-
    cember 26, 1984, p. D-1.
21. Regarding Khadafi's anti-West, anti-Israel stance, see Allister
    Sparks, "Gadhafi Denounces Nonaligned; Vows to Lead Anti-
    Imperialist Army," *Washington Post,* September 5, 1986.
22. This episode is described in detail in Joseph C. Goulden, *The Death
    Merchant* (New York: Bantam Books, 1985), pp. 289-295; see also,
    Peter Maas, *Manhunt* (New York: Random House, 1986), pp. 176-
    177, 179-182. Both appear to rely in part on the testimony of John
    Heath, at Wilson's 1983 trial in Houston, Texas for illegal export of
    explosives. Heath was an employee of Wilson who was present at

the meetings when the nuclear arms were discussed with Libyan officials. Neither Goulden nor Maas had access, however, to the documents describing the nuclear deal offered the Libyans, which were obtained by the author in 1986 under the Freedom of Information Act.

According to Heath's testimony at Wilson's 1983 trial, Wilson was motivated by simple greed in pursuing the deal. Transcript of testimony of John Heath, January 29 and 31 and February 3, 1983, p. 71, *U.S. v. Wilson*, Cr. H-82-139, Federal District Court, Southern District of Texas. In an interview conducted in the fall of 1986, Wilson challenged this version. While confirming that meetings were held with Libyan officials to discuss the nuclear sales, he claimed that Heath "was the one that was really pushing it" because "he wanted to make a commission out of the thing." Indeed, Wilson asserted that he (Wilson) "killed the deal." Interview by Alan Burlow, *National Public Radio*, "All Things Considered," August 14, 1986, 6:30 PM. The jury in Wilson's trial, however, found Heath a credible witness, and U.S. law enforcement officials reject Wilson's account of his role.

23. See preceding note.
24. See Peter Maas, *Manhunt*, pp. 77, 89-90, 94-96. Wilson was convicted in 1983 for the C-4 deal.
25. Joseph Goulden, *The Death Merchant*, p. 290. According to Goulden's account, Donnay claimed that he could obtain the material from a Portuguese associate; the material was said to have come from a nuclear reactor in Germany. Ibid.
26. Sources differ as to the precise date of Donnay's visit. Goulden states that it took place in the "late spring" of 1981, but Maas places it in February of that year. Heath, in testifying on the matter, stated he was not sure of the date but thought it was "around 1980." The contract, discussed below, which Donnay and Wilson presented to the Libyans is headed "Validity: 15/3/1981" suggesting it was drafted in March of that year. (In European notation, the month appears after the day in such abbreviations.)
27. Heath testimony, pp. 74, 77.
28. Joseph Goulden, *The Death Merchant*, p. 291.
29. Goulden states one additional meeting was held; Wilson's attorney in cross-examining Heath at Wilson's trial, however, referred to Wilson's presence at "several" of them.
30. Peter Maas, *Manhunt,* pp. 181. Communication with Lawrence Barcella, summer 1986.
31. Although John Heath ultimately testified against Wilson, he was one of Wilson's most trusted lieutenants in 1981 and had played an important role in transporting quantities of C-4 to Libya. While a master sergeant in the U.S. Army, Heath had been trained in nuclear weapons "design, functioning, and rendering safe proce-

dures," and Wilson used Heath as a technical adviser on the Donnay proposal. Indeed, Heath claimed that from the start he saw that the Donnay project lacked substance, but like Wilson hoped it would pass Libyan scrutiny. Heath Testimony, pp. 81, 83.

One scenario that has long troubled U.S. policymakers is the possibility that a complete nuclear weapon might someday be stolen from the United States or an overseas storage area. An important safeguard against the possible misuse of stolen weapons are mechanisms in the units themselves—combination locks (known as permissive action links) that must be properly set before the weapon can be detonated and devices that can render the weapon unusable if it is tampered with. John Heath would certainly have been knowledgeable about such protective devices, possibly even knowledgeable enough to be able to defeat them. The fact that men with specialized training in such sensitive areas are available for hire by would-be nuclear black-marketeers like Wilson is, to say the least, sobering.

Iraq

1. Paul Power, "The Baghdad Raid: A Retrospect and Prospect," *Third World Quarterly*, July 1986, p. 860; Michael Dobbs, "France Delays On Iraqi Reactor," *Washington Post*, December 3, 1984.
2. Several possible sites for the project were reported to have been identified in 1985-1986, "Iraq Selects Sites," *Nuclear Engineering International*, April 1986, p. 5; "Al-Ittihad: USSR to Select Nuclear Reactor Site," Al-Ittihad (Abu Dhabi), March 11, 1985, p. 6, translated in *Foreign Broadcast Information Service (FBIS)/Middle East and Africa*, March 14, 1985, p. E-3.
3. Two U.S. specialists knowledgeable about nuclear-weapons design, consulted by the author, stated that it would be feasible for Iraq with its limited nuclear skills to make a weapon out of 12.5 kilograms of highly enriched uranium. A third specialist believed as many as three weapons could be fabricated from the material. Several other non-proliferation experts, probably less familiar with the details of weapons design, were more skeptical, however. Most sources use 15 to 25 kilograms as the amount of highly enriched uranium needed for a nuclear explosive, but the amount can apparently be reduced with certain design refinements that are described in unclassified publications. U.S. experts also believe that the fact that Iraq's highly enriched uranium was lightly irradiated in the adjacent Isis reactor in 1980 would not significantly impede the use of the material for a weapon today.
4. Leonard S. Spector, *The New Nuclear Nations* (New York: Vintage

Books, 1985) pp. 44-54.

5. Elaine Sciolino, "Iraq Cited on Chemical Weapons," *New York Times,* March 15, 1986.

6. See Paul Power, "The Baghdad Raid"; Jed C. Snyder, "The Road to Osiraq: Baghdad's Quest for the Bomb," *The Middle East Journal* (Autumn 1983): 565; U.S. Congress, Office of Technology Assessment, *Technology Transfers to the Middle East* (Washington, D.C.: Government Printing Office, 1984), p. 388; Lucien Vandenbroucke, "The Israeli Strike Against Osiraq," *Air University Review* (September-October 1984): 35; Leonard S. Spector, *Nuclear Proliferation Today* (New York: Vintage Books, 1984).

7. Jed C. Snyder, "The Non-Proliferation Regime: Managing the Impending Crisis," *Journal of Strategic Studies,* December 1985, p. 11.

8. See references in note 6 and citations therein. Another controversial aspect of the Osiraq project was the fact that it was to be fueled with highly enriched uranium, material directly usable for nuclear weapons. France originally proposed selling Iraq 72 kilograms of the material, enough for two or three weapons. When, under international pressure, France proposed a substitute fuel that could not be used for nuclear arms, Iraq objected, insisting that only the fuel France originally promised would permit a full range of research activities at Osiraq. This insistence, too, has been taken as an indication that Iraq saw the reactor and its fuel as means for advancing toward the bomb. Ultimately, France agreed to provide highly enriched material, but only in smaller quantities so that once Osiraq began operating, Iraq would not have on hand at any time enough readily available weapons-grade uranium for a single weapon. (Only 25 kilograms of fresh fuel would be in Iraq, half of which would be in Osiraq and thus contaminated with radioactivity, and the other half was to be lightly irradiated in the adjacent Isis reactor, slightly contaminating it with radioactivity at least temporarily.) This left irradiation of uranium targets in Osiraq (to be subsequently reprocessed in the hot cells or an expanded reprocessing unit) as the major proliferation risk posed by the reactor.

9. Ann MacLachlan, "Iraq Nuclear Export Vetoed," *The Energy Daily,* October 2, 1980, p.1; Leonard S. Spector, *The New Nuclear Nations,* pp. 165-166. This episode is also highlighted in Jed C. Snyder, "The Road to Osiraq." Depleted uranium, a leftover of the uranium enrichment process, is uranium from which the precious uranium-235 isotope has been culled.

10. It should be noted that under the Non-Proliferation Treaty, Iraq had the obligation to open the Italian hot cells to periodic IAEA inspections only after it had introduced nuclear materials there; until Iraq made this declaration, IAEA inspectors had the right to check that design information submitted to the Agency was accurate, but no on-going authority to inspect these units or another

Italian laboratory capable of fabricating uranium specimens that could have been inserted into Osiraq. Although Iraq had not yet declared the labs to the Agency at the time of the Israeli raid, using the facilities to produce plutonium clandestinely would still have required defeating the tight safeguards on Osiraq itself. See Jed C. Snyder, "The Non-Proliferation Regime" and references in the next note below.

11. H. Gruemm, "Safeguards and Tamuz: Setting the Record Straight," *IAEA Bulletin* (December 1981); Christopher Herzog, "Correspondence to the Editor," *International Security* (Spring 1983): 196. Iraq could have pursued the manufacture and testing of non-nuclear atomic-weapon components in secret. Regarding the subsequently abandoned Swedish nuclear-weapons program of the late 1950s and the 1960s, see Leonard S. Spector, *The New Nuclear Nations*, pp. 65-77.

12. The setbacks to the Iraqi program included an April 1979 explosion that destroyed the Osiraq reactor's core structures while they were awaiting shipment to Iraq in a warehouse in Seine-sur-Mer, France; the June 1980 murder in Paris of Dr. Yahya el-Meshad, an Egyptian nuclear scientist working for the Iraqi Atomic Energy Commission; and a series of bombings and bomb threats against a number of French and Italian companies supplying nuclear equipment for the Iraqi nuclear program. Some observers attribute these acts to Israel. See Leonard S. Spector, *Nuclear Proliferation Today* (Vintage Books: New York, 1984) pp. 175-178 (also discussing Israeli diplomatic efforts to slow the Iraqi program).

13. Through a series of interim measures at the 1983 and 1984 General Conferences, a final decision on sanctions against Israel had been postponed to succeeding years, enabling the United States to return as a full participant in IAEA activities in mid-1983. See Leonard S. Spector, *The New Nuclear Nations*, pp. 143-146. A motion at the 1986 Conference for sanctions against Israel—made only days before a major press story indicating that Israel has a more substantial nuclear arsenal than previously assumed—was withdrawn after it became clear it would be defeated.

14. Leonard S. Spector, *The New Nuclear Nations*, pp. 44-54. The discussion of this episode is based on European press accounts, a review of the prosecutor's dossier in the case, an in-person interview with one defendant, and a telephone interview with a second.

15. One defendant in an interview stated that he discussed the price of the plutonium with a "general of the Iraqi Army in charge of missiles," during a May 1982 meeting in Rome. A May 7, 1982, cable to him from a second member of the smuggling ring quotes the price for the material, apparently in preparation for the meeting. (The price was $60,572,000 or $1.78 million per kilo.)

16. Claude Van England, "Iran Scores Gains in War with Iraq," *Chris-*

tian Science Monitor, March 13, 1986.

17. Elaine Sciolino, "Iraq Cited on Chemical Weapons"; Michael Berlin, "U.N. Team Says Chemical Agents Used in Gulf War," *Washington Post,* March 27, 1984.
18. Shortly after the U.N. report was issued, Iran accused Iraq of again deploying chemical weapons against Abadan. "Reportage on Combat Operations in War with Iraq; Iraq Deploys Chemical Weapons," Tehran Radio 1930 GMT, April 3, 1986, reprinted in *FBIS/ Middle East and Africa,* April 4, 1986, p. I-3. A month prior to the UN report, Iraq claimed that Iran had fired 500 chemical weapon shells against residential sections of the city of Al-Khasib, near Basra. "Iran Accused of Using Chemical Weapons 12, 13 February," INA, 2030 GMT, February 18, 1986, translated in *FBIS/Middle East and Africa,* February 20, 1986, p. E-1. Outside observers have not confirmed the allegation, however, and according to U.S. and U.N. officials there was no evidence through March 1986 of Iranian use of chemical arms. Elaine Sciolino, "Iraq Cited on Chemical Weapons."
19. See e.g. "U.S. Condemns Iraq, Charges Use of Chemical Weapons," *New York Times,* March 21, 1986.
20. "Iraq to Obtain New Soviet Weapons 'Very Soon,' " QNA 0652 GMT December 19, 1985, translated in *FBIS/Middle East and Africa,* December 19, 1985, p. E-1; "French to Supply 24 F-1 Mirage Aircraft in 1986," *Al Siyasah,* October 31, 1985, translated in *FBIS/ Middle East and Africa,* November 4, 1985, p. E-2.
21. "U.S. Warns Iranians on Threats to Other Nations in Persian Gulf," *New York Times,* March 15, 1986.
22. Indeed, in 1982, Iraqi officials, while denying that their nation had used poison gas, insisted on its right to use any weapon to defend itself against invasion. Thomas O'Toole, "Paris Lists Terms for Rebuilding Reactor in Iraq," *Washington Post,* February 20, 1982.
23. "Nuclear Reactor to Be Built with Iraq, Pakistan," KUNA 1002 GMT, December 9, 1985, reprinted in *FBIS/Middle East and Africa,* December 9, 1985, p. D-1.
24. Although there have been no reports of Iraqi efforts to design a nuclear device or to perform the necessary preliminary tests, such activities would undoubtedly be carried out in secret and might not be apparent to outside observers in any case.
25. David Ignatius and Gerald Seib, "U.S., Iraq to Restore Full Diplomatic Ties; Baghdad Split with Radical Arabs Is Seen," *Wall Street Journal,* November 8, 1984; Bernard Gwertzman, "U.S. Restores Full Ties with Iraq But Cites Neutrality in Gulf War," *New York Times,* November 27, 1984; "Iraq is Breaking Its Ties with Libya," *New York Times,* June 27, 1985.

Iran

1. See pp. 45–55.
2. Daniel Poneman, *Nuclear Power in the Developing World,* (London: George Allen & Unwin Ltd., 1982), p. 96.
3. Thomas Stauffer, "Ayatollah Rediscovers Nuclear Power, With Kraftwerk Union's Aid," *Energy Daily,* October 2, 1984; "German Team Inspects Stalled Bushehr Plants," *Nuclear News,* June 1984, p. 95.
4. See Akbar Etemad, "Iran," in Harald Müller, *European Non-Proliferation Policy* (Oxford: Oxford University Press, forthcoming.) Etemad was the Chairman of the Atomic Energy Organization of Iran during its period of greatest activity under the Shah.
5. See pp. 49–50.
6. Akbar Etemad, "Iran," p. 9; "Iranian Reactor to Go Critical," *Nuclear Engineering International,* (December 1984): 13. (The "reactor" referred to is a subcritical training unit, i.e., one that will not sustain a nuclear chain reaction.)
7. Elaine Sciolino, "Iraq Cited on Chemical Weapons," *New York Times,* March 15, 1986; "Reportage on Combat Operations In War with Iraq; Iraq Deploys Chemical Weapons," Tehran Radio 1930 GMT, April 3, 1986, reprinted in *FBIS/Middle East and Africa,* April 4, 1986, p. I-3.
8. See Akbar Etemad, "Iran," pp. 23-28.

Chapter V:
Latin America

Argentina

1. A bloodless military coup on March 24, 1976 ousted Argentina's
   President Maria Estela Martinez de Peron, wife of two-time president Juan Domingo Peron, and installed a governing junta composed of the commanders of the three armed forces. The coup, led
   by army Gen. Jorge Videla, came after months of rampant inflation, right and left-wing terrorism, and political indecision. Gen.
   Videla was sworn in as president and served until March 1981,
   when he was replaced in rapid succession by Gen. Roberto Viola
   (March-December 1981), Gen. Leopoldo Galtieri (December
   1981-July 1982) and Gen. Reynaldo Bignone (July 1982-December
   1983). This period of military rule was marked by political repression, including suppression of opposition parties and wide-scale detention and slaughter of suspected left-wing activists, and by continued economic hardship. After Argentina's defeat in the 1982
   Falklands war, Gen. Bignone initiated a transition to civilian rule
   that culminated in the election of Radical Civic Union candidate
   Dr. Raul Alfonsín to the presidency in October 1983.
2. The plants are the West German-supplied Atucha I and the
   Canadian-supplied Embalse reactors. Both are natural-uranium/
   heavy-water reactors.
3. One key commodity still needed from abroad is heavy water, used
   in Argentina's power reactors. In a controversial 1980 deal, however, the Swiss firm, Sulzer Brothers, with the approval of the Swiss
   government, agreed to sell Buenos Aires an industrial-scale heavy-
   water production plant, to be built at Arroyito.
     In 1980, Argentina had solicited bids for both the large heavy-
   water plant and for a third nuclear-power plant, Atucha II. Canada
   and West Germany were asked to submit bids for both plants.
   Canada stated that it would not sell the plants unless Argentina
   agreed to maintain all of its nuclear installations—current and future—under IAEA safeguards. Under U.S. urging, West Germany
   agreed to require the same conditions, apparently because a heavy-
   water plant, rarely sold in international nuclear commerce, was involved. At the last minute, however, Argentina announced it
   would split the deal, buying the heavy-water plant from Switzerland, which had not made these "full-scope" safeguards a condition
   for the sale, and purchasing the reactor from Germany, which then
   declared that it, too, would not require comprehensive safeguards,
   since it was no longer selling the heavy-water plant. Canada considered the German action a betrayal of their previous understanding.

Switzerland and Germany did require, however, that the reactor, the heavy-water plants, any plutonium produced through their use, and any facilities based on their technology be placed under safeguards.

    Argentina is also developing an experimental heavy-water facility indigenously. (See chart at end of this section.)

4. Plans to build a large, indigenous research reactor, RA-7, have apparently been abandoned. Richard Kessler, "Argentina Denies It Plans Large Unsafeguarded Research Reactor," *Nucleonics Week,* August 8, 1985, p. 5. The facility's spent fuel could have been reprocessed at Ezeiza without IAEA oversight to produce plutonium that could be used for nuclear weapons without violating any international undertakings. Technically, several of Argentina's existing research reactors are subject to IAEA inspection only because of the presence of imported enriched uranium fuel, and if unsafeguarded fuel (imported from China or produced indigenously) were used, any plutonium subsequently extracted could be available for weapons. The output of these reactors, however, would be insignificant in any event because they are so small.

5. Richard Kessler, "Argentine Government Bides Time with Congress to Revamp CNEA," *Nucleonics Week,* July 10, 1986.

6. Argentina's natural-uranium/heavy-water power reactors do not require enriched uranium fuel and, although it is theoretically possible to use slightly enriched uranium in them, no other country does so. Argentina's research reactors do require enriched uranium but the Pilcaniyeu plant's capacity, as announced, was more than sixteen times that necessary to serve these small research facilities. Moreover, the decision of Argentina's former leaders not to place the plant under IAEA safeguards meant that if it were configured to produce weapons-grade uranium, Argentina would be free to use the material for nuclear arms.

    Commencement of the Pilcaniyeu project coincided with the start of construction of the Ezeiza reprocessing plant, and the two appeared to be a direct response to Brazil's 1975 deal with West Germany, under which it was to receive both enrichment and reprocessing capabilities. (Indeed the then head of the Argentine Atomic Energy Commission acknowledged to one U.S. non-proliferation aide that Argentina could not abandon the Ezeiza plant—then the only one of the two Argentine plants publicly announced—because of the 1975 Brazilian deal.)

    These factors and Argentina's increasing militarism in 1978, as evidenced by its provocation of a near-war with Chile over the Beagle Channel Islands and a major build-up of conventional armaments, strongly suggested that the Pilcaniyeu installation was initiated for the purpose of giving Argentina a nuclear weapons option.

7. Leonard S. Spector, *Nuclear Proliferation Today* (New York: Vin-

tage Books, 1984), pp.257-263. One well-placed Brazilian official, speaking anonymously in 1986 on the earlier sudden disclosure of the Argentine facility, echoed these concerns in a more muted tone: "The people here hadn't expected such a development and felt the Argentines hadn't been quite candid. I believe this has created some uneasiness." Bradley Graham, "Argentine Leader Proposes Moving Capital to Patagonia," *Washington Post,* April 17, 1986.

8. Richard Kessler, "Argentina's Alfonsín Pledges Funding for Fuel Cycle Projects," *Nucleonics Week,* June 5, 1986. The plant has a capacity of 20,000 separative work units per year (twice that of South Africa's Valindaba pilot enrichment plant); in principle this capacity is enough to produce 100 kilograms (220 pounds) of 90 percent-enriched uranium per year, depending on how the facility is laid out. The plant is scheduled to produce its first 20 percent-enriched material (still not suitable for weapons) some time in 1986.

9. Although the Peronists were narrowly defeated by the Radical Civic Union in Argentina's 1983 general elections, they have retained a substantial voice in the nation's domestic political debate. Drawing on the coalition put together by Juan Peron, president of Argentina from 1946 to 1955 and again from 1973 until his death the following year, the Peronists have achieved political support through a platform of intense nationalism and affiliation with labor. Opposition to Alfonsín's economic policies in 1984, for example, was mounted by the Peronists in conjunction with the General Confederation of Labor (CGT), Argentina's powerful trade union. The November 1985 midterm congressional elections, however, showed a growing dissatisfaction with the Peronist opposition, especially with the wing of the party most closely associated with union bosses.

10. Leonard S. Spector, *The New Nuclear Nations* (New York: Vintage Books, 1985), pp.182-183.

11. See e.g. "Alfonsín Proposes CNEA Reforms," *Nuclear Engineering International,* September 1984, p. 10.

12. Richard Kessler, "Argentina May Be Scaling Down Heavy Water Production Plans," *Nucleonics Week,* May 16, 1985, p. 13. The treaty requires parties to accept IAEA safeguards on all their nuclear installations, but the pact does not become binding on a state that ratifies it until all regional states have taken this step; a ratifying country can voluntarily waive this entry-into-force requirement, however, and accept the treaty as binding. Argentina has neither ratified the treaty nor waived this condition, and Cuba has not even signed the pact. With the exception of Brazil and Chile, virtually all regional states have both ratified the accord and waived this entry-into-force requirement. See Appendix E.

13. Richard Kessler, "Argentina, Brazil Agree to Mutual Inspection of Nuclear Facilities," *Nucleonics Week*, March 14, 1985, p. 14. Unlike ratification of the Tlatelolco Treaty, which might have the appearance of a unilateral concession made at least partly in response to long-standing pressure from the United States and others, implementation of the mutual inspection proposal would allow Alfonsín to argue that he had gained something in return for relinquishing Argentina's nuclear privacy.

14. Other regional states were also to be given access to the installations covered and Uruguayan President Julio Maria Sanguinetti, for one, was said to have agreed to participate.

15. But see page 202 in Brazil section, discussing 1985 comments by Brazilian Army Minister Pires Goncalves, suggesting a security basis for a Brazilian nuclear arsenal.

16. Lydia Chavez, "Argentina Plans Stringent Curbs on Economy and New Currency," *New York Times,* June 15, 1985.

17. Lydia Chavez, "Leader Imposes a State of Seige on Argentina," *New York Times,* October 26, 1986. The bombings were apparently an attempt to compel the government to grant amnesty in the trials of Argentina's former military leaders accused of murder and torture while they were in power during the 1970s. These trials were nearing their conclusion when the bombing campaign took place. In mid-December, Generals Emilio Massera, Roberto Viola, and Jorge Videla were convicted and given stiff prison sentences.

18. Bradley Graham, "Ruling Party Leads in Vote By Argentines," *Washington Post,* November 4, 1986. The split among the Peronists was so severe that the party was obliged to run two competing slates of candidates in Buenos Aires province, its traditional stronghold.

19. "Joint Declaration on Nuclear Policy by the Governments of Brazil and Argentina," November 29, 1985 (copy obtained from Argentine Embassy, Washington, D.C.)

    Some important nuclear cooperation has already taken place under the 1980 Brazil-Argentina nuclear trade pact, including Argentina's lease of 240 metric tons (265 short tons) of uranium concentrate to Brazil, which Brazil "returned" after its own uranium-mining operations were expanded; Argentina's sale to Brazil of 160,000 meters (174,978 yards) of zircalloy tubing for nuclear-power-reactor fuel elements; and Brazil's contract to manufacture the reactor vessel for Argentina's Atucha II nuclear-power plant.

20. "Alfonsín Wants Nonproliferation," *Jornal do Brasil,* December 1, 1985, translated in *FBIS/TND,* January 9, 1986, p. 16; Richard Kessler and Jeff Ryser, "Argentina-Brazil Committee to Work Out Details of Joint Inspection," *Nucleonics Week,* December 5, 1986, p. 9.

21. To symbolize the new direction in bilateral relations, at the conclusion of the talks, Alfonsín accompanied Sarney to the Itaipu hydro-

electric dam, built by Brazil and Paraguay; Argentina had not joined in the project, which its military government had claimed represented a threat to Argentine security. Richard Kessler, "Argentine-Brazilian Committee To Work Out Details of Joint Inspections," *Nucleonics Week,* December 5, 1986, p. 9.

22. Richard Kessler, "Argentina and Brazil Will Not Provide the IAEA with Information," *Nucleonics Week,* March 2, 1986, p. 9.

23. "Committee Report On Talks with Argentina, Accord with FRG," *O Estado de São Paulo,* April 18, 1986, translated in *JPRS/TND,* June 13, 1986, p. 44; Richard Kessler, "Panel Favors Mutual Inspections of Facilities by Argentina, Brazil," *Nucleonics Week,* May 1, 1986, p. 6.

24. Richard Kessler, "Argentine-Brazil Protocol Promotes Nuclear Accident Accord," *Nucleonics Week,* July 31, 1986, p. 1.

25. Tim Coone, "Sarney and Alfonsín to Sign Trade Pact," *Financial Times,* July 29, 1986.

26. Martin Anderson, "Alfonsín Faces New Violence," *Washington Post,* June 3, 1986; Shirley Christian, "Military Tensions Rise in Argentina," *New York Times,* June 12, 1986; "Dante Caputo Rules Out Coup Possibilities," Telam, 1157 GMT, June 15, 1986, translated in *FBIS/Latin America,* June 17, 1986, p. B-1.

27. Richard House, "Brazil Steps Back from Race to Build Nuclear Weapons," *Washington Post,* August 28, 1986; Richard Kessler, "Electronic Monitors Eyed for Argentine-Brazil Mutual Inspections," *Nucleonics Week,* September 11, 1986. See section on Brazil below.

28. Richard Kessler, "Electronic Monitors Eyed."

29. Argentina, for example, has long complained in behind-the-scenes negotiations that while the Tlatelolco Treaty permits nations to develop peaceful nuclear explosives to the extent they differ from nuclear weapons, the IAEA precludes all nuclear explosives by treating them as the equivalent of weapons (as they are treated under the Non-Proliferation Treaty) when it negotiates safeguards agreements with individual parties to the Tlatelolco pact. This, Argentina argues, deprives it of an important right. Argentina's public characterization of the dispute, however, has been far more euphemistic. It never mentions peaceful nuclear explosions but only states that the IAEA's stance does not reflect the "particularities" of the Tlatelolco accord. See Foreign Minister Dante Caputo to Senator Charles Percy, February 23, 1984, *Hearing Before the Subcommittee on Energy, Nuclear Proliferation and Governmental Processes of the Committee on Governmental Affairs,* U.S. Senate, June 27, 1984 (Washington, D.C.: Government Printing Office, 1984) p. 20. In May 1985, the Alfonsín government interposed a new objection to its ratification of the accord, claiming that if special inspections at the Pilcaniyeu plant were conducted by a region-

al safeguards group established under the treaty, the results could compromise the facility's secret technology. Richard Kessler, "Argentina Raises New Concern About Impact of Tlatelolco Treaty," *Nucleonics Week,* May 30, 1985, p. 7.

In mid-1986, Alfonsín was considering a unilateral moratorium on peaceful nuclear explosions, as a means for breaking the impasse over this issue, but intended to seek parliamentary approval of such a step. The Peronist opposition is said to oppose it. Richard Kessler, "Argentina May Declare Moratorium Against Peaceful Nuclear Explosions," *Nucleonics Week,* June 12, 1986, p. 6.

30. Richard Kessler, "Electronic Monitors Eyed." In fact both institutions have extensive support in the developing world. The vast majority of Latin American states, for example, have ratified the Tlatelolco Treaty, and indeed, Brazil has taken this step. (The treaty is not yet in force in Brazil, however, because unlike most other adherents, Brazil has not waived the entry-into-force requirement of universal ratification by all relevant states. Argentina has signed but not ratified the pact.)

31. Ibid.

32. Richard Kessler, "Argentina Won't Export Sensitive Technologies Without Safeguards," *Nucleonics Week,* February 27, 1986, p. 7. Buenos Aires would not require recipients to place *all* of their nuclear installations under IAEA safeguards as a condition of supply. Argentina has, itself, refused to accept this condition in its dealings with the United States, Canada, and other supplier states.

33. Concerning trade with Brazil, see note 19. Leonard S. Spector, *Nuclear Proliferation Today,* pp. 212-213, 228; Leonard S. Spector, *The New Nuclear Nations,* pp. 185-187.

34. Ibid.

35. Leonard S. Spector, *Nuclear Proliferation Today,* pp. 211-212, 215-216; "Zhao: China Sold Heavy Water to Argentina," Noticias Argentinas, 2325 GMT, November 7, 1985, translated in *FBIS/Latin America,* November 8, 1985. Argentina initially denied the story, but subsequently confirmed the deal. Richard Kessler, "Argentine Officials Deny Any Purchases of Chinese Heavy Water," *Nucleonics Week,* October 31, 1985; Richard Kessler, "Argentina to Tender for Heavy Water After June Purchase from China," *Nucleonics Week,* September 25, 1986, p. 5.

36. Richard Kessler, "Iran Sending Delegation to Argentina to Explore Nuclear Cooperation," *Nucleonics Week,* May 15, 1986, p. 3. In 1986, Buenos Aires also held talks with Japan concerning uranium mining operations in Argentina. Rik Turner, "Argentina May Turn to Japan for Help in Exploiting U3O8 Reserves," *Nuclear Fuel,* July 28, 1986, p. 5.

37. Atomic Energy Act of 1954, as amended, Section 127.

38. "Speech by President Alfonsín at the Central Atomic Energy Day

Ceremony, Embalse Rio Tercero, May 30, 1986," translated by Congressional Research Service. (Author's files).

39. Ibid.

40. "Official on Nuclear, Other Energy Sources," Noticias Argentinas, 2008 GMT, July 23, 1985, translated in *FBIS/Latin America,* July 26, 1985, p. B-6.

41. "Commitment to Startup for Atucha-2 in 1992," *Nuclear News,* March 1986; Richard Kessler, "The Argentine Nuclear Budget Appears Likely to Increase Significantly," *Nucleonics Week,* February 6, 1986; see also Richard Kessler, "Argentina Apparently Decides to Complete Heavy Water Plant By Early 1988," *Nuclear Fuel,* February 10, 1986.

42. Richard Kessler, "Argentina's Alfonsín Pledges Funding for Fuel Cycle Projects," *Nucleonics Week,* June 5, 1986, p. 3.

43. Arthur F. Manfredi, et al., "Ballistic Missile Proliferation Potential in the Third World," *Congressional Research Service Report* (mimeo) (Washington: Library of Congress, 1986), pp. 16-17.

44. Ibid. Throughout this book Sweden's late 1950s nuclear-weapon design, which was for a bomb weighing 1,300 pounds, is used as a conservative benchmark for estimating the weight of early-generation nuclear weapons that might be built by the emerging nuclear states.

45. Through the "Five Continents" initiative, for example, Alfonsín has played a highly visible role in international efforts to curb the U.S.-Soviet nuclear arms race. See Don Oberdorfer, "Six Non-aligned Countries Offer to Monitor a Nuclear Test Ban," *Washington Post,* October 29, 1985.

46. See e.g. "CGT Says Strike Received Record Support," Telam, 0000 GMT, June 15, 1986, Translated in *FBIS/Latin America,* June 17, 1986, p. B-1.

Brazil

1. See Leonard S. Spector, *Nuclear Proliferation Today,* (New York: Vintage Books, 1984) pp. 239-244.

2. "Angra I Inaugurated," *O Estado de São Paulo,* January 18, 1985, translated in *Joint Publication Research Service (JPRS)/ Nuclear Proliferation and Development (TND),* March 12, 1985, p. 65. The facility first operated in 1982, but has undergone an unusually long period of debugging, which delayed commercial operation for three years.

3. The reprocessing plant was intended to extract plutonium from spent reactor fuel to permit Brazil to recycle the material as a substitute for low-enriched uranium in fresh reactor fuel—it being assumed at the time that an anticipated world-wide uranium shortage would make the substitution essential for the economical operation

of Brazil's power reactors. Today, however, there is a glut of uranium on world markets, and hence the demand for low-enriched uranium fuel will be far smaller than expected, largely eliminating the economic justification for the reprocessing plant.

In any event, the low-enriched-uranium fuel that Brazil is likely to use in Angra I, II, and III will be purchased largely from the British-Dutch-German uranium enrichment consortium, which has required that Brazil place any of the plutonium produced in the fuel and subsequently extracted from it in an IAEA-safeguarded plutonium storage facility that is also under multinational control.

4. The German uranium enrichment plant is being designed to produce only low-enriched uranium, not usable for weapons, although the technology in the plant could, in theory, be used to produce weapons-grade material. IAEA safeguards at the plant, however, should be able to ensure that the facility is not secretly reconfigured to produce highly enriched uranium, and the FRG-Brazil agreement specifies that any facility developed in Brazil using the jet-nozzle technique must also be placed under IAEA supervision. (The latter restriction on "replication" also applies to any reprocessing plant Brazil might build with West German reprocessing technology.)

The West German deal also included assistance to Brazil in conducting uranium prospecting and resource development and the supply of a pilot-scale nuclear-power-plant fuel-fabrication installation, to be followed by a commercial facility.

5. See Appendix E.

6. Richard House, "Brazil Steps Back"; "Navy Carries Out Own Nuclear Research," *Fôlha de São Paulo*, August 26, 1986, translated in *FBIS/Latin America*, September 4, 1986, p. D-1; "Navy Reportedly Manufacturing Nuclear Reactors," *Fôlha de São Paulo*, April 28, 1985, translated in *JPRS/TND*, May 23, 1985, p. 60.

7. "IPEN's UF_6 Conversion Technology Said to Be Ready for Commercial Use in Brazil," *Nuclear Fuel*, July 28, 1986, p. 5.

8. "Cals on Angra Problems, Laser Beam Enrichment Process," *Jornal Do Brasil*, July 7, 1984, translated in *JPRS/TND*, September 24, 1984, p. 48. Additional work on lasers is said to have been conducted at the University of Campinas.

9. "Brazil Says It Now Produces Small Amounts of Plutonium," *Washington Post*, December 18, 1986; see Spector, *Nuclear Proliferation Today*, pp. 247-252, discussing allegations that the unit operated in 1983.

10. "Production of Atomic Bomb Expected in 1990," *Fôlha de São Paulo*, April 28, 1985, translated in *FBIS/Latin America*, May 1, 1985, p. D-1; "Editorial Questions . . . ," *Fôlha de São Paulo*.

11. Spector, *Nuclear Proliferation Today*, pp. 257-262.

12. "Figueiredo Observes IPEN Centrifuge Uranium Enrichment," *O*

Estado de São Paulo, October 9, 11, 1984, translated in *JPRS/TND,* November 2, 1984, pp. 30-32.

13. "Presidential Candidate Neves Comments On Program," *O Estado de São Paulo,* August 5, 1984, translated in *JPRS/TND,* August 28, 1984, p. 26.

14. Alan Riding, "Passing Muster In Brazil: President Woos Army," *New York Times,* January 23, 1986; see also Marc Levinson, "Brazil's Fragile Democracy," *Worldview,* June 1985, p. 4.

15. Richard Foster, "Brazil Introduces New Currency and Price Freeze," *Financial Times,* March 1, 1986; "Brazilians Warm to Sarney's Price Freeze Package," *Financial Times,* March 4, 1986; Alan Riding, "Brazil Marches to War Against Goliath of Inflation," *New York Times,* March 26, 1986; Roger Cohen, "Brazil's Inflation Success Brings New Woes," *Wall Street Journal,* June 3, 1986.

16. "EMFA [Armed Forces General Staff] Opposes Constitutional Restraint," *Fôlha de São Paulo,* June 22, 1985, translated in *JPRS/TND,* September 23, 1985, p. 51.

17. "Piva Confirms Country Able to Make Bomb in Five Years," *O Estado de São Paulo,* August 17, 1985, translated in *JPRS/TND,* October 21, 1985, p. 18.

18. "Army Minister Said To Favor Building Atomic Bomb," EFE, 1431 GMT, September 1, 1985, translated in *FBIS/Latin America,* September 4, 1985, p. D-2; Richard Kessler, "Argentina Had No Official Comment on News Reports Saying that Brazil's . . . ," *Nucleonics Week,* September 5, 1985, p. 9. Goncalves reportedly claimed that Argentina could rapidly advance over 100 miles into Brazilian territory, although Brazil would ultimately have the advantage in men and war materials. The general claimed that Argentina could test an atomic bomb at any time—a considerable overstatement of known Argentine capabilities. Goncalves' comments are also remarkable in that they suggest that, contrary to the view of most observers, support for Brazilian nuclear arming is spurred not by considerations of prestige, but by security concerns.

19. "EMFA Head Denies Interest in Building Atomic Bomb," *O Estado de São Paulo,* September 8, 1985, translated in *JPRS/TND,* December 13, 1985, p. 32; "Setabul Reassures Argentina on Atomic Bomb," *O Globo,* September 5, 1985, translated in *FBIS/Latin America,* September 10, 1985, p. D-1.

20. "Army Minister Stresses Need to Complete Nuclear Cycle," *Fôlha de São Paulo,* September 4, 1985, translated in *JPRS/TND,* September 23, 1985, p. 48, brackets in original.

21. "Navy Minister Said to Support Atomic Bomb Plan," EFE, 0135 GMT, September 14, 1985, translated in *FBIS/Latin America,* September 17, 1985, p. D-1.

22. According to the U.S. Department of State, Brazil is "engaged in a

modest indigenous research program in uranium enrichment. We believe the GOB has made some progress in its research of enrichment by the centrifuge method. It has publicly announced its intention to build a pilot scale enrichment plant. However, the GOB consistently states that it does not intend to build nuclear weapons." *Hearings on Review of 1985 U.S. Government Non-proliferation Activities,* before the Subcommittee on Energy, Nuclear Proliferation, and Government Processes, of the Committee on Governmental Affairs, April 10, 1986 (Washington: Government Printing Office, 1986) p. 25. See note 9.

23. Richard Kessler, "Argentina, Brazil Agree to Mutual Inspection of Nuclear Facilities," *Nucleonics Week,* March 14, 1985, p. 14.

24. "Joint Declaration on Nuclear Policy by the Governments of Brazil and Argentina," November 29, 1985 (copy obtained from Argentine Embassy, Washington, D.C.). Similarly, when interviewed after the talks on the inspection issue, Sarney deflected reporters' questions, in contrast to Alfonsín who expressed enthusiasm for the verification concept. "Brazil, Argentina Discuss Joint Cooperation," *O Estado de São Paulo,* November 30, 1985, translated in *JPRS/TND,* January 9, 1986, p. 15.

25. "Chief of Staff Supports Nuclear Cycle Research," *O Globo,* December 5, 1985, translated in *FBIS/Latin America,* December 9, 1985, p. D-4.

26. Richard Kessler, "Argentina and Brazil Will Not Provide the IAEA with Information," *Nucleonics Week,* March 27, 1986, p. 9.

27. "Committee Report On Talks With Argentina, Accord with FRG," *O Estado de São Paulo,* April 18, 1986, translated in *JPRS/TND,* June 13, 1986, p. 44; Richard Kessler, "Panel Favors Mutual Inspections of Facilities by Argentina and Brazil," *Nucleonics Week,* May 1, 1986, p. 6. The reevaluation committee's recommendations on nuclear cooperation with West Germany were adopted by Sarney and implemented through an August 1986 policy statement discussed below. Many of the reevaluation committee's recommendations were public knowledge in mid-March, and the ministerial participants undoubtedly voiced their support for the inspection concept through internal channels prior to the bilateral commission's March meeting. "Reevaluation Commission Recommendations," *O Globo,* March 27, 1986, translated in *JPRS/TND,* May 19, 1986, p. 34.

28. "Nuclear Inspection Clause with Argentina Rejected," EFE 1517 GMT, August 19, 1986, translated in *FBIS/Latin America,* August 21, 1986, p. D-1. Nevertheless, nuclear cooperation was enhanced as both agreed to notify the other in the case of nuclear accidents. Richard Kessler, "Argentina-Brazil Protocol Promotes Nuclear Accident Accord," *Nucleonics Week,* July 31, 1986, p. 1.

29. Richard Kessler, "Electronic Monitors Eyed for Argentine-Brazil

Mutual Inspections," *Nucleonics Week,* September 11, 1986, p. 9. One Brazilian concern, according to U.S. sources, is that the mutual inspection program could slow Brazil's progress toward mastering the enrichment process—in effect freezing the country in an inferior position compared to Argentina. This would place Brazil at a serious disadvantage if Alfonsín were succeeded by a more militant government that decided to develop nuclear arms—an eventuality Brazilian officials consider all too possible. Communication with knowledgeable U.S. official.

30. *"Further Reportage of Alleged Nuclear Test Site," Fôlha de São Paulo,* August 8, 1986, translated in *FBIS/Latin America,* August 12, 1986, p. D-1; Richard House, "Brazil Steps Back from Race to Build Nuclear Weapons," *Washington Post,* August 28, 1986.

31. Richard Townley, "Brazil Rekindles Reactor Program and Denies Proliferation Plans," *Nucleonics Week,* August 14, 1986, p. 12.

32. Ibid. Brazilian spokesmen also asserted that the sedimentary formations and high water table at the site would make it inappropriate for underground nuclear testing.

33. Communications with knowledgeable U.S. officials, September 1986; cf. *Hearings on Review of 1985 U.S. Government Non-proliferation Activities,"* p. 25.

34. Communication with knowledgeable specialist, Washington, D.C., September 1986. Regarding the Swedish nuclear-weapon design, see Christer Larsson, "Build a Bomb!," *Ny Teknik,* April 25, 1985.

35. See Leonard S. Spector, *The New Nuclear Nations,* pp. 217-218.

36. "Foreign Ministry Consults Brazil on Nuclear Tests," Telam, 2135 GMT, August 19, 1986, translated in *FBIS/Latin America,* August 21, 1986, p. B-1.

37. Richard Kessler, "Electronic Monitors Eyed for Argentine-Brazil Mutual Inspections."

38. "Former Navy Minister Advocates Atomic Bomb," AFP, 2136 GMT, September 5, 1986, translated in *FBIS/Latin America,* September 8, 1986, p. D-2.

39. Paul Lyons, "Brazil Bids in $25-Million Algeria Uranium Exploration Project," *Nuclear Fuel,* August 12, 1985; Peter Bruce, "KWU Signs Preliminary Accord For N-Plants in China," *Financial Times,* June 6, 1985.

40. "Nuclear Power Agreement Signed with Egypt," *Fôlha de São Paulo,* April 30, 1986, translated in *JPRS/TND,* June 13, 1986, p. 46.

41. "Sarney-Betancur Manaus Talks Include Nuclear Accord," *O Estado de São Paulo,* January 31, 1986, translated in *FBIS/TND,* February 21, 1986, p. 45.

42. PRC-Brazil Nuclear Cooperation Agreement, signed in Beijing, October 11, 1984, Article 6; "Nuclear Cooperation Accord Signed with PRC," *Fôlha de São Paulo,* October 12, 1984, translated in

FBIS/Latin America, October 15, 1984, p. D-1.

43. "Libyan Envoy on $1 Billion Trade, Arms Purchases," *O Estado de São Paulo,* December 3, 1985, translated in *FBIS/Latin America,* December 4, 1985, p. D-8; "Iraq to Purchase 250 New Cascavel Tanks," *O Estado de São Paulo,* June 19, 1986, translated in *FBIS/Latin America,* June 23, 1986, p. D2.

44. Atomic Energy Act of 1954, section 127 (1978). The specific facilities not subject to IAEA safeguards apparently are a uranium purification (UD_2) plant at IPEN and a facility for producing uranium hexafluoride (UF_6), the compound which serves as the feedstock for the enrichment process. Paul Lyons, "EXIM Credits to Support U.S. Service and Equipment Sales to Brazil," *Nucleonics Week,* June 13, 1985.

45. Richard House, "Brazil Steps Back"; "Specifications of IPEN Enrichment Facility Noted," *Jornal do Brasil,* October 8, 1984; Charles Thurston, "Brazil's First Enrichment Cascade to Begin Operation In February," *Nuclear Fuel,* November 26, 1984, p. 6.

46. Communication with knowledgeable U.S. officials, September, 1986.

47. Ibid.

48. Angra II is approximately seventy percent complete but work on Angra III has not gone beyond the pouring of some foundations. "Brazil Commission Opts to Continue Nuclear Program," Reuters, April 18, 1986, AM cycle; Robert Townley, "Brazil Rekindles Reactor Program"; Rik Turner, "Brazil's Sarney Defines Emphasis for National Fuel Cycle Development," *Nuclear Fuel,* August 11, 1986, p. 10. Communications with knowledgeable U.S. official. Concerning prior policy see Leonard S. Spector, *The New Nuclear Nations* (New York: Vintage Books, 1985) pp. 197-198.

49. Arthur F. Manfredi, et al., "Ballistic Missile Proliferation Potential in the Third World," *Congressional Research Service Report* (mimeo) (Washington, D.C.: Library of Congress, April 23, 1986) pp. 13-15.

50. Ibid. (This source states the rocket will not have an inertial guidance system); but see, "Brazil's Move Toward the Stars," *Defense and Foreign Affairs* (April 1985): 34; Richard House, "Brazil Pursues Dream in Space," *Washington Post,* December 13, 1984.

51. Richard House, "Brazil Pursues Dream in Space." See also Max G. Manwaring, "Nuclear Power in Brazil," *Parameters* (Winter 1984) p. 44; David M. North, "Brazil Plans to Launch Its Own Satellites," *Aviation Week and Space Technology,* July 9, 1984, p. 60.

52. Richard House, "Brazil Pursues Dream"; John R. Redick, *Military Potential of Latin American Nuclear Energy Programs* (Beverly Hills: Sage Publications, 1972), pp. 25-26; "Space Technology Accord with PRC Explained," *O Estado de São Paulo,* January 29, 1985, translated in *FBIS/Latin America,* February 1, 1985. David M. North, "Brazil Plans to Launch Its Own Satellites," *Aviation*

Week and Space Technology, July 9, 1984, p. 60.

53. *"O Globo:* Nuclear Missiles Possible in Five Years," January 13, 1986, translated in *FBIS/Latin America,* January 16, 1986, p. D-1. According to this analysis, with a liquid-fuel rocket, Brazil could lift payloads of 2,200 pounds—more than sufficient for an early generation of nuclear warheads—and the guidance technology offered by China would provide sufficient accuracy for a military missile. (Throughout this volume, it is assumed that an emerging nuclear state could build a nuclear device weighing 1300 pounds. The judgment is based on the fact that Sweden designed a weapon of this size, in which it had high confidence, as early as the late 1950s, as part of its subsequently aborted nuclear weapons program. Christer Larsson, "Build a Bomb!" *Ny Teknik,* April 25, 1985.)

54. See chart at end of this section.

Chapter VI:
Africa – Introduction

1. "Babangida Remarks on Nuclear Policy," AFP 1633 GMT, April 14, 1986, reprinted in *Foreign Broadcast Information Service (FBIS)/Near East and Africa*, April 15, 1986, p. T-7.
2. Ibid. In 1980, Chuba Okadigbo, a senior adviser to then Nigerian President Shehu Shagari, stated in an address to the Foreign Policy Association in New York that Nigeria could obtain the technology and materials needed for a nuclear bomb and intended to build one "if it is necessary to bring South Africa to the negotiating table." Okadigbo, who declared that he was speaking for the Nigerian government on the matter, continued, "We won't allow Africa to be subjected to nuclear blackmail," and added that it would be "unreasonable to expect" other African nations not to seek a nuclear weapon to meet South Africa's presumed capability. Jonathan Kwitny, "Nigeria Considers Nuclear Armament Due to South Africa," *Wall Street Journal,* October 6, 1980.
3. "Africans Are Advised To Develop Atom Arms," *New York Times,* June 10, 1983. There has also been increasing scholarly interest in the possibility of black African proliferation. See Tunde Adeniran, "Nuclear Proliferation and Black Africa: The Coming Crisis of Choice," *Third World Quarterly* (October 1981): 673; Robert D'A. Henderson, "Nigeria: Future Nuclear Power?" *Orbis* (Summer 1981): 409; Ladi Adenrele, "Models of Nuclear Weapons Decision Strategy in Africa," *Arms Control* (September 1984): 148; Oye Ogunbadejo, "Africa's Nuclear Future," *Journal of Modern African Studies* (1984): 19.
4. As analyzed more fully in Chapter II, discussion of this scenario is not intended to be a prediction that a future South African government will necessarily espouse a radical ideology. Indeed the strongest forces promoting change in South Africa today are moderate ones. Nonetheless, the threat of a radical take-over is one that cannot be ruled out.
5. Mary Battiata, "Author Defends 'Africans,' " *Washington Post,* September 6, 1986. Mazrui expressed similar views during a 1985 interview, David K. Willis, "South African Blacks to Have the Bomb by the Year 2000?," *Christian Science Monitor,* July 1, 1985.

South Africa

1. This has been the prevailing view among non-proliferation specialists, including the author. See e.g. *Blocking the Spread of Nuclear Weapons: American and European Perspectives* (New York: Council on Foreign Relations, 1986) pp. 32, 77-78.

2. Murray Marder and Don Oberdorfer, "How West, Soviets Moved to Head Off S. Africa A-Test," *Washington Post*, August 28, 1977.
3. Interview with author, Spring 1985.
4. David Fishlock, "The South African Nuclear Weapons Scare," paper prepared for the Congressional Research Service, December 1977, p. CRS-5.
5. Marder and Oberdorfer, "How West, Soviets Moved."
6. Caryle Murphy, "South Africa Powers Reactor with Uranium it Enriched," *Washington Post*, April 30, 1981. The Ford administration had suspended shipments of fuel for the U.S.-supplied SAFARI reactor in 1975. Since 1980, U.S. law has prohibited nuclear fuel exports to South Africa because of South Africa's refusal to place all of its nuclear installations under IAEA safeguards. Nuclear Non-Proliferation Act of 1978, P.L. 95-242, amending Atomic Energy Act of 1954, sections 127, 128 (1978).
7. See note 38; below. A widely cited 1980 UN Centre for Disarmament study assumed South Africa was capable of producing 50 kilograms of highly enriched uranium annually, beginning in March 1977. Department of Political and Security Council Affairs, United Nations Centre for Disarmament, Report of the Secretary General, *South Africa's Plan and Capability in the Nuclear Field,* Report A/35/402 (New York: United Nations, 1980). This estimate of the date of the first availability of South African highly enriched uranium, on which the author relied in *Nuclear Proliferation Today* (New York: Vintage Books, 1984), now appears premature.
8. At the time the Kalahari test site was discovered in mid-1977, it may be noted, Washington reacted vigorously, given the clear evidence that a test site was being readied and the uncertainties that then prevailed as to Pretoria's enriched-uranium-production capabilities.
9. The panel's conclusions have remained controversial and were apparently disputed by the Defense Intelligence Agency and the Naval Research Laboratory. Key Carter administration arms control officials continue to view the report of the White House panel as definitive, however. The Reagan administration has declined to reopen the matter.
10. Interviews with U.S. officials, spring 1985. South Africa claims that placing the pilot-scale enrichment plant under IAEA monitoring would divulge industrial secrets. It has never, however, offered to negotiate the question with the Agency to see if such disclosures could be avoided. See generally, summary of IAEA General Conference discussion of South African nuclear program, GC(XXVIII)/724 Annex 2 (Vienna: IAEA 1984).
11. See e.g. Bernard Gwertzman and Alan Cowell, "U.S. Recalls Envoy from Pretoria in Response to Raid on Botswana," *New York Times*, June 15, 1985; Anthony Robinson, et al. "S. African At-

tacks Threaten Bid for Constitutional Talks," *Financial Times*, May 20, 1986.

12. See e.g. Executive Order 12532 (September 9, 1985) imposing economic sanctions against South Africa; see notes 19 and 20 below.

13. Angola, for example, is said to have MiG-21 and MiG-23 jet fighters in its arsenal. The Cheetah, an up-grade of South Africa's aging Mirage IIIa's is said to be able to match the MiG-23. "General Malan Comments," Johannesburg SAPA, 0025 GMT, July 16, 1986, reprinted in *Foreign Broadcast Information Service (FBIS)/Middle East and Africa*, July 16, 1986, p. U-4. See Glenn Frankel, "U.N. Arms Ban Proves Costly to South Africans," *Washington Post*, February 21, 1985; Christopher Coker, "South Africa: A New Military Role in Southern Africa," *Survival* (March/April 1983): 59; "T.V. Reviews Weapons Buildup in Southern Africa," Johannesburg Television Service, 1800 GMT, November 6, 1985, reprinted in *Foreign Broadcast Information Service (FBIS)/Middle-East and Africa*, November 7, 1985, p. U-13.

14. The Final Declaration of the Third Review Conference on the Treaty on the Non-Proliferation of Nuclear Weapons, for example, specifically criticized South Africa's nuclear posture in two separate provisions, calling on it to place all of its nuclear plants under IAEA safeguards. See also "South Africa's Nuclear Capabilities," Resolution adopted during the IAEA General Conference September 27, 1985, GC(XXIX)/Res/442.

15. See note 6.

16. See Leonard S. Spector, *Nuclear Proliferation Today* (New York: Vintage Books, 1984), pp. 295-298; Rick Atkinson, "Reactor Operators Suspected of Working for South Africa," *Washington Post*, January 20, 1985.

17. Leonard S. Spector, *The New Nuclear Nations* (New York: Vintage Books, 1985) pp. 54-59. During 1984, Pretoria also reportedly sought to bypass supplier-country controls in the hopes of eventually obtaining a heavy water plant not subject to IAEA safeguards. Although no supplier nation would sell such a facility without IAEA controls, Pretoria was said to be negotiating with the Swiss firm of Sulzer Brothers to obtain engineering services that would have enabled it to purchase unregulated components for such a plant and assemble them in South Africa. U.S. non-proliferation specialists feared that unsafeguarded heavy water might be used in a clandestine natural-uranium/heavy-water reactor to produce plutonium for nuclear arms. Spector, *The New Nuclear Nations*, pp. 220-222.

18. Preexisting contracts relating to the operation of the French-supplied Koeberg reactors were not to be affected, however. The July 1985 partial state of emergency was lifted on March 7, 1986. However, a nationwide state of emergency was declared on June

12, 1986.

"Nuclear Hardware Not Affected," Umtata Capital Radio, 1100 GMT July 25, 1985, reprinted in *FBIS/Mid-East and Africa*, July 26, 1985, p. U-3.

19. Executive Order 12532. Exceptions were allowed to permit nuclear transfers for humanitarian reasons and in support of IAEA safeguards. These sanctions, originally imposed for a year, were extended in September 1986. Bernard Weinraub, "Reagan Extending Limited Sanctions," *New York Times*, September 5, 1986.

20. The change in the American stance, it should be stressed, was a reflection of public and congressional concerns; the Reagan administration had consistently opposed sanctions of any kind and implemented them only because of domestic political pressure.

It is also worth noting that the most economically painful nuclear-related sanction—a prohibition on the importation of South African uranium—was not imposed at this time, and the United States and Western Europe continued to import significant quantities of the material; Canada, however, banned imports of uranium produced in Namibia, territory which South Africa continues to occupy despite the expiration of its UN mandate to govern the region. James Branscome, "Canada Bans Future Conversion Contracts for Namibian Uranium at Eldorado Facility," *Nuclear Fuel*, July 29, 1985, p. 10; Dinah Wisenberg, "Antiapartheid Measure Poses Distant Threat to South African Uranium Imports," *Nuclear Fuel*, August 12, 1985, p. 3; James Branscome, "South Africa Will Offer SWU On World Market in 1988," *Nucleonics Week*, February 27, 1986, p.1.

South Africa had paid the U.S. Department of Energy in advance for enriching a quantity of uranium to the low level needed for reactor fuel. When it became clear that prohibitions in the 1978 Non-Proliferation Act would prevent the Reagan administration from exporting enriched uranium to South Africa, Pretoria, with U.S. approval, sold off both the natural uranium feed material it had presented to DOE for enrichment and the enrichment rights, the former to the Central Electricity Generating Board of Great Britain and the latter to the Swiss utility, Bernische Kraftwerke AG. Stephanie Cooke, "Britain's CEGB Buys U.S.-Origin U3O8 Owned by South Africa's ESCOM," *Nuclear Fuel*, February 11, 1985, p. 1. At least through mid-1985, American and foreign utilities had also arranged for the importation into the United States of significant quantities of South African uranium to be enriched by the U.S. Department of Energy to reactor-fuel levels. See John Buell and Daniel Horner, "Weapons Implications of U.S. South African Uranium Trade," (Washington, D.C.: Nuclear Control Institute, 1985); updated through interview, June 1985.

In mid-1986, Washington and the European Economic Community (EEC) considered a ban on imports of South African uranium, as part of a second round of sanctions that would be considerably harsher than those imposed in September 1985, and a group of six British Commonwealth countries had agreed to implement such a ban on uranium imports. (Britain, however, refused to adopt this measure.) Neil A. Lewis, "West's Sanction Plans." Karen De Young, "Britain Firm Against Wide Sanctions," *Washington Post,* July 31, 1986; Edward Walsh, "Senate Panel Votes Sanctions on Pretoria," *Washington Post,* August 2, 1986. Ultimately, however, the EEC dropped the uranium import ban from the list of sanctions it adopted, while U.S. legislation, passed in October 1986 over President Reagan's veto, banned importation of only certain forms of uranium (uranium ore and uranium oxide, but not uranium hexafluoride). Karen De Young, "Europeans Vote Weakened Sanctions," *Washington Post,* September 17, 1986; Steven V. Roberts, "Senate, 78 to 21, Overrides Reagan's Veto and Imposes Sanctions on South Africa," *New York Times,* October 3, 1986.

With respect to the termination of U.S. nuclear exports to South Africa, the U.S. legislation, it may be noted, once again linked the lifting of this ban with South Africa's nuclear policies; exports could be reinstituted if Pretoria ratified the NPT or placed all of its peaceful nuclear activities under IAEA safeguards. Anti-apartheid Act of 1986, P.L.99-440 (1986), Section 307 (a).

21. By late March 1986 some 1300 persons had been killed in the nineteen months of civil unrest that had begun in August 1984. Glenn Frankel, "2 South African Police Die in Township Violence," *Washington Post,* March 26, 1986.

22. Anthony Robinson, "South African Guerrillas Blast Strategic Plant," *Financial Times,* November 11, 1985.

23. Ibid.

24. Rob Laufer, "Reactor Components Struck in Bombings at South Africa's Koeberg Station," *Nucleonics Week,* December 23, 1982, p.1.

25. Allister Sparks, "Homeland Official Killed in S. Africa," *Washington Post,* July 31, 1986. When the Botha government in mid-June 1986 reimposed the state of emergency that had been lifted in March, anti-white terror tactics reached new heights, with bombings in the white sections of Durban and Johannesburg and the use of mines to destroy water lines near the former city. But it is by no means clear that stepped-up ANC violence will be confined to such "soft" targets and that further paramilitary operations will not be mounted.

26. During the spring of 1986, Botha attempted to deflect black demands for power-sharing by initiating a series of carefully limited reforms of apartheid. In March, for example, an eight-month state of emergency was lifted and blacks detained under it were released.

In April, Botha introduced legislation to moderate the nation's system of "pass laws," requiring blacks to carry written passes to work in the country's so-called whites-only cities. A second measure introduced at this time sought to restore South African citizenship to some blacks who lost it when the tribal "homelands" they supposedly belong to were declared "independent" by the Pretoria government. Glenn Frankel, "South Africa Presses Apartheid Reforms Spurned by Blacks," *Washington Post*, June 26, 1986. These two legislative proposals were not as sweeping as they appear, however. While the abolition of the pass laws would permit blacks to travel freely in search of work, other laws prohibiting blacks from residing in white areas were to remain in effect. The citizenship restoration proposal similarly benefited only twenty percent of blacks whose South African citizenship had been withdrawn.

27. Ned Tenko, "S. Africa Raids on ANC: Bid to Appease Rightists," *Christian Science Monitor*, May 20, 1986; Anthony Robinson, et al., "S. African Attacks Threaten Bid for Constitutional Talks," *Financial Times*, May 20, 1986.

28. The state of emergency was imposed in anticipation of massive antigovernment protests on June 16 to commemorate the tenth anniversary of an uprising in the black township of Soweto. By late July an estimated 10,000 to 12,000 persons had been detained under the emergency decree. Bernard Weinraub, "U.S. Says It Weighs Limited Sanctions on South Africa," *New York Times*, July 27, 1986.

29. Allister Sparks, "Botha Refuses Plea to Free Mandela," *Washington Post*, July 30, 1986. A British paper summed up Botha's response to Howe's mediation effort more succinctly with the headline, "Get Lost!" Karen DeYoung, "Britain Firm Against Wide Sanctions," *Washington Post*, July 31, 1986.

30. Steven V. Roberts, "Senate, 78 to 21, Overrides Reagan's Veto." See note 20.

31. The six Commonwealth nations were Australia, the Bahamas, Canada, India, Zambia, and Zimbabwe; together with Britain they formed a seven-nation committee charged by the forty-nine member Commonwealth with developing a policy toward South Africa. Although the Thatcher government rejected the sanctions package subsequently passed by the Commonwealth, in so doing it appeared to accept a milder sanctions program proposed by the EEC. The principal differences were that the Commonwealth package included a ban on extending landing rights to South African airlines and a ban on new investment in South Africa. Mrs. Thatcher would not accept the former ban but did agree to "discourage" further British investment. Britain is one of South Africa's two principal trading partners along with the United States. Karen DeYoung, "Thatcher's Sanctions Stance Called 'Pathetic,' " *Washington Post*, August 6, 1986.

32. Allister Sparks, "S. Africa Hits New Sanctions," *Washington Post*, August 6, 1986.
33. As noted above, Congress overrode President Reagan's veto of U.S. sanctions legislation in October 1986, but the matter is unlikely to end there. The legislation will be subject to interpretation and, where it has the discretion, the administration, because it opposes the sanctions in principle, will undoubtedly attempt to mitigate the measure's impact. Moreover, the sanctions legislation itself was far milder than it might have been because of President Reagan's opposition. And, undoubtedly, the administration would seek to block any harsher measures that might be considered in the future. Thus, despite Congress's override of Reagan's sanctions veto, the Botha government would still have something to lose if it alienated the Reagan camp to the point that the president ceased his opposition to such measures. The same is true in the case of the Thatcher government.
34. Regarding right-wing political activities, see Ned Tenko, "S. African Raids on ANC: Bid to Appease Rightists," *Christian Science Monitor,* May 20, 1986; "Pretoria Returns to a Siege Mentality," *Financial Times*, June 7, 1986.
35. Ned Tenko, "South African Ruling Party Tries to Rein in Right," *Christian Science Monitor,* April 10, 1986.
36. See note 7 and, "Former IAEA Official on Bomb Production," *Star,* September 14, 1985, reprinted in *FBIS/Middle East and Africa,* September 17, 1985, p. U-16.
37. Ann MacLachlan, "IAEA Acknowledges Impass in Talks with South Africa Over Safeguards," *Nuclear Fuel,* October 6, 1986, p. 5.
38. Weapons-grade uranium is made up of 90 percent or more uranium-235, a rare isotope that is found in natural uranium in a concentration of less than 1 percent. South Africa's small Valindaba uranium enrichment facility is capable of increasing the concentration of uranium-235 to weapons-grade, but, using natural uranium as a feedstock, it can produce only enough weapons-grade material for two or possibly three nuclear weapons per year. Because of the peculiarities of the uranium enrichment process, a large proportion of the work (and hence of plant capacity) involved in reaching the highly enriched level needed for weapons is expended in upgrading natural uranium to the low-enriched stage (3 percent uranium-235); considerably less effort (and plant capacity) is required to increase the low-enriched material to weapons-grade levels. The Valindaba plant, which uses the jet-nozzle process, is thought to be composed of thousands of nozzle units, each of which incrementally increases the concentration of the material passed through it. After each slight concentration, the improved material is fed into another nozzle for further slight enhancement, a process that is repeated until

the desired enrichment level is obtained. To produce highly enriched uranium from natural uranium, a large proportion of the
available nozzle units must be devoted to reaching the low-enriched
stage. If the enrichment process begins with low-enriched material,
however, a larger proportion of the facility can, in principle, be
devoted to the task of reaching the higher enrichment level needed
for weapons.

39. George Lardner, Jr. and Don Oberdorfer, "China Was Source of
    Atomic Fuel for South Africa, U.S. Believes," *Washington Post,*
    November 18, 1981; "China Says Study Shows It Wasn't Uranium
    Source," *Washington Post,* December 8, 1981. Some U.S. officials
    believe the Chinese material may have been sold to South Africa
    through middlemen.

40. Rob Laufer, "Kaiserangst Purchase Seen As Freeing South Africa
    from U.S. Contract," *Nucleonics Week,* February 18, 1982, p. 1.

41. Christer Larsson and Jan Melin, "Third World Countries Buy
    Swedish Nuclear Weapons Technology," *Ny Teknik,* May 2, 1986,
    p. 12, translated in JPRS/TND , July 30, 1986, p. 1. Flash X-ray
    machines are discussed in detail in the section on Pakistan, above,
    note 29.

42. "President is the Pits," Associated Press, *Washington Post,* July 23,
    1986.

43. The political leverage in this instance would stem both from the
    vital interest of the government in regaining control over its nuclear
    assets as well as from the prospect that a weapon might be used
    against a South African target.

Chapter VII:
Controls and Safeguards

1. See *Nucleonics Week,* issue of August 28, 1986; Walter Pincus, "U.S., Soviets to Sign 2 Pacts Today on A-Power Accidents," *Washington Post,* September 26, 1986; Ann MacLachlan, "Nuclear Safety Conventions Endorsed Overwhelmingly in Vienna," *Nucleonics Week,* October 2, 1986.

2. See Leonard S. Spector, *The New Nuclear Nations* (New York: Vintage Books, 1985) pp. 143-146.

3. See "China," *Nucleonics Week,* February 27, 1986, p. 15.

4. IAEA Annual Report for 1985, p. 59.

5. Ibid, p. 61.

6. The other new parties since mid-1985 are Belize (August 1985), Malawi (December 1985), and Colombia (April 1986). For a discussion of the Third Non-Proliferation Treaty Review Conference, see Leonard S. Spector, *The New Nuclear Nations,* pp. 240-250.

7. See Introduction to Asia chapter.

8. Leonard S. Spector, *The New Nuclear Nations,* pp. 22-44.

9. Communication with Simon Henderson of the *Financial Times,* July 1986. Slebos was given six months' probation and a 20,000 guilder ($8,600) fine in lieu of his one-year jail sentence.

10. Another development relating to the eight prosecutions was the decision of Dutch authorities not to re-indict senior Pakistani nuclear aide Abdul Qader Khan, after his conviction, in absentia, for soliciting classified information was set aside on appeal. Khan, a German-trained metallurgist who had worked in the Netherlands for a subcontractor of the Dutch-German-British uranium enrichment consortium, URENCO, had been convicted in October 1983 for requesting classified data on uranium enrichment technology from two former colleagues in 1976 and 1977. In March 1985, a Dutch appeals court reversed his conviction on the grounds that he had not been properly notified of the charges against him. (The Pakistani government had refused to serve him with the Dutch summons, citing the absence of a formal treaty on this subject with the Netherlands.) Simon Henderson, "Netherlands Drops Proceedings Against Nuclear Scientist," *Financial Times,* July 16, 1986.

11. New data also came to light about a number of incidents that have been previously reported, including Libya's negotiations to purchase (non-existent) nuclear weapons from Edwin Wilson in 1981 and Israel's secret dealings with France during the 1950s and 1960s. These are discussed in the sections on Libya and Israel.

Appendices

Appendix A: Producing Nuclear-Weapons Material – A Primer

It is generally accepted today that designing an atomic bomb—drawing the blueprint—is within the capabilities of most nations. Indeed, a number of American college students have come up with workable designs based on unclassified material.

The major technical barrier to making a nuclear device is obtaining the nuclear material for its core. Twenty-five kilograms (fifty-five pounds) of highly enriched uranium, or eight kilograms (about eighteen pounds) of plutonium are generally considered the necessary minimum, although in both cases more sophisticated designs relying on high compression of the core material, neutron reflecting "tampers," or both, enable a bomb to be built with considerably less material—perhaps fifteen kilograms of highly enriched uranium or five kilograms of plutonium, and even smaller amounts can apparently be used. Neither of these materials occurs in nature, however, and highly complex and expensive facilities must be built and operated in order to make them—an undertaking of considerable difficulty for developing nations without assistance from more advanced nuclear-supplier countries.

Highly enriched uranium. To make a weapon from uranium, the unstable "isotope" of uranium having a total of 235 protons and neutrons in its nucleus (U^{235}) is used. Since natural uranium consists of less than one percent U^{235}, while nuclear weapons use material that is made up of 90 percent or more U^{235}, natural uranium must be upgraded at an *enrichment plant* to achieve this concentration. Uranium enrichment is an extremely complex process and requires considerable investment. For this reason, the uranium enrichment route has been generally considered a less likely path to proliferation than the plutonium option. However, South Africa, Argentina, and (with extensive outside aid obtained mostly by clandestine means) Pakistan have all developed independent uranium enrichment capabilities, and Israel, Brazil, and India are known to be conducting research in the field.

Enriched uranium can also be used as a fuel in nuclear power or research reactors. The power reactors used in the United States and most other countries (called "light-water reactors") use *low-enriched uranium* fuel, i.e., uranium that has been enriched up to three percent U^{235}. Thus a country can have entirely legitimate, non-weapons-related reasons for developing uranium enrichment technology even though the same technology can be used to upgrade uranium to the high enrichment level useful for nuclear weapons. On the other hand, developing a sizable independent uranium enrichment capability is economically justifiable only for nations with large domestic nuclear power programs or significant potential export markets.

Because highly enriched uranium is sometimes used to fuel research reactors, a nation can have legitimate reasons for obtaining small quantities of this material, despite its usefulness in nuclear explosives. In recent years the United States and France have developed lower-enriched uranium fuels that can be used in lieu of highly enriched material in most of these reactors, however, considerably reducing the proliferation risks these research facilities pose.

Producing highly enriched uranium entails many steps apart from the enrichment process itself, and many other installations and capabilities are necessary. For nations wishing to obtain highly enriched uranium without international restrictions prohibiting its use for nuclear explosives, all of these would have to develop independently, or obtained illegally, since virtually all nuclear exporter states are unwilling to sell nuclear equipment and materials unless recipients pledge not to use them for nuclear explosives purposes and place them under the inspection system of the International Atomic Energy Agency. (See Appendix C). For illustrative purposes the basic nuclear resources and facilities that would be needed include:

- uranium deposits;
- a uranium mine;
- a uranium mill (for processing uranium ore containing less than one percent uranium into uranium oxide concentrate, or yellowcake);
- a conversion plant (for purifying yellowcake and converting it into uranium hexafluoride, the material processed in the enrichment plant);
- an enrichment plant (for enriching the uranium hexafluoride gas in the isotope U^{235}); and
- a capability for converting the enriched uranium hexafluoride gas into solid uranium oxide or metal (a capability usually associated with a yellowcake-to-hexafluoride conversion plant).

Plutonium. To obtain plutonium a country needs a *nuclear reactor*. This can be one designed specifically to maximize plutonium production (a "production reactor"), a large research reactor, or a power reactor for producing electricity. *Uranium fuel*, usually in the form of uranium-filled tubes (fuel rods) made of zirconium alloy (zircaloy), is placed in the reactor. For most production, power, and for a number of large research reactors, the fuel itself is either natural or low-enriched uranium, which is not usable for nuclear weapons at this point. As the reactor operates, the uranium fuel is partly transformed into plutonium. This is amalgamated in the fuel rods with unused uranium and highly radioactive waste products, however, and must then be extracted. To do this, "spent" fuel rods are taken to a *reprocessing plant* where they are dissolved in nitric acid and the plutonium is separated from the solution in a series of chemical processing steps. Since the spent fuel rods are highly radioactive, heavy lead casks must be used to transport them, and the rooms at the reprocessing plant where the chemical extraction of the plutonium occurs must have thick walls, lead shielding, and special ventilation to prevent radiation hazards.

Although detailed information about reprocessing was declassified by the United States and France in the 1950s and is generally available, it is still a complex procedure from an engineering point of view, and virtually every nation at the nuclear-weapons threshold that has attempted it—Argentina, Brazil, India, Iraq, Israel, and Pakistan—has sought outside help from the advanced nuclear-supplier countries.

Like enrichment facilities, however, reprocessing plants can also be used for legitimate civilian purposes, because plutonium can be used as fuel in nuclear-power reactors. Indeed, through the 1970s it was generally assumed that as the use of nuclear power grew, worldwide uranium resources would be depleted and plutonium extracted from spent fuel would have to be "recycled" as a substitute fuel in conventional power reactors.

In addition, research and development is under way in a number of nations on a new generation of reactors known as breeder reactors. These use plutonium as fuel surrounded with a "blanket" of natural uranium; as the reactor operates, slightly more plutonium is created in the core and the blanket together than is consumed in the core, thereby "breeding" new fuel.

Like plutonium recycling, the economic advantages of breeders depends on natural uranium becoming scarce and expensive. But over the past decade new uranium reserves have been discovered, nuclear power has reached only a fraction of its expected growth levels, and reprocessing spent fuel to extract plutonium (a critical step in both cases) has proven far more expensive and complex than anticipated. Moreover, concern over the proliferation risks of widescale use of plutonium as a fuel has grown. These factors have led one advanced nation, the United States, to abandon its plans to use plutonium fuel, although Japan, France, Britain, and West Germany are continuing to develop this technology actively. Nevertheless, the advanced nuclear-supplier countries are strongly discouraging plutonuim use in nations of proliferation concern.

The longstanding view that plutonium is a legitimate and anticipated part of civilian nuclear programs, however, has allowed Argentina, Brazil, India, and Pakistan to justify their reprocessing programs—even though they currently provide these nations with a nuclear-weapons capability, or may soon do so.

Like the production of enriched uranium, the production of plutonium entails many steps, and many installations and capabilities apart from the reactor and reprocessing plant are needed. For illustrative purposes, the following facilities and resources would be required for an independent plutonium-production capability assuming a heavy-water research or power reactor, employing natural uranium fuel, is used:

- uranium deposits;
- a uranium mine;
- a uranium mill (for processing uranium ore containing less than one percent uranium into uranium oxide concentrate, or yellowcake);
- a uranium purification plant (to further improve the yellowcake into reactor-grade uranium dioxide);
- a fuel fabrication plant (to manufacture the fuel elements placed in the reactor), including a capability to fabricate zircaloy tubing;

- a heavy-water research or power reactor;
- a heavy-water production plant; and
- a reprocessing plant.

If the option of building a natural-uranium/graphite reactor is used, the needs would be the same although reactor-grade graphite would have to be produced instead of heavy water. A light-water reactor would necessitate use of low-enriched uranium, implying an enrichment capability was available; if so, highly enriched uranium could, in theory, be produced, obviating the need for plutonium as a weapons material.

Appendix B: Nuclear Weapons—A Primer

A nuclear weapon is a device in which most or all of the explosive energy is derived from either fission, fusion, or a combination of the two nuclear processes. *Nuclear fission* is the splitting of the nucleus of an atom into two (or more) parts. Highly enriched uranium and plutonium, when bombarded by neutrons, will release energy and emit additional neutrons while splitting into lighter atoms. In *nuclear fusion*, light isotopes of hydrogen, usually deuterium and tritium, join at high temperatures and similarly liberate energy and neutrons.

Fission Weapons. Many heavy atomic nuclei are capable of being fissioned; but only a fraction of these are *fissile*, which means fissionable by neutrons with a wide range of velocities. It is this property of fissile material, principally U^{235} and Pu^{239}, that allows a chain reaction to be achieved in weapons employing the fission process. In a *chain reaction*, fissile nuclei that have been bombarded by neutrons split and emit two or more neutrons, which in turn induce proximate nuclei to fission and sustain the process. With each successive fission "generation" additional energy is released, and, if the fission of one nucleus induces an average of more than one fission in the following generation, the energy yield of each generation is multiplied. A fission explosion in the range of 1 to 100 kilotons for example, would occur over a few microseconds and involve over fifty generations, with 99.9 percent of the energy released coming in the last seven. The minimum mass of material necessary to sustain a chain reaction is called the *critical mass*. This value may be lowered by increasing the material's density through compression or by surrounding it with "reflectors" to minimize the escape of neutrons; this makes it difficult to pin down the precise amount of uranium or plutonium required for a bomb.

Two basic nuclear-weapon-design approaches that are used to achieve a supercritical mass (i.e., exceeding the critical level) are the implosion technique and the gun assembly technique. In the *implosion technique,* a peripheral charge of chemical high explosive is uniformly detonated to compress a subcritical mass of plutonium or highly enriched uranium into a supercritical configuration. In the *gun assembly technique,* two (or more) subcritical masses of highly enriched uranium (plutonium cannot be used) are propelled together by a conventional explosion, resulting in a supercritical mass. In both cases, a *tamper* may be used to keep the material from exploding before enough generations of a chain reaction have occurred, and this tamper often doubles as a reflector to reduce the escape of electrons.

Fusion weapons. Fusion of light atomic nuclei requires a high density of fusion material and extraordinary heat, both of which are provided by a fission explosion in a "thermonuclear" or "hydrogen" bomb. Lithium-6 deuteride is the most widely used thermonuclear material, serving as a source of both deuterium and tritium, the atoms whose nuclei merge, in a fusion weapon.

In a *boosted weapon,* fusion material is introduced directly into (or next to) the core of fissile material, improving the efficiency of a fission weapon and thus increasing the yield of a given quantity of highly enriched uranium or plutonium. Although energy is released in the fusion reaction of a boosted weapon, the primary contribution of the fusion material to the explosion is that it provides additional neutrons for the fission process and therefore allows a more rapidly multiplying chain reaction to occur.

Other thermonuclear weapons are designed to capitalize on the energy released in a "secondary" fusion reaction triggered by a "primary" fission explosion. In such devices, fusion material is kept physically separate from a fissile or boosted fissile core that compresses and ignites it. Additional "stages" of fusion or fission material may be included to augment the weapon's yield, with each layer being triggered by ones closer to the core. For example, the *hydrogen bomb* includes a third stage or "blanket" of natural uranium, a widely available fissionable but not fissile material, that is fissioned by fast neutrons from the primary and secondary fission and fusion reactions. Hence, the energy released in the explosion of such a device stems from three sources—a fission chain reaction, the first stage; "burning" of the thermonuclear fuel, the second stage; and the fission of the U-238 blanket, the third stage—with, very roughly, half the total energy stemming from fission and the other half from fusion.

Source: Thomas B. Cochran, William M. Arkin, and Milton M. Hoenig, *U.S. Nuclear Forces and Capabilities* (Cambridge, MA: Ballinger Publishing Company, 1984), Chapter 2.

Appendix C: International Atomic Energy Agency (IAEA) Safeguards

The International Atomic Energy Agency, a Vienna-based U.N.-affiliated organization now having over 110 members, was founded in 1957. By the mid-1960s, it had established a program of on-site inspections, audits, and inventory controls know collectively as "safeguards." Today, the IAEA monitors some seven hundred installations in over fifty nations and the Agency is widely regarded as a principal bulwark against the spread of nuclear arms.

The basic purpose of IAEA safeguards is to deter the diversion of nuclear materials from peaceful uses to military purposes through the risk of timely detection. In simplified terms, the Agency monitors the flow of nuclear materials at nuclear installations by auditing plant records and conducting physical inventories. Seals and cameras are used to ensure materials are not diverted while IAEA inspectors are not present.

To date, the IAEA has never concluded that material under safeguards has been diverted. In September 1981, however, the Agency indicated that it was unable to determine whether material was diverted from Pakistan's KANUPP reactor or from a similarly designed reactor in India because the Agency had not been permitted to apply all of the monitoring apparatus needed at these installations. The Indian deficiency was quickly corrected, but it was nearly a year and a half before the safeguards at the KANUPP reactor were declared adequate. It is possible that during this period plutonium-bearing spent fuel was removed from the reactor without detection.

Apart from these unusual cases, the IAEA safeguards system has some well-recognized limitations. First, and most important, key installations in countries of proliferation concern including enrichment and reprocessing facilities, are not under the IAEA system. Thus, Argentina, Brazil, India, Israel, Pakistan, and South Africa all remain free to use unsafeguarded installations to manufacture material for nuclear weapons. (Even in each of these countries, however, some installations are subject to the IAEA system, and nuclear materials produced in them cannot, therefore, be used for this purpose.) Nations that have ratified the Non-Proliferation Treaty or for which the Treaty of Tlatelolco is in force have accepted safeguards on all their nuclear facilities.

Secondly, certain types of facilities, such as fuel fabrication, reprocessing, and enrichment installations, handle nuclear materials in bulk form, i.e., as powders, liquids, or gasses. Such materials are particularly difficult to safeguard since measurement techniques are not accurate enough to keep track of 100 percent of these substances as they move through the facilities processing them. This makes it theoretically possible to divert a certain small percentage of material for military purposes without detection since this could appear to be a normal operating discrepancy. The problem is especially dangerous at fuel-fabrication plants handling plutonium or highly enriched uranium in powdered form, at reprocessing plants where plutonium is dissolved in various liquids for processing, and at enrichment plants, which use uranium hexafluoride gas as feed.

Low IAEA budgets and manpower have also meant that far fewer inspections are conducted at safeguarded installations than needed to meet the IAEA's safeguards objectives fully. Other problems include the fact that it is almost impossible for Agency inspectors to make unannounced visits to safeguarded installations. Nations subject to IAEA safeguards are also permitted to reject particular IAEA inspectors.

It must be stressed, however, that even if safeguards as applied are imperfect, their deterrent value remains strong since would-be diverters could not have confidence that their misuse of nuclear materials would go undetected.

Finally, even assuming that IAEA safeguards functioned perfectly, their usefulness may be limited when applied to highly enriched uranium and plutonium, materials directly usable for nuclear weapons. Here, even if the IAEA system reacted instantaneously to diversion, it might still be possible for the nation appropriating this material to manufacture nuclear weapons within a matter of weeks if all the non-nuclear components had been prepared in advance, presenting the world community with a *fait accompli*. In such a setting, safeguards cannot provide "timely warning" sufficient to allow the international community to react before the nation diverting the material has achieved its objective. For this reason, the United States has worked actively to curtail commerce with nations of proliferation concern involving plutonium, highly enriched uranium, or enrichment and reprocessing facilities—whether or not safeguards would be applied. Virtually all other nuclear supplier nations have adopted the cautious approach of the United States in transferring such items.

In the event of a safeguards violation, the Agency's Board of Governors has the authority to notify the United Nations Security Council, but not to impose sanctions of any kind.

**Appendix D: The Treaty on the Non-Proliferation of
Nuclear Weapons (NPT)**

The treaty divides the countries of the world into two categories, "nuclear-weapon states" (those which had detonated a nuclear weapon before 1967, i.e., the United States, the Soviet Union, Great Britain, France, and China) and "non-nuclear-weapon states" (those which had not). Under this pact:

- Non-nuclear-weapon states ratifying the treaty pledge not to manufacture or receive nuclear explosives. (Both nuclear weapons and peaceful nuclear explosives are prohibited.)

- To verify that they are living up to this pledge, non-nuclear-weapon states also agree to accept International Atomic Energy Agency safeguards on all their nuclear activities (an arrangement known as "full-scope" safeguards).

- All countries accepting the treaty agree not to export nuclear equipment or material to non-nuclear-weapon states except under IAEA safeguards and nuclear-weapon states agree not to assist non-nuclear-weapon states in obtaining nuclear arms.

- All countries accepting the treaty agree to facilitate the fullest possible sharing of peaceful nuclear technology. (In practice this is a pledge by the advanced nations to help less developed countries build peaceful nuclear programs.)

- All countries accepting the treaty agree to pursue negotiations in good faith to end the nuclear arms race, and achieve nuclear disarmament under international control. (In practice, this applies to the United States and the Soviet Union.)

- A party to the treaty may withdraw on 90-days' notice if "extraordinary events" related to the subject matter of the treaty have "jeopardized" its "supreme interests."

In effect, the treaty is an agreement among countries with

differing interests. The less developed countries, for example, give up their right to develop nuclear arms and accept full-scope safeguards. In return, the advanced countries agree to share peaceful nuclear technology, and those with nuclear arsenals agree to pursue arms control.

The treaty does *not* prohibit parties from accumulating nuclear-weapons material (highly enriched uranium or plutonium) as part of their peaceful nuclear energy or research programs as long as the material is subject to IAEA inspection. This means parties to the pact can come dangerously close to possessing nuclear arms without violating the terms of the treaty.

The treaty has also been interpreted to permit parties to make nuclear sales to countries that are not parties, such as India or Argentina, even if these countries have unsafeguarded nuclear facilities. However, the items exported (and nuclear materials produced through their use), must themselves be placed under IAEA safeguards. Thus, for example, U.S. sales of nuclear fuel to South Africa, which has at least one unsafeguarded nuclear installation, are permissible under the treaty as long as the fuel is placed under safeguards in South Africa. (However, U.S. law, the 1978 Nuclear Non-Proliferation Act, prohibited sales to countries with unsafeguarded facilities after March 1980, absent a special presidential waiver. Canada, Sweden, and Australia have also adopted this policy.)

Negotiations devoted specifically to the Non-Proliferation Treaty began in earnest in 1965, when the United States, and later the Soviet Union, submitted draft treaties to the Eighteen-Nation Disarmament Committee. After overcoming a number of potential stumbling-blocks—including disagreement over the form and extent of the proposed safeguards and demands for security assurances by the non-nuclear-weapon states—the treaty was opened for signature on July 1, 1968, and signed on that date by the United States, the United Kingdom, and the Soviet Union, along with fifty-nine non-nuclear-weapon states. The U.S. Senate ratified the treaty in 1970. More than 130 non-weapon states have ratified the treaty, along with the three nuclear-weapon states, mentioned earlier.

France, though not a party, has pledged to behave as though it were. However, China, also not a party, is believed to have taken actions that would be prohibited by the treaty. In the late 1970s and early 1980s, it sold nuclear materials to Argentina and reportedly to India, Pakistan, and South Africa without requiring the application of IAEA safeguards, and it may have directly assisted Pakistan in designing nuclear weapons. In 1983, however, China advised the United States that it would require safeguards on all its future nuclear exports.

Six non-nuclear-weapon states of proliferation concern—Argentina, Brazil, India, Israel, Pakistan, and South Africa—have not ratified the treaty. All have unsafeguarded nuclear activities. Libya, Iraq, and Iran, three additional potential nuclear-weapon states, are parties to the accord.

Three review conferences on the implementation of the treaty have been held in 1975, 1980, and 1985.*

---

* See, generally *Arms Control and Disarmament Agreements, Text and Histories of Negotiations,* United States Arms Control and Disarmament Agency, 1982 edition, pp. 82-95.

A. Parties to the Non-Proliferation Treaty

Afghanistan	1970	Holy See	1971
Antigua and Barbuda	1985	Honduras	1973
Australia	1973	Hungary	1969
Austria	1969	Iceland	1969
Bahamas, The	1976	Indonesia	1979
Bangladesh	1979	Iran	1970
Barbados	1980	Iraq	1969
Belgium	1975	Ireland	1968
Belize	1985	Italy	1975
Benin	1972	Ivory Coast	1973
Bhutan	1985	Jamaica	1970
Bolivia	1970	Japan	1976
Botswana	1969	Jordan	1970
Brunei	1985	Kampuchea	1972
Bulgaria	1969	Kenya	1970
Burkina Faso	1970	Kiribati	1985
Burundi	1971	Korea (South)	1975
Cameroon	1969	Laos	1970
Canada	1969	Lebanon	1970
Cape Verde	1979	Lesotho	1970
Central African Rep.	1970	Liberia	1970
Chad	1971	Libya	1975
Colombia	1986	Liechtenstein	1978
Congo	1978	Luxembourg	1975
Costa Rica	1970	Madagascar	1970
Cyprus	1970	Malawi	1986
Czechoslovakia	1969	Malaysia	1970
Denmark	1969	Maldives	1970
Dominica	1968	Mali	1970
Dominican Republic	1971	Malta	1970
Ecuador	1969	Mauritius	1969
Egypt	1981	Mexico	1969
El Salvador	1972	Mongolia	1969
Equatorial Guinea	1984	Morocco	1970
Ethiopia	1970	Nauru	1982
Fiji	1972	Nepal	1970
Finland	1969	Netherlands	1975
Gabon	1974	New Zealand	1969
Gambia, The	1975	Nicaragua	1973
Germany (East)	1969	Nigeria	1968
Germany (West)	1975	N. Korea	1985
Ghana	1970	Norway	1969
Greece	1970	Panama	1977
Grenada	1975	Papua New Guinea	1982
Guatemala	1970	Paraguay	1970
Guinea	1985	Peru	1970
Guinea-Bissau	1976	Philippines	1972
Haiti	1970	Poland	1969

Portugal	1977	Syrian Arab Republic	1969
Romania	1970	Taiwan	1970
Rwanda	1975	Thailand	1972
San Marino	1970	Togo	1970
Sao Tome & Principe	1983	Tonga	1971
St. Lucia	1979	Tunisia	1970
St. Kitts & Nevis	1983	Turkey	1980
St. Vincent &		Tuvalu	1979
The Grenadines	1984	Uganda	1982
Senegal	1970	USSR*	1970
Seychelles	1985	United Kingdom*	1968
Sierra Leone	1975	United States*	1970
Singapore	1976	Uruguay	1970
Solomon Islands	1981	Venezuela	1975
Somalia	1970	Vietnam	1982
Sri Lanka	1979	Western Samoa	1975
Sudan	1973	Yemen, (Aden)	1979
Suriname	1976	Yemen, (Sana)	1986
Swaziland	1969	Yugoslavia	1970
Sweden	1970	Zaire	1970
Switzerland	1977		

B. Countries that have signed but not ratified the Treaty

Kuwait
Trinidad & Tobago

C. Countries that have neither signed nor ratified the Treaty

Albania	Djibouti	Pakistan
Algeria	France*	Portugal
Angola	Guinea	Qatar
Argentina	Guyana	Saudi Arabia
Bahrain	India**	South Africa
Brazil	Israel	Spain
Burma	Mauritania	Tanzania
Chile	Monaco	United Arab Emirates
Comoros	Mozambique	Vanuatu
China*	Niger	Zambia
Cuba	Oman	Zimbabwe

* Nuclear weapon state
** India has detonated a "peaceful nuclear device."

Appendix E: The Treaty of Tlatelolco

The international non-proliferation regime is strengthened in Latin America by the Treaty on the Prohibition of Nuclear Weapons in Latin America (the Treaty of Tlatelolco), which establishes a nuclear-weapons free zone in the region. Parties to the treaty agree not to manufacture, test, or acquire nuclear weapons or to accept weapons on their territory deployed by others. To verify that these pledges are kept, adherents agree to accept "full-scope" International Atomic Energy Agency (IAEA) safeguards (i.e., IAEA accounting and inspection measures on all of a nation's nuclear activities). In addition, the treaty establishes the Agency for the Prohibition of Nuclear Weapons in Latin America (OPANAL). OPANAL will undertake special inspections at the request of members who have reason to believe that another party is engaging in prohibited activity, a unique investigatory function not available under the IAEA system.

Under its entry-into-force provisions, the treaty becomes effective once it has been ratified by all eligible countries in the region. However, twenty-two nations have ratified the accord and waived this provision so that the treaty has become effective for these countries. Only four countries have yet to make the treaty operative. Part way there, but avoiding the full-scope safeguards and requirements are Brazil and Chile, which have ratified, but not waived the entry-into-force requirement. Further away are Argentina, which has signed but not ratified, and Cuba, which has neither signed nor ratified the accord. Because Cuba has made approval of the treaty contingent upon U.S. withdrawal from the Guantanamo naval base, progress toward full effectiveness has been stymied.

The treaty is supplemented by two protocols that apply to countries outside the region. Protocol I requires that outside nations with territories in Latin America respect the treaty's denuclearization requirements with respect to those territories. Protocol II prohibits nuclear-weapon states from using or threatening to use nuclear arms against treaty parties. All nations with territories in the region, the U.S., U.K., France, and the Netherlands have signed Protocol I, and all but France have ratified it. All nuclear-weapon states have ratified Protocol II.

One highly controversial issue arises from the treaty's definition in Article 5 of a nuclear weapon as a nuclear explosive "which has a group of characteristics that are appropriate for use for warlike purposes." When the United States and the Soviet Union ratified Protocol II they formally stated that in their view this phrase meant that the treaty's prohibitions applied to *all* nuclear explosives, including so-called "peaceful nuclear explosives" since there was no technological difference between them and nuclear weapons. Argentina and Brazil have objected to this interpretation and cited Article 18 of the treaty which states that parties "may carry out explosions for peaceful purposes—including explosions which involve devices similar to those used in nuclear weapons"—under IAEA supervision. Virtually all other treaty parties, however, have accepted the U.S.-Soviet view since they are also parties to the Non-Proliferation Treaty, which expressly prohibits the manufacture of any nuclear explosive.

Treaty for the Prohibition of Nuclear Weapons in Latin America

Country	Year of Signature	Year of Ratification
Argentina	1967	—
Antigua and Barbuda	1983	1983
Bahamas, The	1967	1976
Barbados	1968	1969
Bolivia	1967	1969
Brazil	1967	1968*
Chile	1967	1974*
Colombia	1967	1972
Costa Rica	1967	1969
Dominican Republic	1967	1968
Ecuador	1967	1969
El Salvador	1967	1968
Grenada	1975	1975
Guatemala	1967	1970
Haiti	1967	1969
Honduras	1967	1968
Jamaica	1967	1969
Mexico	1967	1967
Nicaragua	1967	1968
Panama	1967	1971
Paraguay	1967	1969
Peru	1967	1969
Suriname	1976	1977
Trinidad and Tobago	1967	1975
Uruguay	1967	1968
Venezuela	1967	1970

Protocol I to the Treaty

Country	Year of Signature	Year of Ratification
France	1979	—
Netherlands	1968	1971
United Kingdom	1967	1969
United States	1977	1981

Protocol II to the Treaty

Country	Year of Signature	Year of Ratification
China (PRC)	1973	1974
France	1973	1974
U.S.S.R.	1978	1979
United Kingdom	1967	1969
United States	1968	1971

* Not in force because entry-into-force provision not waived.

Source: U.S. Arms Control and Disarmament Agency, *Arms Control and Disarmament Agreements: Texts and Histories of Negotiations* (Washington, D.C.: U.S. Arms Control and Disarmament Agency, 1982), and U.S. Department of State.

Appendix F: Nuclear Suppliers Organizations

Non-Proliferation Treaty Exporters Committee (Zangger Committee)

Shortly after the treaty came into force in 1970, a number of countries entered into consultations concerning the procedures and standards they would apply to nuclear fuel and equipment exports to non-nuclear-weapon states in order to implement the requirement in the pact that such exports and any enriched uranium or plutonium produced through their use be subject to IAEA safeguards. The countries engaged in those consultations, which were chaired by the Swiss expert, Claude Zangger, were parties to the Non-Proliferation Treaty (or have since become parties) and were also exporters or potential exporters of material and equipment for peaceful uses of nuclear energy.

In August 1974, the governments of Australia, Denmark, Canada, Finland, West Germany, the Netherlands, Norway, the Soviet Union, the United Kingdom, and the United States each informed the Director General of the IAEA, by individual letters, of their intentions to require IAEA safeguards on their nuclear exports in accordance with certain procedures described in memoranda enclosed with their letters. Those memoranda were identical in the case of each letter and included a "Trigger List" of materials and items of equipment which would be exported only under such safeguards. (The individual letters and the identical memoranda were published by the IAEA in September 1974 in document INFCIRC/209).

Subsequently, Austria, Czechoslovakia, East Germany, Ireland, Japan, Luxembourg, Poland, and Sweden sent individual letters to the Director General, referring to and enclosing memoranda identical to those transmitted by the initial groups of governments.

The agreed procedures and Trigger List represented the first major agreement on uniform regulation of nuclear exports by actual and potential nuclear suppliers. It had great significance for several reasons. It was an attempt to strictly and uniformly enforce the obligations of Article III, paragraph 2, of the Non-Proliferation Treaty requiring safeguards on nuclear exports. It was intended to reduce the likelihood that states would be tempted to cut corners on safeguards requirements, because of competition in the sale of nuclear equipment and fuel-cycle services. In addition, and very important in light of subsequent events, it established the principle that nuclear-supplier nations should consult and agree among themselves on procedures to regulate the international market for nuclear materials and equipment in the interest of non-proliferation. Notably absent from the list of actual participants or potential suppliers, as from the list of parties to the Non-Proliferation Treaty, were France, India, and the People's Republic of China.

Nuclear Suppliers Group

In November 1974, within a year of the delivery of these memoranda a second series of supplier negotiations were underway. This round, convened largely at the initiative of the United States, was a response to three developments: 1) the Indian nuclear test of May 1974, 2) mounting evidence that the pricing actions of the Organization of Oil Exporting Countries were stimulating Third World and other non-nuclear states to initiate or accelerate their nuclear power programs, and 3) recent contracts or continuing negotiations on the part of France and West Germany for the supply of enrichment or reprocessing facilities to Third World states.

The initial participants in these discussions, conducted in London were Canada, the Federal Republic of Germany, France, Japan, the Soviet Union, the United Kingdom, and the United States. One of the group's chief accomplishments was to induce France to join in such efforts, since France (which had not joined the Non-Proliferation Treaty or the Zangger Committee) could have undercut reforms of nuclear supply. The French, hesitant about becoming involved and uncertain as to where the effort might lead, insisted that any meetings be kept confidential—which was also the preference of some other participants. So the meetings in London were held in secret. But it soon became known that such meetings were taking place, and this led to suspicion and exaggerated fears of what they were about. The group was inaccurately referred to as a "cartel." Instead, one of its purposes was to foster genuine commercial competition based on quality and prices, untainted by bargaining away proliferation controls.

Two major issues were discussed in the series of meetings which led to a new agreement in late 1975. The first was if, and under what conditions, technology and equipment for enrichment and reprocessing, the most sensitive parts of the nuclear fuel cycle from a weapons proliferation perspective, should be transferred to non-nuclear states. The United States, with support from several other participants, was reported to argue in favor of both a prohibition on such transfer and a commitment to reprocessing in multinational facilities. France had already signed contracts to sell reprocessing plants to Pakistan and South Korea, and West Germany had agreed to sell technology and facilities for the full fuel cycle (including enrichment and reprocessing) to Brazil. They successfully resisted the prohibition proposed by others.

The second issue was whether transfers should be made to states unwilling to submit all non-military nuclear facilities to IAEA safeguards, or whether total industry (full-scope) safeguards should become a condition of sales. The Nuclear Suppliers Group came close to reaching consensus on requiring full-scope safeguards in recipient countries as a condition of future supply commitments, but was unable to persuade the French and the West Germans, though they did not rule out later reconsideration and possible changes by unanimous consent. The group did act to expand safeguards coverage by adopting a "Trigger List" of exports, similar to that of the Zangger Committee, which would be made only if covered by IAEA safeguards in the recipient state.

On January 27, 1976, the seven participants in the negotiations exchanged letters endorsing a uniform code for conducting international nuclear sales. The major provisions of the agreement require that before nuclear materials, equipment, or technology are transferred the recipient state must:

1. pledge not to use the transferred materials, equipment, or technology in the manufacture of nuclear explosives of any kind;

2. accept, with no provision for termination, international safeguards on all transferred materials and facilities employing transferred equipment or technology, including any enrichment, reprocessing, or heavy-water production facility that replicates or otherwise employs transferred technology;

3. provide adequate physical security for transferred nuclear facilities and materials to prevent theft and sabotage;

4. agree not to retransfer the materials, equipment, or technology to third countries unless they too accept the constraints on use, replication, security, and transfer, and unless the original supplier nation concurs in the transactions;

5. employ "restraint" regarding the possible export of "sensitive" items (relating to uranium enrichment, spent fuel reprocessing, and heavy-water production); and

6. encourage the concept of multilateral regional facilities for reprocessing and enrichment.

The guidelines have now been adopted by the United States, Great Britain, France, West Germany, Japan, Canada, the Soviet Union, Belgium, Italy, the Netherlands, Sweden, Switzerland, Czechoslovakia, East Germany, Poland, Australia, and Finland.

The Nuclear Suppliers' Guidelines extended the Zangger Committee's requirements in several respects. First, France (which had not participated in the Zangger group) agreed to key points adopted by that Committee, such as the requirement that nuclear export recipients pledge not to use transferred items for nuclear explosives of any kind and that safe-guards on transferred items would continue indefinitely. Secondly, the Suppliers Group went beyond the Non-Proliferation Treaty and the Zangger Committee require-ments, by imposing safeguards not only on the export of nuclear materials and equipment, but also on nuclear technology exports. India had demonstrated the existence of this serious loophole by building its own unsafeguarded replica of a safeguarded power reactor imported from Canada. The Suppliers Group was unable to reach agreement on the application of this reform to reactor technology, however, and so confined its recommended application to "sensitive" facilities—i.e., reprocessing, enrichment, and heavy-water production plants built with the use of exported technology. The group's acceptance of this limited reform was facilitated by the fact that such a condition was incorporated by West Germany in its safeguards agreements for sale of enrichment and reprocessing facilities to Brazil, and the French in their safeguards agreements covering their proposed sales of re-processing plants to the Republic of Korea and Pakistan.

Third, the Suppliers' Guidelines, while not prohibiting the export of these sensitive facilities, do embody the partici-pants' agreement to "exercise restraint" in transferring them, and where enrichment plants are involved, to seek re-cipient country commitments that such facilities will be de-signed and operated to produce only low-enriched uranium, not suitable for weapons.

Several supplier countries subsequently announced poli-cies stricter than those in the guidelines. France, West Ger-many, and the United States all made separate public an-nouncements that they did not, at least for the time being, contemplate any further new commitments to export repro-cessing technology. In addition, the United States, Canada, Australia, and Sweden have all made recipient-country ac-ceptance of full-scope safeguards a condition for nuclear transfer.

* * *

Excerpted and adapted from, Charles N. Van Doren, "Nuclear Supply and Non-Proliferation: The IAEA Committee on Assurances of Supply," A Report for the Congressional Research Service (Rep. No. 83-202-8) October 1983, pp. 61-64; U.S. Congress, Office of Technology Assessment, *Nuclear Proliferation and Safeguards* (Washington, D.C.: OTA, 1977), pp. 220-221; U.S. Department of State, "Report to the Congress Pursuant to Section 601 of the Nuclear Non-Proliferation Act of 1978" (January 1979), pp. 25-27.

Glossary

atomic bomb A bomb whose energy comes from the fission of uranium or plutonium.

blanket A layer of fertile material, such as uranium-238 or thorium-232, placed around the core of a reactor. During operation of the reactor, additional fissionable material is produced in the blanket.

breeder reactor A nuclear reactor that produces somewhat more fissile material than it consumes. The fissile material is produced both in the reactor's core and when neutrons are captured in fertile material placed around the core (blanket). This process is known as breeding. Breeder reactors have not yet reached commercialization, although active research and development programs are being pursued by a number of countries.

CANDU (Canadian deuterium-uranium reactor.) The most widely used type of heavy-water reactor. The CANDU reactor uses natural uranium as a fuel and heavy water as a moderator and a coolant. Recovery of plutonium from its spent fuel is not at present economical. Hence, the CANDU fuel cycle excludes both the enrichment and reprocessing steps.

centrifuge See ultracentrifuge.

chain reaction The continuing process of nuclear fissioning in which the neutrons released from a fission trigger at least one other nuclear fission. In a nuclear weapon an extremely rapid, multiplying chain reaction causes the explosive release of energy. In a reactor, the pace of the chain reaction is controlled to produce heat (in a power reactor) or large quantities of neutrons (in a research reactor).

chemical processing Chemical treatment of materials to separate specific usable constituents.

coolant A substance circulated through a nuclear reactor to remove or transfer heat. The most common coolants are water and heavy water.

core The central portion of a nuclear reactor containing the fuel elements and, usually, the moderator. Also the central portion of a nuclear weapon containing highly enriched uranium or plutonium.

critical mass The miniumum amount of fissionable material required to sustain a chain reaction. The exact mass varies with many factors such as the particular fissionable isotope present, its concentration and chemical form, the geometrical arrangement of the material, and its density. When fissionable materials are compressed by high explosives in implosion-type atomic weapons, the critical mass needed for a nuclear explosion is reduced.

depleted uranium Uranium having a smaller percentage of uranium-235 than the 0.7 percent found in natural uranium. It is a by-product of the uranium enrichment process, during which uranium-235 is culled from one batch of uranium, depleting it and then added to another batch to increase its concentration of uranium-235 in another.

enrichment The process of increasing the concentration of one isotope of a given element (in the case of uranium, increasing the concentration of uranium-235).

feed stock Material introduced into a facility for processing.

fertile Material composed of atoms which radily absorb neutrons to produce fissionable materials. One such element is uranium-238, which becomes plutonium-239 after it absorbs a neutron. Fertile material alone cannot sustain a chain reaction.

fission The process by which a neutron strikes a nucleus and splits it into fragments. During the process of nuclear fission, several neutrons are emitted at high speed, and heat and radiation are released.

fissile material Material composed of atoms which readily fission when struck by a neutron. Uranium-235 and plutonium-239 are examples of fissile materials.

fusion The formation of a heavier nucleus from two lighter ones (such as hydrogen isotopes), with the attendant release of energy (as in a hydrogen bomb).

gas centrifuge process A method of isotope separation in which heavy gaseous atoms or molecules are separated from light ones by centrifugal force. See ultracentrifuge.

gaseous diffusion A method of isotope separation based on the fact that gas atoms or molecules with different masses will diffuse through a porous barrier (or membrane) at different rates. The method is used to separate uranium-235 from uranium-238. It requires large gaseous diffusion plants and significant amounts of electric power.

gas-graphite reactor A nuclear reactor in which a gas is the coolant and graphite is the moderator.

heavy water Water containing significantly more than the natural proportion (1 in 6,500) of heavy hydrogen (deuterium) atoms to ordinary hydrogen atoms. (Hydrogen atoms have one proton, deuterium atoms have one proton and one neutron.) Heavy water is used as a moderator in some reactors because it slows down neutrons effectively and does not absorb them (unlike light, or normal, water) making it possible to fission natural uranium and sustain a chain reaction.

heavy-water reactor A reactor that uses heavy water as its moderator and natural uranium as fuel. See CANDU.

highly enriched uranium Uranium in which the percentage of uranium-235 nuclei has been increased from the natural level of 0.7 percent to some level greater than 20 percent, usually around 90 percent.

hot cells Lead-shielded rooms with remote handling equipment for examining and processing radioactive materials. In particular, hot cells are used for reprocessing spent reactor fuel.

hydrogen bomb A nuclear weapon that derives its energy largely from fusion. Also known as a thermonuclear bomb.

irradiation Exposure to a radioactive source; usually in the case of fuel materials, being placed in an operating nuclear reactor.

isotopes Atoms having the same number of protons, but a different number of neutrons. Two isotopes of the same atom are very similar and difficult to separate by ordinary chemical means. Isotopes can have very different nuclear properties, however. For example, one isotope may fission readily, while another isotope of the same atom may not fission at all. An isotope is specified by its atomic mass number (the number of protons plus neutrons) following the symbol denoting the chemical element (e.g., U^{235} is an isotope of uranium).

jet-nozzle enrichment method A process of uranium enrichment that uses both uranium hexafluoride and a light gas flowing at high speed through a nozzle along curved walls.

kilogram A metric weight equivalent to 2.2 pounds.

kiloton The energy of a nuclear explosion that is equivalent to an explosion of 1,000 tons of TNT.

laser enrichment method A still experimental process of uranium enrichment in which a finely tuned, high-power carbon dioxide$_5$ laser is used to differentially excite molecules of various atomic weights. This differential excitation makes it possible to separate uranium-235 from uranium-238.

light water Ordinary water (H_2O), as distinguished from heavy water (D_2O).

light-water reactor A reactor that uses ordinary water as moderator and coolant and low-enriched uranium as fuel.

low-enriched uranium Uranium in which the percentage of uranium-235 nuclei has been increased from the natural level of 0.7 percent to less than 20 percent, usually 3 to 6 percent. With the increased level of fissile material, low-enriched uranium can sustain a chain reaction when immersed in light-water and is used as fuel in light-water reactors.

medium-enriched uranium Uranium in which the percentage of uranium-235 nuclei has been increased from the natural level of 0.7 percent to between 20 and 50 percent. Potentially usable for nuclear weapons, but very large quantities are needed.)

megawatt One million watts; used in reference to a nuclear power plant, one million watts of electricity.

metric ton One thousand kilograms. A metric weight equivalent to 2200 pounds or 1.1 tons.

milling A process in the uranium fuel cycle by which ore containing only a very small percentage of uranium oxide (U_3O_8) is converted into material containing a high percentage (80 percent) of U_3O_8, often referred to as yellowcake.

moderator A component (usually water, heavy water, or graphite) of some nuclear reactors that slows neutrons, thereby increasing their chances of fissioning by fertile material.

natural uranium Uranium as found in nature, containing 0.7

percent of uranium-235, 99.3 percent of uranium-238, and a trace of uranium-234.

neutron An uncharged elementary particle, with a mass slightly greater than that of a proton, found in the nucleus of every atom heavier than hydrogen.

nuclear energy The energy liberated by a nuclear reaction (fission or fusion) or by spontaneous radioactivity.

nuclear fuel Basic chain-reacting material, including both fissile and fertile materials. Commonly used nuclear fuels are natural uranium, and low-enriched uranium; high-enriched uranium and plutonium are used in some reactors.

nuclear fuel cycle The set of chemical and physical operations needed to prepare nuclear material for use in reactors and to dispose of or recycle the material after its removal from the reactor. Existing fuel cycles begin with uranium as the natural resource and create plutonium as a by-product. Some future fuel cycles may rely on thorium and produce the fissionable isotope uranium-233.

nuclear fuel element A rod, tube, plate, or other mechanical shape or form into which nuclear fuel is fabricated for use in a reactor.

nuclear fuel fabrication plant A facility where the nuclear material (e.g., enriched or natural uranium) is fabricated into fuel elements to be inserted into a reactor.

nuclear power plant Any device or assembly that converts nuclear energy into useful power. In a nuclear electric power plant, heat produced by a reactor is used to produce steam to drive a turbine that in turn drives an electricity generator.

nuclear reactor A mechanism fueled by fissionable materials that give off neutrons, thereby inducing heat. Reactors are of three general types: power reactors, production reactors, and research reactors.

nuclear waste The radioactive by-products formed by fission and other nuclear processes in a reactor. Most nuclear waste is initially contained spent fuel. If this material is reprocessed, new categories of waste result.

nuclear weapons A collective term for atomic bombs and hydrogen bombs. Weapons based on a nuclear explosion. Generally used throughout the text to mean atomic bombs, only, unless used with reference to nuclear weapon states, (all five of which have both atomic and hydrogen weapons).

plutonium-239 A fissile isotope occurring naturally in only minute quantities, which is manufactured artificially when uranium-238, through irradiation, captures an extra neutron. It is one of the two materials that have been used for the core of nuclear weapons, the other being highly enriched uranium.

plutonium-240 A fissile isotope produced in reactors when a plutonium-239 atom absorbs a neutron instead of fissioning. Its presence complicates the construction of nuclear explosives because of its high rate of spontaneous fission.

power reactor A reactor designed to produce electricity as distinguished from reactors used primarily for research or for producing radiation or fissionable materials.

production reactor A reactor designed primarily for large-scale production of plutonium-239 by neutron irradiation of uranium-238.

radioactivity The spontaneous disintegration of an unstable atomic nucleus resulting in the emission of subatomic particles.

radioisotope A radioactive isotope.

recycle To reuse the remaining uranium and plutonium found in spent fuel after they have been separated at a reprocessing plant from unwanted radioactive waste products also in the spent fuel.

reprocessing Chemical treatment of spent reactor fuel to separate the plutonium and uranium from the unwanted radio-active waste by-products and (under present plans) from each other.

research reactor A reactor primarily designed to supply neutrons for experimental purposes. It may also be used for training, materials testing, and production of radioisotopes.

spent fuel Fuel elements that have been removed from the reactor after use because they contain too little fissile and fertile material and too high a concentration of unwanted radioactive by-products to sustain reactor operation. Spent fuel is both physically and radioactively hot.

thermonuclear bomb A hydrogen bomb.

thorium-232 A fertile material.

ultracentrifuge A rotating vessel that can be used for enrichment of uranium. The heavier isotopes of uranium hexafluoride gas concentrate at the walls of the rotating centrifuge and are drawn off.

uranium A radioactive element with the atomic number 92 and, as found in natural ores, an average atomic weight of 238. The two principal natural isotopes are uranium-235 (0.7 percent of natural uranium), which is fissionable, and uranium-238 (99.3 percent of natural uranium), which is fertile.

uranium-233 (U^{233}) A fissionable isotope bred in fertile thorium-232. Like plutonium-239 it is theoretically an excellent material for nuclear weapons, but is not known to have been used on this purpose. Can be used as reactor fuel.

uranium-235 (U^{235}) The only naturally occurring fissionable isotope. Natural uranium contains 0.7 percent U^{235}; light-water reactors use about 3 percent and weapons grade, highly enriched uranium normally consists of 93 percent of this isotope.

uranium-238 A fertile material. Natural uranium is composed of approximately 99.3 percent U^{238}.

uranium dioxide (UO^2) Purified uranium. The form of natural uranium used in heavy water reactors. Also the form of uranium that remains after the fluorine is removed from enriched uranium hexafluoride (UF^6). Produced as a powder, uranium dioxide is, in turn, fabricated into fuel elements.

uranium oxide (U_3O_8) The most common oxide of uranium found in typical ores. U_3O_8 is extracted from the ore during the milling process. The ore typically contains only 0.1 percent U_3O_8; yellowcake, the product of the milling process, contains about 80 percent U_3O_8.

uranium hexafluoride (UF_6) A volatile compound of uranium and fluorine. UF_6 is a solid at atmospheric pressure and room temperature, but can be transformed into gas by heating. UF_6 gas (alone, or in combination with hydrogen or helium) is the feed stock in all uranium enrichment processes and is sometimes produced at an intermediate product in the process of purifying yellowcake to produce uranium oxide.

vessel The part of a reactor that contains the nuclear fuel.

weapons grade Nuclear material of the type most suitable for nuclear weapons, i.e., uranium enriched to 90 percent U^{235} or plutonium that is primarily Pu^{239}.

weapons-usable Fissionable material that is weapons-grade or, though less than ideal for weapons, can still be used to make a nuclear explosive.

yellowcake A concentrate produced during the milling process that contains about 80 percent uranium oxide (U_3O_8). In preparation for uranium enrichment, the yellowcake is converted to uranium hexafluoride gas (UF_6). In the preparation of natural uranium reactor fuel, yellowcake is processed into purified uranium dioxide. Sometimes uranium hexaflouride is produced as an intermediate step in the purification process.

yield The total energy released in a nuclear explosion. It is usually expressed in equivalent tons of TNT (the quantity of

TNT required to produce a corresponding amount of energy).

Sources

1. Congressional Research Service, *Nuclear Proliferation Factbook* (Washington, DC: U.S. Govt. Printing Office, 1977).
2. Energy Research & Development Administration, *U.S. Nuclear Power Export Activities* (Springfield, VA: National Technical Information Service, 1976).
3. Nuclear Energy Policy Study Group, *Nuclear Power: Issues and Choices* (Cambridge, MA: Ballinger Publishing Co., 1977).
4. Office of Technology Assessment, *Nuclear Proliferation and Safeguards* (Washington, DC: Office of Technology Assessment, 1977); Nuclear Power in an Age of Uncertainty (Washington, D.C.: Office of Technology Assessment, 1984).
5. Wohlstetter, Albert, *Swords from Plowshares: The Military Potential of Civilian Nuclear Energy* (Chicago: The University of Chicago Press, 1977).
6. United Nations Association of the USA, *Nuclear Proliferation: A Citizen's Guide to Policy Choices* (N.Y.: UNA-USA, 1983).

Index